Security Risk Management

Building an Information Security Risk Management Program from the Ground Up

Security Risk Management

Building an Information Security Risk Management Program from the Ground Up

Evan Wheeler

Technical Editor
Kenneth Swick

ELSEVIER

AMSTERDAM • BOSTON • HEIDELBERG • LONDON
NEW YORK • OXFORD • PARIS • SAN DIEGO
SAN FRANCISCO • SINGAPORE • SYDNEY • TOKYO
Syngress is an imprint of Elsevier

Acquiring Editor: Angelina Ward
Development Editor: Heather Scherer
Project Manager: Danielle S. Miller
Designer: Alisa Andreola

Syngress is an imprint of Elsevier
225 Wyman Street, Waltham, MA 02451, USA

Library of Congress Cataloging-in-Publication Data
Application submitted

British Library Cataloguing-in-Publication Data
A catalogue record for this book is available from the British Library.

ISBN: 978-1-59749-615-5

For information on all Syngress publications
visit our website at *www.syngress.com*

Printed in the United States of America

11 12 13 14 15   10 9 8 7 6 5 4 3 2 1

Typeset by: diacriTech, Chennai, India

Contents

Preface

I wish that I could start off with some fascinating story about how this book came to be, listing all my altruistic reasons for writing it, but ultimately my motivation for writing this book has been mostly practical and selfish. Several years ago, I wanted to share my own experiences with risk management, so I developed an Information Security Risk Management course for the graduate program at Clark University, and I realized that there wasn't any one book available that covered both the basics of risk assessment and how to build and manage a risk-based program. So, I set out to make my own life a little easier by writing a book that I could use in my courses. My secondary motivation for writing this book actually goes back to the original idea for my course at Clark; my goal was to address the lack of formal risk education opportunities for information security professionals. There is certainly nothing wrong with on-the-job training, but if that is the only option available to educate future risk analysts and risk managers, then we will continue to see the mishmash of risk analysis techniques and weak risk models that is casting doubt on the viability of risk management in general. There just hasn't yet been widespread adoption of comprehensive risk models specific to the information security field, and there are even fewer educational options available to get the few good models more exposure in the security community. Information security programs need to continue to evolve toward a risk-focused approach if they are going to have any chance of keeping up with the growing demands with ever-limited resources. I have seen the success that a risk-based program can produce, and my goal has been to share both my successes and lessons learned with the security community in the hopes that I can provide a solid foundation upon which others may design their own risk-focused security programs.

Most information security training programs churn out security practitioners who know which static security patterns to follow or how to run a tool but, if challenged, they can't explain to you why it should be done that way and they can't adapt to situations outside the template that they learned in class. So many in the field don't see the value in taking the time to understand the principles of information security and how to apply them to a dynamic environment (sorry, the CISSP doesn't count as proof that you can apply information security principles). This constant focus on the operational and technical side of information security is creating a large percentage of security practitioners who have no idea what to do when the situation doesn't fit their static patterns or, even worse, they mistakenly apply the same checklists even if they don't address the actual risks. The next time you are interviewing for a security role, try asking the candidate not only how to implement a security control but also to explain why that control is critical at all. The scary thing is that most people can't explain why. They have just always done it that way or have been told to do it that way and they never questioned it. What if the variables change, would they know what to do? The reality is that most of these practitioners can't adapt. Maybe it is even acceptable for someone at the practitioner level to use security checklists as a crutch, but when you start to consider those professionals who are leading and directing security programs, they need to align their initiatives with the business and adjust their approach at a moment's notice. Blindly applying a checklist or standard isn't going to cut it. Throughout this book, I try wherever possible to provide not only the guidance about how to best manage risks but also the underlying reasoning so that you can adapt the approach to your own needs. I hope that this will encourage a better fundamental understanding of why certain risks need to be prioritized over others and help the reader to think of creative solutions to reduce risk in their organization.

For years, as a consultant, I helped clients to build, assess, and improve their risk management programs. I decided to leave consulting in 2008 to take on the challenge of developing an Information Security Risk Management program for a financial services company. Opportunities as a consultant had allowed a breadth of experience partnering with organizations across many industries, from the largest financial institutions to the manufacturing sector, but I was starting to feel like I needed to prove to myself that I could practice what I had been preaching as a consultant by meeting the challenges that come with managing a risk management program day in and day out. It is one thing to perform risk assessments as an outside consultant, or even to work with a client collaboratively to develop a portion of their program, but at the end of the day, you get to walk away and they are left managing the everyday challenges. This career move has given me a fresh perspective on what works, what doesn't, and how to best optimize limited resources to expand and mature the program to meet ever-increasing demands and expectations. Because of the opportunities I have had to see many different attempts to implement risk-based programs for many different consulting clients, I am confident that this book will be valuable for those who are just starting down the road of developing a program, as well as for those who have a solid understanding of assessment techniques but may not have the experience framing a program around risk.

INTENDED AUDIENCE

This book is intended for anyone who is analyzing new threats or vulnerabilities, performing security assessments, providing a technology audit function, or building an information security program. Even those who are familiar with performing risk assessments will benefit from the tips on how to more efficiently conduct assessments and the programmatic view of risk. Compliance and audit are such a large focus for most security teams, and I believe that anyone who is responsible for an audit function can use the information in this book to better focus their own assessments and more accurately evaluate identified risks. On the flip side, security professionals can also use the tips and techniques in this book to better interface with internal and external auditors and to improve presentation of risks to senior management.

The hope is that this book will help both security professionals and business managers understand how to qualify risk to the organization and make educated decisions about how to handle risk exposures. This topic bridges the gap between the subject matter experts in information security and the business executives with whom they work. Even for IT professionals, it is essential to understand the risk management lifecycle and how it will continue to impact and shape their daily responsibilities.

Finally, although this book is primarily targeted as a guide for information security professionals, I have also been conscious to organize it in such a way that it could be used as a textbook for a risk management course.

ORGANIZATION OF THIS BOOK

This book consists of three main sections, which are as follows:

Part I—Introduction to Risk Management

This book begins with a brief history of how risk management has evolved in the *information security* field and how this organic growth has led to mixed adoption of sound risk management methodologies. After reviewing some fundamental security principles, we jump right into an introduction to the basic concepts of risk management as it is applied to information security, including the fundamental definition of terms and principles that will be used throughout. Next, we explore each phase of the risk management lifecycle, focusing on implementing assessment, analysis, and evaluation techniques that should be used to properly assess and mitigate information risk. Beyond just implementing a risk management program, we focus on how to deeply embed a risk mindset into every aspect of your security program.

- Chapter 1: This chapter summarizes the struggles of checklist–oriented practitioners trying to move security initiatives forward without the clear business focus and lays out a new vision for how risk management can change the dynamic. Once you understand some of the basic security principles, models, and concepts, it will help you to choose risk assessment activities that will most benefit your organization.
- Chapter 2: Whether you are building an entire security program or just designing a risk management function to fit into an existing security program, you will need to know how best to position it with senior management. A well-designed security program can leverage risk models to reduce some level of burden on the organization from the security and compliance requirements. There are some distinct benefits and drawbacks of both qualitative and quantitative analysis approaches that are important to understand before you choose which model to implement in your own organization.

- Chapter 3: Risk management is a combination of on-going profiling, assessment, evaluation, mitigation, validation, and monitoring activities throughout the lifetime of any critical resource. This chapter lays out each step of the risk management lifecycle, which should be used to keep your team focused on the areas of greatest risk for your organization.

Part II—Risk Assessment and Analysis Techniques

The lifecycle workflow that is introduced in the first part of the book will be used as the structure that guides the discussion of risk profiling, risk assessment approaches, analysis methods, risk decision strategies, control selection, mitigation planning, documenting risks, and processing exceptions. This part of the book takes a different spin with an insider's look at techniques for consultants performing risk assessments and essential strategies for working with auditors or regulators. A detailed walkthrough of a recommended risk assessment report and effective techniques to present risk to senior management wraps up this discussion of the risk lifecycle. As a risk manager or analyst, you will need to adapt your approach depending on the scope of the assessment, whether it be an operational, project-based, or third-party assessment.

- Chapter 4: The idea of profiling a resource to determine its value to the organization, or risk sensitivity, is one of the most pervasive concepts in all of risk management. It affects which resources you assess at all, how often you reassess them, how detailed the assessment needs to be, how to prioritize any risk findings, what level of risk is acceptable, and even the level of management needed to approve an exception. Looking beyond the individual asset, it is necessary to know how best to gauge the risk appetite of the organization, which really means assessing the risk tolerance of the most senior leaders.
- Chapter 5: This chapter starts out by focusing on how to construct a risk statement that includes all the necessary details to convey the likely consequences to senior management. Following the formulation of the risk description, it is important to review the many approaches to modeling and analyzing potential threats. A structured approach to threat modeling can provide a great insight into areas of risk that need to be prioritized, but done wrong this activity can become a huge time drain and can easily distract the security team from the imminent threats.
- Chapter 6: The most controversial topic in risk management by far is how to rate the risks. This chapter focuses on simple and proven models for both qualitative and quantitative risk analysis. The majority of the chapter is spent framing out a qualitative risk measure that accounts for the sensitivity of the resource, the severity of the vulnerability, and the likelihood the threat will exploit the vulnerability. The chapter wraps up with a brief review of

quantitative measures, highlighting several implementation challenges and a loss expectancy analysis method.

- Chapter 7: Risk management needs to be more than just a control selection exercise, but there is no denying that controls play an important role in managing acceptable levels of risk. There are many standards and frameworks available that will prescribe the minimal security controls that every organization should have in place, but to really understand the significance of these controls, an understanding of the fundamental security services that all these controls implement in some way is required. After reviewing the basics, some particularly universal control requirements will be introduced along with references to additional resources for further guidance.

- Chapter 8: Once the risks have been assessed, the next step in the risk management lifecycle is to decide how to address those risks. Even more fundamentally, a decision needs to be made about which ones are even worth reviewing and addressing at all. There is more than one way to mitigate a given risk, and the best risk managers are the ones who can get to the root of the problem and find a creative way to limit the exposure. For those risks that can't be addressed, or can only be partially mitigated, robust exception approval process is needed.

- Chapter 9: This chapter focuses on how to organize an effective executive summary that will highlight the most critical themes from an assessment. Especially for risk managers and consultants, or anyone who is working with auditors regularly, this chapter will become an essential reference. Crafting management responses for auditors or regulators is truly an art form and anyone can greatly benefit from the advice throughout this chapter.

- Chapter 10: Once you have a risk model established, you will need to choose different assessment methodologies that match the scope of your assessment. A risk assessment associated with a single project is going to require a different approach than an assessment of an entire other company that is being acquired. There will also be the everyday assessments of newly announced vulnerabilities or quick assessments of the risks discovered during an active incident investigation. This chapter reviews the most common categories of assessments and offers the most effective way to approach each.

Part III—Building and Running a Risk Management Program

Most books and courses about risk management would have ended at this point, but it is critical to show how you can integrate these risk techniques into a comprehensive program to manage risk. To be in *information security* means that you are assessing and prioritizing risks, but without a structure for processing and filtering the risks, even the best assessor will get buried under the flood of risk information. Monitoring and assessing threat trends, daily vulnerability reports, deviations from security baselines, and design oversights are all critical components of your program. The book ends by proposing a roadmap to pull the various aspects of a security program (policy, threat and vulnerability management, incident response, baseline reviews, security architecture, and vendor management) into one cohesive risk management program with a normalized view of risk across the entire organization.

- Chapter 11: A Threat and Vulnerability Management (TVM) program is characterized by constantly revolving short assessments of newly identified vulnerabilities and the processing and filtering of incoming threat intelligence. TVM is the umbrella for the majority of the operational risk assessments including security scanning, patch management, and monitoring of security detection controls. Without a strategy for filtering out the lower risk items quickly, you will drown yourself in information almost immediately.
- Chapter 12: A fundamental control for any organization is a set of security policies and standards that set the tone for how to operate the business securely. The challenge becomes how to assess the organization's current alignment with these standards and determine which gaps need to be addressed most urgently. This gap analysis is one of the fundamental on-going risk assessment activities that will help to gauge the security posture of the organization versus what controls might be documented on paper.
- Chapter 13: According to the experts in secure software development, there are three essential functions: code review, penetration testing, and architectural risk analysis. Of the three, the latter is the rarest, but it is also the most proactive and impactful of the three when done correctly. Security architecture is a big topic, so this chapter will focus on the highlights that risk managers and analysts need to understand in order to work with their architects to develop at least a basic risk assessment model.
- Chapter 14: This chapter pulls together the various risk models, assessment techniques, activities, and processes from the entire book and lays out a strategy for turning this into an actual program. As hard as it might be to assess some risks, the real challenge is integrating all these components into your existing security program and showing real value to the rest of the business. This chapter not only presents several of the prerequisites for a risk management program but also offers one possible roadmap for implementing a program with as little resistance as possible.

Appendices

Appendix A: Sample Security Risk Profile
Throughout the book, there is a large focus on the value of rating the risk sensitivity of information resources through profiling. This appendix presents a sample *security risk profile* questionnaire that can be customized to fit the needs of a particular business or industry.

Appendix B: Qualitative Risk Scale Reference Tables

Many risk analysis techniques, models, and scales are used throughout the book to demonstrate the assessment process with several case studies. This appendix pulls together the final qualitative analysis scales into one place for easy reference.

Appendix C: Architectural Risk Analysis Reference Tables
Chapter 13 provides an overview of the architectural risk analysis process based on a model of assessing information flows. This appendix provides a several tables that are used to determine the appropriate security requirements for each information flow.

Acknowledgments

For a first-time author, having a team of editors available to guide me through this process has been invaluable. Angelina Ward, Heather Scherer, and Ken Swick—I couldn't have done it without you all. Writing this book has given me a chance to reflect on my own career experiences, and each success can be directly tied to the good fortune to find a mentor who saw potential and was willing to give me a chance to prove it. I would like to thank all my mentors for all the selfless hours that they have devoted to developing my career and for their positive impact on my life:

- Elle Douglass first showed me how to channel my passion for technology into something productive, and she set me on the path for success. I will never forget those late nights when I was working on projects, hoping someone would bring us some food. Did we ever see daylight those years?
- Marc Takacs gave me the confidence to take on the hard tasks and was never too busy to teach me something new. Among many things, Marc taught me that you can find the best barbecue in Alabama if you follow the dirt road to the house with the pig tied up out front, take a left, and take another left at the corner where the tree fell over back in 1981, and then follow that road until you get to the house where the Parsons used to live and take a right. It's worth it if you can find it!
- Bill Whittaker gave a former network engineer, but current developer, his first break into the information security field, and I haven't looked back since. More than anything, Bill taught me how to systematically troubleshoot a problem in a real way and that skill has been invaluable in my career.
- Finally, I have to thank my current mentor and boss, Justin Peavey. Without the opportunities that Justin has so selflessly sought out on my behalf and the knowledge he has shared with me, I don't think this book would have been possible. His trust and guidance have made it possible for me to build a risk management program that is worth sharing with the rest of the industry. We've come a long way from our early conversations at the Thirsty Bear.

All these mentors have either set me on the right track or given me a push in the right direction, but the one who gives me the strength to keep challenging myself everyday and inspires me to be my best is my extraordinary wife (and secret editor), Rachel. Despite her own challenging career demands, she has put up with my insane hours and inability to say no to new projects that consume our evenings and weekends, and every step of the way, she has always been my greatest supporter. Clearly, I understand what it means to take risks, but with her as my partner, I am confident that nothing is out of reach. Sorry about making you read so much about risk profiling and exception processing!

About the Author

Working as a security consultant in many industries for over 10 years, Evan Wheeler is accustomed to advising clients on all aspects of *information assurance*. Specializing in risk management, digital forensic investigations, and security architecture development, he offers an expert insight into security principles for both clients and security professionals. He brings years of hands-on experience developing a risk assessment practice for a large security services company serving a diverse client base, designing architectural risk analysis frameworks for several major financial services organizations, and performing risk assessments for organizations of various sizes.

Evan has spoken to many audiences on topics ranging from building a forensic incident response infrastructure to developing security risk management programs from the ground up. He currently leads the information security risk management program as Director of Information Security for Omgeo (A DTCC, Thomson Reuters Company), and he previously spent over 6 years supporting the US Department of Defense as a security consultant.

As a complement to this diverse experience in the field and his Computer Science degree from Georgia Tech, he has earned a Master of Science in Information Assurance from the National Security Agency certified program at Northeastern University. Currently, Evan continues to promote the security industry as an instructor at both Clark and Northeastern Universities and as an instructor and author of the Information Security Risk Management course for the SANS Institute. More details about his work and several free resources are available at: http://www.ossie-group.org.

About the Technical Editor

Kenneth Swick is a 20 year veteran of the IT industry in multiple vertical markets with much of that time involved with Risk and Security. He has multiple industry-recognized security certifications from organizations such as SANS, ISC2, and ISACA. Currently, he is a Technical Information Security Officer and Vice President of Citi, being tasked with reducing risk across the organization. His hobbies include keeping up on the latest infosec news and spending time with his family.

Introduction to Risk Management

The Security Evolution

INTRODUCTION

Before even starting to think about the various steps required to design a program to assess and evaluate information security risks, it is important to briefly review the history of the field and take a quick look at Information Security as a discipline. Even those of you who are already familiar with some advanced risk assessment techniques can benefit from reviewing how we got here or you risk repeating the same mistakes. Information Security (or Information Assurance) needs to be viewed through the lens of business context to see the added value of basing your security program on a risk model. Risk management is by no means a ubiquitous foundation for information security programs, but many visionaries in the field recognize that the future of information security has to be focused on risk decisions if we are to have any hope of combating the ever-changing threat landscape and constantly increasing business demands. From an outsider's perspective, risk management may seem like an obvious fit for information security, but, amazingly, within the profession, there are still debates regarding its merit.

HOW WE GOT HERE

If you attend any industry conference or pick up any information security trade magazine, you will certainly see many references to risk assessments, risk analysis, and risk management. So, how is it possible that many security professionals are still arguing about the value of a risk-based approach to information security? Certainly, all the security products and service vendors have jumped on the risk bandwagon in full force. As a profession, have we fallen behind the vendors or are they contributing to the false perception of risk management? In fact, walking on the expo floor of any major information security conference, the number of vendors touting their so-called "risk management" solutions has increased significantly compared to even 1 year prior. Hopefully, as you look at each vendor's offerings, you will start to ask yourself questions like "is a vulnerability scanner really a risk management solution?" The answer is no, not really; but, the vendors are positioning it that way, and many people are more than happy to follow blindly if they can cross risk management off their compliance checklist. This example highlights a great misunderstanding within the field about what risk management really is. Let's face it—risk management is not a new concept. Several other industries (for example, insurance, economics, finance) have implemented very robust and precise risk models to handle even complex scenarios. Unfortunately, the information security field itself is rather young compared with these other industries, and when you try to apply a mature discipline like risk management to an evolving practice, there will be gaps that need to be overcome. This book is focused on addressing those gaps by providing a solid foundation upon which information security professionals can build a world-class risk management program that is aligned with the business objectives of the organization.

Banning Best Practices

In order to start the transformation into a risk mind-set, we first have to shed some of the baggage of outdated approaches to information security and dispel several misconceptions about how an information security function should operate. A growing problem in the information security field is the emphasis and reliance on checklists and so-called "best practices" as the only basis for many decisions. For the sake of simplicity and consistency, the security field has evolved into a cookbook-type approach. Everyone gets the same recipe for security and is expected to implement it in the exact same way. The fundamental flaw with this strategy is that we don't live in a one-size-fits-all world. Instead of blanketly applying best practices across the board, we should be using some risk analysis techniques to identify the critical focus areas and to select the most appropriate solutions for our organizations.

The motivation behind this cookbook mentality and the value of security checklists are clear when you look at how the information security field has evolved. There has always been a heavy technology focus in the field, and much of the security community got their start in an Information Technology (IT) role. As the discipline developed, implementations of security principles and concepts were inconsistent at best and the need to provide more standardized guidance to the practitioners who were battling it out in the trenches every day resulted in several generic security frameworks, some basic standards, and a lot of operationally focused training. Moreover, there are a wide variety of training options available at the practitioner level, but almost nothing focused on how to build and lead an information security program; most programs are aimed at teaching management activities, but there aren't many educational programs focused on true leadership.

Let's look at a quick example of this problem in practice. A typical information security standard might be that sensitive data needs to be encrypted wherever it is stored. Suppose that you found a database within your organization where sensitive data isn't encrypted. Before you confront the business owner and ask them to implement encryption, start by asking yourself why encryption is necessary. What problem are you trying to solve? What risk are you trying to mitigate? Encryption may not be necessary or appropriate every time. In some cases, it may even conflict with other security needs, such as the desire to inspect all communications in and out of the organization for malicious content or data leakage. Security controls need to provide business value and shouldn't be applied without first analyzing the problem. Your boss may attend an industry presentation, likely by a vendor, where the speaker recommends database encryption for all sensitive data. So, they run back to the office and you find yourself suddenly scoping out the effort to encrypt all your databases, but have you defined the problem you are trying to solve? This book is specifically focused on providing a risk model that will allow you to evaluate the threats and the vulnerabilities for your organization, and make educated decisions about how to address the most critical risks.

Having checklists and baselines does make it easy for security practitioners, and even people outside of security, to apply a minimal level of protection without having to understand the intricacies of information security, but at what expense? How can a single list of best practices possibly apply to every organization in the same way? There are "common practices," yes, but none of us is in the position to claim "best practices." There is too much potential to be lulled into a false sense of security if we base evaluations of security posture solely on a checklist.

TIPS & TRICKS

Try removing "best practices" from your vocabulary whenever you are communicating with others in your organization and really focus on the business drivers to justify any recommended controls or mitigation actions.

To be effective, senior security professionals need to learn how to perform a true risk assessment and not just accept the established security checklists. Even the US federal government seems to be moving in this direction with the latest revision of the NIST SP800-37 guide [1] for managing the security of federal information systems (formerly focused on Certification and Accreditation), which has been overhauled to use a risk-based approach. It is hard to deny that risk management is the future of the information security field, though some still try to argue against it. A risk-based model can provide a more dynamic and flexible approach to security that bases recommendations on the particular risks of each scenario, not just a single pattern for the entire field. Just look at the Payment Card Industry (PCI), given all the breaches in the retail space, it is clear that the PCI requirements have not made retail companies any more secure, just more compliant.

Looking Inside the Perimeter

Another important development in the information security field is the shift from focusing purely on securing the perimeter. Traditional information security practices were primarily concerned with keeping the "bad guys" out. The assumption was that anything outside your network (or physical walls) was un-trusted and anything inside could be trusted. Although this perspective can be very comforting and simplifies your protection activities (in an "ignorance is bliss" kind of way), unfortunately, it is also greatly flawed. As environments have grown more complex, it has even become necessary to separate different portions of the internal environment based on the sensitivity of the resources. It is hard to deny the statistics (according to the 2010 Verizon Data Breach Investigations Report [2], 48 percent of the breaches were caused by insiders) regarding the large percentage of security breaches initiated by malicious insiders or compromises resulting from attackers leveraging exploits on mobile devices to launch attacks on more sensitive internal resources. At this point, it would be hard even to draw a meaningful perimeter line around your organization. You can't assume that the other systems on your internal networks can be trusted or that not being directly Internet-facing excludes a system from needing to worry about external threats.

Early attempts by many organizations to address these issues without a common security framework have lead to the implementation of point solutions and ad hoc levels of protection, which in many cases have not been the best solutions to address the organization's greatest risk areas. We all have seen organizations that spend a lot of money on technology or spend all their time trying to keep up with the bleeding-edge hacking techniques, but miss the big gaping holes that end up being exploited. Critical exposures are overlooked, and breaches occur despite the expensive controls in place. Technology won't fix process and procedural weaknesses, which are what typically contribute to the major disclosures. As the threat landscape continues to shift, the old paradigms for information security just aren't going to cut it anymore.

A RISK-FOCUSED FUTURE

No one can deny that keeping up with the pace of change in this field is challenging at best, and can, at worst, feel impossible. As soon as you feel like you have a good handle on the major threats to your organization, three new threats pop up. So how can you keep up? If you want to stay ahead or even just keep pace, you need not only to understand the fundamental principles of a solid information security program but also to understand how to apply them to mitigate your organization's specific risks.

A New Path Forward

There are many good security advisory services available that can provide a steady feed of intelligence about the latest threats and vulnerabilities, but you will soon discover that keeping up with the pace of information can quickly become overwhelming. Along the same lines, try running a vulnerability scan of any average-sized environment for the first time and see how many hundreds of findings you get back; even if your organization has a mature security program, a typical scan will generate volumes of raw data that need to be analyzed. Unfortunately, many new security managers will start with this approach instead of first establishing the foundation for their program on a robust risk model, so they get lost in the race to combat the latest threats or close out vulnerabilities as quickly as possible without any prioritization. The result is that resource administrators spend all of their time responding to every new vulnerability report and applying every security patch; meanwhile, the security folks spend all of their time processing and tracking every new vulnerability when they should be focusing on prioritizing risks and developing a security strategy. It's easy to get caught up in trying to address each risk finding as soon as you discover it, and in doing so, you lose sight of the big picture. If you don't identify and address the root causes and systemic issues, then you will just keep killing time and resources fixing the same symptoms over and over again.

So how can we manage this better? How do we avoid the information overload? The answer is to develop a risk model that takes into account the particulars of your environment so you can stay focused on your organization's most critical exposures. Risk is, and needs to be, more than just a buzz word that vendors use to sell products. When someone says that a particular system is "risky," what does that mean? Does it mean that it has a low tolerance for risk exposures? Or does it mean that it has a high degree of exposure to threats? Maybe it indicates that the resource has a large threat universe? Potentially, the resource is a particularly attractive target? Does it have known and unmitigated vulnerabilities that are exploitable? Unfortunately, a lack of consistent and accurate terminology has lead to the current state where "risky" might mean any of these things. This makes it very challenging to have meaningful discussions about risk because everyone around the table has something different in mind when they use the word. Just labeling something as risky isn't descriptive enough to differentiate between these possibilities, but it may greatly affect how we manage risk for that resource. This book is one attempt to clarify the terminology and establish a consistent foundation for talking about information security risk and may be used along with other frameworks like OCTAVE and FAIR that include their own terminology and risk assessment techniques. Each of these industry frameworks will be explained in greater detail later in this book.

The Shangri-La of Risk Management

The goal of risk management is to maximize the output of the organization (in terms of services, products, revenue, and so on) while minimizing the chance for unexpected outcomes. There is no mention of eliminating risk because that just isn't a reasonable goal. Some organizations with low tolerance for risk have taken the stance of crushing and grinding any identified risks into the ground. While this is an admirable sentiment, it creates a culture of fear to identify risks because the effort required to eliminate them is often completely out of proportion to the exposure. From a business perspective, being secure is not perceived as being essential to being profitable as many security professionals think that it should. Security leaders must try to define, control, and predict uncertainty, rather than eliminating it.

It is expected that an organization may implement a risk model differently across functional areas, but there needs to be a common language and framework for risk management at an enterprise level. From this common framework, functions can adapt the model to meet their individual needs, as long as there is a clear process defined to normalize the risks across functions (or business units) to get an enterprise level snapshot of the organization's risk posture. For example, a critical risk for the financial liquidity of assets from the accounting team needs to be equivalent to a critical exposure of regulated data from the compliance team. Each function may even use a different implementation of the enterprise risk model, depending on the level of granularity that is appropriate for their domain, but there needs to be a single risk scale at the enterprise level for reporting and comparison's sake. Especially, if there isn't already an enterprise level risk function or committee, you can begin to align the different risk models that may already be in use by starting to establish a common methodology for assessing risk and agreeing upon common definitions for risk terminology.

INFORMATION SECURITY FUNDAMENTALS

The goal of Information Security must be to ensure the confidentiality, integrity, availability, and accountability of the resources for which we are responsible. The desirable level of assurance varies between organizations, between industries, and maybe even between departments within the same organization. Essentially, there is no single approach or standard that will apply to everyone, so we as security professionals need to know how to gauge the risk tolerance of our organization, apply the intent behind the security standards to each situation, and balance the cost of controls against the potential reduction in risk exposure.

Threats can target vulnerabilities when data is at rest (in storage on media of many types), during processing (while they are being input, filtered, parsed, manipulated, and so on) or while in transit (wired, wireless, or even internal to a system). The risks at these three data stages can be very different and therefore need to be analyzed individually.

Safety before Security

The first rule of Information Security should always be that considering controls and procedures to increase security should never come at the expense of human safety. This rule has become even more important as the Information Security field has taken a prime role in defending national critical infrastructure and as technology has taken on such a big role in the medical field. Think that your decisions don't impact human safety? A typical security standard is that all security controls must fail closed. In terms of a firewall, this would mean that when the device fails, it doesn't allow any traffic through. That way no one can take advantage of a control failure (or cause a control failure) to bypass security controls. Now, think about a man-trap that serves as an access control for sensitive areas, such as a data center; in the event of a fire, you can't just trap someone in there to maintain control over entry into the room! Similarly, you wouldn't want to design a critical medical system to stop functioning just because a security control failed.

WARNING

A False Sense of Security

If you think that safety doesn't apply to your security risk management, consider this example of how a high school misused security cameras. Typically, a camera is used as a detective control to catch security violations, but sometimes detective controls can also discourage security violations and abuses in sensitive areas. There was recently a story about a school that chose to save a few dollars by implementing cameras in key areas to discourage students from violating school policies, but they didn't implement the back-end system to monitor or record camera activity. They just put cameras out with cables into the ceiling that didn't actually connect to anything. The thinking was that this would be a good deterrent. The outcome they didn't expect was that when a student was attacked in the halls by another student, the victim ran over to the cameras for help, and of course, none came. By creating a false sense of security, this implementation of the control did more harm than good. All too often we create the same false sense of security in our organizations to save a buck or in the name of compliance.

The Lure of Security by Obscurity

Security by Obscurity is a very common phrase in the field. In the past, many have tried to approximate security by implementing a nonstandard format, encoding, or protocol that outsiders would not be familiar with, therefore making it harder for them to find a weakness or decipher sensitive information. Unfortunately, this tactic provides nothing more than a false sense of security; it has been proven over and over again that very little effort is required to analyze and decode these attempts to make data unrecognizable. There are cases where using a proprietary software or protocol may slow down an attacker, but chances are that once they get past the initial barrier to entry, the weaknesses they will find and exploit will be far more severe than the vulnerabilities generally found in commercial solutions. The benefit to commercial or open-source solutions is that the strengths and weaknesses have been tested over time by an extensive community of users and researchers. In particular, with open-source software, the industry has the ability to inspect the code down to the most fundamental components and identify any weaknesses, thereby increasing the chances that security weaknesses will be discovered and fixed early on.

Redefining the CIA Triad

The three foundational pillars of information security are commonly known as Confidentiality, Integrity, and Availability. However, as the security discipline has evolved, it has become apparent that this model is missing a fourth core requirement: Accountability. Accountability describes the need for the ability to trace activities to a responsible source. For example, digital signing of an e-mail or an audit log would both be controls that ensure accountability. You won't find the concept of Confidentiality, Integrity, Availability, and Accountability (now abbreviated C-I-A-A) on your CISSP exam or in many security publications, but many professionals have been using this expanded view of information assurance goals for years, and it has held up well over time. The concept of four pillars instead of three will continue to grow in popularity as the need for audit trails becomes more pervasive, in no small part due to the increase in regulations. Similarly, accountability requirements have also come to the forefront with supply chain tampering concerns.

Whether you use the original CIA model or the expanded C-I-A-A perspective, you won't see many security or risk models taking full advantage of these core security concepts as of yet. C-I-A-A is more than four security terms to be used in general conversations about security requirements; these concepts can be used to focus risk assessment activities in the areas where the organization or a single resource is most sensitive. Throughout this book, we will use the idea of C-I-A-A as the basis for risk profiling, vulnerability qualification, control mapping, and many other risk-related activities. In terms of determining the business impact of a particular resource, all four variables are independent of each other. For example, any data or resource may require a high level of integrity control and a low level of confidentiality control at the same time. The terms are defined as follows:

Confidentiality Assurance that information is not disclosed to unauthorized individuals, processes, or devices.

Integrity Protection against unauthorized creation, modification, or destruction of information.

Availability Timely, reliable access to data and information services for authorized users.

Accountability Process of tracing, or the ability to trace, activities to a responsible source.

These four constructs comprise the foundational objectives of information security. The term "Information Security" typically focuses on the traditional principles of data protection, confidentiality, and integrity, but the term "Information Assurance" seems to better fit these needs (and is a more popular term in the US federal government) along with expanding the concept to include availability and accountability concerns. That being said, the term Information Security has been chosen for this book, largely because of its greater popularity in the private sector. As used in this book, Information Security should be thought of as including all four aspects of C-I-A-A equally.

Notably, other terms such as "Access Control" or "Authentication" are not included in C-I-A-A because they describe the means to meet security goals and are not security objectives themselves. You would never see an application owner describe password-based authentication as a basic objective for their software, but they might list the need to prevent unauthorized modifications of data, which could be achieved with an authentication control. Access control, authentication, and authorization are all security services that may be needed to ensure some combination of C-I-A-A, whereas a concept such as "Privacy" really includes both confidentiality and accountability concerns that require both technical and process controls to ensure. In essence, C-I-A-A is nothing more than a way to summarize the fundamental assurance objectives on which security professionals should be focusing.

RISK DEEP DIVE

C-I-A-A Independence

Consider this example of putting the C-I-A-A concept into practice when assessing risks. The information on a public Web site is by design meant to be read anonymously, so confidentiality and accountability are not a concern; however, integrity would be important (you don't want someone defacing it) and availability might also be important depending on the service it provides (you don't want someone to get denied access because the maximum number of sessions for your Web server has been exceeded). However, if the information on this site is not of critical importance, availability may not be important. Given this quick analysis, you now know that you should focus your risk assessment efforts on threats and vulnerabilities related to integrity and possibly availability. Another resource may have a very different intended use and, therefore, a different mix of C-I-A-A needs, which would require a different focus when evaluating potential risks.

Security Design Principles

Success in information security has lots to do with striking a good balance. For example, the implementation of advanced security controls can introduce many complexities to an environment. These complexities can lead to errors or make it difficult to detect unauthorized activity and can sometimes create a weakness inadvertently. For example, the more granular and complex your firewall ruleset is, the more you may think that you are improving your organization's security posture with detailed access restrictions (principle of least privilege), but doing so also increases the chance of making an error in logic that could open an unexpected hole in your perimeter controls. These are trade-offs that have to be weighed and made every day as an information security leader.

There are three pervasive principles that will influence many facets of security standards, guidelines, and control designs:

- Least Privilege
- Defense in Depth
- Separation of Duties

This is certainly not an exhaustive list, but these three principles are commonly recognized in the field as being essential.

Least Privilege

This principle specifies that no communications or activities should be permitted unless there is an explicit need for that transaction or access. This guidance can be applied at any level of design and operation. Least privilege truly is the most fundamental of the information security privileges. Very plainly stated, no one should be granted a level of access above what they need to carry out their job function on a daily basis. A common application of this principle is the use of role-based access controls (RBAC) to define the privileges associated with a particular job function; a user is then assigned to that role for authorization purposes.

TIPS & TRICKS

When you are designing an RBAC model, be cautious not to create a distinct role for every possible job function. The RBAC implementation can become unmanageable when you have a large number of roles with granular permissions.

Keep in mind that the minimum should always be granted, and default privileges should be avoided if they won't be needed for everyone. For example, the security team may have an internal Web site where they store documents and resources (an intranet), but a member of the team who isn't responsible for incident response may not need access to the incident case files, even though they are a member of the security team. Some implementations would assign access to the entire site based on your role as a security team member, but this isn't appropriate in all cases. These permissions could get even more granular, down to the level of setting access to each site resource individually. It is better to explicitly assign privileges than lump users into large groups, but a balance must be found with the complexity that granular controls introduce. The trick is to find the balance between what is practical to manage from a provisioning and deprovisioning perspectives versus having very granular and precise restrictions. As you increase the complexity of the restrictions, you may actually start to see the level of security decrease as errors become more frequent.

TIPS & TRICKS

Never assign "read-write" access to a resource by default. Permissions should default to "read-only" unless there is an explicit need to create/modify data. Similarly, access should not be permanent or include all data records by default, often access will only be needed to a subset of the data and for a given time period.

RISK DEEP DIVE

Applying Least Privilege

The following story both illustrates the importance of limiting user access and reinforces the need to focus on accidental threats. There was an intern who was tasked with reconciling the IT team's asset inventory with finance's records. To accomplish this task, the intern requested access to the central database of assets. Being new to databases, the intern established a linkage between his local copy of MS Access and the enterprise database instance and started running queries. Unfortunately, during the course of his work, he accidently ran an update query that was meant to execute against a local copy of the asset data, but instead, he managed to duplicate every record in the enterprise database. The first question you may ask is "how could he have been so careless?" (in fact, his boss chewed him out in front of the entire team for this mistake), but your first thought should be "who gave him write access to the database?" If least privilege had been followed, there wouldn't have been any chance of him corrupting the central database. This situation was damaging to the organization not just because of the work it took to clean up the duplicate data and account for any changes that were made after the duplication but also because this data was used to calculate charge-backs within divisions of the company for IT services. As you might imagine, this was a nightmare to clean up, and restoring from a backup was not an option at the time.

Defense in Depth

This principle recommends the use of multiple security techniques or layers of controls to help reduce the exposure if one security control is compromised or circumvented. This may include several layers of defense using different types of protections or could even include vendor diversity. A simple example of this principle is the implementation of firewalls to protect against external attacks, used along with Intrusion Detection Systems (IDS) to detect any attacks that get past the perimeter controls. Each layer of protection doesn't need to perform the same function. In fact, many layered security controls may look at communications at a network level with one control and then inspect the traffic again at an application level.

RISK DEEP DIVE

Applying Defense in Depth

Relying on defenses at a single layer, or tier, is fundamentally flawed. A good example of how this can backfire is one organization that had a widely used Web application for online gaming. The idea was that the users would submit a game code, and some would be randomly selected to either receive a prize or save up points that could be combined for a larger reward. A user stumbled on a weakness using the Safari browser where a single winning code could be submitted over and over again to score more points. This was detected because the user ended up accruing thousands of points in a single afternoon, which flagged an exception when someone reviewed the account balances. The fundamental flaw in the application was that it was designed to implement all the controls on the client side, and the server didn't track any of it. All filtering, disabling of features, and access controls were implemented by JavaScript code in the browser. When the pages and code didn't behave as expected in the Safari browser (or you just turned off JavaScript in your browser), the user was able to indefinitely submit the page that chose the points rather than the prize and the server accepted it each time. When working with the developers to correct these flaws, their first inclination was to improve the client-side controls in the browser. However, setting up a demonstration of

(Continued)

> (*Continued*)
> how the browser could be easily bypassed altogether with a simple proxy program to submit and modify the Web requests forced the development team to consider server-side controls to complement the client-side restrictions. Sometimes it takes a couple of tries to get developers to understand that just because your submission page limits the number of characters entered to 10 doesn't mean that someone can't submit a longer string to the application. This can certainly be a paradigm shift for the security uninitiated.

Pick up any trade magazine from around 2008 or 2009, and you'll see an article about the downfall of the perimeter defense strategy. It just isn't viable as your sole strategy any more. The reality is that threats aren't just sourcing from outside the organization and the perimeter is getting harder to delineate. Given that employees are commonly working from home and partners need access to extranet sites, where do you draw the magic line of your network's edge? What about mobile devices and wireless networks: how do they fit into a perimeter approach?

A strategy of defense in depth recommends the use of layers of controls so that you aren't relying on a single set of controls, which will likely fail at some point leaving you wide open. Defense in depth recommends implementing layers of controls, different categories of controls (preventative, detective, and responsive), establishing zones of control (or enclaves), and using different technologies at the various layers. An enclave, also called a zone or domain, is an environment of systems all sharing the same risk profile and business function. These are usually logically or physically separated from other enclaves. A typical example of this is a De-Militarized Zone (DMZ). This is an enclave where you can place any directly Internet-facing services, such as e-mail or Web servers.

> **TIPS & TRICKS**
>
> Never let sensitive data reside in a DMZ. Systems in this DMZ zone may be front-end interfaces to applications with sensitive data, but that information itself should never be stored on the DMZ systems, since they are exposed to far more attacks.

A common mistake is to assume that all services in a DMZ should be treated the same. To truly implement a defense in depth strategy, even resources with different risk profiles and business functions in the DMZ itself may need to be separated from other DMZ resources to minimize transitive risk. Transitive risk is the exposure imposed by a resource of lower sensitivity and with looser security controls on a resource with a higher sensitivity. Just because two systems share an Internet connection or user community, it doesn't mean that those systems should have unrestricted access to each other.

The layers of control also need to be more than just implementing several instances of the same control. For example, you may have two layers of Check Point firewalls: one set between the Internet and your DMZ, and the other set between your DMZ and internal network. But if there is a vulnerability announced by Check Point, chances are it can be exploited on all the firewalls, thus not providing any better security than a single layer of firewalls. The trick is to vary the technology and even the control vendor in some cases. Typically, vulnerabilities only affect a certain brand of technology like Cisco or Microsoft; variation in the make of the technologies can increase the complexity of maintenance and management, but it decreases the chances of all your controls being vulnerable at once. This is another example of the conflict between fulfilling the security principle of defense in depth versus the need for operational simplicity that we as security managers need to negotiate on a case-by-case basis.

TIPS & TRICKS

Consider using one anti-malware solution for desktop/laptops and another for servers. There have been several instances of vulnerabilities in the anti-malware software itself, not to mention that each one is successful at detecting different malware. Likewise, use a different vendor's virus scanning on the e-mail server versus your desktop scanner.

Separation of Duties

Just like the three branches of government in the United States, a secure environment requires checks and balances. The principle of Separation of Duties is intended to minimize errors and make it more difficult to exploit access privileges for personal gain. This principle requires the system to be built or process to be implemented so that no one person or group has authority to perform all privileged functions, especially all functions related to the creation and handling of sensitive or critical information. This concept can be applied to operational management tasks and has influenced the three-tier application architecture commonly used in many enterprises.

A simple example of this is the monitoring of system administrator activities on a critical server. You wouldn't want the system administrator doing the monitoring for their own activity; rather you want an objective third party like that person's manager, a member of the security team, or maybe a member of another operational group to do the monitoring. Similarly, a maker/checker control might be implemented in the change management process so that peers can check each others' work for mistakes. A change management system might require a second person to sign off on all changes before they can be implemented.

Other benefits of this approach include preventing single points of knowledge by encouraging cross-training and also by making it more difficult to abuse access privileges without collusion. Someone is much more likely to take advantage of their access if they can do it alone; having to involve another individual greatly lessens this likelihood. Many organizations actually require individuals in a privileged role to take a certain amount of vacation each year so that any questionable activities will quickly surface when someone else has to fill in those job responsibilities for 2 weeks.

Together the principles of Least Privilege, Defense in Depth, and Separation of Duties can greatly shape an organization's approach to security, and it should be incorporated into all security standards and control designs.

Threats to Information

When we talk about securing data, we need to think of the controls in terms of three information states:

In Transit: This refers to the data that is being electronically transmitted between systems or physically transported. Usually, this includes your network security and physical security controls.

In Process: This refers to the protection of data as it is being used by the system or application. For instance, when a user inputs data into a form, how is that data filtered and parsed, how is it stored in memory while being processed, and how is it made available to other users?

At Rest: These protections usually focus on protecting data where it is stored, whether that be a database or a backup tape. Typical controls for this state include Access Controls, Encryption, and Physical Protections.

For every state that data can take, there is a long list of threats to that information. The major categories are

- **Unauthorized Disclosure**, such as a data breach
- **Corruption**, such as an accidental modification of a data record
- **Denial of Service**, such as an attack that makes a resource unavailable
- **Inability to Prove the Source of an Attack**, such as the use of a shared account to perform an unauthorized activity

Notice that the first three categories map to Confidentiality, Integrity, and Availability, respectively, and the fourth category maps to Accountability. Threat assessments and modeling will be discussed in greater detail in Chapter 5.

THE DEATH OF INFORMATION SECURITY

The organization and the structure of security teams are changing drastically. There isn't just one recommended way to organize the security function within an organization anymore. Now, as other parts of the business take more responsibility for protecting information resources, you may start to wonder whether security as a function will be carved up and absorbed into other business units.

Security Team Responsibilities

Security teams should really approach an Information Security program as if they are consultants hired to help guide the business. The majority of their time should be spent interpreting security policies and standards, and helping the organization to understand how and when to apply them. If they are spending all their time with enforcement, then either the educational aspects of the program are failing or they don't have the necessary support from the leaders in the organization.

A major component of your security program will be identifying areas of the organization that don't meet internal policies and standards, assessing the risk of noncompliance, and working with the business owners to address the risks. These basic risk assessments are intended to ensure that established security standards are being followed and to identify any gaps. The goal is not 100% compliance, but rather to identify high-risk areas to prioritize remediation.

The trend is definitely for security teams to have fewer staff members in roles requiring operational/technical management and monitoring of security devices. The role of a security manager is also evolving into more of an oversight focus, providing guidance and tools for the existing operational teams to perform their daily functions, and regularly assessing their effectiveness.

Modern Information Security Challenges

There are several challenges with today's dynamic business environments that can make it difficult to adequately protect the organization's resources. Among these many challenges, the following are worth highlighting:

1. **Blending of corporate and personal lives** – As the work day has less of a distinct start and end, it becomes harder to differentiate between work life and personal life. For example, employees use company e-mail for some personal communications, and some employees may be issued a BlackBerry or cell phone that they use for limited personal use. Many people may not even have a home computer and instead use their company issued laptop for everything, including running personal software, like their tax software or computer games for their kids. On the flip side, some employees may bring a personal laptop into the office and try to plug it in to the company's network.

2. **Inconsistent enforcement of policies** – Many organizations either haven't enforced their policies in the past or have done so inconsistently depending on the position of the employee. This causes many issues when a security function tries to crack down on violators. Hopefully, you don't work for one of those organizations who have buried their security policies on some internal Web site that no one ever reads!

3. **IT doesn't own and control all devices** – We alluded to this issue above regarding the use of personal mobile devices, but what if the organization doesn't provide a PDA to the sales team, so employees buy their own and start storing client lists on it and trying to connect it to your wireless network in the office? What happens when you need to do an investigation on that device—can you? These are questions that need to be considered, discussed with legal, and included in your risk assessments.

4. **Blurring of internal versus external** – The edge or perimeter of the network isn't as clear as it used to be. In the past, we established strong perimeter

controls to regulate access into and out of the network, but now, that perimeter has been pushed out to partners with extranets, to third parties with hosting services, and to employees' homes with VPN solutions that can be used from a personal desktop. Where would you even draw the line now?

5. **Covert attacks are no longer obvious** – It used to be typical for a virus infection to be big and messy, causing severe damage and being immediately obvious when you were infected. Now, however, attackers are silent and stealthy. They don't want to erase your data or take down your system, instead, they want to slowly steal your data or use your computing power to attack other victims. They do their best to be undetectable with rootkits and backdoor Trojans.

6. **Moving target** – As we mature and get better at securing our systems, attackers find new and more creative ways to bypass our controls. As we close the easy ways in, they develop more sophisticated attacks. It is a never ending battle.

The next time you hear about some new exploit being demonstrated at one of the hacker conferences like Black Hat, DEF CON, or ShmooCon, just remember that very few weaknesses or attacks are really new. Old attacks get repackaged and new buzzwords are coined, but in so many cases, hackers and security researchers are just applying the same fundamental attack strategies to new targets. We in the information security field have the habit of making the same design mistakes over and over.

The threat landscape is constantly changing, and it can be easy to fall behind. Techniques and strategies that worked last year may not be enough this year. Some security programs seem to spend all their time analyzing the slightest change in threat intelligence with little actionable results. Your security program does need to be flexible and you do need to be aware of the threat trends, but this doesn't require minute-to-minute monitoring of news feeds. Take advantage of the threat reports and study the major trends, and adjust your approach periodically. Try to avoid the pitfalls and allure of chasing every new vulnerability or hacking technique that makes the news. An accomplished security professional knows how to filter out the noise and focus on the imminent threats.

TIPS & TRICKS

Try signing up for just one threat intelligence feed and set aside 30 minutes every morning to review it first thing.

The Next Evolution

As the field continues to move toward an integrated approach with other parts of the business and a risk-based model that the organization implements outside the security group, it raises doubts about the future of information security as a function and distinct team within the business. Will the Chief Information Security Officer (CISO) exist as a position in 10 years? What about the privacy or compliance officer? No one can say for sure, but it seems likely that these functions and the oversight being performed by the information security team today will be absorbed into existing functions within the organization. Most security awareness programs try to emphasize that protecting the organization's interests is not just the responsibility of the security team, but that every employee is responsible for security. But be careful what you wish for—the realization of this dream may land you out of a job or at least a change in boss. Ultimately, wherever the functions and activities of information security end up in the organization, each business will need someone with vision, leadership, and subject matter expertise to provide oversight and ensure that there is a cohesive approach to protecting the business' interests. Positioning yourself as a risk manager, as opposed to a security manager, may give you more longevity.

SUMMARY

Understanding how the Information Security field has evolved from a technical group focused on perimeter protections will help you to understand some of the current perceptions of the security function that need to be overcome. Performing any of the risk activities in this book, and especially building a program around them, requires a solid foundation in the basic security principles of Least Privilege, Defense in Depth, and Separation of Duties. These concepts will drive many of the security design decisions, just like Confidentiality, Integrity, Availability, and Accountability will inform the requirements for controls to mitigate specific risks. The sooner we stop using the concept of best practices as a crutch to justify security controls, the sooner we can focus on risk-based prioritization.

References

[1] NIST 800-37, Guide for Applying the Risk Management Framework to Federal Information Systems. http://csrc.nist.gov/publications/nistpubs/800-37-rev1/sp800-37-rev1-final.pdf, 2009 (accessed 29.12.09).
[2] Verizon Business, 2010 Data Breach Investigations Report. http://www.verizonbusiness.com/resources/reports/rp_2010-data-breach-report_en_xg.pdf, 2010 (accessed 21.07.10).

Risky Business

2

INFORMATION IN THIS CHAPTER

- Applying Risk Management to Information Security
- Business-Driven Security Program
- Security as an Investment
- Qualitative versus Quantitative

INTRODUCTION

A common view of the Information Security function is that it is all about encryption and firewalls. We are perceived as the group that is always telling the business what they can't do and is constantly screaming about the vulnerabilities that will bring the organization to the state of ruin. This perception has really hurt the profession over the years, but the good news is that this image of security is beginning to change for the better. It is all too easy to fall into the trap of being constantly at odds with the business, but in the end, this will get you nowhere. Many security professionals want the business to operate in the equivalent of medical clean room. It just isn't realistic to address every weakness and neutralize every threat. The goal is no longer to be secure, but it is to be secure enough. The tough part is defining what secure enough means for your organization.

APPLYING RISK MANAGEMENT TO INFORMATION SECURITY

Think of Information Security as a way to maintain the level of risk exposure in the organization within acceptable levels without unduly constraining the growth of the business. In theory, if you reduce the unnecessary risks from people, processes, and technology, then the business opportunities will increase. You want to reduce the risk of operating the business wherever possible so that the organization can take business risks elsewhere. The idea is that every organization has a threshold—or maximum appetite—for risk across the entire business. So, if the organization wants to attempt a risky business venture that might provide a competitive advantage, then you have to reduce the organization's risk in other areas to stay within that healthy range of risk tolerance. The information security function's role is to reduce the organization's operating risk with sound information security practices in order to enable the organization to take business risks that their competitors can't.

Mission of Information Security

Fundamentally, the Information Security field is all about managing the risks to sensitive data and critical resources. For those of us who have been in this field for a long time, we may need to reorient ourselves to embrace the perspective that not every vulnerability needs to be "fixed." The goal of Information Security should be to ensure that the confidentiality, integrity, availability, and accountability of the organization's resources (tangible and intangible assets) are maintained at an acceptable level. Information Security has a broad set of responsibilities, ranging from training and awareness to digital forensics. Given this wide range of job roles, there are many ways to structure your team and position the function within the organization.

Although the level of desired assurance (or tolerance level) varies between organizations, industries, and maybe even between business units within the same organization, the fundamental goals remain constant. Essentially, there is no single out-of-the-box security approach, implementation, or standard that will work for every organization. Any concept of "industry best practices" that is blindly followed will certainly lead to poor-risk decisions. A good-risk model will take into account the specific needs and objectives of the organization and guide the selection of the appropriate strategy to bring the level of risk exposure into an acceptable range.

So if the Information Security isn't all about firewalls and encryption, what is it about? In the current climate of privacy concerns and heavy regulations, you might say that organizations should focus on compliance. Although this approach might look good on paper, any security program with the sole mission of achieving compliance is going to fail to provide any real assurance, which means you will have to take that long walk to the CEO's office at some point to explain the latest major security breach in your "compliant" environment. Regulations are made to fit the lowest common denominator and then are watered down from there. Many security programs tie themselves to a single regulation or standard and check off the boxes on the compliance list, but they never really secure themselves against the threats to their particular environment. We need more than a checklist to defend our environments, which is to say that a quarterly Qualys vulnerability scan, for example, isn't enough to protect your organization.

It is easy to get caught up in the modeling of malicious threats; however, accidental damages are often more common and dangerous. Data entry errors, misconfigurations, and physical blunders (just to name a few) represent a significant headache for most IT functions. Later in this book when threat modeling and risk articulation are covered, you will want to keep accidents in mind along with the more sensational hacker attacks.

Goal of Risk Management

To understand the goal of risk management and how it relates to information security, we must first agree on a definition of risk. Like all the terminology used in risk management, the definitions for "risk" range widely as well. One definition for risk applied to information security specifically is:

The expected loss of confidentiality, integrity, availability, or accountability.

The following is a more general definition for risk from Jack Jones, the creator of the Factor Analysis of Information Risk (FAIR) framework, which will be reviewed in Chapter 11:

"The probable frequency and probable magnitude of future loss" [1].

By combining these two definitions, you can see the intended focus for the information security function:

The probable frequency and probable magnitude of future loss of confidentiality, integrity, availability, or accountability.

We will use this as the definition for risk throughout the rest of this book, so you may want to flag this page and can refer back to it later, when we get into deeper risk discussions.

Given the constantly increasing security demands and quickly changing threats, it is essential for every security professional to understand how a robust risk model can become the cornerstone of a mature information security program. The sophistication of the threat landscape and ever increasing complexities of the legal and regulatory requirements are forcing the information security field to evolve into a more mature discipline that has to make hard choices about where to focus resources and how to prioritize mitigation efforts for the organization. You will quickly discover that the business does not see security as essential for profitability, so it becomes the responsibility of the security team to change that perception by working with other teams of the organization to define, control, and predict the uncertainty of negative events that could impact the organization's business objectives.

As security professionals, most of our daily activities are focused on trying to prevent vulnerabilities from being exploited and identifying new ones, or on bad days, discovering the resources that have already been compromised. There is no single perfect way to organize your security program or reporting structure, but it has become clear that the risk management program needs to be the umbrella for all the daily security activities. Whether it is working with auditors, processing new vulnerabilities from vendors, or reviewing the design of a new application development project, decisions must be closely focused on what is acceptable for the organization. Security professionals need to promote a corporate culture that encourages operating with an acceptable level of risk.

TIPS & TRICKS

Start thinking about managing the everyday risks that you uncover like a police investigation to bring down a large organized crime ring—sometimes you will have to let the little fish go, so you can catch the big fish.

Simply, the goal of risk management is to maximize the output of the organization (in terms of services, products, and revenue) while minimizing the chance of unexpected negative outcomes. You can look at this in terms of minimizing uncertainties related to your organization's products and services or aligning and controlling organizational components to produce the maximum output. The goal should never be zero exposure, but finding the right balance. It all comes down to well-informed decision making. The security program should be filling a governance and oversight role to help identify the risks that have the greatest chance of harming the organization with the most severe impact. If you have properly educated the organization about the likely risk exposures, then you have fulfilled your obligations even if the business chooses not to address the risks.

Architecting a Security Program

If policies are the foundational component of any mature information security program, then risk management needs to be the lens through which you view the organization. The building blocks of a security program are policies, standards, guidelines, procedures, and baselines, which you use to establish expectations about how to secure the sensitive resources. As a security professional, you may not have direct operational responsibility for managing an asset, but it is your job to guide the resource owners and the custodians to better manage their information-related risks. Security policy should set the tone for your security program, and the information security function should help the organization to understand how best to apply it. The security team may even have a more explicit charter within the organization that defines the scope and the expectations for that function. Policies should be of high level and relatively stable (that is, they should not change often). From these policies, you will develop more detailed artifacts, such as standards, guidelines, procedures, baselines, and design patterns, which should all be derived from the policy.

Similarly, the role of the risk management program should be well represented in the organization's security policy. Some of the topics that need to be covered in policies and standards are as follows:

- How the critical resources will be identified?
- The roles responsible for conducting risk assessments.
- The process that will be followed for risk assessments.
- How often assessments will be conducted?
- How findings will be scored and addressed?
- The process for requesting an exception.

Once you establish new policies and standards, be prepared to spend a lot of time interpreting those requirements as individual business cases and scenarios arise. You will always want to think back to the intent of the policy or standard and try to be flexible by allowing the organization to find its creative ways to meet those requirements when the solution may not match the letter of the standard. Having an exception approval process is essential on day one of implementation for any new policies or standards. A formal exception process not only demonstrates proper due diligence and increases visibility of key exposures but also provides a great opportunity for the security team to learn more about how the business actually functions and to uncover weaknesses that otherwise might go unnoticed until it is too late. You will want to promote a culture where other members in the organization are encouraged to identify risks and request exceptions for justified activities. Often, even when you are reviewing an exception request for a low-risk item, you might find that you will discover some other related exposures that are more critical to the organization.

WARNING

Even at the standard level, you need to be careful not to get too prescriptive about the actual implementation details of the risk management program. Instead, reference other internal risk assessment methodologies and established processes that will determine the specifics. For example, a security standard might designate that the frequency of risk assessment will be based on the criticality of the resource, but leave yourself the flexibility to define the criteria for criticality and the actual schedule outside of the standard.

How Does it Help?

When analyzing the threat landscape, it is important not to focus solely on the latest trends in magazines or the news media, but rather to model the threats that are specific to your industry or organization. A vulnerability without a corresponding threat is not a risk to the organization. To put it another way, if you have a weakness, but there is no one to exploit it, then there is no risk. Clearly, a data center in Kansas may be vulnerable to earthquakes, but shouldn't that organization be spending its resources mitigating the threat of tornados, which are far more frequent? Almost every day, we see organizations spending their time and resources mitigating the wrong risks because they haven't taken the time to properly analyze the risks that are most imminent for them. An organization may burn a lot of time and resources securing the wireless network when it is easier for an attacker to walk into a conference room and just plug-in to the wall. To be effective, a risk management program needs to identify these poor allocations of resources and help the organization prioritize the mitigation activities.

RISK DEEP DIVE

Prioritizing Vulnerabilities

Let's say you get an application penetration testing report back for your internal intranet site, and there are two findings as follows:

1. Cross-site scripting vulnerability
2. Privilege escalation vulnerability

(Continued)

(Continued)

Both were rated as high risks by the testing team, but there are only enough development resources to fix one in the next release of the intranet application. How would you advise senior management?

If you aren't familiar with the details of these vulnerabilities, start with a quick Google search. Cross-site scripting on a public-facing application might be a big risk, but for an internal application, it just isn't as exploitable. The privilege escalation has a much higher likelihood of being abused because it would be a more attractive attack vector for malicious insiders.

Keep in mind that risk can never be eliminated unless the threat is completely removed, the weakness is totally fixed, or the scenario is avoided altogether. As opposed to remediation actions that would fix a vulnerability, most mitigation actions are simply going to decrease the risk. For example, putting in a firewall is a mitigation step that doesn't eliminate the risk of a network compromise, but it does reduce the likelihood of this occurrence. Automatically purging sensitive data from a server after 90 days may reduce the severity of a compromise because less data is exposed. The goal is to reduce risk to an acceptable level without hindering business processes. If you get caught up in trying to eliminate (or remediate) every risk, you may be wasting resources. A certain level of risk exposure is almost always acceptable.

Not all risks are created equal. Later chapters in this book will discuss the many ways to rate and evaluate the risks, but the basic idea is to prioritize them. If you're spending time addressing four moderate-level risks while leaving one critical risk unaddressed, then you aren't spending your resources wisely. By defining a risk model with common definitions and ranking levels, you can present risks to senior management with all the information necessary for them to make an informed decision. You may find yourself escalating several critical risks to senior management at the same time, but there may only be enough resources to address some of them right away. So you need to help management understand the differences in urgency and impact to the organization.

As part of any risk evaluation, you should also consider the implications of not being compliant. For most regulations, you can estimate fairly accurately the potential fines that would result from noncompliance. If you are liable for $200k in fines from the regulator, but it is going to cost $800k to implement the required control, then our risk methodology would recommend not implementing the controls. Of course, this example is simplifying the issue slightly because in situations like these, there are probably other factors (like civil lawsuits, loss of business, and so on) to consider. But it still illustrates the point that we need to get away from blindly applying controls, take a step back, and do the analysis first. You just may not want to share that analysis with your regulator!

RISK DEEP DIVE

PCI Risk Example

A good example of a tough risk decision can be found when looking at the Payment Card Industry (PCI) requirements for protecting credit card and personal information. Although not technically a regulation, these standards come close to it for credit card processors and companies in the retail industry. Many of the large merchants have implemented full disk encryption or database level encryption to protect that data on back-end servers based on the PCI Data Security Standards (DSS) published by the major credit card companies:

PCI-DSS: Use of strong cryptography like disk encryption to protect sensitive data [2].

We already alluded to the idea that database encryption may be a suspect control in Chapter 1. Although encryption may be a good solution for mobile devices, it fails to mitigate the real threats of an application-level attack on databases storing card numbers in data centers. Let's look at why this standard may not make sense when applied to database servers.

Think about an attack on an application that stores credit card numbers in a database. In order to function, the application needs some way to decrypt the data regardless of whether it is stored on an encrypted drive or whether the database encrypts at a field level. This means that the best vector for an attacker is to exploit weaknesses in the application and use it to access card numbers in the database. In this case, all you have protected against is abuse of the data by the database administrators if you encrypt at a field level, or physical theft of the server itself if you encrypt at the drive level.

If the database server is in a retail store, maybe there is a real threat of physical theft, but think about databases in secure data centers. Is this control really making that sensitive data more secure? The only viable way to defeat these application attacks is to hash the sensitive data instead of encrypting it, but this only works for certain data types. It works well for an identifier or authentication credential because you can compare it in its hashed form, but for other sensitive data, you will need to present it back to the application in its raw format, which eliminates hashing as an option. Unless you are worried about an attacker physically running off with the drives in your servers, then full disk encryption isn't reducing your risk at all.

If an attacker doesn't target the application as their way in but rather goes after a vulnerability on the database server directly, then the encryption is even more useless. Chances are if they can compromise the server, they will also get access to the unencrypted data fairly easily.

Without a formal risk assessment and analysis methodology, many organizations will implement the controls they need to in order to be "compliant," but really not reduce their risk exposure at all.

Throughout this book, we will examine exactly how to perform a risk assessment inclusive of threat modeling to better evaluate the most applicable risks and choose controls that are appropriate for your organization. The intention is not to exhaustively cover methodologies and techniques for deriving complex likelihoods and frequencies or quantifying risks with a great level of precision. There have already been many publications to address these techniques in detail. The goal of this book is to help security professionals address a critical gap in knowledge about how to identify information security risks and articulate the implications for their organization. If you don't truly understand what questions to ask and where to look for exposures, then it won't matter how sophisticated your measurement techniques are.

To sum up the goal of Information Security even more simply, it is an attempt to ensure that authorized users have access to authorized information at the authorized time. Violations of this can take many forms, many of which we will explore throughout this book. The discipline of risk management will give you the tools to qualify the real risks to your organization and prioritize the remediation of exposures. In the end, you need to be able to articulate the risks and justify the recommended mitigation steps to the organization in terms the nontechnical management can understand.

BUSINESS-DRIVEN SECURITY PROGRAM

As previously discussed, every organization has a certain threshold for risks across the entire business; the challenge is gauging the executive team's risk appetite before an incident occurs. Whenever you join a new organization as a risk manager, it is important to take some time to observe how the business functions and understand the decisions that are being made. With this insight, you should begin to profile senior management's tolerance for risk in different areas. You can expand on this knowledge through direct conversations with the executives about areas of concern or even host more formal tabletop exercises to talk through likely incident scenarios. The important point is to use this as an opportunity to listen and profile the risk appetite of the organization through the lens of senior management. This idea of profiling your organization is explored in greater detail at the end of Chapter 4.

TIPS & TRICKS

Don't underestimate the power of just listening. Security professionals may be used to doing a lot of the talking, but listening and careful observation can be invaluable tools!

Work Smarter, Not Harder

When developing a security program, you need to start with the organization's objectives and identify how the security program can help achieve them, not the other way around. If you can't map a security initiative to a business objective, then you probably shouldn't be spending time on it. It can be overwhelming trying to tackle the hundreds or even thousands of vulnerabilities your organization may have, so you need a consistent and simple way to prioritize remediation for the organization. Limited time, money, and resources are always going to be a reality, so it is important to be strategic and not spend your political capital on the small stuff. If you are escalating a critical issue to the senior management, make sure that it is comparable with other organizational risks that your initiative might be pulling resources away from.

Even the most experienced and disciplined security professionals fall into the trap of information overload. There are just so many sources for potential and realized risk exposures, whether it be vulnerability advisories or actual incident reports, it can be easy to lose focus and try to take on everything at once. Less mature security programs don't establish their foundation on a robust risk model; they just dive in and start attacking every problem that they find until all their resources are exhausted. Even if you manage to keep up with the flood of new threats and vulnerabilities, you can't make any significant progress without a strategic vision for information security. Mature programs go beyond looking at each risk individually and instead begin to analyze the interdependent impact that every risk has on every other risk. For example, three moderate-level risks might all magnify each other and create a higher risk situation. Risk models may not have this level of sophistication on day one, but as your risk model evolves, your goal should be identifying these thematic or systemic issues.

You will often come across situations with regulators and auditors who expect you to assess every single weakness in your environment and have a plan to fix them instantly or be in 100% compliance with every security policy and standard as soon as it is published. Many security programs have tried (and failed) to go broad and deep at the same time, but there are never enough resources available for this approach. It is up to the security professionals to combat these expectations and educate outside assessors about the value of taking a risk-based approach to mitigating weaknesses. However, for this approach to be effective, you will need to demonstrate a comprehensive and repeatable process for assessing and handling risks within your organization. Start by identifying the resources that are most critical to the organization and focus your efforts there first. You may even be able to leverage existing work that has been done for business continuity purposes to rate the resources in the organization by criticality. The annual business objectives of the organization should be the primary factor influencing your information security initiatives. Start by identifying risks that could jeopardize the achievement of the organization's objectives, and you will build more credibility for the security function.

The tendency for new security leaders is to try to tackle a broad set of weaknesses all at once and get to a "perfect" state right away. The problem with this approach is that you may set an unsustainable pace as the demands and requirements keep expanding. It is always better to focus your efforts and establish sound practices on a small scale, and then, expand on these successes. Let's say, for example, that you are brought in to manage an organization that has no security policies or standards established. You could look at the industry recommendations for 10 to 15 policies, implement these, and then start to assess any gaps. Or you could assess the most critical areas of exposure or deficiencies and start with one to two carefully chosen policies. This way, you don't overwhelm the organization with change and out-of-compliance findings all at once. Similarly, you may be starting an initiative to establish regular vulnerability scanning of your environment. Why not start by scanning a single system, processing the results, and then scanning it again? No need to go after an entire network immediately. How you determine the areas of greatest need is what Part II of this book is all about.

Positioning Information Security

The Information Security industry has evolved beyond being able to rely on Fear, Uncertainty, and Doubt (FUD) to scare up money or resources for initiatives. The business is getting savvier, management is learning to ask the right questions, and we need to have good answers ready. Especially, in tough economic times, you may spend a lot of your time and energy justifying the expense of your program and future initiatives. Many organizations have only invested in information security after feeling the bite of a major data breach. Your goal is to avoid being one of those organizations, but this requires doing the upfront analysis work to determine how best to allocate your scarce resources.

When you're making your case to the business managers, you need to speak in terms that they will understand. Start by describing how this weakness will hurt their bottom line and how likely it is to occur. Risk is a common language that the business managers will understand, and you can use that to your advantage. Whenever you are making your case to the senior management, it is important to demonstrate that you have done your due diligence. A gut feeling isn't going to be sufficient justification, for example.

TIPS & TRICKS

Try to shift the image of information security by changing the vocabulary. There should be no such thing as a "security requirement"; instead, position it as a "business requirement."

Ultimately, you need to identify and understand the risks and make a sound business decision based on the information you have about the likelihood and severity of the consequences. You can't plug every hole and fix every issue—and no one expects you to—but you can apply a risk-based approach and address the most critical exposures first. Not every risk needs to be eliminated or completely mitigated; management will always appreciate suggestions for how risk exposures can be reduced to an acceptable level rather than spending a lot of resources trying to "fix" the problem.

WARNING

Regulations and compliance pressures may help in moving forward some of your initiatives, but be careful not to make compliance the end goal. Securing to a regulation only makes you compliant, not secure. Just being compliant shouldn't help you sleep better at night.

Due Diligence

Security programs will always be judged by the outside parties, whether they be auditors, customers, regulators, or even judges in court, so it is important to demonstrate that you have done your due diligence. In general, you will be compared with whatever the standards or common practices are for your industry. For example, no one expects you to implement every new security technology as soon as it hits the market, but if you have ignored a common security feature that comes standard on all the modern devices, then you could be opening your organization up to liability. Ultimately, you need to identify and understand the risks, and then, make a sound business decision based on the information you have about the likelihood and severity of the potential consequences.

A good example of this is in the wireless space: WPA2 protection (replacing the weaker WEP and WPA options) is now an established and readily available option on laptops and access points, so not implementing this level of encryption is not demonstrating due care. Of course, you may have some legacy devices that aren't capable of WPA2 or even WPA, so this is where a risk acceptance comes in. Possibly, you could find another control to further mitigate the risk of not implementing strong encryption and authentication on these legacy devices.

The steps necessary to secure your environment are far too numerous to list here, but some basic guidelines are listed as follows:

- You never want your organization's resources to be used in an attack on another organization.
- Even if you can't prevent a resource from being exploited, it is important to provide the means to recover from the attack.
- A basic requirement for any program is a comprehensive ability to detect and remove malware, and detection needs to be automated even if the removal is manual.
- Establish a standard(s) for remote access into the network—especially if there is a work-from-home program—and require approval for any new methods of remote access.
- Identify and monitor all external connections (that is, entry points into the network); have up-to-date network diagrams of all external connections, and start by deploying network intrusion detection systems (IDS) at these logical access points.
- Implement a patch management system that covers both desktops in the office and any remote or mobile devices.
- Implement some form of host-based security control suite (anti-malware, firewall, and so on) on all desktops and laptops.
- Publish a basic set of policies, standards, guidelines, and configuration baselines—this is a good low-cost control.
- Perform background checks for personnel in privileged roles.

Ultimately, not every vulnerability is serious enough to deserve immediate attention. It all comes down to well-informed risk management decisions. For instance, in the wireless example noted previously, it may be that upgrading all the legacy devices to be WPA2 compatible is a big expense, so instead, you might be able to recommend alternatives that reduce the exposure.

> **WARNING**
>
> Background checks can be implemented for existing employees and new hires, but you need to be prepared for the circumstance when a "trusted" member of the staff with a long tenure will have a black mark on his/her record. Be sure to work out, well in advance, with HR and Legal, how you will handle these situations.

Facilitating Decision Making

Risk assessments aren't only useful when trying to remediate vulnerabilities; it should also be used to make decisions about investments in technology and other IT improvements. Assume that your company is looking to outsource a function to a third party or purchase a new technology platform. It is critical to assess the risks before making a business decision. Risk assessments can also be used to determine whether a project is worth pursuing, what controls might be needed, and to show due diligence in the evaluation process.

Be sure to document who was involved in the evaluation team, what options were considered, and what specific decisions were made. It is important to track these details in case decisions are questioned later. If you don't capture the specifics, it will be hard to remember several months later exactly how you came to a particular conclusion. This is especially useful as evidence to provider auditors and regulators. A risk assessment should be integrated into the process for vendor selection and any acquisitions. Whenever a contract is being signed for a third-party service, a decision should be made about whether it requires a security risk assessment. This decision will generally be based on the type of service being provided and the sensitivity level of data involved. If your organization is considering purchasing an application or hiring a third-party service provider, there are many security considerations that need to be included in the process. When hiring a service provider for example, it is important to know if the service will process or store any sensitive information off-site. The data involved may fall under the current privacy laws, for example, and require additional provisions of which the business owner might not be aware.

> **TIPS & TRICKS**
>
> A good way to ensure that you have proper visibility into the decisions that are being made is to establish a checkpoint for a security risk assessment in the technology acquisition or vendor selection processes. Make sure that there is a formal security approval step in the process.

It is important to be prepared for these situations with a set of questions to quickly assess whether a vendor will meet the organization's security needs for that particular project. Then, define criteria for assessing and approving the vendor. This may include several reviews at different levels of granularity along the process of evaluating vendors. A good tool to use when assessing third parties is the Standardized Information Gathering (SIG) questionnaire, which is published by the BITS organization [3]. BITS is a not-for-profit industry consortium whose members are from 100 of the largest financial institutions across the United States, and they have developed a common information security questionnaire that can be used to assess the security program of third parties at several different levels of detail. You may you use a risk sensitivity ranking of projects to determine the level of questionnaire that is required for each project. A low-sensitivity vendor may require no specific assessment, just the standard contractual controls, whereas a moderate- or high-sensitivity vendor who handles sensitive data or has direct access to your environment may require a SIG Level 2 and full SIG review. These considerations will be covered in more detail in Chapter 10. Essentially, some level of security risk assessment should be performed whenever money is being spent or a contract is being put in place.

PASSWORD LOCKOUT POLICY

Consider a scenario in which you are hosting a Web-based application, such as an e-commerce site. Your corporate standard requires that all user accounts be locked after three failed login attempts, and accounts must then be unlocked by a security administrator. This is a common practice for many organizations; however, this is causing issues for your customers because they have to call support every time they lock out their account. The support managers are looking for other ways to increase the efficiency, so they have recommended that the number of failed attempts be increased from three to five and that the lockout configuration be changed to automatically unlock the account after 15 minutes instead.

- Current configuration:
  - Three attempts before lockout
  - Unlock requires administrator
- Proposed change:
  - Five attempts before lockout
  - Automatic unlock after 15 minutes

So would you approve this proposal from an information security perspective? As you're making your decision, consider the following:

1. Are there any issues with the current configuration?
2. What are the risks with the proposed changes?
3. Is there sufficient business justification?
4. Could additional controls mitigate any risks?

If your initial reaction is to deny this request, then think about how you would justify your decision. Some points to consider for the current configuration are as follows:

1. That it is vulnerable to a denial-of-service attack.
2. There may not be a good way for a security administrator to authenticate a user over the phone when they call in to unlock the account.
3. This puts burden on the support staff to process unlock requests.
4. It is inconvenient for customers.
5. The current controls make it hard for an attacker to perform brute-force password attacks.

Now, consider the new proposal:

1. Is it really viable to execute a brute-force attack against a password at the rate of five tries every 15 minutes?
2. Could logging and alerting be put in place to detect multiple unlocks in a given period of time?
3. It eliminates the denial of service and over the phone authentication issues.
4. It takes all the burden off the support staff to process unlock requests.
5. It would take most customers more than 15 minutes to call support and get their account unlocked anyway.
6. What other password controls like complexity, history, or expiration are in place to further lessen the risks?
7. Will this put you out of compliance with any regulations or customer contracts?
8. If the user got the password wrong for the first three times, is there any chance that the user would get it right the fourth or fifth time?

A reasonable approach might be to accept the proposal to automatically unlock the accounts after 15 minutes, as long as there is adequate monitoring and alerting if a single account is locked several times in a row to catch brute-force attempts. You might also consider restricting the automatic unlock only to user accounts and not system or service accounts. Failed passwords for a system or service account usually indicates a bigger problem than just a user forgetting the password, and it could be better to force an administrator to intervene when those accounts are locked out. Regarding the increase of failed attempts from three to five, you may not feel that this imposes any significant additional risk, but it may still reject that part of the proposal because it would put the organization out of compliance with customers' own policies and expectations. On the basis of this analysis, you may offer the following compromise:

- Three attempts before lockout
- Automatic unlock after 15 minutes for user accounts only
- Unlock requires administrator, for system or service accounts (nonuser)
- Monitoring of lockouts must send an alert when three automatic unlocks occur in a row

This demonstrates how the business needs should be considered along side the actual risks of the proposal and a good compromise reached through a collaborative process.

SECURITY AS AN INVESTMENT

Industry experts are constantly arguing about the existence of a Return on Investment (ROI) for security spending. Thus far, no one has really demonstrated that there is a direct way to show a true ROI in the strictest definition of the term, unless your company sells security products or services. The first Google result for ROI is from Investopedia:

> "*A performance measure used to evaluate the efficiency of an investment or to compare the efficiency of a number of different investments [4].*"

The concept is focused on measuring the profit that results from an investment, and security investments rarely result in profits directly. Rather security investments are made to reduce losses. It is safe to say that, like insurance, security investments should prevent or decrease losses resulting from unmanaged risks, but that they will never directly result in profits that can be measured. A fascinating debate on the subject of security ROI was published in the ISSA magazine in 2008 in an article titled *The Great Debate: Security Spending* [5]. This conversation between Jos Pols and Donn Parker is not only a great discussion about how to frame the value of security investments but also a wonderful illustration of how the security field needs to separate itself from the old guard who focused entirely on best practices and personal experience to guide organizations through the maze of the information security lifecycle.

For most organizations, security is seen as a Cost Center, and the best you can do is try to enable the business to take business risks or add value by differentiating your organization from competitors. We are in the business of preventing and containing disasters. At the very least, you can hope to minimize the cost of security and lessen the impact of any eventual exploit. Your job is to help prevent unnecessary spending to recover from an exploit that could have been avoided, but often times, organizations are willing to take the risk knowing completely well what the implications are.

How you position security in the organization in large part determines the amount of influence you will have in your company. If you simply say the "sky is falling" all the time as justification for security resources, dollars, and initiatives, then your influence will quickly diminish. If you can steer clear of the "Chicken Little Mentality" and instead offer a reasonable approach, derived from an understanding of the organization's mission and what it takes to achieve it, you will be seen as a contributing partner within the organization, not an alarmist. Where the security group in your organization reports into will determine how your funding and budgets are determined, but it is safe to say that most organizations expect you to deliver a lot in the way of protection with very little investment.

The US Secret Service may keep the president safe, but they won't make him/her a better president. The same is true in information security. Just because you are protecting the organization from breaches and other disasters, doesn't mean that you are necessarily adding to the business' bottom line. If we focus on how information security can benefit the objectives of the organization and align our own initiatives accordingly, then we have a better chance of not being perceived as the enemy to progress and a black hole for money.

Whether you look at information security as an investment or as more analogous to an insurance policy, there are definitely ways to show the value of security by reducing risk levels in line with business objectives. It isn't accurate to report on the ROI of security, but certainly, the value of security investments can be demonstrated and tracked through metrics.

Security Metrics

Metrics should be a way for you to demonstrate how the security function is improving over time, and for that, you need a good measurement of your starting point, also known as a benchmark. When you are defining the metrics that you will report to the senior management, make sure that you are first challenging yourself as to why the metric should be meaningful to management. Too many programs produce complex statistics and graphs that are ultimately meaningless. Before you produce and report a metric, question the value of the activity or effort being reported.

Less is more. Choose three to four different metrics to report and focus on improving them from quarter to quarter. Process improvement opportunities always make good metrics (for example, it used to take us 25 man hours per week to analyze log files for attacks, and now after implementing a new security monitoring system, it only takes three man hours).

RISK DEEP DIVE

Going through the Motions

It is important to understand the difference between activity and performance metrics. Just giving the management team a metric of how many times the firewall has blocked traffic on your DMZ is an example of an activity metric and really doesn't demonstrate value. However, if you could correlate that with internal malware infections that were blocked from communicating with their command-and-control host to transfer out sensitive data or download additional malware, and maybe even compare that to a previous malware infection where this firewall wasn't in place to block malicious traffic, now you have a meaningful metric.

What if you report to the management how many suspected incidents your team has followed up on over the last three months? Does this really provide any meaningful data to the management? Not really because those are just activities. It may show how hard your team is working or how busy they are, but it doesn't show your team's value. You really have no good means to measure how many incidents were missed. Instead, consider a metric that shows the number of events that your team caught early and was able to contain before it lead to an incident requiring public notification. Unfortunately, the problem with this metric is that you need bad things to happen each month for your metric to improve.

Another metric might be how often high-risk system patches were applied within the recommended timeframe after being released. You probably won't have to worry about there not being enough patches coming out regularly for that metric to improve over time. Of course, the challenge will be communicating to the management what an acceptable level of patching is. For example, is 90% enough? Should you be aiming for 99%?

Often, we find ourselves trying to prove a null hypothesis. You may spend a lot of time and resources implementing a new preventative security control, and then, you want to show its effectiveness. Even if you see a subsequent improvement, you can never say with 100% certainty that the preventative controls you implemented are related to the decrease in the number of incidents: how do you know that the attackers didn't just use another threat path this month or independently decide to target another organization? However, you can report on the number of attempts that were defeated by that control. This is especially difficult if you implement a control to combat an expected attack and there is no history of exploit attempts in the past. Let's say that you decide to reinforce your physical controls around your data center to prevent someone from driving right up to the building and doing damage to the data center. You install some large cement blocks outside the building that prevent cars from getting within 200 yards. Can you now claim success that no one successfully attacked your data center in this way after deploying the controls? Technical controls should be looked at in the same way.

Occasionally, it is just as important to report to the management about what isn't getting done so that they understand the extent to which your team is under-staffed or how much you need a technology to automate some work. It is important that this be presented tactfully, however, so that it doesn't come across as complaining.

Sometimes, an activity metric (for example, we analyzed 2,000 lines of code or responded to 10 incidents) can hide the varying level of effort behind the work, so it may help to include the number of man hours spent to help quantify the level of effort. Metrics can help if they are accurate and accumulated over time, so it is important to record these data if you want to have any hope of draw-ing meaningful conclusions. There are many useful resources available with recommendations for creating good security metrics. Be sure to keep metrics and reporting in mind as you develop your own risk management program.

WARNING

Remember, that you are protecting your organization's reputation, information, and assets, not yours. Don't take the decisions personally that the business makes about whether or not to protect an asset. It is your job to present all the information and help them make an informed decision. You will win in some cases and lose in others, and there is no time to wallow when decisions don't go your way. Executives have to weigh many concerns when prioritizing initiatives, and you may not be aware of other factors, like long-term strategy shifts or emerging business partnerships, which may be influencing a decision.

The information security group/team needs to be closely aligned with the goals of the organization. All the yearly objectives of the security team should directly map to and support the organization's stated business goals. No security for secur-ity's sake any more. We should always look for opportunities to enable the business and make business processes more efficient. If you can make security a selling point or differentiator to customers, then you will be in a great position. Every orga-nization must determine the best way to give the senior management a view of the organization's current risk posture, without causing information overload.

QUALITATIVE VERSUS QUANTITATIVE

If you're familiar with the almost religious debate between Windows enthusiasts and Apple fanatics, then you can appreciate the debate in the field between Quali-tative and Quantitative risk analysis proponents. In reality, there are benefits and limitations of both approaches, and a lot of room in between for those of us who use some of each. What each approach is trying to calculate is the Risk Exposure value. Essentially, risk exposure is a measurement of our risk, which we defined previously as the probable frequency and probable magnitude of future loss of C-I-A-A. Another way to look at risk exposure is that it is a measurement of the probability that a threat will occur and the impact the threat will have on a given business process or mission. As you begin to analyze risks, keep in mind that each combination of threat and vulnerability may have a different risk exposure even if they share a threat or vulnerability in common.

Qualitative Analysis

Most commonly, you will see professionals in the security field using a qualitative approach to rate risks, either because there just isn't enough accurate historical data to calculate the probabilities and magnitudes of risks, like an insurance actuary would, or because it is just more approachable for those who are new to the discipline. Most qualitative approaches use a relative scale (for example, Low–Moderate–High) to rate risks based on some predefined criteria for each level and rely on the knowledge and experience of the assessor for accuracy. The downside is that this makes a qualitative approach very subjective and prone to inaccuracies and imprecision.

On the other hand, many quantitative models have been proposed over the years with very complex equations for calculating risk, but this relies heavily on having accurate historical data about previous breaches, and in some cases, understanding some advanced mathematical concepts. An alternative to the quantitative approach is to build a simple model around a qualitative scale and use a mapping table (also called a risk matrix), as shown in Figure 2.1, to determine the final risk exposure level. One such model is to take a three-level scale for Severity on the x-axis and three-level scale for Likelihood on the y-axis.

Especially, when you are building a risk management program from the ground up, anything more complex than this has a good chance of never getting off the ground or stalling out in the early stages. You need to be aware of the

	Severity		
	High	**Moderate**	**Low**
High	High	High	Moderate
Moderate	High	Moderate	Low
Low	Moderate	Low	Low

(Likelihood on the y-axis)

FIGURE 2.1

Basic qualitative mapping table.

culture and maturity of your organization. For many organizations, explicitly reviewing and rating risks at this level will be overwhelming enough for them, and if you try to push forward a more complex quantitative model, you risk losing them completely. Like everything in information security, start small and get some successes under your belt before tackling the more complex (and more precise) quantitative models. All the program elements in this book have been designed and presented in a modular way, so you can always substitute a quantitative analysis methodology down the road when you're ready.

The benefit of the qualitative risk matrix is that it is easy for the business to visualize and understand how changes in either the likelihood or severity will change the end result. It also provides a good reference for making decisions about accepting risks or approving exceptions. Let's assume that you have identified a risk with Moderate likelihood and Moderate severity. Using the mapping table in Figure 2.1, that combination of severity and likelihood would result in a Moderate risk exposure, but imagine that the business wants to accept the risk as is without any further mitigation. Depending on the sensitivity of the target resource, this may or may not be within the acceptable tolerance range. We will look at more in depth risk assessments in later chapters once we have established some more basic risk concepts. For now, keep in mind that these simple scales for risk give you a lot of flexibility for prioritizing risks and making consistent decisions regarding mitigation actions.

The simple mapping table in Figure 2.1 gives you a mechanism to rate the risk exposures, but notice that it doesn't account for the sensitivity of the asset itself. So you may end up with a high-level risk exposure on both your benefits application and a printer in the mailroom, but clearly those assets aren't equal in importance even if the risks have the same severity and likelihood scores. These considerations will be covered in Chapter 6.

Quantitative Analysis

Quantitative analysis approaches will focus on hard numbers and calculations to determine the risk exposure. Generally, this will result in some kind of dollar value. Most of the models take advantage of probability theory and statistics to measure risk exposure. Many formulas for risk have been proposed, including:

- Sensitivity $\times$ Severity $\times$ Likelihood = Risk Exposure
- Exposure Rating = Severity^2 $\times$ Threat

  One industry researcher has even offered a formula that includes six variables:

- Vulnerability
- Popularity
- Exposure
- Threats
- Asset Value
- System

Meanwhile, the Common Vulnerability Scoring System (CVSS) [6], which is used to rate the risk of most publicly released vulnerability notifications, uses a formula so complex that it requires a scoring tool to be usable. Clearly, there are many factors to consider when measuring risk, and most of these sample equations account for these factors in some way. The following is the most common calculation that you will see in a textbook:

Single Loss Expectancy × Average Rate of Occurrence = Annualized Loss Expectancy

However, like many textbook concepts, this one isn't commonly used in the industry. It calculates an Annual Loss Expectancy based on a Single Loss Expectancy and Annual Rate of Occurrence. For example, if you expect to lose five BlackBerries this year, and the cost to replace one BlackBerry is $50, then your ALE is 5 × $50 = $250. If you only lost one blackberry every 2 years, your ALE 0.5 × $50 = $25.

The challenge is that it is very difficult to quantify the value of our assets when we consider reputational loss and other intangibles, much less predict the rate of occurrence without large volumes of historical data. But don't lose hope; there is actually a lot of great research being done in the space of quantitative risk analysis specific to information security. If you would like to get involved in this work, a good resource is the Society for Information Security Risk Analysts (SIRA) [7].

Whether you use a qualitative or quantitative model really doesn't matter, just as long as the model provides accurate determinations of risk that the organization can use to make consistent decisions about priorities. As the quantitative methods evolve and hopefully more tools like CVSS become available, you will likely see more adoption of these models, but most organizations will have their hands full with simpler qualitative models for a long time.

Both qualitative and quantitative analysis approaches will be reviewed in more detail in Chapter 6, and a particular qualitative risk model will be used throughout the book to rate risk examples.

SUMMARY

Whether you formally align your information security program with a risk management methodology or not, you are forced to make risk decisions every day as part of your function. You will see greater success and encounter fewer obstacles if you can learn how to look at your organization through the lens of acceptable risk. Even starting with the most basic qualitative analysis model will immediately produce measurable improvements in the efficiency and effectiveness of your program. When properly packaged, these metrics can be presented to the senior management to demonstrate the value of security investments for the business.

Action Plan

After reading this chapter, you should consider taking the following actions in your own organization:

- Map each of your security program's annual objectives to at least one of your organization's objectives. If you can't find a match, remove it from your list.
- Integrate "acceptable risk" into your everyday vocabulary.
- Before you say no to any business initiative because of security concerns, make yourself a list of all the likely risks and propose a compromise instead.
- Pick one solid metric that demonstrates the performance improvements being made by the security team and regularly present that metric to the senior management.
- If you don't already have a risk model, immediately adopt a simple qualitative risk model and start prioritizing your risk activities.

References

[1] J. Jones, An Introduction to Factor Analysis of Information Risk (FAIR). www.risk managementinsight.com/media/docs/FAIR_introduction.pdf, 2010 (accessed 06.03.10).
[2] PCI Security Standards Council. www.pcisecuritystandards.org, 2010 (accessed 02.02.10).
[3] Standardized Information Gathering Questionnaire (SIG). www.sharedassessments.org, 2009 (accessed 16.11.09).
[4] Investopedia. www.investopedia.com/terms/r/returnoninvestment.asp, 2010 (accessed 30.01.10).
[5] D. Parker, J. Pols, The Great Debate: Security spending, ISSA Magazine, April 2008.
[6] A Complete Guide to the Common Vulnerability Scoring System, Version 2.0. http://www.first.org/cvss/cvss-guide.html, 2010 (accessed 30.01.10).
[7] Society of Information Risk Analysts (SIRA). www.societyinforisk.org, 2011 (accessed 05.01.11).

The Risk Management Lifecycle

INTRODUCTION

If you think about risks in your own organization, you might think about a weakness that is found during the software development process, an unknown dependency that is discovered during a disaster, or maybe a manual process that is prone to human error. In all these cases, the risk will certainly change and evolve over time. You may assess that exposure as being a critical level risk to the organization today, but in 6 months the risk may be reduced as the result of mitigation efforts. You are likely to see shifts in threats and priorities of the organization over time that can greatly affect a previously assessed level of risk. A SQL injection attack may be your biggest threat today, but tomorrow it might be the spread of malware through iPhone applications. Similarly, the sensitivity of your resources will likely change over time, so your risk management process needs to account for these shifts by monitoring changes in the threat landscape, the effectiveness of risk mitigation efforts, and asset changes.

STAGES OF THE RISK MANAGEMENT LIFECYCLE

The risk management process is made up of several point-in-time assessments of risk that need to be re-evaluated as risks evolve. The process begins by profiling your resources (assets) and rating them on a sensitivity scale similar to a traditional Business Impact Assessment (BIA) exercise. The goal is to identify critical resources that need to be protected. You then identify the threats and vulnerabilities for these critical resources, rate the risk exposure, determine appropriate mitigation strategies, implement controls, evaluate the effectiveness of those controls, and finally monitor changes over time. Sounds easy, right?

Of course, each of these steps can be very complex depending on your environment, the scope of your assessment, and how detailed you want to get. Having a clear scope for each assessment is crucial. You may find yourself assessing a single data flow in and out of an application or performing a much broader assessment of a service provider's entire environment. At a workflow level, these assessments will be the same, but as you will soon see, the tactical approaches may vary based on the scale of the assessment.

Risk Is a Moving Target

The environments that you protect are constantly changing, and this means that you need to account for shifts in threats and exposures in your risk management workflow. There are many times when a re-evaluation is needed (basically starting the assessment cycle over) including the following:

- A change in the sensitivity of the target resource
- A significant shift in the threat landscape
- A change in legal/regulatory requirements
- A change in security policy
- On a schedule, based on the resource's sensitivity to risk

It is important to keep in mind that the sensitivity of a resource may change over time if the intended use for that resource changes, new types of sensitive data are added, or the priorities of the organization change. It is up to the resource owner to notify the security team of any significant changes that might require an out-of-cycle assessment, and it is up to the security team to stay well informed about changes in the threat landscape so they can educate the resource owners. Any major changes to the design, intended use, customer base, or implementation should trigger a new assessment. Think of it like managing the classification of a document. You may declassify it if the information is no longer the same level of sensitivity, which means that the required controls will also change. The same goes for your resources: if the sensitivity of the data being processed changes, then the controls around that resource need to be re-evaluated. You may approve certain controls for a server or application knowing that it doesn't process any sensitive data; then, down the road, someone decides to expand the scope of that system to include a sensitive function. The intended use is so important when trying to understand why controls have failed in several breach cases; you will often find out that the controls were appropriate for the original use of the system, but that the controls didn't evolve as the scope of the system changed.

For example, a system may have started out being a simple FTP server that was used to distribute software updates to internal devices, and then somewhere along the way the business needed a server to receive billing data dumps from clients and this system was the fastest solution to get operational. Now the server has gone from only being used internally, to accepting sensitive financial data from clients across the Internet using an unencrypted connection with weak password controls. Every organization has these chinks in its armor, and you either find them by accident or discover them when a breach occurs. Likely, you can think of five different controls that would either prevent this case from happening or immediately detect it; but no organization has the time or resources to put in the comprehensive control environment that we would all like to have.

TIPS & TRICKS

The information security team should be involved in the review and approval process for all firewall change requests, not just to catch nonsecure rule changes, but also to be aware of any new flows that might indicate a change in a system's intended use. These requests should be reviewed at more than just a ports and protocol level.

It is important to have a mix of preventative and detective controls to catch scope creep situations, but risk management also needs to be embedded into the culture of the organization. Professionals often debate how to measure the success of risk management. If you have individuals in the business escalating risks to you on their own, or even better, notifying you of a risk and how they are already addressing it, then you are well positioned for success. If you want a useful metric for your program, track how many issues are self-identified versus being discovered by the security team.

Of course, you can't ever rely solely on the resource owner to be aware of every possible shift in the risk landscape, so you also need to reassess critical resources on a periodic basis according to their importance. Here again you need to be careful to avoid the fix-everything mentality. Even the low hanging fruit can often distract you from the more critical exposures. Not all assets in your organization have the same value, and they need to be treated differently according to their sensitivity to risk. Your most critical assets might require an annual evaluation, whereas less sensitive resources might be assessed every 2 to 5 years. Having established levels of sensitivity and criteria for the degree of due diligence required for each will really help you to maximize your resources.

Let's look at vendor management as an example. Suppose you have a third-party service provider who comes in once a year to organize your annual offsite sales retreat. You may require a high-level assessment of that vendor when you first sign the contracts to ensure that their onsite personnel aren't going to expose the organization to any risks, but it wouldn't be worth your time to reassess them every year. Chances are their security program won't change much over time, and assessing a vendor who handles outsourced payroll is certainly more worthy of your time. Establish this schedule up front with the resource owners and make sure it is one of their objectives to ensure it is performed on a timely basis. Part of delegating security functions within your organization is getting the resource owners to take responsibility for protecting their own resources, identifying risks, and owning the remediation. The security function shouldn't own every information security risk that is identified.

Over time you may also discover additional weaknesses in your controls or new threats that pose a new risk to a resource. This information needs to be funneled into the risk management process through threat and vulnerability management, incident management, and other security activities to help identify when a reassessment is necessary.

A Comprehensive Risk Management Workflow

There are a few well-established risk management frameworks for Information Technology, and even several more emerging ones that focus on managing information security risks specifically. All these frameworks use a very similar lifecycle approach, although there are some slight differences in terminology and how they distinguish the steps of the process. Essentially, you need to start by profiling the requirements of the resource that will be the target of the assessment, then assessing the risks, deciding how to address any exposures, implementing any changes, and finally monitoring the effectiveness of the controls. This process continues for the lifetime of the resource.

A basic risk management process flow is shown in Figure 3.1. Each stage in the process includes a short description along with the responsible party for that step in the process. Responsibilities for many of these steps are shared between

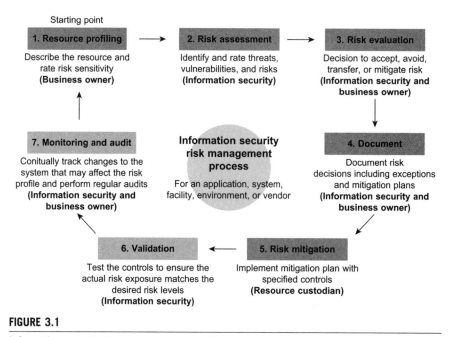

FIGURE 3.1

Information security risk management workflow.

the information security team and the business owner because the security function can't be the sole team managing risk for the organization. The security team can guide the process, provide oversight, and make recommendations, but ultimately it is the business that owns the risk.

Notice that the workflow begins with *resource profiling* then goes to *risk assessment* and *risk evaluation* stages. You will certainly see these terms used interchangeably (and often inconsistently) by many people in the field; however, there is an important distinction between them. *Risk assessment* is the function of identifying the threats and vulnerabilities for a given resource, articulating the risk, and rating that risk exposure on a given scale. In this workflow, the *risk assessment* step includes Risk Analysis, which is considered the process of measuring (or rating) the likelihood of the undesirable event occurring and the expected severity of that event. Some kind of vulnerability assessment is generally used as part of the risk assessment to identify technical weaknesses, along with threat modeling. The next stage of *risk evaluation* is the function of determining the proper steps to manage that risk, whether they be to accept, mitigate, transfer, or avoid the risk exposure.

During the *risk evaluation* stage, newly identified risks need to be compared to the existing list of risks for the organization, and priorities should be determined based on the big picture of all risks across the enterprise, taking into account available time and resources. It may not be appropriate to mitigate every risk; so, armed with the information from the risk assessment, management can make an educated risk decision, which may include a temporary exception or a mitigation plan. Think of yourself like an advisor to the executives. It is the risk manager's job to provide accurate information about the potential magnitude of consequences, likelihood of occurrence, and what steps are recommended to address the exposures. The leaders of the organization then need to make the hard decisions about how to balance available resources.

In the *risk mitigation* stage, the plan of action is implemented to address the risks, including the controls that were selected in the documentation stage. Addressing a risk does not necessarily mean that the vulnerability is "fixed" or the exposure is eliminated. Organizations have several options to address a risk, the most common being the execution of a plan to mitigate or reduce the exposure in some way. Frequently, however, there will be risks that can't be mitigated at all, aren't worth the effort to reduce the exposure any further, or just won't be addressed in the short term due to other priorities. Risk exceptions become a crucial tool to formally track the acceptance of risks for a defined period of time. Often, mitigation plans will be submitted along with a temporary exception so that the organization can formally document the acceptance of the risk exposure while work is being done to mitigate it.

Once this plan has been completed, the *validation* stage includes the testing of the controls to ensure the desired reduction in risk has been achieved. It is not uncommon for controls to be implemented incorrectly, or for a control to fall short of the desired level of risk reduction. You will see this often when trying to affect the behavior of users. You might select a deterrent control that isn't as effective as hoped, or that has unintended results creating problems in another area. For example, you may increase the logging level on your servers to provide better detail about unauthorized activity by your system administrators and discover that this has significantly impacted the performance of a critical business service running on those servers. Another classic example is how enforcement of stricter password complexity requirements will cause users to store their passwords in spreadsheets or on sticky notes because they can't remember them anymore.

Finally, in the *monitoring and audit* stage, the resource and its threats/vulnerabilities are monitored for any drastic changes that would require an out-of-cycle reassessment or adjustment of the controls. When a resource is first profiled, it should be assigned a schedule for periodic reassessments, but often there will be unanticipated changes that require more immediate action.

The workflow cycles through the steps again starting back at the profiling stage during the next assessment. As any heavily regulated organization will tell you, there is no end to audits and risk assessments, you are always either working on the mitigation plans from the last assessment or preparing for the next one.

The workflow in Figure 3.1 is loosely based on both the NIST and Octave Allegro risk management models, taking the best of each. There are many different frameworks for both IT and security-focused risk assessments, including NIST SP800-37, OCTAVE, ISO 27005, COSO, FAIR, CRAMM, and so on, but all of these include the same general activities, even if each uses its own terminology.

BUSINESS IMPACT ASSESSMENT

A traditional BIA will result in a binary assessment of your resources; either a resource is critical or it isn't. This differentiation is then used to guide activities by the business continuity teams who need to plan for disruptions and disasters that may affect the organization's core services and processes. In information security, you can leverage the results of a BIA, but they need to be adapted to categorize resources into more than just two buckets.

Resource Profiling

Before any risk assessment can be performed, a *security risk profile* must first be created for the resource in question. Resource profiling is the first step of the seven-part workflow that was introduced earlier in Figure 3.1. If you think about your own organization, you can probably come up with a list of critical resources without very much effort. So how can you generate a list so easily? What criteria are you using to distinguish the critical from noncritical, maybe without even knowing it?

In general, you may think about the resources that the organization is most dependent on to function, or maybe the resources with the most sensitive data, or even those that are the most visible to the public. Whatever your criteria are, the idea is to operationalize them into levels of importance to your organization, and use this information to prioritize any subsequent assessment work. Creating categories or tiers of resources based on their importance to the organization, or the potential impact if their security were breached, will help to inform your decisions about where to focus your efforts. It can be hard for security professionals to purposely set aside resources with known vulnerabilities, but this discipline is necessary to keep focused on the organization's critical functions. It is all too easy to get distracted by the ever-growing list of vulnerabilities and threats at any given time. The only way to effectively work your way through this list is to attack the problem strategically. In the first year of your program, select a small group of assets that are most important to the organization and focus your risk assessment efforts there. Set clear objectives detailing which resources will be assessed, how the findings will be addressed, and by when. Holding to this plan can be tricky as you encounter external pressures from auditors, regulators, customers, and so on, to shift the assessment focus to other areas, but you need to hold firm. Without this diligence, you risk missing some devastating exposure while you are busy knocking off the more satisfying "low hanging fruit."

Often, the target resource will be an application, but it may also be necessary create a risk profile for a system, environment, facility, business unit, or vendor. How you organize your profiles will have a lot to do with how the organization itself is structured, but some typical targets to profile might be a Partner Extranet system, a Client-Facing DMZ network, the Human Resources department, a critical data center, or a specific third-party provider. Depending on your business, you may spend a significant amount of your time creating profiles for business units, key processes, service providers, and so on. The *security risk profile* is another term that can have many meanings and uses in the industry. Strictly speaking, the security risk profile gathers information about the resource to help rate its sensitivity to security risks. This is considered independently of any particular threats or vulnerabilities for that asset. It may not seem like an important distinction right now, but as you start to profile a few resources, you will quickly discover how easy it is to muddle the difference, and mixing up these concepts can totally skew your risk ratings down the road, so be cautious. For example, you may be inclined to include a question about whether the application is Internet-facing in your profile, but this question is really an evaluation of the threat landscape and not the inherent sensitivity of the application. Why does it matter if the application is on the Internet or internal only? Does it make it any more important to the organization? Not likely! Most likely, you were thinking that it makes it more likely to be attacked, but this doesn't make it any more important to the organization. If, however, the question is intended to capture the visibility of a potential breach, that might be a good question for the profile. In this case, it may be more damaging for the organization if a public rather than an internal application is exploited. Maybe a better question would be who the audience for the application is, rather than simply asking if it's Internet-facing. Then, you can make distinctions between the value of visibility to different groups like employees, clients, vendors, partners, and so on.

Factors that should be considered in any risk profile include financial, legal, and reputational damages or regulatory constraints/restrictions that may result from a security violation. The idea is for the business owner to rate the resource's importance to the organization from an information security perspective and relative to all of the organization's other assets. This profile should be at a high-enough level so that it can be completed even before any implementation decisions are made for the resource. Since it isn't tied to specifics about implementation, like the environment or the type of encryption, it can be assessed at a business level at a very early stage of development or acquisition. The security team will usually establish the risk profile format and questions, but it is the business owner's responsibility to provide the answers and business context. For example, as a security professional, you should be able to make a quick list of regulations that may apply to a system or business sector, but it is the business owner who needs to understand the impact to the organization if that regulation is violated. Security will generally need to guide this process the first couple of times through and help the business owners to articulate the value of each asset.

Risk profiles can vary in detail and format, but there are some basic data points that you will want to capture in each profile:

- General description
- Function and features
- Information classification
- Criticality to organization
- Applicable regulations

We will dive into more detail about how exactly to define and rate sensitivity for a resource in Chapter 4.

A VULNERABILITY ASSESSMENT IS NOT A RISK ASSESSMENT

The next time you are hiring for an open-information security position, if you want to watch the candidates squirm, ask them to describe the difference between a vulnerability assessment and a risk assessment. It may seem like splitting hairs, but this casual use of terminology is usually a symptom of information security inexperience that leads to some very ineffective security programs. Just like running a vulnerability scan isn't a penetration test, it isn't fair to equate a vulnerability scan to a risk assessment. Too many organizations think that if they get a pretty report out of Qualys or Nessus scanners listing all the running services, missing patches, and possible vulnerabilities that they have performed a risk assessment. For every one vulnerability that you might discover during a security scan, there could be two or ten risks associated with that single vulnerability, and all of them may have different risk exposure ratings. Take, for example, an organization that has no central identity and access management system, so the accounts on all 100 of their servers are managed individually. This single issue is going to have several possible consequences, including users being given too much access, being given access to the wrong resources, inconsistent access controls, or maybe just how difficult it is to properly audit. Do all these risks have the same likelihood of resulting in a data breach? Probably not, but a scanner would report the use of local account management as a single finding with a single risk rating. That just isn't good enough.

Vulnerability Assessment

All too often, security professionals confuse the terms *risk assessment* and *vulnerability assessment*, but they really are different activities. A typical vulnerability assessment will identify weaknesses and flaws through some kind of active means such as scanning or configuration analysis. Vulnerabilities are identified and rated based on a very general knowledge of how they might be exploited; however, no real analysis of applicability or threat analysis is included. In addition, a vulnerability assessment assumes a single finding per vulnerability, but in reality, there could be several combinations of different threats with a single vulnerability that will result in several distinct risks. This level of detail isn't captured in a vulnerability assessment.

Vulnerability assessments are good tools to be used as part of an overall risk assessment process. They can produce good metrics to measure the effectiveness of current control measures like patch management processes or hardening of servers. They are also useful if you need to identify resources that are susceptible to a particular exploit or running a prohibited service. Attackers typically use vulnerability scans as part of their reconnaissance, so it is good to run the same tests yourself to identify which weaknesses would be visible to an attacker.

Risk Assessment

In general, a technical risk assessment is going to include a vulnerability assessment of some kind; however, there is much more to a risk assessment than just identifying weaknesses. If you just want a list of things to fix, do a vulnerability assessment, but if you really want to understand your exposures and prioritize remediation efforts, then you need a risk assessment.

A *risk assessment* is the superset of activities for taking that vulnerability data, mapping it to likely threats, evaluating the severity for the given environment, and articulating the risk(s) that might result. A risk assessment should also take into account the sensitivity level of the resource that has the vulnerability, whereas a typical vulnerability assessment would assume the same risk level no matter where it is found. If Microsoft announces a new vulnerability in Windows, they don't list it as a high risk for servers and moderate risk for desktops. Similarly, any scanning or assessment tool may provide some guidance about the applicability

3 SSL Server Has SSLv2 Enabled Vulnerability   port 443/tcp over SSL

QID:	38139	CVSS Base:	4 [1]
Category:	General remote services	CVSS Temporal:	3.6
CVE ID:	-		
Vendor Reference:	-		
Bugtraq ID:	-		
Service Modified:	07/07/2009		
User Modified:	-		

THREAT:
The Secure Socket Layer (SSL) protocol allows for secure communication between a client and a server.

There are known flaws in the SSLv2 protocol. A man-in-the-middle attacker can force the communication to a less secure level and then attempt to break the weak encryption. The attacker can also truncate encrypted messages.

These flaws have been fixed in SSLv3 (or TLSv1). Most servers (including all popular Web servers, mail servers, etc.) and clients (including Web-clients like IE, Netscape Navigator and Mozilla and mail clients) support both SSLv2 and SSLv3. However, SSLv2 is enabled by default for backward compatibility.

The following link provides more information about this vulnerability:

Analysis of the SSL 3.0 Protocol (http://www.schneier.com/paper-ssl.html)

IMPACT:
An attacker can exploit this vulnerability to read secure communications or maliciously modify messages.

SOLUTION:
Disable SSLv2.

FIGURE 3.2

Sample QualysGuard vulnerability finding.

of a vulnerability, but you are going to get a very one-dimensional risk score from a vulnerability assessment. For example, Figure 3.2 shows a typical vulnerability finding from a scan of a Web server, using the QualysGuard vulnerability scanning tool. The impact statement describes two potential threat activities, unauthorized reading of communications and intentional modification of messages in transit. This would be included in a vulnerability report as a single item, but even without analyzing this weakness any further, it is clear that there are at least two possible risks associated with it. One threatening the confidentiality of the data and other affecting the integrity.

Further, a comprehensive risk assessment needs to account for any compensating controls that already exist. These controls may not neutralize the vulnerability, but they reduce the inherent risk in some way. In the case of the Web server supporting weak SSL ciphers, a compensating control might be that the Web server is only ever accessed over a secure VPN connection, thus not relying on the SSL encryption to protect the communications.

By the end of the risk assessment stage, the risk exposure should be determined for each threat/vulnerability pair. The combination of the likelihood that the threat will exploit the vulnerability, and the severity of the exploit, combined with the sensitivity of the asset itself yields the risk exposure rating. The risk exposure describes the outcome of a successful exploitation of the vulnerability by the threat. Sometimes the risk exposure is referred to as the "impact" or "consequence" of the risk, and it should always be tied to a particular threat/ vulnerability pair.

For example, the risk exposure resulting from the exploit of a weak SSL cipher could be described as follows:

"communications could be intercepted in transit and decrypted by a malicious party resulting in an unauthorized disclosure of sensitive data for all customers in the United Kingdom, which would require a breach notification to regulators and affected clients, costing the organization 2 million dollars in lost revenue and financial sanctions."

Notice that this description helps us rate the severity of the exploit by indicating how much data (all client data from the United Kingdom) will be affected, and the sensitivity by the scope of which data will be disclosed (sensitive, regulated customer data). It also indicates that a notification to clients will be required which affects reputation, costs money, and could expose the organization to civil legal action. A dollar value of financial loss is also stated in order to quantify the impact to the organization.

When articulating a risk, it is not enough to just describe the lack of a control and call it a risk. For example, you may see someone with no formal risk assessment training describe the risk in the previous example as "TLS/SSLv3 is not required for all communications." The lack of strong encryption is not a risk; in fact, there may be plenty of other ways to protect information from disclosure in transit. We need to be careful not to assume the solution when describing the risk. It is a common tendency to have the control in mind when you are assessing a risk, but this will often be too prescriptive. In our earlier example, SSLv2 may be required by the business to support a specific set of clients with older browsers. Especially, as an auditor or outside consultant, you should avoid locking the client into one solution to address a risk and rather focus on the root cause or intent of the finding.

MAKING RISK DECISIONS

If the number one rule of risk management is that you can't eliminate all risk, the number two rule of risk management is that you shouldn't try to "fix" every vulnerability. Limited time and resources are a reality whether you have a security staff of 150 dedicated specialists or just two part-time staff members. At the other extreme, everyone has been a part of or done business with an organization that uses the head in the sand approach to risk management. There are many ways to address a risk, and just ignoring it really means that you are accepting the exposure as it is.

Risk Evaluation

After you have assessed all the risks, you also need to weigh and prioritize them, so that you can make well-informed decisions about which risks need to be addressed, and to what degree it is appropriate to mitigate the risks. There are several options for addressing a risk:

- **Accept** A decision to accept the risk.
- **Avoid** Ceasing (or not engaging in) the activity that is presenting the risk altogether.
- **Transfer** Shifting the responsibility or liability for a risk to another party.
- **Mitigate** Limit the exposure in some way.

Of course, if you are going to weigh these options, you need to have some idea about what it would take to mitigate the risks. At this stage, it doesn't need to be a detailed mitigation plan, but you should aim to have enough information to be able to estimate the cost of mitigation. Our inclination may be to settle for nothing less than reducing the risk to its lowest possible level, but we really need to learn how to take a step back and consider the risks in light of the organization's risk posture overall. There is more to consider than just the direct financial impact of a risk; in addition, it is important to strongly consider these indirect control costs:

- Implementation
- Additional support resources
- Education and training
- Reduction in operational effectiveness due to complexity or performance degradation

All these costs need to be balanced against the likely cost of not implementing the recommended control. We have all been guilty of purchasing the perfect solution to mitigate a critical risk exposure, only to see it become shelfware because there does not exist the expertise to implement it, the resources to maintain it, or the training to optimize it. There is the initial cost of hardware, software, professional services, and so on, but don't forget to calculate the cost of maintenance and support over time. Security solutions, especially technical controls, need to have an operational support plan baked into the cost of mitigation. Any new technology may require additional resources to run and maintain it, and possibly training for staff if it is a new technology.

Without a true sense of the cost of the controls over time and impact to the organization to support them, the organization can't make educated risk decisions. The total expense of the controls should never cost more than the asset is worth or the potential impact of the risk. When deciding on a risk mitigation strategy, it's important to consider the cost of implementing controls and also the potential costs of not doing so. You might consider a process or procedural control instead of a technical control, but you have to account for how that decision may affect operational effectiveness. For example, you may choose to implement procedural checks rather than an automated control system, but this could become a drain on the staff.

Document

Can you remember what you had for lunch last Tuesday? Do you think you have any chance of remembering 6 months from now what your justification was for rating a risk a certain way? What factors did you take into account? Were there any compensating controls that affected your assessment of the risk? There are tons of new risks being processed every day, and each finding has its own intricacies making the chance of you remembering the details without good documentation slim to none.

For anyone who is in a regulated or highly audited environment, you know that documentation and evidence are crucial for demonstrating a level of due diligence. The documentation of risk is listed as an explicit stage in the workflow, but really you need to be documenting your assessment and evaluation steps all along the way. When that annual audit comes up, how will you remember why you rated the likelihood of a particular risk as moderate instead of high? It is likely that you won't remember unless you have been documenting your rationale along the way.

At a minimum, you want to capture the following details of your analysis for each risk finding:

- Why a rating was given
- Compensating controls considered
- Business justification
- Mitigation plans—long- and short-term
- Policy exceptions/risk acceptance

If you choose to address a risk with some kind of mitigation plan, the business owner needs to document the agreed upon steps, target dates, and responsible parties. It is generally security's job to oversee and track the progress of the mitigation plan, but it is up to the business owner (and resource custodian) to execute on it. You may even need a temporary exception in place while the mitigation plan is being executed. A combination of long- and short-term action items may also be appropriate. Maybe some short-term action items reduce the risk from critical to high, and the long-term plan will further reduce the risk exposure to moderate. A phased mitigation plan could be tracked in an exception by setting an expiration date for each milestone of the plan. When the exception expires, the progress toward the plan will be reviewed, and the exception extended to the next milestone date until completion.

Whenever a risk is being accepted (even temporarily), a formal policy exception or risk acceptance form should be filled out with senior management approval. If no action is being required to mitigate the risk, this could be a very simple summary of the risk evaluation decision, or may include details of the current compensating controls. Exception processing is a critical component of any risk management program, and strategies for implementing an exception process will be discussed further in Chapter 8.

MITIGATION PLANNING AND LONG-TERM STRATEGY

Once you have gotten to this stage, the assumption is that you have already decided, in the *risk evaluation* stage, how you want to address the risk at a high level (that is, accepting, mitigating, transferring, or avoiding the risk, and so on), and that you have documented your decision in step 4: Documention. Any of these decisions is going to involve some activity to implement and possibly further flesh out that plan, with avoidance requiring the least planning. The ability to identify the most appropriate mitigation steps for a given risk is a skill that can make or break your security program. It is crucial to find the right mix of controls, both technical and nontechnical, to reduce the likelihood of occurrence or limit the effects enough to be acceptable without putting any undue burden on the organization. This is definitely the time to be creative and think outside the box!

Risk Mitigation

There are many options for mitigating a risk, and again the focus is not always on trying to eliminate the risk, but rather to reduce the risk exposure to an acceptable level. To mitigate a risk, you either have to

1. reduce the likelihood of occurrence, or
2. limit the severity of the impact, or
3. decrease the sensitivity of the resource.

The first two choices are the most common, but in some cases, it may be possible to change the sensitivity of the resource. For example, imagine a Web server in your DMZ with credit card numbers and client names on it. Just by removing the credit card numbers from that server and placing them on an internally protected database tier instead, you could reduce the sensitivity of that Web server significantly without addressing any vulnerabilities or threats.

Another option for this example might be to reduce the threat universe by implementing firewall rules to limit source networks that are allowed to connect to the Web server. Again, this option would not limit the severity of the exposure or change the sensitivity of the Web server, but it would reduce the likelihood of abuse by reducing the number of entities who can access the server. There are many other examples of how to reduce the threat universe, for example, implementing authentication controls to limit access to a smaller user community.

To limit the severity of an exploit, you need to somehow contain the potential compromise. This approach to risk mitigation recognizes that you can't necessarily prevent the exploit, but you can limit the scope or quickly react to prevent further escalation. Most controls in this category will be detective and recovery focused. An active alert triggered from a log file that detects brute forcing of user account passwords may be too late to prevent someone from compromising a single account, but you may be able to quickly disable the account before any damage is done or the attacker is able to move to another system. Another typical example is limiting the scope of access the attacker would have when exploiting the account. If you can limit the access to a standard "user privilege" level as opposed to an "administrative privilege" level, then you have reduced the potential magnitude of the exposure.

The most common risk decision is *mitigation*, which involves limiting the likelihood or effects of the exposure in some way. In contrast, risk *remediation* refers to the actual removal or patching of the vulnerability. If you remediate a risk, you would be fixing the underlying issue, whereas a mitigation action reduces the exposure but does not eliminate the vulnerability. Most of your time will be spent planning efforts to alleviate or limit the risk, but acceptance and transference of risk are also important strategies. As discussed previously, there needs to be a well-established and formal process for requesting a security exception. This is the vehicle for implementing the acceptance of any risk. Most times, it will require an exception to a particular security standard that the organization has established. Any mitigation plans are most easily tracked by tying them to a temporary exception. That way, you get the proper approvals and visibility to accept the current risk level while the plan is being executed. Alternatively, all these approvals could be included as part of the mitigation plan itself.

Finally, if the decision is made not to mitigate the risk, transferring the risk can take many forms, from insurance to cover a possible financial loss, to trying to transfer the liability for a process or service that may have high rates of risk exposure. For example, you may engage a third party, shift the responsibility within a contract, or implement a self-service feature to transfer the risk to another party. In Chapter 8, we will go into much more detail about how to manage and plan the mitigation steps and track any exceptions.

Validation

Once controls have been implemented to mitigate a risk, you need to verify the adequacy of these controls through active testing or review. There are many different levels of testing, including vulnerability scanning, penetration testing, or even configuration review. Depending on the vulnerability being addressed, the approach to testing may be different, but the intent is to detect any areas where the controls don't satisfactorily mitigate the risk or may have been misconfigured.

Often organizations will establish a *certification and accreditation* (C&A) process to formally document the controls and validation of those controls before the application/system is allowed to "go live" or be released. This ensures that the responsible parties are maintaining consistency and quality of the required controls. This is also a common control in software development environments so that someone with a security role is reviewing new releases before they are implemented and made available to users.

Monitoring and Audit

This final step of the risk management lifecycle represents all the time after the formal risk assessment has been performed and the execution of the mitigation plans are completed (or at least underway). There is no rest for the risk management program: we are constantly either assessing a risk, tracking the mitigation, evaluating an exception request, or monitoring for new and changing risk exposures.

The most common triggers for a reassessment of risks are as follows:

- Significant resource changes
- Changes to the threat landscape
- Shifts in business focus
- Changes to the regulatory or legal requirements
- Detected weaknesses in current controls
- Predetermined period of time has passed

Typically, a predetermined schedule is established for each resource to catch any changes that should have prompted a reassessment along the way. The schedule should be based on the sensitivity level of the resource: 1 year for highly sensitive resources, 3 years for moderately sensitive resources, and 5 years for low-sensitivity resources is a good place to start. It is always the responsibility of the business owner to identify changes requiring a reassessment and to lead the periodic assessments, but the security team needs to provide oversight and guidance.

From time to time, threats will also significantly shift their focus, maybe from one attack vector to another, or maybe from targeting one industry to another, so we need to monitor these trends and adjust our risk assessments accordingly. Many organizations perform regular assessments of the threat landscape to determine any areas that require additional focus. There are many sources of security intelligence in the public domain that can help to inform these decisions. Try not to get too caught up in everyday trends; it just isn't practical to adjust your controls so often based on the latest flavor of attack. What the media may package as a "brand new" threat is generally just a variation on an old attack method. Get the fundamental controls in place, and you should avoid being so vulnerable to the latest variant.

It is also critical to feed the results of detective controls into your risk assessment process. As you detect attempts to bypass existing controls or even successful compromises of controls, you should be using this knowledge to adjust your preventative controls and guide future assessments. We see this often with application-based firewalls, where it is possible to detect activity that is not expected by the application and possibly prevent a compromise. If you can then feed that knowledge back to your architects and developers, you should be able to account for these scenarios in the application itself and alleviate the need for the firewall to block that exploit. The focus of information security used to almost always be on preventative controls, but the focus is shifting significantly toward monitoring and auditing controls to catch abuses. This recognition that there are too many abuse vectors to effectively prevent them all is evident in rise of the Security Information and Event Management (SEIM) systems. The security monitoring infrastructure really becomes the heart of your technical security program, providing the intelligence about the effectiveness of controls, new threats, trends in noncompliance, and so on.

PROCESS OWNERSHIP

There are a lot of different teams and roles involved in the risk management lifecycle. For example,

- Business owner
- Custodian
- Information security.

The information security team can't take sole responsibility for every step in the process and be successful. The risk management lifecycle (Figure 3.1) pictured earlier in this chapter lists who will generally be the responsible parties under each stage of the workflow. Notice that in some cases, illustrated in Table 3.1, the responsibility may be shared and that not every step is lead by the security team.

The emerging model for information security management is more and more decentralized. The security team has limited staff and a growing scope of responsibilities within the organization (physical security, privacy, legal concerns, and so on), so we need to start leveraging other parts of the organization to perform their own risk management. Ultimately, these are not our information resources, so we need to empower the business owners to understand and manage their own risks with our assistance.

With this approach, the security team's role shifts to one of policy maker, overseer, and internal consultant, rather than being operationally responsible for protecting every resource. The business owner is the subject matter expert when it comes to defining the needs of their resource, and often the Information Technology team assumes a role of custodian for that resource and fills the role of implementing and

Table 3.1 Risk Responsibilities and Roles

Responsibility	Role
1. Resource profiling	Business owner
2. Risk assessment	Information security
3. Risk evaluation	Business owner Information security
4. Document	Business owner Information security
5. Risk mitigation	Resource custodian
6. Validation	Information security
7. Monitoring & audit	Information security Business owner

maintaining the controls. It is the security team's responsibility to ensure the risk assessments are being performed accurately and on a timely basis, but we should leave the business owner some flexibility as to how they want to assess the risk.

Establishing ownership for each stage of the lifecycle is critical, and it may take a few tries to find the right balance for your organization. In Table 3.1, the business owner is intentionally listed first for steps 3 and 4 of lifecycle because they should be driving those risk activities with support and guidance from security. For example, the information security team doesn't need to draft the mitigation plan or submit the exception request. Nor should we take responsibility for making the risk decisions about how to address an exposure. Security is a stakeholder in the decision-making process, but the business owner needs to feel empowered to control their own destiny. Essentially, the business owner needs to take responsibility for protecting their assets, and the security team needs to help them to understand the risks and ensure that the process is being followed.

SUMMARY

Your security policies and your program need to be designed with a multistep risk management lifecycle in mind. The seven-step workflow in this chapter offers one option for representing the various phases of the lifecycle of constant risk management. Start by profiling your critical resources, assess the most likely and severe exposures, determine the most appropriate way to address the risk, document your findings and justification, implement your mitigation plan, verify the risk has been reduced as expected, and monitor the environment for changes that will require reassessment. To make the best use of this process, clearly define responsibilities and roles for both the business owners and the information security team.

Action Plan

After reading this chapter, you should consider taking the following actions in your own organization:

- Ensure your information security policies and standards outline the high-level process for ongoing risk assessments.
- Establish a schedule of assessments based on the sensitivity of the resource.
- Educate business owners regarding their responsibilities to protect their own resources, and specifically their role in the assessment process.
- Implement a process to formally approve and track mitigation plans with visibility to the senior management level.
- Whenever scoping or planning an assessment, clearly distinguish between vulnerability assessment activities and the overall risk assessment process.
- Formally integrate security risk assessment checkpoints into your internal SDLC process.

Risk Assessment and Analysis Techniques

Risk Profiling

INFORMATION IN THIS CHAPTER

- How Risk Sensitivity Is Measured
- Asking the Right Questions
- Assessing Risk Appetite

INTRODUCTION

If you think about your own organization, you can probably come up with a list of critical resources without much effort. You may or may not have formal criteria established to distinguish critical resources. Depending on the industry and business model of your organization, this may be an easy exercise. You probably think about the organization's intellectual property or infrastructure that supports a core service. Whatever your criteria are, the idea is to categorize resources into levels of importance and use this information to prioritize your assessment efforts. In risk management, this evaluation of importance is called *risk sensitivity*.

HOW RISK SENSITIVITY IS MEASURED

Before any risk analysis can be performed, you must first determine the sensitivity of the resources you are assessing. Think about a resource's risk sensitivity as a measure of its importance to the organization. Risk sensitivity is defined as follows:

> *A relative measurement of the resource's tolerance for risk exposures, similar to an evaluation of criticality or importance to the organization, independent of any particular threat or vulnerability.*

From an operations perspective, you will often focus on assessing an application or system, such as a specific server, infrastructure device, or piece of software. Although it is valuable to get to this level of granularity, and even go deeper to the point where you are assessing components of systems and applications (for example, a Java library), it can be difficult to tackle this level of detail right out of the gate. It may be less precise, but you should probably start by profiling environments instead of individual systems. For example, assign a risk sensitivity score to your

DMZ network, desktop environment, and server farm rather than trying to profile every individual system and application in those environments.

Let's say that, to start, you assign your printers a low sensitivity, your user PCs a moderate sensitivity, and your servers a high sensitivity. Is this going to account for every nuance, such as the printer in the Human Resources department having a higher sensitivity for confidentiality than the general network printer? Well, no—but you need to start somewhere. The alternative will lead you down a path of trying to perfectly profile every component in your organization, which can take a very long time. If you are having trouble with making these generalizations in the early stages, keep in mind that risks will be going unaddressed while you are building perfect profiles for every system in your environment. It is better to grow your program slowly and improve your precision as you go. This practical approach to building a risk management program is a recurring theme throughout this book: start small and build on success.

Making a Resource List

We started this section by asking you to list out the most critical assets for your organization. Did you include any of these in your resource list?

- Physical site, building, or facility
- Data types like *social security numbers* or *credit card numbers*
- Employees
- Reputation
- Trash
- Firewall

Each of these items presents its own difficulties in assessing risk. Usually, when someone lists one of these as an asset, they are actually thinking of it in the context of a control. The physical building could be considered a resource if you are thinking about risks that could result in damages to the building, which will cost the organization money, but generally that would fall outside of an information security discussion. Chances are you are thinking about the physical protection that a building provides, which puts it in the security control category, not asset. Similarly, a firewall is usually not an asset that you would assess for risks. A firewall may be a control to protect a resource, like the production server, or may be the source of a vulnerability, but generally isn't a critical asset in the same sense as the production server. In the security context, employees are more often threats than resources (for example, a disgruntled employee who decides to take out their anger on company resources), or they are the vulnerability in a social engineering attack. Safety is an important consideration, in which case employees are a resource to be protected, but that is also outside of the purview of information security. Whenever you are dealing with intangible assets like reputation, there is no value in focusing on these as explicit assets to protect directly. It is better to consider reputation as a component of the consequences of a breach rather than a resource to profile and directly control. Data should never be overlooked as a critical resource; however, you need to put data in the context of their container. To say that you are going to profile financial account numbers independently, for example, would not be a productive exercise. Instead, you would look at a mobile device or database that serves as the container for that information, and focus on the container as the resource whose sensitivity will be defined in large part by the data it processes, stores, and transfers. There is no definitive list of what should and shouldn't be considered a resource in terms of risk profiling, but a simple guideline to follow is to try to think of a single direct vulnerability for each item that you want to put on your resource list. If you can't think of a vulnerability that could put that target at risk, then the resource probably can't be assessed directly. Later in this chapter, you will see the factors included in a risk profile, such as reputation or financial impact, and hopefully this will eliminate the need to track the intangible assets directly.

Sensitivity, Not Exposure

At this point, let's bring our focus to measuring a resource's risk sensitivity. A resource's risk sensitivity should take into account the potential impact of a compromise to the organization for that class of resource. To qualify this, you will want to gather at least the following information about each resource or a class of resource:

- General description
- Function and features
- Information classification
- Criticality to organization
- Applicable regulations
- User community

All these attributes will help you differentiate the importance of each asset to the organization. Notice that the profile is not evaluating the resource's level of exposure. We don't care whether it is directly accessible on the Internet or in a locked room with no network access. Whether data are going across an untrusted network or kept safely in an encrypted database says nothing about the data's sensitivity. Risk sensitivity measures the asset's importance and inherent value to the organization, which shouldn't depend on the particulars of placement or implementation.

Another way to think about the risk sensitivity is as a measurement of the resource's tolerance for risk; it identifies an acceptable range of risk exposure for that resource. The risk threshold is always inversely proportional to the risk sensitivity level. If you have a high sensitivity to risk, then you should have a low threshold for risk. Think about a biomedical company. Their most critical asset is likely the research for the next drug being developed before a patent has been issued. Any server storing these research data is going to have the highest confidentiality requirements for the business. You would categorize these data, and any

Table 4.1 Risk Tolerance Range Example

Information Resource	Risk Sensitivity	Risk Tolerance	Risk Threshold
Drug research server	High	Negligible-Low	Low
Printer in mail room	Low	Negligible-High	High

containers such as file servers and databases, as being highly sensitive to risk. Likewise, these data have a low tolerance for risk exposure. This relationship is illustrated in Table 4.1 for the biomedical company's drug research server and a printer in the *mail room*.

If you are using a simple sensitivity scale of Low-Moderate-High, you would say that the acceptable level range of risk exposure is from Zero (or negligible) to Low for the server storing the research data. On the other hand, a printer in the mail room, which is only used to print timesheets, might have a low sensitivity to risk. It would have a high tolerance for risk exposure, or an acceptable risk-exposure range of Zero to High. If the Low-Moderate-High scale isn't granular enough for your organization, you can always expand the scale.

Security Risk Profile

Once you have identified your list of targeted resources to be profiled, you are ready to begin creating *security risk profiles* for each one. The security risk profile gathers information about the resource to help rate its sensitivity to information-security risks. Factors that are considered include *financial*, *legal*, and *reputational* damages or *regulatory* constraints/restrictions that may result from a security violation. The idea is for the resource owner to rate the resource's importance to the organization from an information-security perspective and relative to all other assets in the organization. This profile tracks information at a business and function level and is not necessarily specific to implementation decisions. For example, if you are designing a new system, you should know what types of data will be processed and what the basic functions being performed will be before you decide on technologies or placement in the network. You may not have defined the specifics of how the functions will be performed, but having business and functional requirements defined is enough to complete the security risk profile.

The best way to profile a resource is with a simple questionnaire. This questionnaire uses a series of targeted questions to measure the potential impact to the organization of a generic security violation for the target resource. It should include questions that are designed to identify:

- Resource ownership
- Sensitive data processed, stored, and/or transmitted

- Sensitive functions performed
- Applicable laws and regulations
- Financial, legal, and reputational implications of a security violation
- User community
- Support and hosting model
- Access administration model
- Audit trail and maker/checker controls
- Overall confidentiality, integrity, availability, and accountability requirements
- History of previous risk assessments and requirements for future assessments

Ideally, this resource owner should be able to complete the questionnaire in 15 to 30 minutes at most. Resource owners are not expected to directly rate the sensitivity of their resource; rather, their answers to the questionnaire items are rated in the background and the final risk sensitivity score is calculated either manually by an analyst or, ideally, automatically using a rating mapped to each question. This risk-sensitivity value will be used to inform the frequency and depth of risk assessment required initially, as well as throughout the lifetime of the resource. The risk sensitivity is most commonly rated on a scale of Low-Moderate-High.

RISK DEEP DIVE

Profile Design

When you are designing your profile questionnaire, it is important to note that not every question needs to be used in the calculation of the risk sensitivity. Some questions are meant to capture other pertinent information about the resource for reporting purposes and do not directly contribute to the risk-sensitivity score. For example, you may ask a question about where the system is hosted. The answer to this question doesn't affect the sensitivity of the asset, but you may want to prioritize assessments of third-party hosted systems because of increased risk exposure, and the answer to this item will give you the desired information about which systems are hosted internally versus externally. You may also want to ask a couple of high-level questions about whether basic security controls are in place (for example, roles-based access, encryption, and audit logging). Again, the answers to these questions may help you to focus your efforts on resources that don't meet the most basic security control requirements. Similarly, you may want to ask if the system uses a common or central infrastructure for authentication and authorization or logging to eliminate the need for assessing those areas any further. Systems using one-off solutions for these core security services may have more potential for risk exposure. Again, these are not factors that change the sensitivity of the resource, but they can help with prioritization. As a final example, whether or not a vulnerability test has been performed on the resource does not affect its sensitivity, but this knowledge is important for identifying resources that may have undiscovered vulnerabilities that are readily exploitable. You will often find yourself trying to choose between several high-sensitivity resources to assess, and these other factors can help you decide which ones to focus on first.

The security risk profile questionnaire should include several questions about the resource to help determine the sensitivity and criticality of the application in comparison to others. It is essential to evaluate a resource's sensitivity on a relative scale. Start by identifying the resource that is most crucial to the organization, and use this as a reference point. This is important because the tendency is to rate resources too high. If you end up with all resources being rated as high sensitivity and none as moderate or low, then the scale becomes worthless.

An example questionnaire is included in *Appendix A: Sample Security Risk Profile.*

Profiling in Practice

Using risk profiles in this way can also help you to structure your program around an assessment frequency. Higher sensitivity resources should undergo evaluation more frequently than lower risk resources. Also, as risk findings are discovered, you will use the risk sensitivity as one variable when calculating the risk exposure. The other two variables are the severity and likelihood of the risk. To use the earlier example of the biomedical company, the identical threats and vulnerabilities could exist on both the drug research server and the mail room printer, but the resulting risk exposure will be very different because of the difference in risk sensitivity between the two resources. By including risk sensitivity as its own independent variable, we can account for identical security weaknesses that will have a bigger impact on a critical asset than they will have on a lower importance asset and therefore need to be addressed in a much more immediate time frame.

To really assess the sensitivity of a resource, you need to first define a sensitivity scale. For example, you could start with a qualitative scale, as shown in Table 4.2, with detailed criteria to help differentiate between the sensitivity levels.

Table 4.2 Qualitative Risk Sensitivity Scale	
Level	**Criteria**
Low	A compromise would be limited and generally acceptable for the organization, resulting in minimal monetary, productivity, or reputational losses
	There would be only minimal impact on normal operations and/or business activity
Moderate	A compromise would be marginally acceptable for the organization, resulting in certain monetary, productivity, or reputational losses
	Normal operations and/or business activity would be noticeably impaired, including the potential for breaches of contractual obligations
High	A compromise would be unacceptable for the organization, resulting in significant monetary, productivity, or reputational losses
	The ability to continue normal operations and/or business activity would be greatly impaired, potentially resulting in noncompliance with legal or regulatory requirements and/or loss of public confidence in the organization

Table 4.3 Sensitivity Ratings by Environment

Environment	Sensitivity
Research lab	High
Web server farm	Moderate
Sales laptops/mobile devices	Low
Backup servers/network	High

By utilizing a risk ranking methodology based on sensitivity, you can focus your energy on the most critical resource and hopefully avoid the constant distractions of the "low hanging fruit." So, many of the most well-known security breaches have resulted from organizations simply focusing their efforts in the wrong places. Take vulnerability and patch management, for example. There are two ways to approach sensitivity ratings: the first is to look at each category of resource (printer, PC, server, network device, and so on) and assign each a single sensitivity value for the category; the second option is to examine resources based on environment (campus network, server farm, database tier, Web-facing DMZ, partner extranet, and so on) and assign each environment a sensitivity rating. If you choose the latter and assign the sensitivity by environment, it might look like Table 4.3 for the biomedical company.

If you are instead focusing on vendor management, you might look at rating the sensitivity of each vendor or outsourced service. For example, say that you are using an outsourced employee benefits portal. It is a common practice for many organizations to allow their employees to manage their insurance and financial benefits through a Web portal hosted by a third party. You would go through the same profiling exercise for other third-party providers like offshore development groups or, potentially, vendors who are part of your supply chain. Whatever the service being provided, you would want to assess the sensitivity for the function being performed by that vendor.

TIPS & TRICKS

When you are assessing a vendor, start by looking them up on the Privacy Rights Clearinghouse [1] for any history of data breaches or disclosures. This doesn't directly affect sensitivity, but it is a good indicator of what to be concerned about.

Everyone's inclination is to think of their own function and responsibilities as being critical to the organization. If you surveyed the resource owners in your organization and asked them to rate the importance of their functions or assets to the organization, you are probably going to get few responses of low or moderate. Because of this, you need to assess resources relative to the most important asset or process in your environment. If, for example, the mainframe holds all your sensitive data and runs all your critical applications, then you certainly couldn't justify rating your desktops and laptops as being in the same category of sensitivity. As you rate the resources in your organization, you may have to keep reminding yourself that you aren't evaluating its risk exposure, just its sensitivity to risk. The distinction between exposure to risk and sensitivity to risk is crucial for any program. If you take the same server and move it from an Internet-facing network to an internal closed network, has the sensitivity of that server changed? No, but the level of exposure has changed. The confidentiality, integrity, availability, and accountability needs are the same regardless of the threats, vulnerabilities, and controls surrounding it. The same goes for data. No matter where you move the data or what controls you put around them, the sensitivity of the data doesn't change just because the container has changed.

> **WARNING**
>
> Be careful not to over-rate the sensitivity of your resources. Always keep one extremely critical resource in mind while you are profiling and compare everything to it.

There are a few categories of resources that you will want to profile:

- Applications
- Infrastructure
- Environments
- Facilities
- Business units
- Vendors

Where you focus first is going to depend on your organization and industry. If you are an *Internet service provider*, you might start by profiling your infrastructure such as network devices, DNS servers, and so on. But if you are an *application service provider*, you would likely start with the applications that you host. Similarly, an organization that makes heavy use of offshore developers might focus its efforts on vendor profiling first. Understanding the business you are in will help guide your priorities. You don't need to address all these areas right out of the gate. Pick your battles!

Once you are certain that your profiling process is running smoothly, you can break out of your focus on these high-level categories of assets and start assigning more specific sensitivity scores. For example, you may begin by profiling an entire environment, but later discover that there are aspects of that environment that should be treated differently. A typical first step is to profile environments like your production server network versus your desktop environment. This will get you started, but you'll quickly discover that not all production servers are equivalent, nor are all desktop environments. So you could further break down those environments by business function, profiling the desktops used by researchers in the lab separately from those used by administrative staff. The key is to start broad and set reasonable goals or you will quickly get overwhelmed.

You will want to include additional ownership and administration information in the profile, even though it doesn't directly affect the evaluation of the resource's sensitivity because it will help you to manage the assessment process. For example, be sure to also capture:

- Resource owner
- Business unit
- Resource custodian
- Environment and/or location

These administrative details will help with the execution of your risk program and can also make reporting metrics easier. These may seem like simple details, but your job will be that much harder if you don't establish this information from the start. Although the risk profile doesn't need to be a list of every security control related to that resource, you should also capture some general details about access methods, interfaces, and basic security controls like:

- Support and hosting model
- Access administration model
- Audit trail and maker/checker controls
- History of previous risk assessments and requirements for future assessments

You do not need to obtain the techie details about control implementations for each of these items, but you can use these guidelines to capture a very basic baseline that will be used to prioritize areas of greater exposure. You may also want to explicitly assign members of your own team to be responsible for the profiling and assessment of particular resources or categories. This could be another field in your security risk profile. In the end, you should be building an inventory of sorts based on the risk profiles.

ASKING THE RIGHT QUESTIONS

The *security risk profile* needs to ask several questions about the resource to help determine its sensitivity and criticality in comparison to other resources within the organization. How can you take these likely financial and reputation outcomes and map them to different resources? You need to develop questions for the business owners that will help you to rank the various assurance needs of each resource.

Risk Impact Categories and Examples

To qualify the sensitivity of a resource, you will need to think about impacts to the organization if the resource were compromised in some way. Security compromises can take many forms, ranging from intentional service disruptions to accidental disclosures of confidential information. But this information doesn't really describe the consequences of these incidents. To really measure the sensitivity of a resource, you need to understand what it would mean to the organization to suffer a service disruption or breach of data. It is the impact to the organization that determines the sensitivity rating of any given resource. Consider, for example, a services disruption: it could cause the organization to pay fines to clients if the Service Level Agreement (SLA) is violated. Potentially, it could result in reputational damage that hurts new sales or even loss of current customers who lose confidence in the organization. In some cases, it could even lead to regulatory sanctions or increased oversight. Similarly, a data breach can result in costs associated with notifying customers of the breach, lost productivity during the investigation and aftermath, loss of market shares, or even the cost of litigation. These are all tangible outcomes that can be analyzed and measured.

As noted earlier, the most common categories of impact that should be included in a security risk profile are as follows:

- Financial
- Legal
- Reputational
- Regulatory

The financial and legal damages are fairly straightforward and include monetary impact from loss of business, fines, direct theft of funds, damages paid to injured party, legal fees, or even productivity loss during an incident investigation. The consequences could even include jail term or other criminal penalties if a law is broken. Because of the emergence of Sarbanes Oxley compliance and more recent privacy laws, these consequences are a real possibility for most organizations. Organizations with a global footprint need to be especially well informed about the applicability and implications of international data protection laws.

Reputational consequences can be far less direct and tangible than financial and legal penalties. A security compromise could include damage to the perception of your organization by clients or within your business' industry. You will also need to consider damage to your reputation with regulators that might decrease their trust in your organization and increase scrutiny. If you have to self-report to regulators or, even worse, have the regulators discover a breach before you do, they can make your life miserable with sanctions and additional oversight.

When it really comes down to it, all these categories will eventually result in some financial impact to the organization, whether it is direct or not. The categories suggested here can help you to organize these consequences so that you can better compare the profiles of different resources. Some security incidents will have greater long-term effects than others and it isn't always clear how customers or regulators will react to them. Mapping out the chain of events that would result from a compromise and trying to anticipate the backlash is an important exercise when creating both your sensitivity scales and the security risk profile template. Your risk model needs to account for how the scope, duration, and visibility of a security compromise affects the degree of impact to the organization.

Profile Design

There are many questions that you could ask in a *security risk profile* questionnaire. In general, you want to ask direct questions with set answers. Giving free-form questions/answers will make scoring the questionnaire very difficult. For example, you might ask who the target user community is for this resource and offer several options to choose from (shown in Figure 4.1).

Some examples of items you might want to include in your profile questionnaire are as follows:

* Are there any contracts that require specific levels of security protection?
* How long could this resource be unavailable?
* Are audit trails required by a regulation?
* Would someone go to jail if data were intentionally modified?

Also, try not to ask subjective questions like "how sensitive is the data being processed by this resource?" As noted previously, everyone always wants to think that their resources are important, so you'll end up with everyone selecting "High." Instead, ask them to check off all the data types that apply to their resource and use a backend calculation to measure the sensitivity of those data types. For example, if you wanted to gauge the sensitivity of the data in a particular application, you might use the question setup shown in Figure 4.2.

In the background, you may have each selection mapped to a level of sensitivity (for example, Medical Information = High; Hire Date = Low). This way, the

1. Please select which groups of individuals have access to your application:
   - ☐ Employees
   - ☐ External clients
   - ☐ Partners
   - ☐ Outsourcers
   - ☐ Regulators
   - ☐ Government agencies
   - ☐ Vendors
   - ☐ Others

FIGURE 4.1

User community form.

2. Please specify the employee data used or collected (select all that apply):

Employee data	Contains data value (Yes/No)
Birth date	
Credit card information	
Cultural information (racial or ethnic origin, political opinion, religion, trade union membership, sexual preference, criminal record)	
Dependents or beneficiaries	
Financial institution deposit information	
Hire date	
Home address	
Home or cell phone	
International identifying number (e.g. Social security)	
Marital status	
Medical information	
Performance reviews / evaluations	
Personal private information (e.g. mother's first/middle/maiden name, city of birth, first school, etc.)	
Salary/compensation information	

FIGURE 4.2

Data sensitivity form.

business owner filling out this profile doesn't need to make any judgments about the level of sensitivity directly; they just identify the applicable application data types. You could even take this a step further and code the questionnaire such that combinations of data types yield higher sensitivity levels. The combination of data often makes something sensitive, whereas the data on their own may be of lesser importance. Maybe the biomedical company keeps sensitive medical records for participants in their research studies. If this data are stored with only a generic participant number, instead of a full name, on each record, then there would be no HIPAA or privacy concerns. However, as soon as you combine that with a list of associated names, it suddenly becomes more sensitive.

Let's look at an example of a resource and think about how to assess its sensitivity. If you wanted to rate the sensitivity of the general workstations and laptops in your organization, you might ask some of the following questions:

- Is availability important for each device?
- Are any sensitive data stored locally?
- Can the organization function without them?

To properly rate this resource, you will need to think about many aspects of a desktop/laptop's criticality to the organization. This is going to vary between businesses depending on how the system is used. For example, a laptop for a scientist in a biomedical research lab may have intellectual property that is very valuable to the company and is very sensitive to unauthorized modifications, whereas the receptionist's workstation may not contain any sensitive data. A member of the sales team may lose access to his laptop for 2 days without any major impact to the business, whereas the availability of the company's e-mail server may be critical for the business to function.

If you are looking at rating the workstations/laptops in general, you will need to think about the average sensitivity level as compared to servers or network infrastructure devices. Would a breach of each have the same impact on the organization? From an availability perspective, the loss of a single workstation versus a single server would be greatly different. Chances are that a user could find a workaround for losing access to their workstation, such as using a loaner system or temporarily working off their BlackBerry. Conversely, the disruption of most servers would impact far more users and potentially critical services. But if, on the other hand, you think about a malware outbreak that infects many workstations and laptops, making them unusable, you are going to see a much higher productivity loss for the organization. Still, the loss of multiple servers will tend to be more damaging than even multiple workstations or laptops. Even if you think about this comparison in terms of dependencies, the workstations and laptops are dependent on the servers for many services that cannot be performed locally, but very few production services would be hindered by the unavailability of the desktop environment.

Another good example of a resource is printers. When considering a risk profile for printers, a few of the following questions might come to mind:

- Will confidential documents be printed?
- Could the printers themselves be hijacked?
- Is availability an issue?
- What about accountability?
- Are any sensitive data stored in memory or persistent storage locally?
- How does this resource compare with a Mainframe or File Server?

In general, the sensitivity level for printers is going to be low compared with other resources, but you can't ignore the sensitivity of certain printers in your environment. The printers that are used to print out paychecks or checks to vendors may be very sensitive to both confidentiality and integrity threats. Certain departments in your organization, like HR and Finance, may even have dedicated printers for this reason.

Sometimes, it may not even be the function of the resource itself that makes it sensitive, but rather the ability to use it as an attack vector against more sensitive targets. Think in general about the impact of a compromised printer. Would an attacker be targeting the printer itself or would they be using it as a vector to compromise a more valuable system?

Another common resource to profile is the organization's Internet connection. Consider what will drive the sensitivity of this resource:

- What services rely on this connection?
- Are sensitive data transferred through the Internet?
- Is it needed for e-mail?
- How do the availability requirements compare with confidentiality, integrity, or accountability needs?

Availability concerns are probably the most obvious, but there are certainly other areas to consider as well. Organizations do use their Internet connections differently, but it is safe to say that the majority of traffic will likely be e-mail or Web browsing. These functions may have a reasonable tolerance for disruptions. If an e-mail takes 30 minutes to be delivered rather than 1 minute, it may not have any measurable impact of productivity. However, consider the difference if your organization uses the Internet for its VOIP infrastructure or to receive critical files from clients? Then, how would you rate the availability needs of the Internet connection? Maybe your organization doesn't rely on outside connections to function. It could have dedicated connections to its clients for all critical and sensitive functions instead. All these factors will need to be taken into account in your security risk profile.

When considering the factors on which to focus your profile, it's important not to forget about the sensitivity of data. Is it critical that the data going through the Internet connection is protected from eavesdropping? Most likely, the answer is yes. Is it important that there be protection from intentional modification, deletion, or insertion of data? This answer is also is likely to be yes, but the level of needed integrity will vary. Consider how the importance of preserving confidentiality and integrity would compare with an internal network. In terms of accountability needs, you might ask the business owners how important it is that you can verify the source of traffic and confirm the validity of what is sent, say via e-mail or file transfer through the Internet connection. All these are important factors to include in your questionnaire.

One final example we'll consider is a management console or device. Because of the nature of the privileged access such a device has to other critical resources, these typically are rated very highly for risk sensitivity. As you might expect, whenever you are assessing the sensitivity level of a management device (a system that is used to administer another resource), the sensitivity level is going to be at least as high (and maybe higher) than the sensitivity level of the resource being administered. But even within this general guideline, the sensitivities may vary. For example, the direct console access may have high-accountability needs to assure that an audit trail accurately tracks all privileged activities, but it may not actually transfer data that is very confidential. However, you wouldn't want anyone to be able to modify commands sent between the console and the resource being managed. Login credentials to management devices certainly require a high level of confidentiality, but do other data on the system also require a high level of confidentiality? Typically, a management device will contain configuration information about the resource being managed, which you obviously wouldn't want disclosed to an attacker, but is it as sensitive as, let's say, a database server that stores privacy data about employees? Well, if you think about a management console for your firewalls, the configuration and rule-set data may be classified in your highest level of confidentiality. Anyone with access to your entire firewall policy is fairly likely to find a significant hole in your perimeter defenses.

If confidentiality and integrity sensitivities are high, how important is availability for management devices? This probably depends on whether there is an issue that needs to be repaired at the time. How long could this system be down on average before it hurts the organization? It is likely that if the resource being managed is up and running, having the management console down may not be an issue for short periods. Longer periods may prevent support personnel from tuning and maintaining the system, leading to a disruption on the managed device.

Hopefully, these examples begin to illustrate just how many factors need to be considered when profiling any resource. The key is to carefully and thoughtfully design the profile to assess each resource's sensitivity in these areas through consistent and straightforward questions. You should also include a couple of verification questions to ensure that your calculation of risk sensitivity is close to the business owner's intuitive assessment of the resource's importance. These questions won't be included in any calculations, but rather will be used to identify any mismatches.

RISK DEEP DIVE

Criticality of Unstructured Data

One of the tricky challenges in classifying the sensitivity level of data is that risk changes over time and based on other independent factors, such as what other information is available with the data. For example, a list of bank account numbers alone is of little use to an attacker. There is some risk because now the attacker has a list of valid numbers to try and may be able to discover a pattern in the creation of the account numbers, but, overall, this list would be classified as low sensitivity. A list of account numbers with the names of the account holders, however, would be classified as high sensitivity. It is the mapping of the two lists (numbers and names) that needs to be protected, but how would you control access to the lists on their own?

Similarly, a list of user passwords with usernames would certainly be considered high sensitivity, but what if the list was from 6 months ago and all accounts must change their password every 6 months? In this case, time really matters. Why is this important? Well,

(Continued)

> *(Continued)*
> think about backup tapes. What if they contained unencrypted user password lists from 6 months ago and were stolen? Is this a risk you should be spending a lot of time trying to mitigate? Of course, there certainly could also be data on the backup tapes that isn't time dependent, which would need to be protected regardless of how old it is.
>
> Think about profiling a database server that stores medical information for several hospitals. Doctors may use these data in their daily work to review a client's medical history, or administrators may use the data when working with insurance companies. The database itself will likely have high sensitivity for confidentiality and integrity, at least. Say that now an administrator exports a partial report of one client's history to provide to the insurance company. Does this deserve the same high-sensitivity rating from a profiling perspective? What if a doctor prints out a report of the medical history for the last year for 100 patients to use in a research study, but each patient's name is masked. How will this affect the value of those data?
>
> In the security field, we can't always apply a blanket standard or baseline of controls to all cases. The risks need to be identified for each scenario and carefully analyzed. Data leakage prevention is a difficult problem to solve unless your organization's sensitive data are very distinct from the nonsensitive data elements.

Calculating Sensitivity

It is no coincidence that the examples in the previous section focused on the confidentiality, integrity, availability, and accountability (C-I-A-A) needs of each asset. Although you ultimately want to assign each resource a single sensitivity score, this will be made up of independent ratings of each aspect of C-I-A-A. Rather than guessing at an overall sensitivity level for each resource, it is more accurate to look at the asset's individual assurance needs for confidentiality, integrity, availability, and accountability and use that to guide the overall assessment of sensitivity. Earlier, in Table 4.1, we compared the overall sensitivity of the *drug research server* to the *mail room printer*. Do you think that all four aspects of C-I-A-A were high for the server? Probably, only integrity and confidentiality were high. Once you account for sensitivity at this level, you can have more meaningful and targeted risk discussions.

A sophisticated risk model should allow you to analyze the threats and vulnerabilities associated with any resource and determine an acceptable level of exposure to each aspect of C-I-A-A. In terms of determining business impact, all four variables are independent of each other, meaning, for example, that any data or resource may require a high level of integrity control and a low level of confidentiality control at the same time, or a high level of availability and a moderate level of accountability.

Most of the questions in the profile form should be organized to match your chosen sensitivity scale. For example, if your sensitivity scale is based on a Low-Moderate-High model, then a question about financial consequences should be similarly structured to have three choices, as shown in Figure 4.3.

With this approach, you aren't asking the business owners to explicitly differentiate between a high and a moderate sensitivity because that mapping is all

3. If information was disclosed to an unauthorized outside party, select the resulting level of potential damage:

❑ <$500,000

❑ $500,000–$999,999

❑ >$1,000,000

FIGURE 4.3

Financial penalty form.

4. Please rate the overall confidentiality needs (the consequence of unauthorized disclosure or compromise of data stored, processed, or transmitted by the application) of the resource:

❑ High

❑ Moderate

❑ Low

FIGURE 4.4

Confidentiality reliability check.

handled in the background. They just need to represent the business impact of specific scenarios. You might have a second question with a slight variation that gauges the impact of an intentional manipulation of information rather than a disclosure. It all goes back to your four basic security requirements of confidentiality, integrity, availability, and accountability and finding a way to measure each resource's needs in those areas.

Anyone who has tried to conduct a survey or design a questionnaire knows that you need a control built in to highlight inconsistency in the answers or problems with the setup of the questions themselves (referred to as inter-item reliability). For example, if you include several questions requiring the resource owner to select the financial impact of data disclosures and they consistently choose the lowest range of impact, but then tell you they think their resource is highly sensitive to confidentiality threats, then what went wrong? Is the business owner inflating the importance of their asset or did you perhaps not include questions that covered all the applicable aspects of confidentiality consequences? One solution is to include some "gut check" questions, like in Figure 4.4.

This gives you a good comparison point for the rest of the confidentiality-related questions. When reviewing the profile, you should always flag it for follow-up if there is a gap between this answer and your more targeted questions. Including a definition of each choice (high, moderate, low) will also help you get better results.

When we measure a resource's sensitivity to risk, we look at all four of these assurance needs (C-I-A-A) and rate each one. For example, a resource may be subject to a particular regulation that requires the protection of data confidentiality, but says nothing about availability. Another asset may need to comply with SOX, which is more concerned with the integrity of data than the confidentiality. This is why it is important to rate each component of C-I-A-A separately.

Figures 4.1 through 4.4 show just a few examples of the questions you might ask as part of a security risk profile. Notice that we don't ask the business owner to rate the application's sensitivity directly or identify any risk exposures (except in the gut check question shown in Figure 4.4); we just ask simple and straightforward questions that can easily be mapped to sensitivity levels when scoring it later. In the background, we can score the answers like *international identifying number* as being in the high-confidentiality category, or *serious injury* as a result of mis-handled data in the high-integrity category. One approach is to score the resource based on the highest sensitivity option chosen for each question. If the business owner chose three categories of data that all have a Moderate risk sensitivity and no other options were chosen in the profile, then the resource would be assigned an overall sensitivity of Moderate. However, as soon as an option that maps to a High sensitivity is chosen, the resource's sensitivity rating would also go up to High.

Another alternative would be to assign each question/answer a numeric score and either take the sum of all the answers or use an average. Although this approach can provide a more granular sensitivity score, the outcome will depend on how many questions and answers are in your profile, so it is easy to skew your results using this method. Because of this, using the first method of taking the maximum is the recommended place to start. Numeric scores can always be added to supplement this down the road.

BIOMEDICAL/DRUG RESEARCH COMPANY

Because there are so many aspects to consider, effectively profiling resources can take some practice. Having a structured profile questionnaire will really help, but for the purposes of this example, let's assume that we don't have set questions yet. What would you consider when profiling a *research data server* for a biomedical/drug research company? Assume that your organization researches, develops, and markets medical drugs to consumers. Start with your four major categories of impact, and then jot down a few questions for each. For example, you might ask the business owner questions concerning the following:

- Financial damages
  - Any funds processed by this resource
  - Any fines or penalties associated with a breach
  - Potential revenue loss
- Legal implications
  - Contract violation
  - Civil lawsuit or criminal case
- Reputational damages
  - Visibility of this resource
  - If it would affect customer or industry perceptions
  - If the organization is sensitive to reputational damage
- Regulatory implications
  - Sanctions
  - Increased compliance requirements
  - More frequent and obtrusive audits

Let's look at the *financial damages* first. Would there be any fines or penalties associated with a breach of the research server? Probably not. What about direct theft of funds? Also, likely not. What about revenue lost due to loss of competitive advantage? Yes, this is likely. The tricky part now is how to qualify that loss. That will likely depend on how competitive your industry is and how differentiated your products are from competitors; so, you may want to build a scale based on percentage of revenue lost. For example, the loss of Coke's secret ingredient would be devastating, but the premature disclosure of their new holiday package design might have a low impact, financially speaking. There is no one-size-fits-all solution for qualifying these answers. With the latest drug research, the company may spend millions of dollars in research and development of a single drug product, only to have it stolen by a competitor before they patented it. All that investment could be lost with a single data breach.

What about legal implications? It doesn't seem likely that there would be any legal implications for the organization directly resulting from a breach of this server unless the data were modified covertly. Someone could maliciously change research data or safety test information that would cause an unsafe drug to be released to the public. That could certainly have severe legal and regulatory implications for the company.

It is always going to be hard to predict the implications for the organization's reputation if a security breach was made known to customers or company's industry. In this example, it may hurt their standing with regulators who review and certify their drugs for distribution. Or, it may cause customers to seek alternatives products, but the chances of a consumer making a drug decision based on the publicized data breach are low. Also, consider whether this would be different if the business were a monopoly or a government agency. Suppose there is no alternative drug to treat or cure a serious disease, would you let a known data breach of the manufacturer stop you from taking the drug? There are many organizations that enjoy the benefits of either having no competition in a market or being part of a government. The reputational hit won't result in the same loss of business for these organizations.

So, in this case, financial damages due to loss of competitive advantage are most likely. Possibly, legal or regulatory implications are also likely, but theft of the intellectual property would be the primary focus. Depending on the risk scale being used, this would probably warrant a risk sensitivity rating of high for confidentiality and integrity.

Higher sensitivity resources will undergo evaluation more frequently than lower risk resources. Also, as risk findings are generated, you should pull the risk sensitivity into the risk exposure calculation, since a security issue may have a bigger impact on a critical asset than it would have on a lower importance asset, and might therefore need to be addressed in a much more immediate time frame. By utilizing a risk ranking methodology, you can focus your energy on the most critical resource, saving time and money while improving your security posture.

ASSESSING RISK APPETITE

On day one of any job as a security professional, you should be observing how the organization manages and reacts to risks, and try to gauge the organization's appetite for risk. As a security leader, one of your primary tasks when joining an organization should be to understand your CEO's tolerance for risk exposure.

Clearly, some organizations are more sensitive to risks and have more to lose during a security breach than others. Risk management choices are often influenced by the corporate culture and the tone for risk acceptance is usually set from the top down.

Assessing the C-Level

You can categorize an organization as either risk accepting or risk averse, but there is a large continuum of risk tolerance in between on which most organizations' risk appetites lie. Organizations that accept risk are generally those that are in a growth mode, whereas larger, more well-established organizations are typically more averse to risk taking. For example, you might hear large banking institutions' approach to risk management as "find all the risks, and crush them into oblivion." This would be characteristic of a risk-averse approach. However, a small start-up company might be willing to operate with a lot more exposure, knowing that they can capitalize on opportunities and have less to lose.

Regardless of whether you approach risk management from a quantitative perspective or focus on qualitative methods, you will discover that risk management can be as much an art as it is a science. This should be no real surprise to anyone who is familiar with similar disciplines such as economics. We like to think of our field as being closer to the science of economics than, say, weather forecasting, but there are the days when we're not quite sure. After all, providing even a 10-day forecast for information security can sometimes feel daunting. The art of risk management becomes most critical when you are trying to gauge the risk tolerance of your executive team. The failures of many young information security officers can be directly attributed to their failure to properly profile their own senior leadership and adapt to the organization's culture.

Sadly, you will hear many horror stories about the security leaders who didn't even attempt to assess the risk appetite of the organization before plowing ahead with security initiatives and "fixes" that weren't at all in line with the executive's priorities. Whether you are interviewing for a senior position on a security team, or you are a new security leader joining an organization, or an existing security officer who has been tasked with building out a risk program, you need to focus on drawing out information from the most senior executives about their priorities and tolerance for risk. The most typical approach is to schedule a few sit-downs with executives to discuss past incidents and current concerns and to talk through how they would want to handle a few likely risk scenarios.

You may be inclined to start the scenario discussion by focusing on a couple incidents that you foresee occurring at this organization, but it can be more productive to start with a couple of hypothetical risk decisions. Present a few risks to the executive with some trade-offs in terms of cost to mitigate and resource constraints and listen to how they would want to address these risks. Pay very close attention to the questions they ask to help make their decision because this is a great indicator of how they think and can help you prepare answers when there is a real decision to be made down the road. For example, if you present a sample risk during this conversation and the executive's first question is whether this risk remediation plan can be outsourced to a consulting company, then you now have valuable information about how to present mitigation plans in the future. As much as possible, it is important to listen primarily and to only speak up when you need to move the discussion forward or to better understand their reasoning.

Present several scenarios—this may need to be over the course of several sessions—with each risk having different levels of exposure and focusing on different aspects of the business. That way, you have some information you can use to compare the executive team's priorities relative to one another. Try translating your risk scales into threshold statements that will be meaningful for senior managers. For example, ask the CEO if a risk that will likely cause an outage of a major service for up to four hours in the next year needs to be escalated to the executive level or not. How about an exposure that will likely cause an outage for thirty minutes? You may want to start this process with your direct boss, whether that be the CIO or another C-level executive, and also be sure to engage the CEO if you don't report to him or her directly. Any meetings that you can attend where decisions are being made about priorities or objectives that are being set will also provide you with invaluable insight into the values of the organization that can help you to focus your own efforts.

These sessions don't need to be formal; you may even extend this exercise to include some table-top sessions where you get several leaders in a room to work through a hypothetical scenario. The goal is to consciously spend some time profiling the organization outside of any information-resource-focused assessments on the ground and to gauge how the senior leadership approach risk decisions.

Setting Risk Thresholds and Determining Tolerance Ranges

As part of the security risk profiling process, each resource needs to have *risk sensitivity*, *tolerance*, and *threshold* values defined. Table 4.4 shows the relationship between sensitivity, tolerance range, and threshold for a basic low-to-high qualitative risk scale.

Think of the *risk threshold* as the highest level of acceptable risk exposure for that resource. If you remember, back in the beginning of this chapter, we stated that the risk threshold is always inversely proportional to the risk sensitivity level.

Table 4.4 Risk-Tolerance Levels		
Risk Sensitivity	**Risk Tolerance (Risk exposure range)**	**Risk Threshold (Risk exposure upper bound)**
Low	Negligible-High	High
Moderate	Negligible-Moderate	Moderate
High	Negligible-Low	Low

If you have a high sensitivity to risk, then you should have a low threshold for risk. A resource with a low sensitivity to risk will have a high threshold for risk exposure. The risk threshold is the upper bound for the *risk tolerance* range. The risk tolerance range defines the lowest and highest levels of acceptable risk for that resource. There is nothing magical about the relationship between sensitivity, tolerance, and thresholds; we use it as a way to inform risk decisions and as a simple criterion for which risks need to be escalated. If a particular exposure is outside the acceptable tolerance range, then this may require an escalation to address the risk exposure. Likewise, you can use this same concept to define threshold risk levels for an environment. For example, when making an implementation decision for a new system, you may determine that it can't be placed into the existing server farm because of the exposures it might introduce to existing systems in that environment. The risk that one system imposes on another is referred to as *transitive risk*. This should be a primary factor when determining the proper placement and segmentation needed in your environment.

Just because a risk exposure is within an acceptable level, it doesn't mean an organization shouldn't choose to mitigate it further. Similarly, just because a risk is outside the tolerance range, it doesn't mean that it can't be accepted. These levels are merely guidelines for making risk decisions and should be used to determine the level of executive sign-off needed to deviate from recommended tolerance levels. These concepts will be particularly important when we start to discuss policy exceptions and risk acceptance in later chapters.

SUMMARY

Risk sensitivity is such a crucial concept in your risk program. At first, it appears to be a fairly simple concept to prioritize your resources based on several factors of criticality, but then you will discover that this evaluation becomes the basis for all your future risk decisions. It affects which resources you assess at all, how often you reassess them, how detailed the assessment needs to be, how you prioritize any risk findings, what level of risk is acceptable, and even the level of management needed to approve an exception. Designing a comprehensive and accurate risk profile form may take a couple tries before you find the right mix of questions, so you should use the sample questions and recommended fields in this chapter to get you started. Don't forget how important it is to gauge the risk appetite of the organization early on, which really means assessing the risk tolerance of the most senior leaders.

Action Plan

After reading this chapter, you should consider taking the following actions in your own organization:

- If you don't already have a risk sensitivity scale, integrate the qualitative scale from this chapter into your program.

- Implement a *security risk profile* form including the basic fields recommended in this chapter.
- Make a list of the resources that seem the most critical to the organization and profile them to verify your assumptions.
- Establish a schedule of risk assessments based on the risk sensitivity of the resource.
- Implement risk assessments with varying levels of detail and invasiveness, and map them to risk sensitivity levels.
- Publish a table of acceptable risk exposure levels based on the sensitivity of the resource and use this to inform, but not dictate, management's risk decisions.
- Schedule time with your senior executives to gauge their risk appetite through some informal discussions about potential risks.

Reference

[1] Privacy Rights Clearinghouse. www.privacyrights.org (accessed 31.01.10).

Formulating a Risk

## 5

INFORMATION IN THIS CHAPTER

- Breaking Down a Risk
- Who or What Is the Threat?

INTRODUCTION

Believe it or not, accurately describing the risk can be one of the hardest parts of any risk assessment. How many times have you had a so-called risk presented such as "the file transfer between the client and application doesn't use encryption" or "that vendor doesn't have an independent audit function?" Are these really risks? Is it really as easy as stating the lack of a control and calling it a risk? In actuality, this is merely a clear sign of an unseasoned assessor. Risk assessments are about more than running through checklists of controls and identifying gaps. Likewise, a risk assessment needs to have more substance than just a list of all the worst-case scenarios that you can imagine. Yes, two simultaneous hurricanes could hit both of your data centers on each coast of the United States on the same day, taking out your operations for several days, but just because it is possible doesn't make it probable. Let's explore how to really break down a risk into its individual components and accurately assess the level of exposure. Remember, it is all about educating the organization about the top risk exposures and helping to set priorities.

BREAKING DOWN A RISK

If you went on Google and looked up *risk management*, *risk assessment*, *risk analysis*, or any similar terms, you would find a lot of different definitions, some of which are significantly different from one another and others that just vary in terminology but use the same core concepts. Even if you narrow your search to *information security risk management*, you are going to find a vast array of interpretations and perspectives. This is not only problematic for beginners as they try to get a grasp on the discipline, but it also makes it very hard to have a productive conversation with anyone in the field because you will find yourself constantly tripping over terminology. After a few minutes of Google searching for risk topics, you may start to get the idea that almost anything can be called a risk assessment. Certainly, there are those in the field who are sorely misusing the terminology or basing their approach on fundamentally flawed models and assumptions, but there is also a lot of fantastic research emerging everyday and solid risk models being applied by information security professionals. Don't worry—there is hope for us yet! Risk management is finally starting to get the focus that it needs, and with that will come more mature risk models.

Finding the Risk, Part I

We will start by defining some terms to describe the key components of a risk, and then we will use these terms as we analyze some simple risk scenarios. The end goal is a model that will accurately articulate, categorize, and rate risk exposure. Consider the following assessment finding:

> *"Network administrators use telnet to manage network devices and their passwords never expire."*

Assume that you are a security manager for a retail company and you identified this finding. How would you break down this scenario into risk components? What is described above is certainly a finding, but does it describe the risk? For example, you should be able to answer the following questions from a well written risk statement:

* Who is a threat we are worried about?
* Why is this vulnerability causing the exposure?
* What is the potential impact to the organization?

A detailed assessment would also take into account any compensating controls that might lower the risk. Already, we have thrown out a lot of terms that may not be clear yet: threat, vulnerability, impact, exposure, and compensating controls. These need to be clearly defined before we can break down our Telnet finding. Once we define some key terms, we will come back to our discussion about the network administrators.

Terminology Is Key

The core elements of a risk exposure and risk rating are as follows:

* **Sensitivity** of the resource (importance or criticality to the organization)
* **Threats**, and threat countermeasures
* **Vulnerabilities**, and vulnerability countermeasures
* **Inherent Risk** (the value of the unmitigated risk exposure)
* **Compensating Controls** (controls currently in place that reduce the exploitability)
* **Residual Risk** (the value of the net risk after mitigation)

In simple terms, an information security *risk exposure* should describe the outcome of a successful exploit of the *vulnerability* by the *threat*. Sometimes, this combination of threat and vulnerability is referred to as the "impact" or "consequence" of a risk exposure. A simple way of remembering the differences between the risk terminology is that the *threat* describes the "who," the *vulnerability* explains the "why," and the *risk* the "what" consequences the business will experience. This may seem very simplistic, but it really helps to conceptualize the differences.

Given those factors, a risk exposure value can be calculated. Chapter 4 discussed risk sensitivity in great detail, so the remaining elements of threat and vulnerability still need to be explained. Risk qualification and especially quantifications can get very complex, but at the most basic level, the magnitude of the vulnerability is measured by *severity*, and the probability of the threat occurring is measured by *likelihood*. Together, sensitivity, severity, and likelihood are the three variables in your measurement of risk exposure. Specific risk qualification methods and risk calculations will be covered in more detail later in this book, but for now, it is important to understand what each term is describing.

To qualify a risk, you need at least three ratings, which are defined by the SANS Institute [1] as follows:

- **Sensitivity** A value relative to the resource's tolerance for risk exposure.
- **Severity** Measures the magnitude of consequences from a threat/vulnerability pair being realized.
- **Likelihood** Measures the probability that the threat/vulnerability pair will be realized.

The severity is a measure of the magnitude of the weakness that the threat can exploit. If the risk describes the consequences if the vulnerability is exploited, then the severity is a measure of the magnitude of the exploit. For example, it may describe the extent of the penetration into your network or the amount of data exposed.

The likelihood is a measure of how probable it is that the threat/vulnerability pair will be realized. If the risk describes the consequences if the vulnerability is exploited, then the likelihood is a measure of the chance that it will happen. Some risk models distinguish between the probability that a risk will occur, and the frequency with which it is likely to occur. Although this is an important distinction, we will include both considerations in likelihood for now to keep the model simple. As you get comfortable with the basic model, you can expand on this.

For example, an exploit of easily readable backup media could lead to "an unauthorized disclosure of sensitive credit card data for all customers, which would require a breach notification to the major credit card companies and affected clients." Notice that this description helps us rate the severity of the exploit by indicating the amount of data that will be disclosed (all client data) and the sensitivity of the asset by indicating which data will be disclosed (sensitive, "regulated" customer credit card data). It also indicates that a notification to clients will be required, which further qualifies the sensitivity of the asset we are assessing by gauging the effects on reputation, financial loss, and possible exposure to civil legal action. You would also want to qualify the likelihood by how attractive these data would be to an attacker, how easily the backup media could be intercepted or lost, and how readily it could be read by a malicious party.

This type of risk qualification can help you determine your mitigation priorities by identifying the mission critical functions that have the most residual risk because, presumably, you will work on these first. It is also important to note that, without a threat, the vulnerability results in no risk exposure.

Envision the Consequences

When you need to present a risk to senior management or a client, it is critical to articulate the risk accurately. Mixing up threats, vulnerabilities, outcomes, and controls will ultimately confuse your audience. When you are describing a risk exposure, think about the consequences for the organization, not just the immediate exploit activity. What would happen if the vulnerability were to be exploited? Remember that the risk exposure description needs to detail the impact to the organization. For example, if sensitive data were disclosed unintentionally or stolen from the organization, what would happen?

If you are having trouble getting started, try to answer these questions:

- Would the organization lose its clients?
- Would they go out of business?
- Would they have to notify all their customers about the unauthorized disclosure?
- Could they recover from a breach?

If your risk description doesn't answer these questions, then you haven't fully covered the components of the risk.

The risk description should include the outcome of a successful exploit of the vulnerability by the threat. To avoid the error of mixing up threats, vulnerabilities, and risks, try using a structured format with required elements to provide a three-part risk statement:

"As a result of <one or more definite causes>, <uncertain event> may occur, which would lead to <one or more effects on resource(s)>"

Consider what would happen if sensitive data were disclosed unintentionally or stolen from the organization. Your risk description needs to address the consequences or outcomes in business terms. For example, you could apply this statement format to a data breach risk:

"As a result of lost backup tapes, an unauthorized disclosure of sensitive credit card data for all customers may occur, which would require breach notifications to regulators and affected clients."

Always take a critical eye to any of your risk descriptions and try to anticipate whether your description conveys the importance of the risk to senior management. Read over your risk description and if you don't think it quickly tells the reader why they care about some security weakness and how this affects their bottom-line, then it needs to be rewritten. Also, be very careful not to include too much commentary or narration in your risk description when presenting it to management. They are going to want the facts without the color of additional opinions or commentary.

It is easy to confuse the threat and vulnerability with the risk itself. Think of the risk as a description of the consequences. What would happen if the vulnerability were to be exploited? Remember that the risk details the impact to the organization.

For example, read through each of these statements and decide if you think that they describe the risk:

- Anyone who could compromise the access controls could have access to a tremendous amount of business information.
- Transmitted information like passwords, e-mails, and business data are subject to eavesdropping.

Carefully read these two statements and decide whether you think that they pass the test of conveying the who, the why, and the what. Both of these analyses seem to have stopped short of the point of the risk. They just don't describe the business consequences for the organization. Without context, there is no way to really qualify the impact to the organization in terms of productivity loss, loss of revenue, regulatory sanctions, and so on.

Let's try rewriting these analyses. Does the following statement better describe the first risk?

> *"Anyone who could compromise the access controls could have access to view regulated financial information for clients numbering around 20,000 records. A breach of this information would require mandatory reporting in over 40 states, and a $200 fine per record for Massachusetts residents."*

Notice how this risk description now provides a very clear picture of how the organization will be impacted. This analysis not only describes the type of data at risk but also includes the quantity and the type of access (read-only in this case). It goes on to describe the obligation to disclose this breach to clients in many states and the expected dollar amount loss for clients residing in Massachusetts. This gives management a pretty good picture of the impact to the organization.

Now let's try rewriting the other example. Does the following statement better describe the risk?

> *"Transmitted information like system administrator passwords for production servers are subject to eavesdropping across the network internally. Access to these passwords could allow a malicious insider to cause an outage of all client-facing services that would last for up to 24 hours."*

Notice that e-mails and other business data have been left off; it is best to focus on one risk at a time. The eavesdropping of other types of sensitive data may have a very different impact on the organization and should be listed separately. Notice that this analysis describes the scope of the outage that results both in the number of clients affected and the duration of the potential outage. It also limits the scope of the source to insider, which would help someone reading this analysis to qualify the risk and understand the potential threat vector. This analysis also assumes some mitigating controls that would allow them to get the service operational again in no more than 24 hours.

The value of clear and concise communication cannot be overstated in risk management. No matter how accurate your risk models or how thorough your threat analysis is, it will all be meaningless if you can't effectively present it to the business.

Finding the Risk, Part II

We have laid out some basic risk concepts for you so far—now let's put this into practice. Remember the network administrator scenario from earlier part of the chapter:

> *"Network administrators use Telnet to manage network devices and their passwords never expire."*

How would you begin to assess the sensitivity, severity, and likelihood of this exposure for a typical retail organization?

Let's start with the vulnerabilities. What is wrong with using Telnet to manage network devices? If you aren't familiar with the technical details of the Telnet protocol, a quick Internet search should turn up plenty of reasons that using Telnet is dangerous. As a quick hint, just referencing a "lack of encryption" is not good enough for our risk description; as discussed in previous chapters, you should never accept "best practices" as a reason to do anything. The use of Telnet makes such a good example because the limitations are easily explained to even the most nontechnical person. Using Telnet to manage any system is problematic because all communications between the client and server are transmitted in cleartext (or in the clear), meaning that anyone who can intercept the traffic can read everything without the sender or receiver knowing they have done so. The information at risk includes the username and password used to log into the system. If you are using Telnet across an untrusted network like the Internet or your local Starbucks wireless, you can assume that the data have been disclosed. In the case of the network administrator, this would include the username and password used to log into and manage a network device such as a router or switch. The consequences of this weakness should be clearer now.

Now let's consider the threats. You will want to identify both the *threat actor*, who or what could exploit this vulnerability, and the *threat activity*, how the weakness will be exploited by the actor. To qualify the most likely threats, you will want to do some basic threat modeling. Start with a few basic questions to identify the threat actor first:

- Are you worried about external mass attacks, such as a general virus that isn't meant to compromise any one organization? Or, would it need to be a targeted attack on your organization to be of concern? Are internal employees a concern or are you mostly worried about outsiders?

- Are you more worried about intentional abuse of this weakness or accidental damages?

Next, a few simple questions can help you to qualify the threat activity:

- Can this weakness be exploited from anywhere or is a certain level of access needed?
- Would the vulnerability be exploited with a physical or technical attack or a combination of the two?
- Is there a level of business knowledge or information about the environment needed to successfully exploit the weakness?
- What is the technical skill level required to exploit it?

For the threat activity, you will want to describe the most likely vector for abuse of the weakness. Vulnerabilities will often exist for a long time without ever being abused, so what threat makes this one likely to be exploited?

Next, you will want to qualify severity. Think of this as the magnitude or scope of the weakness, not necessarily the consequences of the exposure. This is a very important distinction. When you profiled your resource and determined the sensitivity level, you considered all the possible impacts to the organization if it were violated. That potential impact exists regardless of the threat/vulnerability combination, but what you want to measure with the severity is the extent of the compromise. A disclosure of a single sensitive record from your database will have a much smaller impact than 1,000 records from that same database. This is an example of severity levels for confidentiality. Availability severity levels might be distinguished by the length of a disruption, the number of users affected, or the extent of the disruption from degradation of service up to a full outage of services. Another aspect of severity is the level of access the attacker could have over your systems. For example, some network devices have multiple levels of authentication, from a normal read-only user with limited functionality to a full privileged user. On other systems, this would be the difference between the scope of access a restricted user might have to perform everyday tasks versus that of an administrator with full control of the system. The vulnerabilities with the highest severity will provide that unrestricted level of access—what we call "owning the system."

Returning to the Telnet example, you will also want to think about how the lack of any password expiration controls might compound the problem of using Telnet. The fear is that not only would the administrator's credentials be compromised but the attacker could also use them indefinitely. At least if the password expired every 30 days, the attacker might not have the opportunity to intercept the next password and the length of the exposure would therefore be shortened. Of course, if the attacker stole the password once, they can probably steal it twice, which makes the cleartext Telnet Protocol the primary weakness.

So far, the discussion has looked at the risk exposure without considering any compensating controls that might already be in place. You may hear this referred to as the "raw risk" or inherent risk, meaning that you look at the risk naked of any controls or constraints that may lower the likelihood or limit the severity. Again, going back to the Telnet example, if we assume that this organization has a typical corporate network installation, there may be a few controls already in place that make it more difficult or less desirable to exploit this weakness. Suppose the administrators only access the network devices from the local network and never remotely; in that case, an attacker may need to be already connected to the internal network to intercept the Telnet traffic. This could greatly affect your assessment of the likelihood depending on the physical access controls that are in place. At the very least, you might focus your analysis on internal employees, contractors, and guests. For a retail company, however, you need to consider how the networks in any of the stores might be connected back to the corporate offices. Potentially, network administrators need to remotely manage the network devices in the stores, which increases the opportunities for someone to intercept their communications.

To rate the sensitivity of the network devices, you will want to consider the most likely outcomes of any breach. The sensitivity level should be an indication of how bad it would be for your organization to have unauthorized individuals accessing a core infrastructure device like a router or switch. An attacker might be able to view sensitive data that pass through the network device unencrypted. Possibly, a competitor or disgruntled employee could cause a disruption or degradation of critical network services.

The earlier analysis may seem like a thorough exploration of the Telnet risk scenario, but in reality, we have only scratched the surface. These basic qualifying questions are a good place to start whenever you come across a risk in your organization, but—not to worry—we will be introducing a more methodical approach soon. Based on the discussion so far, would you recommend the Telnet risk as a priority issue to be addressed by the retail company?

Let's go through the discussion one more time and capture the specifics. There are really too many possible threat scenarios associated with this one vulnerability to list them all here, so we'll choose one example assuming the organization is a typical retailer:

- **Vulnerability** Commands and authentication credentials are sent to the network device in cleartext, which could allow for eavesdropping or manipulation of data in transit between the user and the network device.
- **Threat** Internal abuse. A savvy insider could intercept and steal the credentials of an authorized administrator with the intention to steal sensitive data as it traverses the network.
- **Severity** Payment card information traverses these network devices between the Point of Sale system (in the stores) and back-end servers (in the corporate data centers). In the event that the attacker gained access to the network device, they would have full access to view any of this sensitive data.
- **Likelihood** Although it is possible to view any data in a Telnet session, it is not trivial to sniff traffic on a switched network. The attacker would need to

be in the path of the communication between the network device and the administrator, or the attacker would need to exploit a vulnerability on another network device in the path. Additionally, the attacker would need some knowledge of the network device technology in order to capture and view data traversing the network device after gaining access. The probability of the attacker gaining access once the credentials have been stolen is further reduced by the use of Access Control Lists (ACLs) on the network device to limit Telnet connections to certain source IP addresses used by network administrator's workstations. Given that the password never expires and is therefore likely not ever to be changed, the chance of interception and successful exploitation increases over time. The attack vector with the most the highest probability of success would be from the store network.

- **Sensitivity** A breach of this sort would require the organization to publicly report the incident, costing the company over $500,000 directly in the form of fines and lawsuits and also indirectly when approximately 10% of clients switch their business to a competitor.

So given this analysis, do you still think that this is a priority item to address? Of course, there may be more likely or severe risks associated with this vulnerability, but based on this risk, how would you rate the risk overall? Take a quick gut assessment of the overall risk on a scale of Low, Moderate, or High. Think about how it compares with other risks in your own environment. If this issue existed in your organization, should it really bubble to the top of the list or would it come out somewhere in the middle? It really is hard to say with any confidence until you have a more structured model for evaluating the level of risk exposure, but these threat scenarios are a good first step to get you thinking about how many factors will affect the end risk exposure level.

WHO OR WHAT IS THE THREAT?

In the context of information security risks, the threat generally describes the source of the "attack" (attack is in quotes because it will not always be an intentional or malicious threat) and also the activity or means of the attack. Essentially, the threat source has the potential to harm the resource, and the threat activity is the way in which it will be harmed.

Defining Threats

Any information security threat can be grouped into one of a few high-level threat categories:

- Natural disaster
- Infrastructure failure

- Internal abuse
- Accident
- External targeted attack
- External mass attack

It is generally in the nature of a security professional to assume that threats will be malicious attackers, but we also need to account for user errors and accidents that can lead to security breaches. As scary as an organized hacker group is, most security teams spend less time dealing with these threats and much more of their time dealing with manual errors that are part of everyday processes or other employee mistakes that can unintentionally damage the organization just as badly. Each category of threat will have different likelihoods of occurring in general. For example, many organizations deal with mass attacks such as general viruses and phishing campaigns more often than the "sexier" and more well-publicized targeted attacks.

There are many ways to measure threat. You can use the concept of the Threat Universe that defines the magnitude of threat surface, like the number of users, networks, or systems that can reach a vulnerability. If your Web server is accessible to the general public on the Internet, you might define the threat universe as close to infinite (such as >1,000), but if it is only available to three partner companies through an extranet, maybe the threat universe may be assigned a value (such as 1,000) representing the number of employees in all three partner companies. A threat universe that only includes internal employees would then be assigned a smaller value (such as 200), depending on the size of the organization. The scale you choose to use is up to you, but this approach provides a quick and dirty way to quantify the scope of a threat, usually on a network or application level. Using real numbers allows you to demonstrate reduction in risk exposure as you decrease the percentage of users/systems to which a vulnerability is exposed. You could also assign qualitative descriptors such as Very High or Moderate likelihood to further describe the threat.

You might want to base your threat calculations on the sophistication of the attacker, the availability of exploit code, or the attractiveness of the target. These are going to be softer criteria and ultimately lend themselves better to a qualitative analysis. You always hear about those attack techniques that have only been demonstrated in a lab environment, running in a configuration that is impractical in 99% of environments, and with a level of existing access where another attack vector would be easier anyways. Your threat analysis needs to separate the "cool" but purely theoretical threats from those that are actionable today. The important thing is to understand the real threats to your organization and to sift through all the hype. A threat needs to be more than just possible; it needs to be probable to be worth assessing any further.

RISK DEEP DIVE

Emerging Threats

Over the years, the threat landscape has really shifted from the individual hacker trying to make a name for themselves with flashy and noticeable exploits that are hard to miss, to the organized and financially motivated attacker who uses stealthy techniques to evade detection while slowly stealing data from corporations for profit. A few emerging threats may not be at the top of our list of concerns yet, but they certainly need to be on our radar: *information warfare, cyber terrorism, organized crime*, and *sophisticated insider attacks*.

Information warfare is a term that has been in the vernacular for the military for many years but is just now starting to make its way into popular culture. Basically, this is the use of information security attacks for military purposes instead of private financial gain. Typically, these attacks would be conducted by a nation state against another nation state. Information systems in this case would be the source and target of attacks rather than just the mechanism. There haven't been many documented cases of information warfare on the global stage, but it is likely just a matter of time before this category of threat emerges as a critical concern. Private companies have been recognized as key components of the nation's critical infrastructure, and they could easily find themselves the subject of such attacks in the future or just part of the peripheral damage.

Cyber terrorism is basically the move from physical acts of terrorism to terrorism in the digital sphere. Although there have not been any large-scale acts of *cyber terrorism* to date, the threat is real and the large terrorist groups certainly have the capability to carry these out. They have built out their own technology groups and even their own tools, such as proprietary encryption programs, to further their efforts without discovery. Every country knows that their critical infrastructure is vulnerable to this kind of attack, and it is just a matter of time before this becomes the attack of choice for terrorists. For the most part, cyber terrorism is a more likely threat than information warfare against the United States at the moment because the nation states who would conduct information warfare are too highly invested in the economy of the United States to risk disrupting the global economy, whereas terrorists generally do not exercise this kind of restraint.

The emergence of *organized crime* in the digital world has also changed the game significantly. The motivation and innovation of these cyber criminals seems to be endless. Today, you can go on the Internet and rent a botnet or purchase malware complete with technical support. If you think that organized crime is still just like what you saw on the Sopranos (© HBO), then you are very much mistaken. The networks of cyber criminals are more sophisticated in many ways than many large enterprises. They have distributed management models and formal software development methodologies that would rival those of many corporations. Unfortunately, their resources seem to be endless and they don't stop to sleep or go home at the end of the day, so we have our work cut out for us. It is crucial to understand their motivation to truly model your most pressing risk exposures.

It used to be that system breaches and malware were loud and messy as they wreaked havoc on your environment, but the targets have changed for the attackers. They don't want to delete your data and take down your systems any more, they want to use your resources to further their attacks on others and quietly infiltrate your environment while stealing your sensitive data. In particular, as the economy suffers, *sophisticated insider attacks* are a concern (though there is no research data to support the assumption that the rate of insider attacks is on the rise). The IT manager who is being fired might install a backdoor on the CEO's computer on his way out or a disgruntled employee may sell sensitive data to a competitor. Whatever the specific case, these attacks are far more subtle and sophisticated

(Continued)

(*Continued*)

than ever before. Do you ever get the feeling that every day that you don't have a security incident, you might be missing something? The situation probably isn't that bad, but you need to be just a little paranoid and pessimistic to be a good risk analyst!

Even though full-out information warfare hasn't taken center stage yet, more covert attacks have been documented, although rarely can the source be conclusively linked back to the initiating national government. The Stuxnet worm in 2010 demonstrated how specific nuclear power plant systems could be targeted in Iran and leading experts believe that this sophisticated and targeted attack was likely supported by another country. Along these lines, the term *advanced persistent threat* seems to be the latest buzzword that is getting attention in the field. This is a more long-term attack that might be intended to bring down the infrastructure of a country or to steal intellectual property from another country. As the term indicates, this type of threat is differentiated by the longevity of the attack attempts and generally the resourcefulness of the attacker to attempt many attack vectors until successful. These nation states have even been known to infiltrate your workforce with their own personnel to get the insider vector. The stakes are rising and even a defense in-depth approach to protecting your organization may not be enough on its own.

When you start to look at the number of computer crimes on the books (see summary from the HTCIA [2] in Figure 5.1), you get a real appreciation for just how diverse the threat landscape can be.

As you go through your threat-modeling exercises, keep this list in mind and try to think about the vulnerabilities in your environment that may be targets of these crimes. The good news is that there are more and more information available every year that can help you to estimate the frequency of threats and successful exploits. These are just a few sources of good information:

- Verizon Business Data Breach Investigations Report [3]
- CSI Computer Crime & Security Survey [4]

Personal crimes	Property crimes	National protection	Financial crimes
Cyber threats	Cyber larceny	Cyber theft of government secrets	Online credit card fraud
Cyber identity theft	Cyber fraud	Online economic espionage	Electronic funds transfer fraud
Cyber harassment	Cyber theft of trade secrets	Cyber terrorist activity	Computer desktop forgery
Cyber violations R/orders	Cyber vandalism/destruction	Cyber threats to government officials	Electronic counterfeiting
Cyber stalking	Cyber copyright infringement	Cyber attacks to critical systems	Online auction fraud
Computer hacking	Theft of computer services	Online criminal disorder and anarchy	Corporate identity fraud
Possession/dissemination child porn, luring-enticing minors	Internet counterfeit products/labels	Internet bomb making and weapons of mass destruction	Internet scams/phishing

FIGURE 5.1

Computer crime summary.

- Trustwave Global Security Report [5]
- Symantec Internet Security Threat Report [6]
- Sophos Security Threat Report [7]
- Trend Micro Future Threat Report [8]
- Arbor Networks Network Infrastructure Security Report [9]
- US-CERT Coordination Center [10]
- Internet Storm Center [11]

Each is worth taking some time to review, not to capitalize on the fear factor, but to justify your priorities and focus in one area versus another. It is also useful to compare your organization's own incident history to these reports to identify where you may be in line or vary from the norm. You may find that the profile of your organization varies from the statistics in these reports, which can tell you several things. First, it reinforces the need to evaluate each vulnerability and threat for your organization and not just blindly accept industry standard risk ratings as gospel. Second, you may discover that you aren't actually experiencing fewer incidents in that area but that you just don't have the right controls in place yet to detect the violations that are occurring. Finally, it should influence your strategy and focus areas for risk assessments, as well as preventative controls like awareness and training. Other good sources of information are the various security advisory services and professional organizations, like the FBI's InfraGard [12] in the United States, which provides threat intelligence to their private industry members through a secure portal site.

Threat Analysis

When measuring threat, we are really trying to evaluate the likelihood (or probability) that a particular vulnerability will be exploited by a specific source population (the threat source). If there is no threat, then there can be no risk no matter how many vulnerabilities you have. Having zero threats may seem like a theoretical state; after all, experience tells you that every weakness is found and exploited eventually. But you also have to consider that we are measuring likelihood, not possibility. For example, a major retailer will be more likely to be exploited than a local business with a single credit card machine, even if the two organizations have the same vulnerability. Why is that? It isn't that the weakness couldn't be found just as easily in both companies' systems, it is because the attractiveness of the target and the motivation of the attacker need to be taken into account. Sometimes, it can be beneficial to be operating under the radar and not drawing attention to your organization; but if your organization happens to be a household name or an attractive target for hackers, then you have to assume that you will be targeted sooner rather than later.

Additionally, don't underestimate the importance of understanding the motivation of the threat source. If the rewards for attacking the major retailer are greater, then the smart attacker would spend their time there. There may be no demand for the small business' internal data, but there is certainly always a market for credit card information. In reality, no one is safe. If an attacker is just looking for resources to control, the small business' systems may fit the need just as easily as the major retailer. In fact, that information might lead the small business owner to focus on external mass attacks, whereas the security team at the large retailer might be more focused on protecting against the targeted attackers, external and internal.

There are several factors that are more closely tied to the details of the vulnerability than the organization itself, for example, the skill level needed to complete the exploit. If the attack is so complex that it requires a Ph.D. in Computer Science to complete, then the threat universe will quickly shrink to the few people in the world who can pull it off. However, if the attack scripts or tools have been published on the Internet for any novice to execute, then the likelihood will increase. For instance, as soon as the attack is included in an automated tool like Metasploit [13], you know that you have a wide audience of potential exploiters.

There are often reports about vulnerabilities that can be exploited in very specific configurations or lab settings that aren't typical for production deployments. These need to be analyzed for the practicality of the attack. Ask yourself how likely it is that the moons will align in just such a way as to allow this exploit to be successful. Maybe the attacker can capture some portion of memory using an exploit, but only one time out of a million is it any useful data. Think about how you would rate the likelihood of a successful attack, assuming that attack success includes not just accessing any garbage data but must include sensitive information.

You may also come across vulnerabilities or attack methods that have not been proven in the field yet and are still considered theoretical. These may be flagged by advisories or security scanning tools as "zero day" vulnerabilities, but if there is no evidence that an exploit exists in the wild, you are going to need to adjust your likelihood rating accordingly. Again, an effective risk-management program needs to sort through the hype and flag the actionable and imminent threats to the organization.

Threats Are Different from Risks

It is important that you can clearly define risk terms and describe the aspects of a risk without confusing them. Of the following, which do you think describe a threat source or activity?

1. Disgruntled employee
2. Password cracking
3. Internet-facing router
4. Cleartext passwords being sent over the Internet

This type of exercise can really trip you up if you aren't careful to think about the distinctions in terminology and purpose. The first two items describe a threat source and activity, respectively. The last two items are not threats; so, what are they? The "Internet-facing router" is considered an asset. If you thought it was a threat, it is likely that it was the "Internet-facing" that threw you off-track.

Regardless of its locations, it is just a resource that needs to be protected. The last item describes a vulnerability, not a threat, which we have used in previous examples. Again, there could be several threat sources associated with this vulnerability of sending the cleartext passwords over an untrusted network like the Internet.

To be a threat source, the item in question needs to describe the "who." Let's try it again—which of these could be considered a threat source?

1. Interruption of operations
2. Untrained personnel
3. Loss of data from virus infection
4. Spear-phishing attack from Russian Business Network
5. Lightning strike on the data center

Did you mark the first item as a threat? Ask yourself who or what would cause the interruption of operations. If you can't answer that question, then you haven't identified the threat source yet. Compare that to the spear-phishing example where the organized crime group, the Russian Business Network, is defined as the source. Untrained or unqualified personnel could certainly be the source of accidental destruction, corruption, or disclosure of data. Also, a lightning strike would fit into our *natural disaster* category of threats (even though "who" is loosely applied to a lightning strike), but loss of data from a virus infection is a tricky one because the "loss of data" isn't the threat, just the virus infection.

Keep in mind that if you find yourself describing the consequences, then you are probably describing the risk, not the threat. The threat is independent of the risk outcome. You can have the same threat against 10 organizations and have different consequences for each.

Threat modeling will be covered in more detail later in the book, but let's wrap up the threat analysis discussion with a quick preview. One technique for modeling threats is to analyze the actors, motives, and outcomes in a threat tree for each critical asset. Start by identifying the source of the threat. In the case of human actors, it can either be an insider or an external party. If you are looking at nonhuman threats, you would consider things like natural disasters, infrastructure failures, and so on.

Next, identify the potential motives for each actor, whether they be accidental or deliberate (malicious). The example in Figure 5.2 shows the possible outcomes of threat modeling for each actor/motive pair; however, it is likely that the outcomes will vary depending on the source and motivation.

For example, as you are modeling different threats, a malicious insider may have nothing to gain by interrupting service for the retailer's Point of Sale system so that will not be a likely outcome; however, an insider may intentionally delete sensitive data from the system resulting in a moderate-level risk exposure. These threat-modeling trees will cover the majority of cases and can simplify your threat-modeling process. Especially, when you are trying to get a handle on large areas of concern like privacy or data leakage, building a threat tree can be a very helpful exercise. If you map out all the possibilities and talk through the scenarios, you will start to see certain scenarios rise to the top and others fall to the bottom.

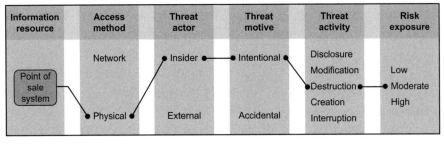

FIGURE 5.2

Threat-modeling tree example.

Remember that perception is reality in the security business. It often isn't enough to be secure. If people think you lack security, then they will treat you as if you do. Alternatively, if attackers think that you are boasting of overly strong security, you may quickly become a prime target.

SUMMARY

The ability to describe and articulate the risk exposure is even more important than implementing a risk-rating technique because without a clear risk statement, there is no way to communicate the potential consequences to management with any meaningful insight for them to make a decision. If resources are limited, and they always are, management may need to choose between mitigating two risks, and a rating on its own won't help them to choose if the risks both have the same rating. A significant activity in any risk-management program is modeling and analyzing potential threats. A structured approach to threat modeling can give you a great insight into areas of risk that need to be prioritized, but if done wrongly, this activity can become a huge drain on your time and easily can distract your team from the imminent threats.

Action Plan

After reading this chapter, you should consider taking the following actions in your own organization:

- To avoid reporting risk exposures to management that are really a description of a vulnerability or a threat, require that all identified risks follow a structured risk statement format (until the organization is comfortable articulating risks properly).
- Establish a risk registry that allows anyone in the organization to identify and escalate a risk, whether it be directly related to information security or not. Market this opportunity to the employee community internally and use this as another source of potential risk information to feed your program.

- Work with your peer groups in the organization (such as *legal, compliance, operations, vendor management, audit,* and so on) to model the top threats to the organization, and use these to focus your risk assessments. Repeat this exercise each year.
- Read through one of the industry threat reports (such as Verizon Breach report or CSI/FBI study) and note the trends that may apply to your own organization if you haven't already done it. Use this data to inform your own internal threat modeling and focus risk assessment activities. Repeat this exercise each year.
- Sign up for at least one daily summarized feed of security threat, vulnerability, and breach information. Set aside a small amount of time every morning to review the daily summary.

References

[1] SANS Institute, Building a Risk-Based Security Program in 10 Easy Steps. www.sans.org/security-training/course_sums/1467.pdf (accessed 03.10.10).

[2] HTCIA New England Chapter Website, Computer Crimes Table. www.htcia-ne.org (no longer available).

[3] Verizon Business, Data Breach Investigations Report. http://www.verizonbusiness.com/resources/reports/rp_2010-data-breach-report_en_xg.pdf, 2010 (accessed 21.07.10).

[4] Computer Security Institute, CSI Computer Crime & Security Survey. http://gocsi.com/survey (access 02.12.10).

[5] Trustwave Global Security Report. https://www.trustwave.com/downloads/Trustwave_WP_Global_Security_Report_2011.pdf (accessed 19.01.11).

[6] Symantec, Internet Security Threat Report. www.symantec.com/business/theme.jsp?themeid=threatreport (accessed 01.04.10).

[7] Sophos, Security Threat Report. www.sophos.com/sophos/docs/eng/papers/sophos-security-threat-report-jan-2010-wpna.pdf (accessed 01.04.10).

[8] Trend Micro, Future Threat Report. http://us.trendmicro.com/us/trendwatch/research-and-analysis/threat-reports/index.html (accessed 09.12.10).

[9] Arbor Networks, Network Infrastructure Security Report. www.arbornetworks.com/report (accessed 01.02.11).

[10] US-CERT Coordination Center, Mailing Lists and Feeds. www.us-cert.gov/cas/signup.html (accessed 30.01.11).

[11] SANS Internet Storm Center, RSS/XML Data Feeds. http://isc.sans.edu/xml.html (accessed 30.01.11).

[12] FBI InfraGard, National Website. www.infragard.net (accessed 30.01.11).

[13] Rapid7, The Metasploit Project. www.metasploit.com (accessed 30.01.11).

Risk Exposure Factors

6

INFORMATION IN THIS CHAPTER

- Qualitative Risk Measures
- Risk Assessment

INTRODUCTION

Whether you are using a qualitative or a quantitative approach to analyze risks, you need to base your approach on a solid model. In his book *The Failure of Risk Management: Why It's Broken and How to Fix It*, Douglas Hubbard observes that several risk analysis methods, which are pervasive across several industries, are no more accurate than astrology [1]. Possibly weather forecasting is a more fair comparison, but either way the effectiveness of several common risk analysis methodologies is questionable. The goal of this book, and this chapter in particular, is to improve on the overly general qualitative models in use throughout information security, by removing some of the room for error and subjectivity. Implementations of this model have been proven to improve risk decisions in several organizations.

Throughout this book, we have focused on three aspects of rating a risk exposure: the sensitivity of the resource, the severity of that exploited vulnerability, and the likelihood of the threat exploiting the vulnerability. We will start with some basic qualitative risk scales that demonstrate how to rate each of these variables and then expand this approach to include more comprehensive criteria for rating risk exposures. Chapter 5 set the stage for this discussion by establishing what is considered a risk statement and the basics of modeling threats and Chapter 4 focused in depth on how to rate the sensitivity of your resources. Now, we combine the risk sensitivity and threat modeling with vulnerability analysis to determine the appropriate likelihood and severity scores.

QUALITATIVE RISK MEASURES

So far, we have talked about the severity and likelihood of a risk in general terms, but this isn't sufficient to really compare the exposure levels of different risks across the organization. You need to have a structured model, whether it be made up of qualitative ratings or quantitative measurements. Let's start with a qualitative approach and see if it meets our needs. The goal is to implement a model that goes beyond just labeling a situation or issue as "risky." A well-designed qualitative model can help us to identify the most likely impact to the organization by clearly defining the sensitivity of the resource, the severity of the vulnerability, and the likelihood of the threat.

The first step is to define risk scales for both the likelihood that a vulnerability will be successfully exploited and the severity of the exploit. Each threat/vulnerability pair may have different likelihoods and severities, so don't assume that all threat/vulnerability combinations will have the same risk exposure rating. Each needs to be evaluated separately. Most often, you will see that the details of the threat will affect our rating of likelihood and the details of the vulnerability will affect our rating of severity. Although this is not true as a rule, it can be helpful to think of it this way as you first start to develop your qualitative criteria. We will point out where this association breaks down later in the chapter.

Most qualitative approaches use a relative scale to rate risk exposures based on predefined criteria for each level and rely on the knowledge and experience of the assessor to apply the scale to the risk exposure in question. This makes a qualitative approach very subjective and prone to inaccuracies. Typical qualitative models will have a relative scale based on descriptive criteria and some sort of mapping to determine the end risk exposure value. Although qualitative scales are subject to inaccuracy, you can reduce the room for error or bias by implementing detailed criteria to guide the analysts.

This chapter starts off by introducing the most simple Low-Moderate-High scale that includes only two variables, severity and likelihood; then, we will expand on that model to include a more granular scale. Finally, we will also integrate sensitivity into the model later in this chapter. Hopefully with this progression of building the model, you will better understand the significance of each choice that has been made about what to include and how to present it so that you are in a better position to choose aspects of this model, or other risk models, that work best for your organization.

Defining Severity

As we discussed in Chapter 5, the severity is a measure of the magnitude of the vulnerability or weakness, independent of any details about the threat source or the resource sensitivity. As you read through this section of the book, it is crucial that you keep in mind the distinction between severity and sensitivity. The severity rating is meant to describe the extent or scope of the exposure, not list all the consequences. For example, from an operational perspective, a vulnerability with a high severity might equate to the potential to cause the entire loss of connectivity to several company offices at the same time, whereas a moderate severity might be defined as the loss of connectivity to just one office. However, sensitivity is meant to describe the consequences for the organization, typically in terms of financial loss or penalty of some sort. If you start to look at the difference in revenue loss between disruption of connectivity to a primary data center versus a small sales office, then you are starting to qualify the sensitivity of the offices; this is not included in our severity variable. A security risk profile of each office would account for differences in the importance of the data center versus the small office, so we wouldn't include that consideration in our severity rating. Think of severity as being asset agnostic.

TIPS & TRICKS

Assessing severity is fundamentally asking the question: "What is the magnitude of exploited the weakness?" From a quantitative perspective, think of severity as a measuring the degree of damages or how pervasive the exploit is.

The criteria for severity levels depend on the aspect of confidentiality, integrity, availability, or accountability being affected. Our earlier example of losing connectivity between offices focused on risks affecting the availability of a resource. On a qualitative scale, these vulnerabilities would be rated by the degree of disruption, ranging from a complete shutdown of services to just delayed response times. When rating the availability aspects of severity, you might also look at the length of the disruption (for example, 2 hours or 2 weeks). On the other hand, confidentiality severities would depend on the amount of data exposed.

Availability Severity

Let's start building our severity scale by focusing first on availability criteria for all three levels (low, moderate, and high). When you are framing out a risk scale, you will probably find that it is easier to start with the worst case and work your way down. There are two factors that we want to consider:

1. The scope of resources affected
2. The length of time

When it comes down to it, every organization is providing some kind of service or producing a product. Even the creation or manufacturing of a product can be thought of as a series of internal services or processes. Your qualitative risk scales are a great opportunity to design a business focus right into your model. For this reason, we focus on affects on the business service being provided, such as a vulnerability that would disrupt all users of the service. If your organization isn't very focused on external services to clients, you might instead focus your severity descriptions on internal business processes. So, a vulnerability that disrupts services for all users would be your highest level of severity (high severity) and then the next logical step down from that would be a disruption that only affects some of the user community (moderate severity). Finally, the lowest level wouldn't be a complete disruption of service; it might just be a degradation or noticeable decrease in performance for any number of users (low severity).

Table 6.1 Qualitative Severity Scale for Availability—Part 1

Level	Description
Low	May result in a degradation of service and/or a noticeable decrease in service performance.
Moderate	May result in a disruption of service for a part of the user community.
High	May result in a disruption of service affecting all users of the service.

Table 6.2 Qualitative Severity Scale for Availability—Part 2

Level	Description
Low	May result in a degradation of service and/or a noticeable decrease in service performance.
Moderate	May result in a short disruption of service and/or denial of service for a part of the user community.
High	May result in a prolonged outage affecting all users of the service.

So let's review our scale so far; the criteria from low to high severity is shown in Table 6.1.

Once we have measured the degree of disruption from full denial of service for all users to degradation of service for some part of the user community, we need to also include the length of the disruption. On a scale of this size, it is best to differentiate between a prolonged and a short disruption of services. By combining this with the previous criteria, you start to see in Table 6.2 how the scale for just availability severity would look.

With a scale such as this in Table 6.2, having both clear criteria for each level and visible distinctions between the levels is essential for success. If you often find yourself guessing at the rating or unable to decide between two ratings, then you need to revise your scale to provide clearer guidance to your analysts.

Notice that the description of a low severity really didn't change much from Table 6.1 to Table 6.2 because it was designed from the start to capture a fairly generic case. If you want to be more specific for how long the performance affects will last or how many users are affected, then you will have to expand your scale. For now, let's stick with the three-level scale and add in confidentiality criteria.

Confidentiality Severity

If you think about vulnerabilities that could put the confidentiality of a resource at risk, the focus will be on unauthorized access to view sensitive data. Risk sensitivity would rate the importance of that information, so your severity criteria will describe degrees of data disclosure from one record to an entire dataset. On a three-level scale for confidentiality, the highest level would include all the data associated with the target resource, moderate level would be some limited subset of that data, and the lowest level would be a weakness that contributes to unauthorized

Table 6.3 Qualitative Severity Scale for Confidentiality

Level	Description
Low	May indirectly contribute to unauthorized viewing of data.
Moderate	May allow limited access to view only certain data.
High	May allow full access to view all data.

access but doesn't directly lead to the disclosure. A possible severity scale to rate confidentiality-related weaknesses is shown in Table 6.3.

RISK DEEP DIVE

Rating Indirect Vulnerabilities

When we developed the availability scale in Table 6.2, the lowest severity level still had a distinctive scope and was a degree lower than the moderate level, but now for confidentiality, we have introduced the concept of an indirect contribution to a weakness. This is a very important concept to understand because it can cause confusion for analysts. Suppose, for example, that the current process for on-boarding a new employee is to send their initial password for the Expense Reporting Application (ERA) to them over e-mail, but that the e-mail encryption being used is weak. You might rate that weak encryption vulnerability as Low because it doesn't allow a direct compromise of ERA. Someone would need to intercept the password, break the encryption, and have access to ERA in order to exploit the stolen password. Many of these factors actually are aspects of likelihood, but in terms of severity, consider that the weak password encryption is not a direct vulnerability for ERA, so it wouldn't be rated as High or Moderate because it doesn't directly lead to an exposure of the sensitive data stored in ERA. Several other primary controls would need to fail before the weak e-mail encryption would affect ERA.

However, if the vulnerability were a weak login page for ERA itself, which could allow anyone to bypass the login controls, this would be rated as at least a Moderate severity vulnerability. Now, consider that the direct login vulnerability could allow someone with administrator-level access to ERA. Suddenly, the potential scope of the breach has gone from the scope of one user's access to unlimited access to the system, pushing our severity rating to High.

We still have two more factors to consider in our severity scale: integrity and accountability.

Integrity Severity

Integrity concerns will primarily focus on unauthorized access to modify, delete, or create data. The difference may be significant between a vulnerability that only allows for unauthorized creation of data versus one that also allows for modification or destruction of data; however, designing a scale to account for these differences will get complicated. To keep with the three-level severity scale, we will lump modification, destruction, and creation together, but you can always break these out later if you feel it is appropriate. The degrees of unauthorized integrity

Table 6.4 Qualitative Severity Scale for Integrity

Level	Description
Low	May indirectly contribute to unauthorized modification, destruction, or creation of data.
Moderate	May allow limited access to modify, destroy, or create only certain data.
High	May allow full access to modify, destroy, or create all data.

Table 6.5 Qualitative Severity Scale for Accountability

Level	Description
Low	May indirectly contribute to unauthorized access that bypasses activity tracking.
Moderate	May allow limited control of functionality that enforces the ability to track activity on the system.
High	May allow full control of functionality that enforces the ability to track activity on the system.

access, as shown in Table 6.4, will closely follow the levels we already defined for confidentiality in Table 6.3.

Accountability Severity

Finally, accountability needs to be included before we combine all these factors into one qualitative scale. Weaknesses that affect accountability usually involve the ability to hide the identity of the attacker or the ability to bypass activity logging. A direct example of this might be a vulnerability that allows the attacker full control over the system so that they can delete or modify system logs to cover their tracks. An indirect example might be that activity logs are not sent to any other system for backup and are only kept locally, thus allowing an attacker to cover their tracks if they first get access to the local log files. Another direct example could be a vulnerability that allows a malicious insider to disable the logging function entirely, while they perform some unauthorized activity. One possible scale to capture accountability severity levels in shown in Table 6.5.

Combined Severity Scale

Now, if we combine all four factors of severity (C-I-A-A) into one scale and expand our language to account for resources that include a system, application, or communication, you will get the qualitative scale in Table 6.6.

An important point to keep in mind is that you may want to establish different severity level criteria, or at least more specific guidance for the analysts, depending on the focus of the risk assessment. If you are assessing a vulnerability from a scanning report, the scale in Table 6.6 might work very well. But if your assessment is

Table 6.6 Qualitative Severity Scale, 3-Level

Level	Description
Low	May indirectly contribute to unauthorized activity or just have no known attack vector. May result in a degradation of service and/or a noticeable decrease in service performance.
Moderate	May allow limited access to or control of the application, system, or communication, including only certain data and functionality. May result in a short disruption of service and/or denial of service for part of the user community.
High	May allow full access to or control of the application, system, or communication, including all data and functionality. May result in a prolonged outage affecting all users of the service.

focused on policy or procedural controls for an out-sourced service provider, you may want to tailor the language to focus less on attack vectors and control of systems. Chapter 10 will cover different kinds of assessments in greater detail, but for now, keep in mind that you will likely have different qualitative scale criteria depending on the focus of the assessment (for example, you might have different criteria for an assessment of a vulnerability advisory than an architectural assessment of an application), but the base model should remain consistent.

RISK DEEP DIVE

Choosing a Scale for Your Assessment

As we expand on the basic severity, and likelihood, scales later in the book, you will see how the levels of the scale stay constant, but that you may apply different criteria depending on the kind of assessment being performed. For example, a more program-level assessment of a third-party service provider may require different severity descriptions than the scale in Table 6.6, whereas an assessment of a security advisory about a vendor's products would fit this scale very well. A high-level assessment of a service provider likely won't get down to the detailed level of missing patches or poor security settings on a particular device, but it should evaluate policy, process, and procedures. Even if the service provider doesn't enforce industry standard security baselines for all its critical devices, it may not directly lead to "loss of control" for the system, but it is an indication of the provider's maturity. So, instead, you might structure the Low-Moderate-High scale for a third-party assessment in terms of missing tertiary, secondary, or primary controls, respectively. With any qualitative model, it is crucial to have descriptions that are detailed and differentiated enough that an analyst can easily and consistently rate the vulnerabilities that are identified. This may require you to specify criteria for a penetration test that doesn't apply to baseline gap analysis. As long as the levels of the model stay constant, don't be afraid to enhance the descriptions as needed.

Defining Likelihood

The likelihood is meant to be a rating of both the probability that a threat will successfully exploit a vulnerability as well as how often that might occur. We mentioned before that these two factors are often separated into two different variables, but for the sake of simplicity, we will start by combining them for now.

The criteria for likelihood levels usually depend on several factors:

- Size of the threat universe
- Motivation of threat actor
- Sophistication of attack or skill level required
- Knowledge of organization or other insider information required
- Level of controls in place to deter or impede exploit
- Attractiveness of the target

Each of these factors will be included in our final qualitative likelihood scale, but we will only review threat universe and the effects of existing controls at this point so that we don't go too deep too quickly. Other factors will be analyzed when we start to apply this scale to actual risk assessments later in the chapter.

Threat Universe Likelihood

The first factor, and the most easily measured, is the threat universe. The threat universe describes the scope of the user community that can access a vulnerability. For an application, you could rate this aspect of likelihood by the size of the user community from a small well-defined group of system administrators to anyone on the Internet. An example of a likelihood scale that includes criteria based purely on the size of threat universe is shown in Table 6.7.

This kind of scale can be very useful in the context of assessing information flows in an architectural risk analysis or looking at the exposure for a new technical vulnerability found in a commercial product. Suppose you have a known weak service or protocol running on one of your critical servers. Will it be less likely to be exploited if you reduce the threat universe from the entire Internet to just a single subnet on your internal network? Yes, of course. The possibility of a successful exploit still exists, but you have reduced the threat surface, thereby decreasing the likelihood of an attack.

One of the aspects of this likelihood scale, detailed in Table 6.7, which might not be obvious the first time you review it, is that this is also taking into account the difference between the likelihood of a weakness being exploited when the vulnerability is only available to authorized users. When performing risk assessments, we often forget to adjust our ratings for a weakness that is publicly available on

Table 6.7 Qualitative Likelihood Scale for Threat Universe

Level	Description
Low	A small, well-defined group of users/systems
Moderate	All employees or systems in the organization, or a defined community of clients, partner, or vendors
High	The entire Internet, or unrestricted

Table 6.8 Qualitative Likelihood Scale for Existing Controls

Level	Description
Low	Controls are in place to prevent the vulnerability from being exercised without physical access to the target.
Moderate	Controls are in place that may impede successful exercise of the vulnerability without significant inside knowledge.
High	Controls to prevent the vulnerability from being exercised are ineffective.

the Internet versus one that requires an authorized login to reach. There is also the factor of anonymity here. If an attacker can attempt to exploit the vulnerability remotely, and seemingly anonymously, they are much more likely to try than someone who knows there might be an audit trail of them logging in and attempting an unauthorized function. You might even include in your likelihood scales the ability to exploit a vulnerability across the Internet from anywhere versus needing physical access to the resource.

Existing Controls Likelihood

No matter how bad an exposure may seem, there is almost always some level of existing controls in place that affect the likelihood of a successful exploit. This might be a detective control that can't prevent the exploit, but will catch it happening and alert the response team. Or, you might have a more proactive control that doesn't make it impossible to exploit, but makes it more difficult to abuse. Even a weak or relatively ineffective control might provide some benefit in making it inconvenient to exploit a given vulnerability, but be careful not to overestimate the level of protection these controls provide. You could fit all of these considerations into a qualitative scale as shown in Table 6.8.

Often, proactive controls like firewalls, authentication, or even encryption might slow down an attacker or make them jump through several hoops to access a weakness, but a sophisticated attacker can still bypass these existing controls. If you think about this in terms of threat universe again, the capability or skill level of the attacker may decrease the threat universe from the amateur running scripts to only a handful of elite hackers. It may also eliminate external attackers as your most likely threat source if significant inside knowledge is needed. Then, you would want to focus your assessment on controls to prevent or deter malicious insiders.

Combined Likelihood Scale

Once you combine the factors of the scale for the threat universe and effectiveness of existing controls, you get the final qualitative likelihood scale in Table 6.9.

Two factors that you might find lacking in Table 6.9 are the motivation of the attacker and also the attractiveness of the target. In large part, these considerations

Table 6.9 Qualitative Likelihood Scale, 3-Level

Level	Description
Low	The threat source is part of a small and trusted group, or controls are in place to prevent the vulnerability from being exercised without physical access to the target.
Moderate	The threat source is part of defined community of users, and controls are in place that may impede successful exercise of the vulnerability without significant inside knowledge.
High	The weakness is accessible publicly on the Internet, and controls to prevent the vulnerability from being exercised are ineffective.

were already included earlier in the threat modeling discussions, but they are certainly important factors to keep in mind. For the sake of maintaining a simple three-level scale, these have been excluded for now, but we will come back to these again when we apply this scale to some sample risk assessments later in the chapter.

Qualitative Risk Exposure

Now that you have a methodology to rate both the severity and likelihood of a compromise (albeit a simplified scale for both), you need some way to pull it altogether to calculate the final risk exposure. The simple mapping table shown in Figure 6.1 gives you a mechanism to quickly rate the risk exposure level, by combining the three-level scales for severity on the x-axis and likelihood on the y-axis. This mapping table, also referred to as a risk matrix, doesn't account for the sensitivity of the target resource itself, which will be discussed later in this chapter.

Severity

Likelihood		High	Moderate	Low
	High	High	High	Moderate
	Moderate	High	Moderate	Low
	Low	Moderate	Low	Low

High – Corrective action must be implemented in 30 days
Moderate – Corrective action must be implemented in 90 days
Low – Corrective action must be implemented in 1 year

FIGURE 6.1

Qualitative mapping table, 3-level.

There are many benefits to using a qualitative risk matrix (like the one in Figure 6.1). First, it is nice and simple, thereby minimizing the time it will take for your peers in other business units and functions to get comfortable using it. Second, it makes directing the actions of the resource owners/custodians very easy. When new vulnerability announcements come out from Microsoft, for example, you can easily determine the risk exposure and communicate that to your Windows administration team. That team then has very clear instructions that a High exposure needs to be remediated in 30 days, and applying a patch for a Moderate exposure can take up to 90 days. Even within this structure of assigning remediation targets to each risk level, you include flexibility in your process to allow for appropriate risk acceptances to be requested and approved.

You can even use this risk-mapping table to drive the exception approval workflow. For example, it may require C-level sign-off to accept a high-level risk exposure without any further mitigation. In contrast, a lower level exposure risk may be acceptable as it is or only require a manager to accept the risk. These mapping tables can therefore be a useful mechanism for quick and consistent risk decisions based on exposure levels.

Applying Sensitivity

At this point, you may be thinking that not all resources are created equal, meaning you may want to patch your domain controllers before you patch the workstation in the mail room. That's where risk sensitivity comes back into our calculations. Using a two-variable formula or mapping for risk exposure is nice when the audience manages resources with all the same sensitivity level, but eventually you are going to need to normalize/standardize the risks across the organization. For this reason, it is recommended that the mapping table be expanded to include a third variable, risk sensitivity.

There are two ways to include the sensitivity of the resource in the qualitative assessment of risk exposure: sensitivity factors can either be included in the definition of severity or the mapping table can be expanded to include all three variables. The problem with including the concept of sensitivity in the definition of severity is that this really mixes two independent conditions. The importance of the resource is not going to be any different regardless of the threat or vulnerability, but the extent to which it is violated will certainly vary with the vulnerability. Mixing these together therefore becomes problematic at best.

As you can see in Table 6.10, applying sensitivity can really increase the complexity of the qualitative mapping table.

Ultimately, you will want to use the three-variable mapping to normalize the results across environments when presenting to senior management. Let's say that only risk exposures with a rating of high on this scale are escalated to the senior management level. Then, looking at the mapping table, you can see that most of the risks that will be presented to senior management will be

Table 6.10 Qualitative Mapping Table, 3-Level

		Risk Sensitivity		
Severity	Likelihood	Low	Moderate	High
Low	Low	Low	Low	Low
Low	Moderate	Low	Low	Low
Moderate	Low	Low	Low	Moderate
Low	High	Low	Moderate	Moderate
Moderate	Moderate	Moderate	Moderate	Moderate
High	Low	Moderate	Moderate	Moderate
Moderate	High	Moderate	Moderate	High
High	Moderate	Moderate	High	High
High	High	Moderate	High	High

associated with your highly sensitive resources, which is appropriate. At a metrics level, senior management are also going to want an overall view of the organization's risk posture, and by including sensitivity in your risk exposure rating, you can provide this perspective. There might be a high likelihood of a moderate severity event, which would have been considered a high risk in Figure 6.1, but this risk exposure will not be escalated to senior management unless it also affects a highly sensitive resource. This is exactly how risk escalations should be filtered.

RISK DEEP DIVE

When Three Levels Isn't Enough

One point to keep in mind as you are reviewing the combinations of severity and likelihood, using Table 6.10, is that you may identify several risks with a potential for a high severity, but there may be no way to reduce the severity of the risk any further. So you might need to focus on the likelihood of the risk instead or, in rare cases, on lowering the sensitivity of the target resource. Notice in the mapping table that the combination of a high severity and low likelihood produces a moderate overall risk exposure for all resource sensitivities. To understand the implications of this, think about any actions you might be asked to recommend in order to lower the exposure of that risk; the likelihood is already at its lowest level, so you have nowhere to go from there.

If you are in a situation where the vulnerability can't be eliminated (remediated) and likelihood is already at its lowest level, but the organization really wants to decrease the risk exposure, the only choices will be to either implement a control to limit the scope of the vulnerability and reduce the severity or you need reduce the sensitivity of that resource. In the case of the high severity and low likelihood, even changing the sensitivity of the resource will have no affect on the final risk score, so you are only left with the option to affect the severity. This is something to keep in mind as you start to think about mitigation plans and the value that a mitigation action will have to reduce the risk in a measurable way.

RISK ASSESSMENT

Now that we have explored the various ways of rating the components of risk exposure, we need to start applying those scales to actual risks. As described in Chapter 3 when we reviewed the Risk Management Lifecycle, step 2 of the workflow, *risk assessment*, includes several activities, including identifying threats and vulnerabilities and then rating each combination to produce a final risk exposure value. Chapter 10 will go into even greater detail than we have already about different techniques to identify weaknesses, but for now let's focus on how to rate each risk. We start with a qualitative approach and then graduate to a quantitative approach at the end of this chapter.

Qualitative Risk Analysis

Limited time and resources are a reality, so imagine risk analysis as if it were a triage system for injuries in the emergency room. You don't have the time or resources to run elaborate blood tests or MRI on every patient in the waiting room. You need to quickly assess the presenting symptoms based on some standard criteria and make some quick decisions about which ones are a priority. The same thing is true in risk management. It would be nice if we had the time to do a detailed analysis of every risk we came across. Ideally, we would map out every possible threat and outcome, do lengthy research to calculate a precise likelihood of occurrence, and perform hands-on testing of every compensating control for effectiveness. But, unfortunately, this just isn't practical. You need a quick, yet accurate and consistent, methodology to separate the critical risks from the ones you just have to live with. This is qualitative analysis. It will never be as precise as a quantitative approach, but it can be structured and flexible at the same time.

Estimating Severity

Earlier in the chapter, we used a three-level qualitative model to illustrate how to develop a severity scale, but now we are going to expand on that to include a fourth level of Critical. This is needed to provide enough granularity in our assessments to differentiate between the issues that are show-stoppers and those that don't even need to make it on our radar. The criteria for the expanded scale are described in Table 6.11.

Any risk at the Critical level is always going to be an extreme case and should therefore be relatively rare. This should be your "the sky is falling" level.

It definitely takes some time to get used to the differentiation between assessing sensitivity and severity, but the value of having these variables remain independent will become even clearer when you have to process large amounts of risk data. If you are having trouble qualifying the severity of a vulnerability, try asking some of these questions:

1. What is the scope after exploitation (full, user, and so on)?
2. How much data will be disclosed?

Table 6.11 Qualitative Severity Scale, 4-Level	
Level	**Description**
Low	May be a deviation from recommended practice or an emerging standard. May lack a security governance process or activity, but have no direct exposure.
Moderate	May indirectly contribute to unauthorized activity or just have no known attack vector. May result in a degradation of service and/or a noticeable decrease in service performance.
High	May allow limited access to or control of the application, system, or communication, including only certain data and functionality. May result in a short disruption of service and/or denial of service for part of the user community.
Critical	May allow full access to or control of the application, system, or communication, including all data and functionality. May result in a prolonged outage affecting all users of the service.

3. Will the breach allow for the modification/destruction or just viewing of data?
4. What degree of service shutdown will occur?
5. Can the attacker execute arbitrary code or are they limited to specific functions?
6. Does the vulnerability allow for information that helps exploit a system to be disclosed?
7. Does the vulnerability involve deviation from best practices?
8. Is the vulnerability an internal or external exposure?
9. Does the weakness present a direct threat or require a combination of vulnerabilities?

Remember that severity is a measurement of the scope, degree, or magnitude of the exploit's potential. It doesn't matter what the target or threat is.

QUALITATIVE SEVERITY EXAMPLE

Suppose that you work for a regional bank that offers a Web portal for clients to perform online banking and this customer portal is hosted by a third-party provider. Keep in mind the qualitative severity scale from Table 6.10 while you look at each of these examples for customer portal:

- A weakness in a Web form could allow for the Web site to be defaced.
- Due to storage limitations, audit logs for the back-end server that stores client financial transaction data are only retained for 1 day.
- The hosting company does not employ an independent third-party audit function to evaluate their information security program.
- Default administrator passwords are being used on a system that is used to manage server configurations.
- Customer accounts for portal access are set up manually by the client support staff at the bank, and human error sometimes results in data disclosures between customers.

Using the qualitative scale in Table 6.11, how would you rate the severity of the weakness in the Web form? If you are starting to think about the value of the financial data and the laws regarding data breach notification, remind yourself that severity is a qualification of the magnitude of the breach, not an evaluation of the Web server's sensitivity. Based on the brief description of the vulnerability in the Web form, this seems like a weakness that directly puts the integrity of the Web site at risk; so, Low and Moderate ratings are eliminated. Does it seem like the weakness would allow the attacker full control of the Web server? Likely not, given that defacement is the only attack that is listed. Based on this reasoning, the vulnerability would be rated High on the severity scale. Easy, right?

Now, try the next vulnerability. Will the lack of historical audit trails lead to a credit card breach directly? Clearly, this lack of data may hinder an investigation into a security breach if audit logs aren't available, but it won't directly cause a compromise. That pretty much eliminates Critical and High ratings from our consideration. Audit logs are important for a few reasons; they will help you prove or disprove an event, but they can also serve as a deterrent for unauthorized activity. Therefore, not keeping audit logs for more than a day can really hurt security operations, so this vulnerability would be considered Moderate on the severity scale.

The next vulnerability, the lack of an independent third-party audit function, is very different than the others. It doesn't present a direct opportunity to compromise the customer portal, nor will the absence of such a function hinder the operations of the security team. In fact, the organization could have an internal audit function that provides excellent oversight of the security program, but it is recommended practice to keep that function separate and objective. This would therefore be a good example of a Low-severity rating.

The use of default administrator passwords may allow for full administrator access to the management server and, likely, privileged access to the servers that it manages. In most cases, this would also include access to any sensitive data on the servers. Notice that it doesn't matter what kind of data are involved for this assessment; the severity rating is measuring the scope of the compromise (remember, it is sensitivity that measures the differences between credit card numbers and the office phone list). Given the scope of access that would result from exploiting this vulnerability, a Critical severity rating is most appropriate for this scenario.

Looking at the last example, the manual setup of accounts by the client support staff, the exposure would likely be limited to one client accidentally getting access to another client's data. Since the disclosure would be limited to a subset of data, and not the entire database, this would be rated as a High severity.

Estimating Likelihood

As with severity, we need to start by expanding on the three-level risk scale for likelihood before we can start assessing risks. In this case, we need to add two additional levels of granularity, one at the top (Very High) and other at the bottom (Negligible). One motivation for this change is to allow for a closer mapping to the typical categories of threat universe and another is to account for the near zero level at the bottom that signifies those exploits that are theoretically possible, but not at all likely.

It is easy to confuse factors that will affect the severity and likelihood of a threat/vulnerability pair. One possible qualitative likelihood scale is shown in Table 6.12. There are so many factors to consider, from the sophistication of the attacker to the attractiveness of the target. For example, if exploit code is freely available on the Internet, your likelihood rating is going to go up. You may also

Table 6.12 Qualitative Likelihood Scale, 5-Level

Level	Description
Negligible	The threat source is part of a small and trusted group, controls prevent exploitation without physical access to the target, significant inside knowledge is necessary, or purely theoretical.
Low	The threat source lacks motivation or capability, or controls are in place to prevent, or at least significantly impede, the vulnerability from being exercised.
Moderate	The threat source is motivated and capable, but controls are in place that may impede successful exercise of the vulnerability.
High	The threat source is highly motivated and sufficiently capable, and controls to prevent the vulnerability from being exercised are ineffective.
Very High	Exposure is apparent through casual use or with publicly available information, and the weakness is accessible publicly on the Internet.

want to look at historical incident data within your own organization or industry as a factor. For instance, employees are constantly losing their BlackBerries, so the likelihood of this event may be easy to qualify. These are some good starter questions to ask when you are trying to qualify likelihood:

- What is the size of the population or threat universe?
- Is there a location requirement for exposure?
- Are information and/or tools available about exploit specifics?
- Does exploit require tricking someone?
- What skill level is required for exploit?
- Can the vulnerability be exploited anonymously?
- How attractive is the target?
- Does exploit require another vulnerability to be present?
- Has it happened before?

TIPS & TRICKS

If these have been a documented occurrence of a vulnerability being successfully exploited within your organization, unless further mitigations have been put in place since the incident, then the likelihood rating should be increased by one level from the initial rating. A documented incident in your same industry should set the minimum likelihood rating at Moderate.

If you are still having trouble qualifying the likelihood of a vulnerability, here are some additional questions to consider:

1. *Is it applicable in our environment?* If vulnerabilities are being identified through some kind of active testing, then this question might not be useful, but when you are sorting through new security advisories, this should be the first question you ask before you do any other risk analysis

2. *Is there a virus or IDS signature for it?* Compensating controls can reduce the severity or likelihood of a threat/vulnerability pair, but most often, they will affect the likelihood. Say, there is a new vulnerability announced and virus code has been detected on the Internet. The likelihood of a compromise would be rated lower if your anti-virus vendor has already distributed a signature for that virus versus if they have not.

3. *Is authentication required prior to exploit?* Often, especially in application penetration testing scenarios, testers will identify high-severity vulnerabilities that require a valid user to log-in before they are exploitable. This might lower the threat universe to a known population of authorized users.

4. *Does it affect servers as well as desktops?* All of the Adobe vulnerabilities that leverage specially crafted PDF documents to infect systems are a good example of this factor. Is an Adobe Acrobat Reader vulnerability as likely to be exploited on servers as it is on laptops? How often do users download and view PDF files directly on a production server? Generally, not very often. How often does this happen on a typical laptop? Likely, everyday or multiple times per day. Laptops are also more likely to roam outside the perimeter protections of the organization than servers, further increasing the chances of a successful compromise. Even if the PDF successfully executed on the server, would other controls prevent the attack from being successful? For an exploit to be truly successful, the attacker still has to get the stolen data out of the network or get control of the system entirely?

5. *How widely deployed is the vulnerable software or system?* If a critical Solaris vulnerability is announced, but your organization is primarily a Linux shop, how will this affect your likelihood rating? Do you think it would make a difference? If we are looking at pure probability, the Solaris server is less likely to be breached in this scenario than the Linux systems, making a breach less likely in this case than if the vulnerability also affected the Linux systems.

Of course, this list of considerations is not exhaustive, and these are just a few of the factors to take into account. Hopefully, however, it will give you a good starting point for assessing likelihood, and you can then build on these questions as appropriate for your organization and the risk being assessed.

Estimating Risk Exposure

Now that we have expanded our severity scale to four levels and likelihood to five, we need a new qualitative mapping table to determine the appropriate risk exposure rating. Starting with just severity and likelihood, you can use the risk matrix in Figure 6.2.

However, you will also want to account for sensitivity for your enterprise view of risk. This is where it starts to get a little complicated. Figure 6.3 shows a risk mapping table with all the possible combinations.

Although this may seem complicated, it is still fairly easy to take any combination of sensitivity, likelihood, and severity and determine the resulting level of risk

		Severity			
		Critical	**High**	**Moderate**	**Low**
Likelihood	**Very high**	Critical	Critical	High	Moderate
	High	Critical	Critical	High	Low
	Moderate	High	High	Moderate	Low
	Low	Moderate	Moderate	Low	Low
	Negligible	Low	Low	Low	Low

FIGURE 6.2

Qualitative mapping table, 4-/5-level, no sensitivity.

Likelihood	**Severity**	**Risk sensitivity**		
		Low	**Moderate**	**High**
Negligible	Low	Low	Low	Low
Negligible	Moderate	Low	Low	Low
Low	Low	Low	Low	Low
Negligible	High	Low	Moderate	Moderate
Low	Moderate	Low	Moderate	Moderate
Moderate	Low	Low	Moderate	Moderate
Negligible	Critical	Low	Moderate	Moderate
High	Low	Low	Moderate	Moderate
Very high	Low	Low	Moderate	Moderate
Moderate	Moderate	Moderate	Moderate	Moderate
Low	High	Moderate	Moderate	Moderate
High	Moderate	Moderate	Moderate	High
Low	Critical	Moderate	Moderate	High
Moderate	High	Moderate	High	High
Very high	Moderate	Moderate	High	Critical
High	High	Moderate	High	Critical
Moderate	Critical	Moderate	High	Critical
Very high	High	High	Critical	Critical
High	Critical	High	Critical	Critical
Very high	Critical	Critical	Critical	Critical

FIGURE 6.3

Qualitative mapping table, 4-/5-level.

exposure. This final score has also been expanded to include a Critical level that indicates a serious situation that needs immediate attention. Especially, if you use any kind of automated tool to track your risk assessments, even a spreadsheet, you can easily include this logic to calculate the rating for you.

Quantitative Risk Analysis

Most commonly, you will see professionals in the security field using a qualitative approach to rating risk exposures because we just don't have enough easily accessible historical data to calculate the probabilities and magnitudes of risks like an insurance actuary or financial analyst would. Many quantitative models have been proposed over the years with very complex equations for calculating risk, but this relies heavily on having both accurate historical data about previous breaches and a lot of time to devote to the analysis. For example, a textbook quantitative model is the calculation of the Annualized Loss Expectancy (ALE):

- If it costs $2,000 to replace a lost laptop (Single Loss Expectancy)
- And history shows that one laptop is lost or stolen every 2 months (Annual Rate of Occurrence)
- Then, Annual Loss Expectancy = $12,000

So, the next logical question is, how would you gather this information for other risk scenarios? In the qualitative analysis discussion, we discussed several vulnerabilities associated with a bank's customer portal. Let's look at two of them again from a quantitative perspective:

- Due to storage limitations, audit logs for the back-end server that stores client financial transaction data are only retained for 1 day.
- The hosting company does not employ an independent third-party audit function to evaluate their information security program.

Using the ALE approach, how would you estimate the Single Loss Expectancy (SLE) for the first vulnerability? We aren't talking about the value of the data on the server, nor would the cost to replace the server itself be relevant. If the poor retention policy affecting the security team's ability to perform an investigation is the risk, then you would need to quantify that impact on the organization. Would the cost of a forensic expert at $300 per hour compensate for the lack of an audit trail? Could it prevent the organization from pursuing criminal charges against a hacker who breaks into the server because the organization has no record of the breach? Would the organization have to announce a potential data breach to all customers without knowing the scope of which accounts were even accessed or defrauded? All these are possibilities. Now, think about the effort it would take to put a dollar value on each consequence and compare that to the security risk profiling process that is used to determine the qualitative risk-sensitivity value.

The next step is to estimate the impact of this incident on the organization, but to do that, you still need to calculate the probability of occurrence. Do you think there is a study out there that has measured the number of times the lack of sufficient logging has either slowed down an investigation or halted it altogether? Especially, before the breach laws were enacted, no one was even willing to share information about their own breaches. Even with anonymous surveys, it was questionable whether respondents were being fully honest, and often these studies were skewed toward particular industries that participate more in studies more often than others.

Clearly, this is not an easy problem to solve, but let's not give up on the quantitative approach just yet. The goal is to calculate the risk exposure, which is basically a measurement of the impact and probability of a threat/vulnerability pair. We purposely use impact and probability rather than severity and likelihood to draw attention to the fact that impact and severity are not equivalent. Using more quantitative language, you could define risk exposure as "a measurement of the probability that a threat will occur and the impact the threat will have on a given business process or mission." Clearly, there are many factors to consider when measuring risk exposure and we have already discussed a few popular formulas that account for these factors in some way. As we have already demonstrated, the challenge is that it is very difficult to quantify the value of your assets when you have to consider reputational loss and other intangibles, much less predict the rate of occurrence without large volumes of targeted historical data. It isn't easy to quantify how often the lack of an independent audit function will directly lead to a compromise of sensitive data, or at least contribute to it, without some targeted research studies. Unfortunately, there is no easy way to quantify our two identified risk exposures for the regional bank.

Until there are better data to cover the many cases that you will come across, the best you can do most of the time is to establish a qualitative model and influence the ratings using actual data gathered over time within that organization through incident tracking. You can assign numbers to a qualitative scale, but that doesn't make it quantitative. Not many quantitative models have seen wide acceptance or use, but one that has great potential to be the first to break through those barriers is the FAIR framework, which will be introduced in Chapter 11 in the context of operational assessments such as technical vulnerabilities.

SUMMARY

If you are going to use a qualitative model to assess risks, then it is certainly important to have well-documented scales with clear differences between each level, but it is also critical to understand how these scales were developed so that you can properly apply them to risks. When you think about risk exposure as only including three variables, it seems simple. But in reality, this chapter illustrated just how many factors go into assessing just likelihood or severity. Especially, if you come across a technical risk where you don't understand the vulnerability or a business risk where you don't understand the impact to the organization, knowing the right questions to ask is going to be invaluable. You can use any of the qualitative models in this chapter to assess your own risks, and in Chapter 11, we will review an emerging framework that takes the quantitative loss expectancy model and makes it practical for information security programs to implement.

Action Plan

After reading this chapter, you should consider taking the following actions in your own organization:

- If you are starting with no-risk model, take the simple three-level likelihood and severity qualitative model and use that to assess a sample of your risks. When you find risks that need more granularity, expand to the final qualitative model.
- If you already have a model in use, take the sets of questions for severity and likelihood and validate that your model accounts for all those factors. If it does, and it can account for risk sensitivity, then stick with it. Otherwise, look to migrate to one of the models in this chapter.
- Review some other risk models and decide whether any of them might better fit your needs (the most promising frameworks, NIST, OCTAVE, FAIR, and FRAAP, are reviewed later in this book).

Reference

[1] D. Hubbard, The Failure of Risk Management: Why It's Broken and How to Fix It, Wiley, Hoboken, New Jersey, 2009.

Security Controls and Services

INFORMATION IN THIS CHAPTER

- Fundamental Security Services
- Recommended Controls

INTRODUCTION

By the title of this chapter, you might expect to find a short discussion of basic security services like authentication and authorization, then followed by a detailed discussion of all the must have security controls that you should be implementing. And you might be right to expect this, except that this isn't a book about auditing, so you will actually find that the opposite is true. In many respects, this chapter starts where Chapter 1 left, continuing to review the fundamental security concepts, principles, and models. After this, the majority of the chapters are devoted to understanding the important distinctions between the security services. Ultimately, if you don't understand what each service provides, you are bound to choose the wrong controls to mitigate your risks.

FUNDAMENTAL SECURITY SERVICES

As first discussed in Chapter 1, there are three pervasive principles that should influence security guidelines, standards, designs, and control decisions: Least Privilege, Defense in Depth, and Separation of Duties. In information security, we have only three categories of controls: Preventative, Detective, and Responsive. Whether you are considering a technical control to mitigate a risk or a nontechnical solution like a new procedure, training, or a policy, the control will need to focus on protecting the sensitive information in one of the following states:

- Data at Rest
- Data in Transit
- Data in Process

These information-centric categories define the different states of being that a control needs to affect. The threats and vulnerabilities will likely change based on the state of the data, but the sensitivity will not differ solely based on the movement between states, and this should be considered when selecting the appropriate controls. Together with the concept of information states, the security design principles in Chapter 1 are the foundation for information security control design and selection.

Security Control Principles

Security Control Principles describe the general requirements and objectives for any technical controls, which will be recommended as part of risk mitigation. These principles include the following:

- Failure Condition
- Modularity
- Standardization
- Compartmentalization
- Balanced Operational Constraints
- Default Configuration

Taken together, these considerations should guide the design or selection of any technical security controls.

Failure Condition

According to the principle of failure condition, controls should have the capability to be shut down gracefully and restored automatically to the conditions prior to shut down. In redundant configurations, this would include provisions to ensure stateful failover between system components or devices, meaning that any current connections or sessions would be maintained when one device fails and another device takes over as active. If there is a complete failure and another device cannot take over, then the controls should be designed to fail closed, meaning that communications or processing should not be allowed to bypass the control when it fails.

Modularity

The principle of modularity specifies that safeguards should be modular so that they may be removed or changed as the system and enterprise risk profile changes, without requiring the replacement of major components of the infrastructure.

Standardization

The principle of standardization states that selection of controls should take into account the ability of the control to be applied uniformly across the enterprise, thereby minimizing exceptions. This principle applies to both technical and process-based controls. Any new designs/implementations should leverage the control selections made by previous initiatives in order to reduce the complexity of the environment, simplify management, and maximize economic benefits.

Compartmentalization

The principle of compartmentalization can be defined as the grouping of like resources or components to provide boundary definitions, isolation from dissimilar entities, and logical constraints on relationships with other entities. The use of this principle can help to minimize the spread of a security breach, reduce transitive risk to other resources, and provide a logical decision point to implement boundary controls. Isolation of sensitive resources is always preferred when practical and cost-effective.

Balanced Operational Constraints

The principle of balanced operational constraints states that controls should not impose unreasonable constraints on business functionality or operate in a manner that causes an unreasonable response time. The desired strength of the control and any associated impact on service delivery must always be balanced. Where security controls may affect performance of a critical business function, the added value of the control needs to be compared with the potential cost to the business.

Default Configuration

According to the principle of default configuration, controls should default to the most secure condition. Modifications to the strength of a control should require a formal acceptance of the associated risk. Therefore, a less secure configuration is an unacceptable default for any control. This can be viewed as an extension of both the concept of Least Privilege, discussed previously, and the Positive Security Model, which will be defined in the next section, Assurance Models.

When taken together, these security control principles form the basis for the security requirements, which should be defined in any level of architecture and design.

Assurance Models

When defining a control framework, it is important to understand the basic objectives of security controls (technical and process), and to use a common terminology to describe these goals.

The C-I-A-A Model

The C-I-A-A model has already been covered in Chapter 1 and referenced often throughout the book, but for ease of reference, we will quickly summarize the important points here. The four foundational pillars of information security are Confidentiality, Integrity, Availability, and Accountability. Information security not only encompasses the traditional principles of data protection, confidentiality, and integrity but also expands this concept to include availability and accountability concerns. In terms of determining business impact, these variables must be considered independently of one another, meaning that any data or resource may require a high level of integrity control and a low level of confidentiality control at the same time, for example.

Positive Security Model

A related model to the principle of Least Privilege is the "Positive Security Model." In contrast to a negative (or blacklist) security model, which defines what is disallowed, while implicitly allowing everything else, the positive model denies all activity by default, requiring specific acceptance defined for permitted activity. The positive security model can be applied to a number of different application security areas.

For example, when performing input validation, the positive model dictates that you should specify only the characteristics of input that will be allowed, as opposed to trying to filter out every possible bad input variation. In the access control area, employing the positive model would mean denying access to everything by default and only allowing access to specific authorized resources or functions.

Access Control Models

There are many approaches to access control and each is designed to support particular functions and environments. The following four models are used in most environments in some capacity.

Discretionary Access Control

A Discretionary Access Control is a way for the data owner to restrict access to resources based on the identity and need-to-know of users and/or groups. Controls are discretionary in the sense that an owner, or user with a certain access permission, may be capable of passing that permission (directly or indirectly) to any other user. This access control model is most often used in peer-to-peer file and print-sharing environments.

Role-Based Access Control

A Role-Based Access Control (RBAC) is designed around the user's actual activities. In other words, RBAC uses roles, or job responsibilities, to define who has access to a resource. A common example of this is restricting access to read-only if the user isn't responsible for updating data. Or read access may be restricted to a subset of data that is needed to perform a specific function, but not the entire dataset. This type of access control is typically used in application systems where each role is granted access to specific privileges and data in order to perform a particular job function.

Rule-Based Access Control

This type of control model defines specific conditions for access to a requested resource. Typically, this model is implemented in filtering devices, such as firewalls or routers, through the use of policies or Access Control Lists (ACL). This model is also used by many application systems to determine whether access should be granted or denied by matching a resource's sensitivity label and a subject's sensitivity label. Unlike the previous two models, access is not granted based on the rights explicitly assigned to the user or based on a role associated with that user. In the simplest case of a firewall, communications filtering decisions are made based on rules that specify which ports and protocols are allowed from one network source to another network resource.

Content-Based Access Control

Content-Based Access Control expands on the Rule-Based Model by not only examining network layer and transport layer information during filtering decisions but also examining the application layer protocol information (such as FTP connection information) to learn about the content of the network session. In many cases, these controls will use intuitive logic rather than static rules to evaluate application communications. Looking more deeply into the communications stream can help prevent common attacks using disguising techniques or abusing ambiguity in standard protocols, but this may also add more overhead and latency to inspection functions.

In order to provide true defense in depth, there must be a diversity of controls, which sometimes require using multiple access control models in combination. For example, a firewall that only implements rule-based controls can often be circumvented by an unauthorized service over a permitted network port and protocol. By adding content-based controls to this network flow, undesirable application protocols or activity can be blocked by inspecting the actual data content of the transmission. Similarly, a combination of models can prevent data leakage, in many cases by using a role-based control to determine access to a document repository while using content-based controls to prevent copying of data that match certain sensitivity criteria.

Security Services

To the greatest extent possible, security services (such as authentication and authorization) should be standardized and centralized. They should be presented as common services and should support standard communications protocols that can be used across several application and system types. Wherever possible, new authentication and authorization mechanisms should be avoided, giving preference instead to standardized methods and existing security services. Optimal efficiency, performance, security, and economic benefits are achieved when these services are centralized and standardized for interoperability.

As shown in Figure 7.1, the fundamental security services include communications inspection (for example, malware scanning or anomaly detection), communications validation (for example, protocol standards validation), communications filtering (for example, Access Control Lists), policy enforcement (for example, host-based health checks), authentication, authorization, auditing & logging, cryptography (including PKI, encryption, digital signing, and so on), resilience (for example, high availability), security event monitoring, and vulnerability management.

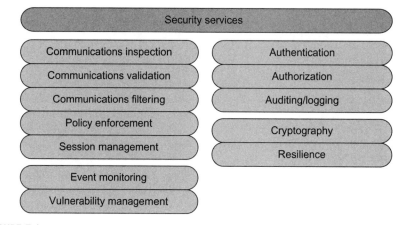

FIGURE 7.1

Security services.

Like the OSI model for networking, this list is meant to be conceptual; so, many services you are familiar with like access control or nonrepudiation aren't listed because they each include combinations of the fundamental security services. For example, the function of access control can include the following security services: authentication, authorization, auditing/logging, cryptography, inspection, validation, filtering, and policy enforcement services. On the other hand, nonrepudiation is comprised of authentication, auditing/logging, and cryptography services. Most security controls will include many different combinations of these services, depending on the intent and function of the control.

Communications Inspection

There are many different layers of depth at which communications traffic can be inspected. From a network perspective, the OSI model provides several layers, from the physical up to the application level, and inspection can be performed at many levels. Typical network security controls interact either at a media access, network, or transport layer and do not inspect the application layer protocols or data portions of the packets. Inspection at these higher levels will provide a more sophisticated view of the actual contents of communications, but it will also result in higher levels of processing and delays. To satisfy the defense-in-depth principle, inspection at all levels should be utilized.

Encrypted channels may require decryption and re-encryption for proper inspection. Depending on the level of inspection and the corresponding level of encryption being used, this may be necessary to truly determine the nature of the communications that have been encapsulated. A common technique for circumventing security controls is to establish a covert channel for communications. This could take the form of encapsulated or encrypted traffic using a permitted service or hiding data within another data type, which requires special tools to detect. An example of the latter is stegonography, which hides data within image, video, or audio files. Similar to the performance concerns of inspecting communications at the application layer rather than the network level, additional processing and delays will typically be associated with decrypting traffic for inspection, and the impact of this additional burden will, therefore, also need to be considered. A threat is also introduced to the communications path whenever data is processed in an unencrypted format on intermediary devices. Local storage, caching, or even the live processing of data in cleartext form can put sensitive data at risk if the security control itself is compromised. Even beyond unauthorized access to the control, this approach potentially increases the threat universe to include system administrators, security staff, and so on. All these considerations need to be weighed against the benefits of performing in-depth inspection.

Another specific goal of inspection services is to identify any malware that may be included in a transmission. This is another opportunity to implement a defense-in-depth strategy. Rather than just relying on malware detection/prevention at the endpoint or recipient, security controls can also be implemented to inspect communications in transit for signs of malware. This includes more than just scanning e-mail attachments—any file transfer or activation of remote code could be checked for infections or malicious functionality.

The criteria for inspection will vary with the particular needs of the information flow and scenario. In some cases, the traffic will be inspected for certain data types or patterns that are indicative of an exploit attempt; this scenario may be thought of as a ruleset for permitted traffic. The primary services that will require inspection functionality are validation, filtering, and policy enforcement. Inspection of communications does not always imply that any filtering is being performed. In fact, often, passive controls may inspect traffic, detect an event, and generate an alert without blocking the communications automatically. Moreover, the use of the term "communications" is not restricted to network communications. Inspection could also be applied to communications within a system, such as between memory spaces of a mainframe.

Communications Validation

In addition to filtering traffic based on a set of rules or some other predefined criteria, the protocols themselves need to be validated to ensure they meet standard specifications. Weaknesses or vague protocol definitions are often abused for malicious purposes. Any communications outside the standard parameters should be rejected unless a known exception has been defined by the organization to meet a particular business need. Even within the standard specifications, weaknesses have been found that can make the protocol vulnerable to unintended uses. Common attributes to validate include the following:

- Size of data units (such as packet, header, or field sizes)
- Unexpected parameter values

- Session or state identifiers out of sequence
- Consistency or integrity checks
- Overall data unit and negotiation format (such as header organization, encoding, flags, parameters, and so on)

Any known cases of protocol exploits should be checked at all layers, from physical to application.

Communications Filtering

This function provides the mechanism to distinguish authorized and expected information flows from unauthorized communications. Often, a rule-based access control model is appropriate to achieve this goal. Attributes of the flow itself will be examined to determine if it meets a predetermined set of criteria. Any unauthorized flows will be denied/rejected in one of several ways depending on the implementation and the protocol layer it is filtering against.

Filtering functions may not necessarily always deny unauthorized traffic. In some cases, filtering logic may look for sensitive data that is not authorized to traverse the control point so that rather than blocking the entire flow, that particular data item can be removed or masked to satisfy any confidentiality requirements. This is just one approach to combat sensitive data leakage.

Even attributes of the flow, like the rate of transmission of certain packets, may become a trigger for a filtering decision to combat Denial-of-Service (DoS) attacks. Filtering rules may not always be just an absolute definition of what communication is allowed between two end-points, but rather it also includes thresholds for acceptable activity levels.

Policy Enforcement

In this context, policy can apply to several areas of information security. It may refer to verifying that standards set for endpoint devices have been met, limiting access to a certain time schedule, or determining the health of the endpoint. The two primary functions of policy enforcement are Assessment and Enforcement.

Common examples of policy assessment checks include the following:

- Current anti-malware software is installed, active, and current
- Current patch levels are applied
- Device is owned/controlled by the organization
- Device meets a common configuration standard
- Device is free from current infections
- A threshold or preset number of uses has not been exceeded
- Access is occurring during certain preset date and time range or schedule

This is not meant to be an exhaustive list; rather, it is provided to illustrate the variety of controls that may be needed. In some cases, a filtering function is implied as a result of the policy assessment portion of this service. However, in other cases, a policy assessment may result in following enforcement actions:

* Blocking or rejection (this could be temporary or permanent)
* Limitation of privileges
* Segregation or quarantine to limit risk exposure
* Automated remediation to bring the entity into compliance
* Reporting or tracking of the policy violation if it is determined not to pose an unacceptable risk to the organization

Enforcement can take many forms, depending on the risk sensitivity and needs of the resources involved.

Session Management

Sessions allow applications to maintain state. After the user logs in, the server and client will operate together to maintain an authenticated state until the user logs out. Usually, a value is used to identify each unique session, and this identifier is either passed as a parameter or even saved in a cookie by the client. However, when the session identifier is stored, it is crucial to protect this value with strong cryptographic mechanisms. Unauthorized interception of the session identifier in plaintext will compromise the session entirely. Proper implementation of the session identifiers should provide integrity to both the server and the client. During a session, it is important to verify that both the client and the server are still authentic, meaning that the entities are the same as when they first authenticated. This will help prevent session hijacking attacks. Some highly risk-sensitive functions may even require reauthentication before completing a request to verify that the session is still secure.

Other common threats to the session identifier include caching or bookmarking of the identifier, inclusion of the identifier in error states, using predictable identifier values, or including sensitive credential information with the identifier on the client. Applications should always consider how session identifiers are passed and presented to the user. When Web applications include these values in URLs or part of HTTP requests, they can be vulnerable to interception.

The following principles of Session Management should be enforced universally, although the details of implementation may vary:

* **Concurrent Session Control** The information system limits the number of concurrent sessions for any user.
* **Session Lock** The information system prevents further access to the system by initiating a session lock after a period of inactivity, and the session lock remains in effect until the user re-establishes access using an appropriate authentication method or an administrator removes the lock state. Permanent locks are generally not recommended because they can be used to perform a denial-of-service attack against systems.
* **Session Termination** The information system automatically terminates a local or remote session after a period of inactivity or after a threshold for

the maximum session duration is exceeded. The server should never rely on the client to properly destroy the session identifier, but rather the server should invalidate the session immediately upon "logout" or termination of the session.

- **Session ID Cycling** The information system will cycle the session identifier periodically throughout the session to limit the effects of a successful hijacking attack and provide a means to detect hijacking attempts.

Standards for concurrent session thresholds, idle timeouts, maximum session durations, and lockout periods should be covered in your organization's Information Security Policy or an associated standard set. This standard applies both to remote sessions over a network and direct access to a system locally.

Another important aspect of session management is the handling of a session that crosses application or system borders without requiring the user to re-present their credentials. A Single Sign-On (SSO) infrastructure provides transparent access to all services resources for a user by extending the user's session across applications. After a single authentication, the established session and trust are passed along to other services, which then perform authorization decisions based on the session passed to them by a trusted SSO service. The user's identity and authentication information is stored by a centralized service, which is trusted by all other services in the environment.

A single sign-on approach has several advantages over having many disparate logins for each service:

- Improved productivity since a user only needs one SSO authentication credential to access every service.
- Easier and more consistent administration of both users' and applications' security profiles.
- Simpler and more secure integration of security features during application programming since only standard library calls to the SSO-API are needed.
- Integration of authentication and credential administration for disparate resources.
- Improved credential transmission security is achieved by implementing a standard for how authentication credentials and sensitive data will be transmitted and managed.
- Users are less prone to write down their multiple passwords when they have fewer credentials to remember.
- Lower cost of implementing and maintaining authentication services across the enterprise. These services are consolidated and can scale more easily.
- Better visibility into assignments of privileges and tracking of activity in a central location.

Several methods for implementing a single sign-on infrastructure exist, including a central authentication and authorization system that is trusted by all resources or a credential synchronization approach. It should be noted, however, that the latter is often limited in terms of the strength and flexibility of the authentication method used.

Authentication

This service provides validation of an individual or system's identity for the purposes of protecting data against unauthorized access and establishing accountability. In most cases, a requester will use a digital identifier that the authentication service can verify to associate the entity with the store of information about the requestor's identity. Strengths of authentication vary based on the number of different factors checked, and the complexity, uniqueness, and difficulty of duplication for the credentials. The three accepted factors of authentication are as follows:

- Something you know (password, PIN, passphrase, personal information)
- Something you have (smartcard, token device, and so on)
- Something you are (physical attribute)

It is not recommended to use Personal Identifiable Information (PII) or other sensitive data about a user as the user's unique identifier or username. Old practices of using Social Security Numbers or other such information as a username or unique identifier can impose additional protection and privacy constraints on handling of such information and can facilitate identity theft attacks. Unique identifiers, such as an employee number, would be appropriate.

The standards for strong authentication and acceptable mechanisms for establishing multifactor authentication levels should be defined in your organization's Information Security Policy or an associated standard set.

In some instances, authentication may not be required for a resource. The term "identification" defines the process of asserting one's identity without any validation being performed. Simple examples of this would be entering an e-mail address to access a resource or restricting access to a resource based only on IP address. These easily spoofed or impersonated attributes are not sufficient to validate identity and, therefore, are not considered authentication factors. They can, however, be another layer of protection in addition to authentication or may be used in scenarios with looser security requirements. All resources should at least establish some form of identity for its users for accountability purposes.

Components of an authentication infrastructure may include the following:

- Identification & Authentication Policy and Procedures
- User Identification & Authentication
- Device Identification & Authentication
- Identifier Management
- Authenticator Management
- Authenticator Feedback
- Cryptographic Module Authentication

Although this is not an exhaustive list, it does cover the primary components needed to implement an authentication infrastructure.

Authorization

Authorization is really the primary component of the composite service of Access Control, addressed later in this section. Once the requestor has been identified or authenticated, the authorization function defines types of access allowed and to what resources that access should be applied. Various access control models are typically employed to provide authorization services. This function provides the means to determine the level and the scope of privilege an authenticated user should be granted. The actual mapping of rights to identity will depend on the access control model being used. Authorization services not only govern on which resources or functions an entity has rights to but also govern on which data or objects the allowed functions can be performed. As a security service, authorization mediates the scope of privileges an entity can exercise. Authorization services are not limited to human users either; in fact, automated processes and objects within a system itself should be required to pass authorization controls before being permitted to perform an action.

Auditing/Logging

This service relates to the capturing of significant events on a system, in an application, or on a network. These events may be records of administrative activity that is captured for auditing purposes or an unexpected condition that may indicate malicious activity. Differentiating between nonsecurity-related events such as errors or operational information is the most challenging aspect of this service. In some cases, it is not possible to determine which events relate to a security incident until a wider picture is examined. Seemingly, innocuous entries like an administrator logging into the system or a user input error may be part of an attack when looked at in a broader context.

Standards for logging on systems should include the following:

- A limited local log storage exists in case connectivity to central logging is disrupted.
- All log entries are sent to a central log repository.
- Logging is enabled up to informational levels, or equivalent.
- All administrative activity is logged.
- Logging is enabled on all devices, systems, appliances, and so on.
- No sensitive data (such as passwords, personal identifiable information, account numbers, and so on) is captured in log entries. System times are synchronized regularly with a trusted source.
- All entries are time-stamped using the system's internal clock.
- Event sources are identified in all log entries.

It is critical to implement off-system logging capabilities to prevent privileged users or malicious attackers from modifying the log entries on a system to hide traces of accidental or unauthorized activity. Both capturing too much data and not enough information can create problems when trying to investigate a potential incident or even when determining if an incident is occurring. When configuring particular systems' logging capabilities, reference the organization's Information Security Policy or an associated standard set for detailed requirements. At a minimum, logging functionality must be capable of providing sufficient information to establish which events occurred, the sources of the events, and the outcomes of the events.

Log records will typically be used to audit the activity on a system in order to identify unauthorized or mistaken activity, as evidence in an investigation, to either prove or disprove a theory, or for troubleshooting purposes, to find the source of an error. The function of nonrepudiation often relies on proper logging being in place to prove an entity performed a certain action at a given time. For these reasons, audit records should be archived to write-once media when possible in order to minimize the chance of tampering. Similarly, modification and deletion privileges to central logging systems should be strictly limited. Logging and auditing are really the primary means to deliver accountability services.

Regular logging and auditing of user and administrator activities can support later troubleshooting, incident response, and forensic efforts, and it is also essential for establishing accountability. In many cases, security incidents and legal issues may not present themselves immediately, so it is important to keep data records long enough to facilitate investigations several months after the fact and to include provisions to preserve records during the course of an investigation. For example, it has become a recommended standard to either take a forensic image of an employee's system upon termination or quarantine the system drive in case of future investigation. This could facilitate a wrongful termination suit or allegations of data theft by that employee after they have left the company and their system (minus the storage drive) has been repurposed to another user. For specific guidance regarding data retention policies and timelines, reference your organization's Data Retention Policy or an associated standard set.

Of course, logging as a control is only effective if auditable events are defined and monitored. Most critical systems and applications will generate a large volume of log entries that will need to be filtered, correlated, and monitored for security events. See section "Event Monitoring" of this chapter for further explanation of this process.

Cryptography

Typically, encryption is the most readily associated implementation of cryptography, but really, this discipline encompasses mechanisms to verify integrity, provide nonrepudiation, and validate identity strongly. Seen in a broad sense, cryptography provides many essential tools for providing security controls that preserve the integrity, accountability, and confidentiality of data. The two most basic functions in cryptography are encryption and hashing. All the other complex tools and mechanisms in modern security controls leverage these functions either individually or in combination. For instance, a standard digital certificate object in a Public Key Infrastructure (PKI) is really just a combination of public and private keys. The private key is used to decrypt incoming communications and digitally sign outgoing communications, whereas the public key is used by other parties to encrypt communications to you. There are, of course, additional attributes of certificates beyond just these two functions, but the basic functionalities are encryption and hashing. Hashing is basically a one-way encryption function, meaning that it cannot be decrypted. This is typically used to protect sensitive data that doesn't need to be viewed in its raw form, like a password or Social Security Number in a database.

The basic process of encryption begins with a plaintext (or cleartext) value, which is run through an algorithm that renders it unrecognizable from its original form. The result of the encryption function is the cipher text. Depending on the methods used for encryption, the length of the cipher text may vary from the original or it may use a different representation of the values. In a simple example, characters might be converted to numeric digits. The function of decryption would then take the cipher text as input and result in the recovered plaintext value. For both the encryption and decryption functions to work properly, a key value must also be used to differentiate between instances of the encryption algorithm. Access to the key(s) is limited to the parties involved in the communications, and along with the identity of the algorithm being used, the key serves as the unique value needed to unlock the cipher text. Many commonly used methods for achieving encryption systems in enterprise environments rely on symmetric and asymmetric models.

The symmetric model predated the asymmetric model, and in some ways, it is simpler and faster because the same key is used for both encryption and decryption. However, distribution of the secret key can be complicated because each end of the communication must be given the key without interception. There are easy solutions between two parties; but as information is shared with three (or 50!) people, the challenge becomes evident. In fact, key distribution and management are the primary challenges for any encryption system. This model is best used when there are large volumes of data or high performance is needed.

The asymmetric model requires two distinct keys: the public and private keys. The public key is freely distributed, whereas the private key must be highly protected and is the essence of identity assertion. For the most part, the mutual creation of keys is easier with asymmetric encryption; however, the distribution systems themselves, like a PKI environment, can be just as complicated. This model is commonly used in e-mail and SSL technology.

Resilience

Threats to the availability of critical resources can be just as costly and disruptive as attacks on confidentiality or integrity. Resource resiliency can be implemented at several levels, from operating systems to applications and from the network infrastructure to the physical infrastructure that supports it. At a physical and network level, provisions should include redundancy and high-availability configurations.

Physical

Power sources and other physical components of the systems should provide some level of built-in redundancy in the device; in some cases, spare parts will be stockpiled to provide quick replacement of failed components. For systems that can suffer short periods of downtime, it may be sufficient to keep spare hardware available and establish a quick imaging and rebuilding process. At a macro level, site redundancy, disaster recovery plans, and business continuity plans should all be in line with the value of the resource to the organization. Many factors go into this planning that is beyond the scope of this architecture.

Logical

Many of the same concerns are applicable at the network, operating system, and application levels. These include the following:

- Multiple data paths
- Bandwidth throttling and traffic rate limiting
- Traffic and process prioritization
- Session, connection, and state table bounding & rotation
- Memory & buffer allocation and bounding
- Proper implementation of protocol specifications
- Isolation of processes and memory
- Data validation and filtering

Following the above practices will defeat most denial-of-service attacks at a logical level. Developers of technology need to account for even the unexpected events and handle them without overrunning available resources. In some ways, it is impossible to design a system that is impervious to Distributed Denial-of-Service (DDoS) attacks. No matter how much processing power, memory, and bandwidth you implement, there is always a way to generate enough traffic to overwhelm the resources. The key is to choose measures appropriate to the value of the service the resource provides and implement multiple layers of choke points and redundant paths to ensure a level of resiliency.

Event Monitoring

Once events have been captured in a central repository, the next step is to analyze and correlate that information across sources to identify signs of notable activity. In the case of security event monitoring, notable entries will point to abnormal or unauthorized activity that may indicate a security violation. Event monitoring may also take the form of live monitoring of systems, as opposed to observing trends in the log events generated by the system itself. This will often involve polling the device for health information, periodically checking an active service to verify that the correct response is received, or monitoring live traffic to and from that system.

Some of the important security requirements for event monitoring include the following:

- Log entries should be normalized into a common format
- Event monitoring services should account for differences in time zones

- Original log entries should be preserved in native format for forensic purposes
- Logs should be correlated across source systems and locations
- Should include live monitoring and alerting on significant events
- Severity should be rated on a common categorization scale
- Log records should be stored offsite and regularly backed up; maintenance of log records should comply with the Data Retention Policy/Standard (at least 3 months)

Finally, operational groups may manage the monitoring of devices on a daily basis, but this information needs to be readily available to incident response staff as well.

Vulnerability Management

This service is intended to perform live monitoring of the environment for emerging vulnerabilities and also to execute regular in-depth assessments to identify new weaknesses. This will include checking for the following:

- Patch levels
- Unauthorized or vulnerable services
- Unauthorized or vulnerable software
- Unauthorized or vulnerable configurations
- Insufficient or weak security controls
- Weak authentication credentials
- Vulnerable protocols

On the basis of these findings, records of identified vulnerabilities should be stored in a central repository and action items should be assigned based on priority of the finding to remediate the vulnerability. The results of the discovery, action taken, and remediation verification should all be tracked and stored for historical trending. Each finding should be mapped to the affected system in the vulnerability management system. Any reports generated from this system that include vulnerability information should be considered restricted information and handled according to your organization's Data Classification and Handling Policy.

Pre-requisites for an effective vulnerability management capability include established:

- Risk Definitions and Scales
- Risk Assessment Processes
- Security Categorization Standards
- Asset Inventories

Once these have been established, trusted services for threat and vulnerability information need to be engaged to provide regular updates that are prioritized based on an industry vulnerability impact rating such as CVSS (an industry-standard vulnerability-rating methodology). Scanning and assessment functions can then be used to identify systems that are vulnerable and remediate them where possible. For those vulnerabilities that cannot be remediated, further risk analysis needs to be performed to determine the actual threat to the organization given the compensating controls that may be in place. Factors such as the likelihood of exploit execution, the sophistication needed to perform the exploit, the actual sensitivity of the systems affected, and the practicality versus theoretical nature of the vulnerability should all be considered when prioritizing remediation steps or accepting a known risk.

Composite Services

The following security services leverage functions of the previously mentioned core services, from Figure 7.1, will provide necessary security capabilities.

Access Control

The primary purpose of access control is to limit access to information system resources only to authorized users, programs, processes, or other systems. Access control can include the following security services: authentication, authorization, auditing/logging, cryptography, inspection, validation, filtering, and policy enforcement services. Complex access control can govern, for example, whether a specific user has updated access to a particular file on weekdays between 9:00 A.M. and 5:00 P.M. while executing a specific program from a workstation at a specific network address.

Access control usually relies on some form of identification (or preferably authentication) of the entity requesting access, some mapping of privileges associated with that entity, such as the entity's role or location, or some attribute of the resource being accessed, such as classification level or current state. Several models of access control that are widely used for information systems were discussed previously in this chapter. Any form of communications filtering policy or the privileges associated with the file system could be considered a form of access control.

The principles of Least Privilege and Separation of Duties are especially relevant when determining the access levels that are appropriate for a resource. All access should always default to the minimum necessary to perform legitimate business functions.

Session management is another security service that complements access control directly. Persistence of sessions, reauthentication, session lockouts, and session termination controls are all related to maintaining access control. Attackers have often abused or exploited weak session controls to bypass access controls.

A common mistake that information security professionals make is to treat access control like an objective or goal, when controlling access is really only a means to achieve one of the primary business goals of assuring confidentiality, integrity, availability, and accountability. Placing access control on the same level as the C-I-A-A principles tends to encourage the security for security's sake approach, which does not take into account the needs or requirements of the organization.

Nonrepudiation

Nonrepudiation provides an assurance that the sender of data is provided with proof of delivery and the recipient is provided with proof of the sender's identity, so neither can later deny having processed the data. Further, this concept can apply to any activity, not just the sending and receiving of data; in a more general sense, it is a mechanism to prove that an activity was performed and by whom. Nonrepudiation is typically comprised of authentication, auditing/logging, and cryptography services. A common application of this service would be digital signing of e-mail messages to prove that the message received was actually sent by the purported sender.

Since access control and nonrepudiation share so many common components, they are frequently implemented together in controls or else closely interrelated. For example, once an access control function has been performed, it may provide sufficient data to facilitate nonrepudiation or at least partial nonrepudiation data.

RECOMMENDED CONTROLS

Now that we have reviewed all the basic security services, you should have an appreciation for how controls are designed to address very specific needs, as well as the fact that some controls can serve several purposes. As you are reviewing industry-accepted control standards, like ISO 17799 Standard, COBIT, NIST SP800-53, or even the SANS Top 20 Critical Controls list, make sure that you note the assurance that each control provides. For example, if your resource is most sensitive to confidentiality threats, then you will want to focus on controls that address this need rather than those meant to address integrity or availability threats. It is really unfortunate when we see so-called security professionals who want to solve every risk with the same two controls—encryption isn't the answer to all your problems any more than anti-virus detection has proved to be.

Fundamental Security Control Requirements

Thus far, this chapter has introduced several foundational security principles that translate into fundamental requirements that need to be implemented in all security controls. As a high-level review, these requirements are as follows:

- The information system or control should prevent the unauthorized accessing of information or any unauthorized activity when there is an operational failure of the control mechanism.
- Controls should be modular so that they may be removed or changed as the system and enterprise risk profile changes without requiring the replacement of major components of the infrastructure.
- Any new designs/implementations should leverage the control selections made by previous initiatives in order to reduce the complexity of the environment,

simplify management, and maximize economic benefits. In many cases, specification documents will be made available listing preferred or acceptable products and solutions for use.

- The information system or control should enforce the grouping of like resources or components to provide boundary definitions, isolation from dissimilar entities, and logical constraints on relationships with other entities. Grouping resources into security zones or logical network segments are examples of applying this requirement in practice.
- The information system or control should not impose unreasonable constraints on business functionality or operate in a manner that causes an unreasonable response time. Strength of control and impact on service delivery must always be balanced based on an impact assessment and risk analysis decisions.
- The information system or control should always default to the most secure configuration. Any configuration setting should default to the most restrictive value.
- The information system or control should enforce separation of duties through assigned access authorizations.
- The information system or control should enforce the most restrictive set of rights/privileges or accesses needed by users (or processes acting on behalf of users) for the performance of specified tasks.

We will go into even greater detail about these requirements in Chapter 13 when we discuss Security Architectural Risk Analysis methodologies. Any good architecture will leverage reusable patterns of design. Although now a little dated, there is a good repository for basic security patterns and guidelines in the Security Patterns Repository [1]. What is nice about this document is it will help you understand the design choices being made as opposed to a typical configuration baseline from a vendor or organization like the Center of Internet Security (CIS).

You may notice that this chapter is ending without really providing a list of must-have controls; this is intentional. Just remember that risk management isn't the practice of creating a list of controls and then trying to find opportunities to implement them. You need to define the problem before prescribing the solution. Control lists from ISO, COBIT, NIST, and SANS are fantastic references, but only as long as you don't turn your risk management program into a checklist exercise. Don't look for risk exposures to justify a control, find the right control to solve the business problem. The better you understand the real exposure, the more effective you will be at recommending controls that don't impose an unnecessary burden on the organization.

SUMMARY

This may have seemed like a long discussion about general security services and controls without a lot of guidance about which specific controls should be implemented as a priority. This focus was intentional to ensure that you are prepared to find solutions that might be outside your usual bag of tricks. With this knowledge, you should now be able to properly map the protection requirements of a certain risk exposure to the security control that would best mitigate that risk. It is important to really understand the significance of these controls and how best to apply them even if you don't understand every technical aspect. The basic security control requirements at the end of this chapter should serve as a good reference, when you are assessing the general posture of your organization. Risk management needs to be more than just a control selection exercise, but there is no denying that controls play an important role in managing acceptable levels of risk.

Action Plan

After reading this chapter, you should consider taking the following actions in your own organization:

- Take the bulleted list of fundamental security control requirements from the last section of this chapter and make yourself a checklist to use whenever you are evaluating a new security control.
- If you haven't already, read the SANS Top 20 Critical Controls list and review your own organization against these recommendations.
- Bookmark the security patterns Web site from the last section of this chapter and reference this whenever you need to design a new security solution or can't remember why an existing control is important.

Reference

[1] D.M. Kienzle, M.C. Elder, D. Tyree, J. Edwards-Hewitt, Security Patterns Repository. www.scrypt.net/~celer/securitypatterns/repository.pdf (accessed 19.06.09).

Risk Evaluation and Mitigation Strategies

- Risk Evaluation
- Risk Mitigation Planning
- Policy Exceptions and Risk Acceptance

INTRODUCTION

If you like banging your head against the wall and having to fight for every security improvement in your environment, then your best bet is to force your organization to fix every risk that you uncover. If you would rather have at least a day or two of peace per year, then start reciting the mantra "prioritize, reduce, plan, and accept." Even now, there remains a culture of close every gap and eliminate every risk within the information security industry. Hopefully, by the time you are finished reading this book, you will be converted to the religion of risk management instead. In this new world, exceptions and mitigations plans are your friends, and the only sure thing is that everything won't get fixed today.

RISK EVALUATION

So, if we can all agree that flawless security is an illusion and not a reasonable goal, where does that leave us? Certainly, not all risks are equivalent. You have already been introduced to many ways to measure and rate risks, but the next step is to evaluate them, meaning that you prioritize which risks need to be addressed and how. As we discussed earlier, if you're spending time addressing several moderate-level risks while leaving a critical risk unaddressed, then you aren't spending your time or resources wisely. Try using the "so what?" test. So what if that password isn't encrypted on the server? So what if the administrators are using a shared account? So what if compilers are installed on the production application server? So what if the client passwords aren't forced to be complex? Bottom line, if you answered any of these questions with "it is best practice," then you have failed. We need to explain the consequences and justify our recommendations in terms the business can understand and appreciate.

Security's Role in Decision Making

Traditionally, security practitioners have used Fear Uncertainty and Doubt (FUD) or the big hammer approach to compliance to force through their own initiatives and basically strong arm the business into implementing certain controls or changing an undesirable practice. Unfortunately, this approach has usually been pushed through without really analyzing the potential impacts to the organization or the probability of occurrence in their environment. What may be the latest threats making headlines may have no relevance to your business or may be far less severe than another weakness that is also not being addressed.

Back in Chapter 3, the risk evaluation stage of the risk management lifecycle was defined as the function of determining the proper steps to manage risk, whether it be to accept, mitigate, transfer, or avoid the risk. During this stage of the lifecycle, newly identified risks need to be compared with the existing list of risks for the organization and priorities determined based on an enterprise view of risks across the organization. This process needs to account for risks to information security, as well as other risk domains, such as financial liquidity, or brand and reputation. Demonstrating the understanding that resources are often pulled away from these other risk areas to address information security risks will add credibility to your program. On its own, an information security risk may seem critical and a no-brainer to throw resources at immediately, but taken into context with other enterprise risks that may threaten the stability or viability of the business, it might need to be de-prioritized. Remember, that risk management is not about a checklist, and it may not be appropriate to mitigate every risk. As a risk manager, your responsibility is to help management to make well-informed risk decisions in the best interest of the organization.

For some reason, there is a perception in some circles that an exception or mitigation plan is a failure. In reality, just the opposite is true. Well-documented, justified, and tracked mitigation plans and exceptions are the signs of a mature and functioning risk management program. That is not to say that an exception on its own has any intrinsic value. Exceptions need to include sound business justification, be reviewed and approved by an appropriate level of management, and include a plan to address the risk. It is the risk manager's job to filter out the risks that have no chance of occurring, will have a negligible impact on the organization or are already well mitigated, and will help senior management to focus on the actionable and imminent threats to the success of the business. In the end, you are making recommendations about how to best manage an acceptable level of risk; you then need to let the other leaders of the organization make the hard decisions about how to balance available resources.

As part of your obligation to escalate the most critical risks to senior management, it is the information security function's responsibility to educate the organization about the most likely and severe risks, without being perceived as an alarmist. As security professionals and risk managers, it is your responsibility to present the results of risk assessments with enough detail so that senior management can make an educated decision about how to manage the exposure. It is very important that you don't take this personally. Often, management will decide not to address a risk that you consider to be critical or just plain embarrassing for the organization. First, consider that there may be other priorities in the organization that present an even bigger risk to their bottom line; also consider the possibility that you need to find a different strategy for presenting the risk findings. For example, mapping a risk exposure to your organization's annual business objectives will immediately get more attention than referencing ethereal security implications or the dreaded "best practices" justification.

RISK DEEP DIVE

Weighing the Soft Costs

Think about your organization's public-facing Web site and how your senior management would react if someone was able to exploit a vulnerability that allowed them to deface some of the site for everyone to see. Continuing with this example, let's now weigh out the costs and benefits of implementing controls to prevent this Web site defacement. Ultimately, Web site defacement may not have direct consequences for the organization that are as costly as, for example, credit card data being stolen. However, even if there is no requirement to report the breach, no regulatory fines, and no payments to clients or contract violations, the reputational damage can still be devastating for the business. For example, one major financial services institution invested heavily in a Web-Application Firewall (WAF) for their public Web site that for the most part only had static pages, like directions to their office and general information about the company. If you know anything about Web application vulnerabilities, you know that the richest vulnerabilities exist in interactive Web sites, whereas static Web pages present far less of a risk. When questioned about why they were investing in such expensive technical controls, they said that they couldn't afford the perception of weakness. If their public Web site could be defaced, clients would lose faith in their ability to protect more sensitive systems. In addition, they believed that any sign of weakness would open the flood gates for attackers to begin trying to break into much more sensitive resources. For them, the potential impact to reputation justified the cost of the controls. This is a good example of an organization choosing to ignore not only the likelihood of occurrence but also the sensitivity of the actual resource being protected. Instead, they were focused on protecting their reputation, not the Web server itself, and for them, money was almost no object when it came to their public perception. They understood that the WAF would add only a trivial reduction in likelihood of a breach, but they wanted to demonstrate to senior management that everything possible was being done to prevent any public display of weakness.

Once the risk exposure has been calculated in the risk assessment step of the risk management lifecycle, risk evaluation is the next task. There are several options for addressing a risk:

Avoid – this option is probably the least frequently used approach; however, it is important to keep it in mind as an option. Avoidance basically involves ceasing the activity that is presenting the risk altogether (or never engaging in the activity at all). So, if it is a new business venture or maybe a technology deployment, avoidance would be abandoning those efforts entirely.

Accept – many risks may be unavoidable or just not worth mitigating for the organization, so in this case, management needs to make a formal decision to accept the risk. Many organizations choose to ignore certain risks, which is really just an implicit form of acceptance.

Mitigate – most commonly, mitigation of a risk or remediation of a vulnerability is associated with risk management; however, remember that this is just one option. To mitigate a risk really means to limit the exposure in some way. This could include reducing the likelihood of occurrence, decreasing the severity of the impact, or even reducing the sensitivity of the resource. Mitigation does not imply a complete elimination of risk, just a reduction to an acceptable level.

Transfer – this option is gaining in popularity as organizations start to really understand where the responsibilities for risks lie. The classic example of this approach is purchasing insurance to cover the expected consequences of a risk exposure. Data breach insurance is just starting to emerge as an option for organizations, the idea being that you transfer the risk to the insurance company. Risk can also be transferred through contracts with partners and clients or by pushing functions out to the customer.

As security professionals, it is in our nature to try to fix all the risks we identify, but we need to strongly consider all our options in each case. The best meetings happen when you can go in and the business folks start making assumptions about what you won't let them do or which controls "security" is going to make them implement. Just sit back and listen to them discuss all the additional controls and process or shoot down each others' ideas, which they perceive as not being secure. In many organizations, you will find that the business still doesn't really understand the intricacies of when certain controls are appropriate, so you may have an opportunity to be the hero who gets to say "no you really don't need all that at all, you can do it much more easily this way ..." and wait for it to sink in. Finding the right controls for the level of risk is the key and that is where you should be providing the most value to the organization.

The term "trusted partner" may be overused at this point, but it does describe how you want to present yourself to the business. The security team needs to work with the business to compare the cost of the safeguard versus the actual value of the resource or impact of a breach. The threshold is clear: if the controls cost more to implement and maintain than the cost of the risk exposure, then the risk isn't worth mitigating. It sounds simple, but as we discussed in Chapter 6, calculating the impact of the risk exposure in terms of a dollar value isn't always so straightforward!

When presented with a risk, the security team, together with the resource owner and maybe even members of senior management, needs to negotiate a plan to reduce the risk or accept it. This can often be the longest step in the risk management workflow because budgets may already be set for the year, resources may be allocated to other projects, and other security risks may pull on the same resources. The bottom line is, there is going to be some negotiating. All of the constraints need to be balanced, and informed decisions need to be made. The security team will meet with each resource owner or Subject Matter Expert (SME) to discuss any outstanding risks and decide how to address them. A risk should be considered "addressed" from a tracking perspective when any of the following criteria are met:

- Approval of an Exception Request (accept)
- Approval of a Mitigation Plan (mitigation or transfer)
- Elimination of the Vulnerability (remediation, a form of mitigation)
- Activity Causing the Exposure is Ceased (avoid)

Documenting Risk Decisions

The artifacts of the risk evaluation step will include either a documented mitigation plan or a policy exception, or, more than likely, both. The exception request becomes the mechanism, not just to track the acceptance of risks but also to document the temporary acceptance of a risk while work is being done to address it. Policy exceptions will be covered later in this chapter; but essentially, you need to at least document the following information during this step:

- Action (avoid, accept, mitigate, transfer)
- Mitigation/Remediation Plan (with dates and owners)
- Status (draft, under review, pending approval, approved, expired, not active, and so on)
- Risk Description
- Risk Rating
- Risk Exception Details (will be covered later in this chapter)

Depending on your preferred approach, you might want to capture all this in some kind of risk inventory or risk register, or, alternately, you can capture the data right in the exception request. This process can be tracked in spreadsheets, MS Word documents, SharePoint, databases, or GRC (Governance, Risk Management, and Compliance) applications; it really doesn't matter where it is captured, as long as the right information is documented and can be made available to the people who are on the hook to fix the risks. This visibility is the key.

Chapter 5 explained how to write a good risk description, but it is worth noting that you will also want to capture some analysis of the current compensating controls. Remember that a compensating control is one that meets the intent of the standard by reducing the exposure to an acceptable level, but it may not match the prescribed control in the standard or policy. Think of it as an equivalent control that needs to be assessed and formally approved as being sufficient. In terms of the format for your risk register, you can choose to include this in the risk description field, with mitigating controls, or in a separate field to document the compensating controls and how they meet the intent of the protection requirement. An exception still needs to be documented for these scenarios to document the formal agreement that the intent of the standard has been met. Alternatively, you can also modify the standard or policy to allow for other controls.

Assuming there are no compensating controls in place, you are left with two basic options: (1) accept the risk as is and (2) develop an action plan to reduce the risk to an acceptable level. If the risk is acceptable to the organization, then an exception must be filed. It is a good idea to base the level of approval needed for the exception on the risk exposure rating. This prevents you from bothering senior management with the low-risk items, but it still ensures that the proper visibility is on the higher exposure risks. Keep in mind as well that no exception should be granted indefinitely. Even for those scenarios where compensating controls are in place, you will want to make sure the risk is being re-evaluated regularly to determine if the solution is still an acceptable one. The threat landscape changes frequently, and so do business objectives, so what might have been an equivalent control today may be found to be lacking in a year from now.

Finally, if the current risk exposure isn't acceptable, you need to work with the business to develop an action plan to address the risk. An action plan can include any combination of the following long- and short-term solutions:

- Mitigation (alleviation, limitation, planning, or remediation)
- Transference
- Avoidance

Mitigation plans aren't all about patching vulnerabilities and installing firewalls; there are many ways to reduce the exposure for the organization.

MAKING THE RIGHT DECISION

If we return to our example of the multiple vulnerabilities on the banking customer portal from Chapter 6, you can think about your options to address these risks in terms of three main choices:

1. Consider the current compensating controls as sufficient, meaning that they may not meet the letter of the standard, but they provide equivalent protection.
2. Accept the risk as is, which will require a formal policy exception.
3. Develop an action plan to address the risks with additional mitigating controls, a transference of risk, or plan to avoid the risk entirely.

In the previous example, the following weaknesses were identified:

- A weakness in a Web form could allow the Web site to be defaced.
- Default administrator passwords are being used on a system that is used to manage server configurations.
- Customer accounts for portal access are setup manually by the client-support staff at the bank, and human error sometimes results in data disclosures between customers.

There are many ways in which you could address each vulnerability; let's start by looking at the weakness in the Web form. Avoiding the risk might seem like a good course of action, but that would involve a plan to shut down the customer portal altogether or at least remove the Web form that is vulnerable. Likely, the online banking service is essential for this regional bank to be successful, so shutting down the service is probably out of the question. A more reasonable approach would be to develop a remediation plan that would involve fixing the vulnerability in the code of the Web form so that it was no longer vulnerable at all.

Changing the default administrator password might seem like the easy fix for this next vulnerability, but let's say there is some technical constraint that prevents you from changing the default administrator password on the management server for another 6 months. There could be some dependency that needs to be fixed and tested, for example. What are your options in the meantime? First, you will want to get and document approval for the acceptance of the risk exposure for 6 months while work is being done to fix the default password issue. Combine this with a short-term mitigation plan, and it will be easier to justify. Maybe you can restrict the source for the administrator account down to one or two workstations? That preventative control would reduce the likelihood of compromise. A detective control might also be appropriate to monitor usage of the administrator account for unusual activity. Any of these controls should be documented in the mitigation plan and that plan should be included in the exception request.

Thus far, we have eliminated avoidance as a solution, recommended one plan to remediate a vulnerability and also a temporary acceptance of risk with a short-term mitigation plan. That just leaves transferring of risk. An example of a plan to transfer the risk of manual customer account configuration would be to empower the customers to setup their own accounts through the Web portal and to take your support staff out of the process altogether. That way if a mistake is made during the setup, you have transferred the liability to the customer to protect their own data. Hopefully, these examples illustrated just how many options are available to address a given risk.

Calculating the Cost of Remediation

When deciding on a risk mitigation strategy, it is important to consider both the cost of implementing controls and the potential costs of not doing so. You might consider a process or procedural control instead of a technical control, but you will then have to consider how that decision may affect operational effectiveness. Consider the cost of

- not implementing a control
- reduction in operational effectiveness
- implementation
- additional resources
- education and training

Whenever you are recommending technical security controls to mitigate a risk, you need to account for both direct and indirect costs. There is the initial cost of hardware, software, professional services, and so on, as well as the cost over time of maintenance and support. Any new technology may require additional resources to run and maintain it, and may require training for staff if it is a new technology. Too many organizations implement high-touch technologies like Intrusion Detection Systems (IDS), Security Information Event Management (SIEM), or Web-Application Firewalls (WAF) without considering the operational needs to support and respond to the events it will generate. When calculating these costs, having some sort of template is helpful so that you can consistently include all the indirect costs, such as licensing, storage space, cost of expansion over time, long-term support, and so on, in your calculations. The total expense of the controls should never cost more than the asset is worth or exceed the potential impact of the risk.

Residual Risk

Residual risk is the remaining risk exposure level after implementing the recommended controls. The process of calculating the residual risk is similar to the previously described rating methodology for calculating the risk exposure given the existing compensating controls. You should be able to provide the business with before and after snapshots of how the recommended controls will lower the risk to the organization. Assess the raw risks, without controls applied, and then again with the controls in place to demonstrate the value of the control by the reduction in exposure. You should be able to predict this even before a control is actually implemented, but you will want to verify that it is behaving as expected.

RISK MITIGATION PLANNING

We have already touched on several aspects of mitigation planning throughout the book because it is such an important focus in the risk management lifecycle. This stage of the workflow is defined as the process of implementing controls and safeguards to reduce the likelihood of occurrence or to limit the effects of the exposure. The goal of a mitigation plan is generally to lower the likelihood of a risk being realized, but it may also aim to contain the exposure by reducing the scope (severity), or provide some means to recover from a successful exploit, thus reducing the impact to the organization.

Mitigation Approaches

There are many options for mitigating a risk, and again, the focus is not always on trying to eliminate the risk, but rather to reduce the risk exposure to an acceptable level. To mitigate a risk, you either have to reduce the likelihood of occurrence, limit the severity, or decrease the impact (sensitivity of the resource). The first two are the most common, but in some cases, it may be possible to change the sensitivity of the resource. Consider an instance of a development database that is used for testing new releases of a bank's customer Web portal application. The developers may want some data that matches production as closely as possible, so someone copies the entire production database onto the development server. This would mean that the development database now needs to have the same level of protection as production because of the sensitivity of the data. The sensitivity could be reduced, however, if the data from production was scrambled in some random manner before being copied to development. This way the data would still be good for testing, but a few of the sensitive fields like customer name or account number could be obfuscated.

Another option for this example might be to reduce the threat universe by implementing firewall rules to limit source networks that are allowed to connect to the database server. Again, this option would not limit the severity of the exposure or change the sensitivity of the database server, but it would reduce the likelihood of abuse by reducing the number of entities who can access the server. There are many other examples of how to reduce the threat universe, such as implementing authentication to limit access to a known user community. We will explore more options for reducing the likelihood of a threat later in this book.

To limit the severity of an exploit, you need to somehow contain the compromise. This approach to risk mitigation recognizes that you can't necessarily prevent the compromise, but you can limit the scope of the breach or react quickly to prevent further escalation. Most controls in this category will be detective and response focused. An active alert triggered from a log file that detects brute forcing of user accounts may be too late to prevent someone from compromising the account, but you may be able to quickly disable the account before any damage is done or the attacker is able to move to another system. Another typical example is limiting the scope of access the attacker would have when exploiting the account. If you can limit the access to standard "user privilege" level as opposed to an "administrative privilege" level, then you have reduced the severity of the exposure. Think about the difference between high and critical on the qualitative severity scale from Chapter 6. Preventing an attacker from getting full control of the system with a quick detection of the initial compromise and a response to contain the breach would lower the potential severity rating from critical to high. There are many examples of how this reduction in severity can be achieved. Three general categories of risk mitigation are as follows:

> **Risk Alleviation** – implements controls to prevent the threat/vulnerability (such as patching a software weakness).
> **Risk Limitation** – limits likelihood or effects with controls (such as the examples given above).
> **Risk Planning** – develops a formal plan to prioritize, implement, and maintain controls (this doesn't directly change the risk exposure level, but it assumes some plan to address the risk in the near future, therefore, limiting the timeframe for possible exposure).

The fourth mitigation option, remediation, isn't applicable for all risks because not all risks have a vulnerability that can be removed. This is a typical solution when presented with a software bug or unnecessary service. As you develop your risk management program, you will want to establish a template for mitigation plans. In addition to the basic information already discussed, it is also helpful to require that the expected reduction in risk exposure be specified. This allows you to compare the effort for a given mitigation action to the expected reduction in risk.

Choosing Controls

If we think about the effects that controls can have on risks, we can agree that they can potentially lower any one or all of the variables used to calculate the risk exposure. A preventative control may change the likelihood of a vulnerability being exploited, but do nothing to change the severity of a successful exploit. In contrast, a reactive control may not lessen the likelihood at all, but it could limit the severity by constraining the scope of the exploit once it is detected. Detective controls can sometimes have the effect of a deterrent that lowers the likelihood, but generally, they will limit the impact of the exploit by allowing the organization to quickly respond to the attack.

There are many good references for control lists including the following:

- ISO 27002 Standard
- COBIT
- NIST SP800-53

Each of these frameworks contains an extensive list of both technical and non-technical controls. Think back to the security services and controls discussed in Chapter 7 and you will see that all the specific controls recommended in these information security standards frameworks are derived from these fundamental services. Each control may have any of the following effects on the risk exposure (and sometimes a combination of two or more):

- They can limit the threat universe (likelihood).
- They can increase the difficulty of exploit (likelihood).
- They can reduce the scope of the exploit (severity).
- They can remediate (negate) a specific vulnerability.

Assume that you may be filing a short- or long-term exception along with your action plan, so you will need to specify the mitigation steps that will be taken to lower the risk of each finding. Be sure to state the action item in the form of an action statement, such as "Contact ...," "Implement ...," "Enforce ...," and so on. You also need to include specific steps that will be taken, responsible parties, and timeframes for delivery for each action.

POLICY EXCEPTIONS AND RISK ACCEPTANCE

Risk exceptions serve many purposes, including documenting when

- a risk exposure can't be remediated or mitigated
- the business chooses to accept a risk as is
- the cost of mitigation outweighs the impact of the exposure
- compensating controls already exist
- a risk exposure needs to be accepted temporarily while it is being addressed

Whenever any of these situations occur, an exception request will need to be filed and approved. Keep in mind that an exception is not a permanent approval to ignore a policy. In fact, most exceptions will be temporary and set to expire based on some mitigation strategy. Even in the case of compensating controls, exceptions should be re-examined regularly to ensure they are still adequate.

Exception Workflow

The level of approval needed for an exception depends on the level of risk being introduced by the deviation from policy and can be directly mapped to the qualitative risk exposure mapping table that we have been using.

One possible exception request and approval workflow can be implemented as follows:

1. Anyone can submit an exception request.
2. Someone reviews the exception for their functional area, selects the appropriate member of management to approve for that functional unit, and forwards it to the information security team.
3. Information security team reviews and enters a risk rating and expiration date, then forwards to the member of management to approve the exception request for the affected functional area.
4. Depending on the level of risk, senior management reviews and approves the exception request and/or the mitigation plan.
5. Depending on the risk level, the head of information security or a combination of corporate officers approves the exception request.
6. Exception is finalized, and any actions are tracked until it expires.
7. Information security team reviews updates from requestor and either closes the exception or extends it.

One possible workflow for this exception handling process is illustrated in Figure 8.1. Once the exception expires, it will need to be reviewed by the information security team in conjunction with the submitter to determine if the risk still exists and whether the exception needs to be updated. If there was a mitigation plan associated with it, the deliverables would be reviewed at that time. Each step in this workflow is designed to promote awareness within the organization's leadership of the risks in their area. It may seem like a lot of reviews and approvals, but it is important to ensure that everyone responsible for approving and potentially allocating resources to mitigate a risk understands the implications.

Ultimately, step 3 becomes the point at which the exception wording and ratings are finalized. This gives the security team the opportunity to enhance the risk analysis that was originally submitted and also challenge it if they don't agree with the risk decisions. It is then sent along through the levels of management approvals.

The exception request form should capture the following information at a minimum:

- Target Resource (application, system, environment, business unit, or vendor)
- Submitter

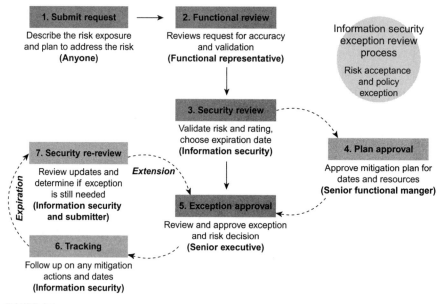

FIGURE 8.1

Risk exception approval workflow.

- Functional Unit
- Workflow Status
- Expiration Date
- Risk Active Status
- Individual Finding(s)
- Standard(s) Impacted
- Source of Findings
- Description of Exception
- Scope of Risk
- Risk Description
- Compensating and/or Mitigating Controls
- Severity
- Likelihood
- Risk Exposure Ranking
- Mitigation Plan
- Approval Tracking

The workflow for approval should require that the submission is reviewed by the information security team before being submitted to management for approval. During this review, the security team will review the submitter's evaluation of the risk and work with the submitter to clarify any sections of the form as needed. In some cases, the information security team may even change the risk evaluations based on these discussions. Next, the request will be submitted to management for approval. The level of management approval needed will depend on the risk exposure ranking of the request. If a mitigation plan is included in the exception request, a specific management approval from the function performing the mitigation steps may also be added. This process has been intentionally designed so that functional management has to review all exceptions and mitigation plans for their functional area, thus ensuring that they are aware of all the identified information security risks for their function. When an exception includes a mitigation plan, the functional manager is really approving the plan, not the exception; however, when a risk is submitted as-is with no mitigation plan, the functional manager is acknowledging their acceptance of the risk for their area.

Notice, too, that this workflow includes two types of actions: review and approval. Steps 2 and 3 require that by reviewing and forwarding an exception request, the representative for that function and the member of the information security team, respectively, attest to having reviewed and validated the risks and safeguards and deem that no further action is necessary beyond what is outlined in the request.

In contrast, steps 4 and 5 represent a decision by senior management that the issues, risks, and associated safeguards have been evaluated with all information available by sources trusted to be competent. By approving this exception, they deem the level of risk acceptable and agree to commit the necessary resources to the execution of any action plans in the request.

Signature Requirements

We have already stated that the approvals should be based on the level of risk exposure, so now let's look at how that might be implemented. Suppose you are using the simple risk matrix from Chapter 6, shown again in Figure 8.2.

Severity

Likelihood		High	Moderate	Low
	High	High	High	Moderate
	Moderate	High	Moderate	Low
	Low	Moderate	Low	Low

FIGURE 8.2

Risk mapping table for exceptions.

In practice, this might be used as follows to determine the exception request's path through the workflow after a member of the security team has reviewed it for completeness and accuracy:

1. For risks that are outside the range of acceptable risks (high on the simple risk matrix), any two of the following signatures will serve as acknowledgment and acceptance of risk and related mitigation plans for the organization:
   a. Chief Information Security Officer, Chief Compliance Officer, Chief Privacy Officer, or Senior Legal Counsel, and also
   b. any C-level executive or officer of the company
2. For risks that are on the line of acceptable risk ranges (moderate on the simple risk matrix), any two of the following signatures will serve as acknowledgment and acceptance of risk and related mitigation plans for the organization:
   a. Chief Information Security Officer, Chief Compliance Officer, Chief Privacy Officer, or Senior Legal Counsel, and also
   b. Senior management for the functional area or business unit
3. For risks that are in an acceptable range (low on the simple risk matrix), any combination of the following signatures will serve as acknowledgment and acceptance of risk and related mitigation plans (if applicable) for the organization:
   a. Either a Senior Manager from the information security team or the Chief Information Security Officer

If a mitigation plan is included as part of the exception request, the plan must be submitted by or approved first by the functional unit management to ensure there is really a commitment to address the risk.

It is also recommended that for exceptions where the business is choosing not to address a risk that has been identified by either the audit function or an outside regulator, or that would violate a legal obligation, signatures from several corporate officers, such as the Chief Executive Officer, Chief Information Security Officer, Chief Compliance Officer, Chief Privacy Officer, and Senior Legal Counsel, must be obtained.

This process helps to ensure that the appropriate visibility and approval are obtained for exceptions with different levels of risk to the organization. If this workflow is followed, no one can say that they weren't aware of an issue and hopefully the process itself will spark some good discussions about priorities. Of course, if your organization already has an enterprise risk function or an established exception process, you could leverage that as well.

WARNING

Given the potential complexity of an exception approval process like this, it is common to try to over-automate it. Meaning that you establish a system with a scripted workflow that puts all these steps into place based on the risk and automatically sends it to the next reviewer. This may seem like a good idea in the beginning, but it quickly becomes clear that every risk may have a slightly different context and it isn't always so consistent who needs to review or approve it. A risk owner may be in a totally different function than the mitigation plan owner. Or you may decide that the Chief Compliance Officer really needs to sign-off on this one exception. Leave the security team the flexibility to dynamically select the approval path as appropriate.

Expiration and Renewal

A good rule of thumb is for all exceptions to be valid for a year from the approval date by default; alternatively, the information security team can select an expiration date based on the specific mitigation plan for that exception. Ninety days prior to the expiration of an exception, the submitter should be notified of the pending expiration and asked for a status update. At this time, the submitter should provide the information security team with a status report for any mitigation plans in progress and indicate whether the risk is still active. An active exception is one in which the risk still exists, as opposed to having been fully remediated or eliminated.

At the point of the status update, the submitter has the option to request an extension of the exception. The approval process for an extension or renewal of an exception should follow an abbreviated version of the original approval workflow. Depending on the level of risk and progress of the mitigation plan, an extension can be approved by any of following individuals:

- Either a Senior Manager from the information security team or the Chief Information Security Officer, as well as
- Senior management for the functional area or business unit if the mitigation plan has changed.

During the renewal process, all parties involved in the exception will be consulted and an appropriate plan of action will be determined. Significant additions or modifications to the risk rating or mitigation plan may require the exception to be resubmitted through the entire approval process.

SUMMARY

There are so many options available to you to choose from when presented with a risk. Guaranteed that remediation will not be the best choice for most of the risks that you will see, outside of the standard patching risks, so you need to staff your risk team with individuals who have an aptitude for creative problem solving and critical analysis. The business will always appreciate it when you work with them to find a lower impact solution that still meets the required risk reduction criteria. As a risk manager or analyst, you will spend a significant amount of your time tracking mitigation actions and getting status updates on active exceptions, so do yourself a favor and setup a formal process to handle these requests and capture the actions with owners and dates. Like the security risk profile, the exception approval process quickly becomes a core component of your program that will be leveraged by several other security activities and functions.

Action Plan

After reading this chapter, you should consider taking the following actions in your own organization:

- Your number one priority should be to implement a formal exception approval process if you don't have one already.
- Implement an internal template, with the minimal fields recommended in this chapter, to document the justification for every risk decision that your team or senior management makes.
- Require that all risk mitigation plans be formally approved by a functional manager, and that at a minimum, it specifies milestones with committed dates for each.

Reports and Consulting

INFORMATION IN THIS CHAPTER

- Risk Management Artifacts
- A Consultant's Perspective
- Writing Audit Responses

INTRODUCTION

Whether you are a risk manager who is engaging outside consultants to perform risk assessments or the consultant who is framing out a risk offering, this chapter includes some essential guidance for how this can be done optimally. We start out with a brief review of the basic artifacts of a risk management program and end with an in-depth look at how to bring risk analysis into the audit process. Even if you don't ever plan to be a consultant or hire them to supplement your team's abilities, the concepts in this chapter can really help you improve your risk-presentation skills.

RISK MANAGEMENT ARTIFACTS

You may remember back in Chapter 3 that the documentation of risk was listed as an explicit stage in the risk management lifecycle; in actuality, you need to document your assessment and analysis steps all along the way. Six months from now, are you really going to remember why you rated the likelihood of a particular risk as moderate instead of high? It is not likely without documenting your rationale along the way. This documentation needs to capture all the factors that you took into account when rating the risk and deciding on the appropriate way to address it. For instance, there may have been compensating controls that affected your assessment of the risk, or maybe a related risk that contributed to a higher than usual rating. Especially, if your organization is regulated or the security program is subject to internal or external audit, this process is critical. No matter what risk model you use, there is some level of subjectivity when rating the risks and making decisions about the best ways to address them.

Your risk assessment template should at least capture the following information:

- Brief risk description
- Risk rating
- Why a rating was given
- Compensating controls considered
- Risk owner
- Risk decision (mitigation plan, accept risk with exception, transfer risk)

If you choose to address a risk with some kind of mitigation plan, the business owner needs to document the agreed upon steps, target dates, and responsible parties. It is generally the security team's job to oversee and track the progress of the mitigation plan, but it is up to the business owner (and resource custodian) to execute it. It is a good idea to ask the business owner to submit a temporary exception request while the mitigation plan is being worked on. Any mitigation plan may include a combination of long- and short-term action items, so it is important to make sure that each milestone is clearly documented and approved by the responsible parties. It won't always be possible to get to the desired reduction of risk right away, so you should be actively looking for some short-term action items that can reduce the risk from, say, critical to high exposure, with a long-term plan in place to further reduce the risk exposure to moderate. It is this type of flexibility and creativity that can win you points with the business while still resulting in a significant reduction in risk. Just be cautious to make sure that all steps of the mitigation plan are clear; otherwise, you could end up with those long-term actions that linger out there forever once the most critical actions are completed. In addition to the data captured in your risk assessment template, exceptions and mitigation plans need to include the following information:

- Business justification for the risk
- Mitigation action items, long- and short-term
- Policy exceptions/risk acceptance approval and timeframe

Whenever a risk is being accepted (even temporarily), a formal policy exception or risk acceptance form should be filled out with senior management approval. You can refer back to Chapter 8 if you need to refresh your memory about the exception process.

Besides the documentation of a risk finding, mitigation plan, or exception request, these are some other artifacts that you should expect to create:

- Security risk profile
- Questionnaires
- Risk inventory (also called a *risk register*)
- Enterprise risk assessment
- Architectural or design analysis

Most of these have been discussed throughout the book already, but it is important to note here that it is essential to have templates for all these documents so that they are not being created ad hoc. A risk inventory could be a simple listing of identified risks, some of which are already assessed and others of which are still in the process of being qualified. This should be at a higher level than a simple risk finding. These risks should describe systemic or thematic risks that typically combine multiple findings from different sources. Similarly, an enterprise risk assessment template would include the appropriate fields to capture and present a risk discovered by the information security team to the executive level. Architectural and design analysis will be covered in Chapter 13, but for now, just keep in mind that this should follow a consistent format to ensure all the necessary areas are reviewed for security flaws.

In terms of internal reviews of your own organization, or assessments of your own service providers and partners, those listed earlier are the most common artifacts that you will need to develop. If, however, you are performing risk assessments as a consultant or other outsider, then you will also need a formal assessment report template, which you will use to present your findings and recommendations.

A CONSULTANT'S PERSPECTIVE

So far, our discussions have focused on internal risk assessments and reviews of your third-party vendors. Now, let's suppose that you are a consultant or an auditor performing an assessment of another company. Your approach is going to be slightly different when you are an external party who has been hired to review the risks for an organization, but the same general risk principles and models apply. Rather than mapping the steps to a typical lifecycle, your assessment will follow more closely the steps of an engagement and needs to be organized in a format that is presentable to management as well as the more technical staff.

This chapter presents one approach for structuring a risk assessment project as a consultant and this process has been loosely based on the methodology in OCTAVE Allegro, a popular industry framework for risk assessment. Let's start by briefly reviewing some of the very basic components of OCTAVE Allegro and then how to streamline the process to fit an assessment engagement.

Octave Allegro

Coming out of CERT and Carnegie Mellon's Software Engineering Institute (SEI), the Operationally Critical Threat, Asset, and Vulnerability Evaluation (OCTAVE) Allegro methodology takes a more software development lifecycle approach to risk management, as opposed to some of the more operation-focused approaches for assessing system risk like NIST's Certification and Accreditation process. There have been many revisions to the framework including OCTAVE (first published in 1999), OCTAVE-S (published in 2003), and now OCTAVE Allegro (published in 2007). Even OCTAVE-S, which was designed to be more streamlined and lightweight than the original OCTAVE framework, was too formal and cumbersome for many organizations. OCTAVE Allegro finally provides an approachable solution that can be implemented even by organizations with less structure around their application development and system deployment lifecycles. Although the NIST documents are sometimes referred to as a framework, NIST actually provides guidelines for risk management and OCTAVE is the first full risk framework specific to information security.

A Phased Approach

In particular, the artifacts provided by OCTAVE Allegro are an extremely good place to start for those just beginning to implement formal risk assessments within their organization. OCTAVE can help you to

- develop qualitative risk evaluation criteria that describe the organization's operational risk tolerances
- identify assets that are important to the mission of the organization
- identify threats to the mission of the organization through threat modeling
- identify vulnerabilities associated with the likely threats and critical assets
- determine and evaluate the potential consequences to the organization if threats are realized
- develop a mitigation plan for each critical asset

The four phases of OCTAVE Allegro are shown in Figure 9.1 with a brief highlight of each step's focus areas listed.

Gathering Business Requirements

One of the strengths of this methodology, for a consultant, is that it is strongly focused on gathering business requirements and tailoring the assessment to those priority areas. It is essential to understand an organization's mission and objectives if you are going to design a risk assessment that really addresses the areas of highest exposure.

OCTAVE Allegro relies on Subject Matter Experts (SME), typically consisting of three to five people per assessment team, being closely involved in the assessment process. Each SME should have strong working knowledge of the critical assets, security requirements, threats, and security practices of the organization. Like previous iterations, OCTAVE Allegro provides several worksheets and questionnaires for conducting a structured assessment. Unlike previous OCTAVE versions, Allegro focuses primarily on information in the context of how and where data are used in storage, in transit, and in process. This level of involvement from the SMEs and the detail level of the requirements and threat analysis steps make the methodology less desirable for the everyday internal assessments, but the perfect fit for an assessment as part of a large phased project, like software development project or consulting engagement.

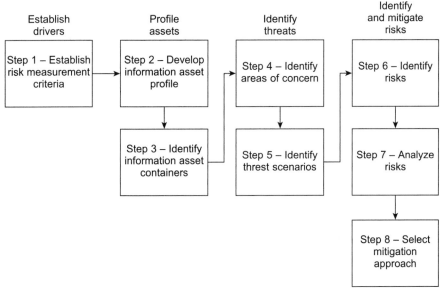

FIGURE 9.1

OCTAVE process flow [1].

The methodology includes extensive questionnaires for profiling threat exposures and vulnerabilities. Specific objectives are as follows:

- Develop risk measurement criteria that are consistent with organizational drivers.
- Profile assets including information containers.
- Identify threats through a structured process.
- Identify risks and develop mitigation strategies.

Step 4 begins the risk identification process by brainstorming about possible conditions or situations that can threaten an organization's assets. These real-world scenarios are referred to as areas of concern and should represent threats and their corresponding outcomes. The purpose of this step is not to identify an exhaustive list of all possible threat scenarios for an asset; instead, the idea is to quickly capture those situations or conditions that come immediately to the minds of the analysis team. If you get the right people in the room during this activity, the issues that jump to peoples' minds will typically be the most critical risks to the organization. Often times, these risks are well known, but there is no mechanism to escalate risks in the organization, so they go unaddressed.

The eight-step process shown in Figure 9.1 follows the same basic steps of profiling the asset, modeling the threats, analyzing the risk, and selecting a mitigation approach that was included in the risk management lifecycle from

Chapter 3. Notice that this process is not depicted as a cyclical process and doesn't cover any steps after the selection of a mitigation approach. This is one reason that the OCTAVE methodology is better suited for a project-based assessment such as an enterprise risk assessment or application development project. Because of the detailed steps, activities, and documentation, it isn't as well suited for brief or ongoing operational assessments. The NIST guidelines provide a better structure for operational assessment activities, as you will see in Chapter 11.

Risk Assessment Engagement

This section of the book really should have started with the following warning:

> *"Be 100% sure that when a client asks you for a risk assessment, they know what a risk assessment is."*

More often than you would think, a client requests a quote or scope of work for a risk assessment only to find out that they really wanted a penetration test or vulnerability assessment, but didn't really understand the difference. This happens often when consultants have to respond to Request for Proposals (RFPs) from customers who aren't very security savvy. The wording and language may say "risk assessment," but you will do well to ask many pointed questions about the expected scope and desired results of the engagement, or else risk being burned by an unhappy customer. Depending on the scope of the project, a risk assessment may not even include any hands-on or active testing of an environment. You will need to make sure that the scope of the engagement is crystal clear and that you fully explain to the customer what the difference between a security scan and a risk assessment is early in the engagement negotiations.

Once you have established the desire for a risk assessment, the secret to pulling off any successful assessment or audit is following a structured and strategic assessment process. Think about breaking up the assessment into three phases:

Phase 1: Build Asset-Based Threat Profiles
- Identify organizational information
- Create threat profiles

Phase 2: Identify Vulnerabilities
- Examine the critical resources
- Examine the supporting infrastructure

Phase 3: Evaluate Risks and Develop Security Strategy
- Identify and analyze risks
- Develop protection strategy and mitigation plans

For risk assessments, a very simple workflow can help you to keep the engagement focused and comprehensive. This assessment format has been adapted and optimized from the OCTAVE Allegro methodology, through years of consulting experience.

Phase 1: Build Asset-Based Threat Profiles

It is always important to start by profiling the organization and their critical resources. When you start scoping out the engagement with your client, you will likely come across two scenarios:

1. The client wants you to identify the critical assets that should be included.
2. The client will already have specific assets identified in the scope of the engagement.

Either way, it is still important to conduct the profiling step to validate the assumptions made about the importance of the assets or environments being assessed. This will also give you valuable insight about where to look for weaknesses and which vulnerabilities and threats present the most exposure to the organization. This phase of the project should include the following steps:

- Identify organizational information
  - Establish impact evaluation criteria
  - Identify organizational assets
  - Evaluate organizational security practices
- Create threat profiles
  - Select critical assets
  - Identify security requirements for critical assets
  - Identify threats to critical assets

The steps in this phase are based on similar activities in the OCTAVE Allegro risk methodology, but have been customized to fit the consulting engagement needs. The steps in this phase are very similar to the exercise of creating a *security risk profile*; however, remember that as an external risk assessor, you will likely have even less context or knowledge of the resources being profiled when you begin. As a consultant, you should already have risk models and evaluation criteria established that you can offer to your clients. For example, the qualitative scales for sensitivity, severity, likelihood, and risk exposure used throughout this book can easily be applied to any risk engagement. Next, you need to work with the customer to identify potential assets that should be assessed as part of the project. The final list will depend on the customer's goals, the nature of their business, and the areas in which the client has already performed significant analysis. Some common resources are as follows:

- Internet-facing services
- Common infrastructure services like DNS, DHCP, and so on
- Servers supporting a critical business process
- Servers storing or processing sensitive data
- Desktop environment, including workstations, laptops, and printers
- Network and security devices
- Physical facilities

It may or may not be obvious during initial discussions with a client which areas are most critical to the organization. In part, this is where you can add value, either to validate their focus or help direct it. Then, like in a security risk profile, you will need to document the assurance needs of the assets in terms of whether confidentiality, integrity, availability, and/or accountability are important and, if so, to what degree.

Next, you will need to help the organization to articulate their business security requirements. It is important to keep these requirements at a high level. Don't get down into the detailed level of technologies or implementations of controls, just talk about the expected levels of information assurance. Otherwise, you risk losing your audience.

Table 9.1 shows a simple example of how security requirements can be gathered through discussions with the client and organized by the category or applicable security principle affected. Having a preset list of the categories will help to ensure that you capture a broad range of requirements and don't focus all of your efforts in one area. Without security requirements stated, you cannot properly assess the risk exposure of any one threat/vulnerability pair.

Early on in the assessment, it is a good idea to perform a general assessment of the organization's security practices. The results of this review will inform where you need to focus your efforts, what you can skip, and how deep you need to dig into each area. A good approach is to treat this evaluation like you would treat a high-level third-party assessment. This should be focused on a small number of program level security questions, and cover the most basic security practices and controls that can raise a red flag if missing.

From this point, you have two choices for building threat profiles:

1. Focus on the observed weaknesses and then model threats that could exploit those weaknesses.
2. Model the most likely threats and then start to identify any related weaknesses.

Although the second approach results in a lot of possibilities that you will eliminate because they aren't really practical or probable, it runs less of a risk of being overly influenced by the obvious vulnerabilities and possibly missing more serious

Table 9.1 Examples of Security Requirements

Category	Security Requirement
Auditing	System events should be audited according to industry best practices and regulatory compliance.
Authentication	Access to the system must use strong authentication for all users.
Authorization	Only authorized users should be allowed to access the system.
Availability	System availability is required 24/7. The criticality of availability is rated as medium.
Confidentiality	Sensitive customer and company data should be kept confidential (restricted on need-to-know basis).
Integrity	Only authorized users should be able to modify data.

issues under the surface. On the other hand, the first approach has a better chance of identifying more pertinent risks, but it tends to be greatly influenced by the experience of the assessor and therefore some less obvious weaknesses may be missed.

> **WARNING**
>
> If you are the one hiring the consultant to perform a risk assessment, you need to make sure that you choose a knowledgeable consultant with extensive experience in assessing a wide variety of organizations. Don't just look for someone with experience in your own industry.

Since both approaches have their pros and cons, it is best to use a combination of these methods. As is shown in phase 1 of the workflow earlier, it is a good idea to start by identifying the major threats to the critical assets, but not to try to make this a comprehensive list. You can then use those threats to influence any additional areas of assessment that may be needed later in the engagement.

Before any testing begins, you need to interview management and any other key stakeholders to identify their primary areas of concern. The concerns that you identify during this phase can greatly affect the testing activities that you choose to include or even where you look for weaknesses and attack vectors. Once you understand the pressures and motivation that are driving the organization to conduct this assessment, then you can properly focus your efforts. For example, Figure 9.2 is a worksheet

Organizational level	Areas of concern
Manager	Compliance The system configuration and security measures must adhere to all pertinent regulations.
	Disclosure Personnel might download company confidential information to noncompany assets such as home computers.
	Disclosure All system communications must be properly protected using encryption and other security methods.
	Interruption Power outages, floods, and other external events can lead to a denial of access to this system.
	Protection The e-mail system must be protected from unauthorized access.
Consultant	Disclosure When accessed from public or shared systems such as kiosks, residual sensitive data could be left behind.
	Disclosure Customer sensitive data stored in public folders could be copied to unauthorized systems without any tracking/auditing capability.

FIGURE 9.2

OCTAVE areas of concern worksheet.

from the OCTAVE Allegro risk methodology and demonstrates a good way to quickly and succinctly capture the concerns of management.

The example in Figure 9.2 shows the information that was gathered from management when performing a risk assessment of a remote access e-mail environment for a regional bank. It is also important for the assessor, in this case a consultant, to identify any areas that may have been overlooked; these are listed at the bottom of the table. Most organizations may not be familiar with the latest regulations or attack vectors, so you may need to include your own areas of concern as well.

Phase 2: Identify Vulnerabilities

Once you have finalized the scope, defined the requirements, and mapped out the likely threats, you will need to develop a testing approach to best identify the vulnerabilities that might apply to those resources and be affected by the threats. When designing a testing plan, it is important to attempt to think like an attacker and try to target the areas that are most exposed to external connections or internal use, depending on the threat focus. For example, you might decide to run a vulnerability scan or conduct a penetration test twice, once from the Internet with no prior knowledge of the environment and then again from an internal network after studying network diagrams and system documentation. In this way, you can get two different perspectives on the risk exposures and rate them independently.

This phase has a singular focus: to assess the applicable vulnerabilities related to the critical resources and any supporting infrastructure. You might think of this phase as being comprised of two steps:

1. Examine the critical resources
2. Examine the supporting infrastructure

In reality, it is sometimes hard to separate the supporting infrastructure from the critical resources being targeted; so, typically, a single testing activity will cover both at once. However, it may be desirable to target the critical resources first, perform an initial analysis of the results and then decide if you need to change your approach to testing the supporting infrastructure based on your findings. The testing activities will likely consist of a combination of assessment methods, such as the following:

- Analyze operating environment
- Internet reconnaissance
- External vulnerability scanning
- Internal LAN-based port scanning
- Network device configuration analysis
- Web application penetration testing
- Firewall rulebase audit
- Wireless security scan
- Application whitebox testing

This is certainly not an exhaustive list, but hopefully it will give you a flavor of the breadth of testing options available. Further, when choosing the appropriate testing activities, don't just limit your options to active technical options (for example, port scanning). You should also consider other methods, such as interviewing key staff members. Even when conducting a more technical test, be careful not to rely on scanning tools alone, as often times, you will gather the best information by sitting down with staff members and asking them questions about the environment and their practices before you start banging away at the environment. Having a few staff members in the room will usually elicit more insightful discussions than one-on-one interviews, but you may find that people are less willing to identify weakness if management is present.

In addition to interviews, other assessment techniques like *physical walkthroughs* are great tools for identifying ways to bypass technical controls. The activities that you include will depend on the scope of the assessment. An extensive discussion of security testing and assessment techniques is outside the scope of our risk discussion, but there are plenty of resources available on these topics from the Open Source Security Testing Methodology Manual (OSSTMM) [2] to various technical courses taught by some expert security testers at the SANS Institute.

Phase 3: Evaluate Risks and Develop Security Strategy

Once a list of the vulnerabilities has been compiled, the bulk of the analysis work begins. This phase of the project includes two very distinct steps:

1. Identify and analyze risks
2. Develop protection strategy and mitigation plans

You might look at step 1 and think that the "identify" portion seems misplaced— after all, didn't you already identify vulnerabilities in the last phase of the project? The distinction is an important one; in phase 2, you made a list of vulnerabilities, but now you need to identify the risks which are a combination of a vulnerability and a threat. This methodology accounts for the possibility of several different threats being combined with one vulnerability to result in several possible risks. Simply put, you may identify several risks associated with one vulnerability, and likewise you may identify several vulnerabilities that all contribute to a single risk. For example, not using encryption for confidential data on mobile devices could have several associated threats, each with a slightly different risk exposure. An employee may leave his/her mobile device in a taxi and accidently expose that confidential data to someone who then reports the incident to the press. The same device could be purposely stolen from the employee and the confidential data may be used to commit fraud. So you can see that with the same vulnerability, we can see two very different consequences, each of which must be addressed in our assessment.

The risk evaluation step should include the following:

1. Determine likelihood of threat/vulnerability
2. Determine severity of threat/vulnerability

3. Determine risk exposure (including *risk sensitivity*)
4. Identify safeguards
5. Determine residual risk level

Each threat/vulnerability pair needs to be analyzed and rated. This includes the analysis of the likelihood that the vulnerability will be exploited, the severity of that exploit, and, finally, taking into account the sensitivity of the impacted resource. Don't forget to note any existing controls that may already mitigate the chance or magnitude of the exploitation.

If you want to demonstrate the value of controls that are already in place, you may choose to include a raw risk score that doesn't account for any compensating controls and then also include the residual risk levels after applying the compensating controls. Whether or not this option is useful will depend on the goals of the engagement.

Finally, you will need to work with the client to develop a mitigation strategy. This will typically include several activities, including the following:

1. Recommend protection strategy
2. Select risk mitigation steps
3. Identify near-term action items
4. Update status of mitigation plan

This phase of the engagement will include several action plan steps to lower the risks to an acceptable level. As the consultant, you would never want to present a list of issues to a client. Instead, you will want to carefully package the assessment results in such a way that management has meaningful information with which to make decisions about which risks need to be addressed and how. All risks need to be tied back to the potential business impact and your report needs to make it clear to management how their business will be impacted if these risks are not addressed.

Always start by including recommendations of your own, taking into account what you have learned about the organization's mission, culture, risk appetite, and available resources. It can help to have some informal discussions with your project contacts to float some ideas by them and get a sense of what might be reasonable for the organization to absorb. It is generally helpful to include at least one mitigation action per risk finding; however, several actions may be needed to adequately mitigate a single risk. Along with each action item, you should always describe how this action will reduce the risk exposure to a desirable or acceptable level.

Once you have a list of recommendations that maps to your list of risks (and not all recommendations need to be for mitigations; they could be for acceptance or transference instead), you should meet with the customer to review the results and begin to build a mitigation plan. Mitigation steps will generally fall into two categories: long-term or short-term strategies for addressing the risks. The near-term action items should always focus on the most critical risks first, but you may also find yourself prioritizing a systemic risk or focusing on a control that will address several risks at once, even if the individual risk exposure levels are rated lower.

Consultants are always looking for value-added services that can differentiate them from competitors and ways to encourage clients to consider them for work on future projects. One great way to stay close to your client is to include a 6-month checkup in the scope of the assessment engagement. This is a good opportunity to take the near-term action plan, or even the long-term strategy, and update the status of each item and discuss any shifts in the strategy that might be appropriate. For example, if the client had decided to implement a control as part of their near-term action plan to address a high-risk exposure, you may find that they have changed their minds by the time you check back in. Either the timeline for the mitigation step may have been pushed out due to other priorities or they may have decided to accept the risk. Another possibility is that they may have decided to mitigate the risk in another way. It can be a useful exercise to review the action plan and update the residual risk levels for the items that have been mitigated. This will give the client a better view of their current security posture and provide the consultant a chance to identify additional possible project work; you might even include limited re-testing of new or updated controls in the check-in.

Structure of a Risk Assessment Report

There are many ways to format and organize a risk assessment report. Shown here is one organizational style:

1. Executive summary
2. Asset-based threat profiles
3. Risk findings
4. Security strategy and plans
   Appendix A: Updated Action Plan Status
   Appendix B: Risk Assessment References
   Appendix C: Third-Party Resources List
   Appendix D: Additional Project Data

We will review each section of this outline in the order it would be in the report itself and mostly, we will focus on the contents of the executive summary, which is the most important section.

Executive Summary

This approach starts with the *obligatory executive summary* section, describes the threat profiles for critical resources, then details the results of the risk evaluation, and finally includes the recommended mitigation steps. The executive summary should include four basic elements:

1. Purpose of analysis
2. Scope of analysis

3. Assessment steps

4. Findings summary

Let's go through each section one by one.

Purpose of Analysis

You will want to start the *executive summary* by describing why you were hired to perform this assessment. This is a great opportunity for you to demonstrate that you understand the motivation behind the engagement and have a clear focus on this organization's specific objectives. Customers are very sensitive to what may be perceived as a boiler plate or template-based assessment report that doesn't focus on their particular environment.

For example, you might include this context about why the project was initiated in your report:

The newly appointed Director of Information Security initiated a risk assessment of XYZ Government Agency. The purpose of this analysis is twofold:

- *Protecting the agency's critical assets*
- *Maintaining compliance with federal directives*

This example describes a possible motivation for XYZ Government Agency to engage a consulting firm to perform a risk assessment of their environment. Including a short mention of the organization's mission can also help the report resonate better with the business audience outside of the security team.

Scope of Analysis

After describing the purpose of the analysis, you will want to include a description of the scope. Be very clear about what is and what is not included in the scope of the assessment. If the client requested that any aspect of the environment be excluded, then state that explicitly. For example:

It is common to exclude some physical security considerations from an assessment that is focused on logical controls. For example, the scope of this assessment included all of XYZ Government Agency's critical assets, such as, production servers and the network infrastructure, but did not include personnel, buildings, and facilities. The following existing documentation was leveraged during the assessment:

- *Prior risk assessments*
- *Threat studies*
- *Applicable internal control reports*

It is also a good idea to include a short statement that the assessment is a point-in-time snapshot of the environment at the time of the engagement and that no guarantees can be made about the state of the environment after that time.

Assessment Steps

Next, you want to provide a high-level breakdown of the steps that were followed during the assessment. This gives the reader a good sense of the due diligence being performed and the thoroughness of the assessment. For example:

The following steps were followed and documented when conducting the assessment of XYZ's environment:

- *A list of all XYZ's critical resources was compiled, including a brief description of the business value to XYZ. Each resource was assigned a value according to its risk sensitivity.*
- *Using a series of different testing techniques, all vulnerabilities were identified for the critical resources, including a brief description of the weakness, how the weakness could affect XYZ, and the categorization of the threat.*
- *A severity and likelihood rating was calculated for each threat/vulnerability pair and a final risk exposure rating was determined based on the* confidentiality, integrity, availability, *and* accountability *(C-I-A-A) needs of each critical resource.*
- *For each of the identified risks, an action was recommended that would bring the risk into an acceptable range of exposure.*

Although the first report format rated the risk exposures based on a single sensitivity value for each critical resource, another way to organize this section of the executive summary would be to focus more on the *confidentiality, integrity, availability,* and *accountability* sensitivities for each resource and the evaluation of the threat/vulnerability pairs for each aspect of C-I-A-A. For example:

To come up with a plan to mitigate and contain these threats, a detailed and systematic information security risk assessment was undertaken to identify the specific exposures that present the highest degree of risk to the organization. The following assessment approach was undertaken:

- *First, company assets (both tangible and intangible) were identified and related business values were documented.*
- *Then, depending upon the criticality of the resource's business value, these assets were evaluated for importance in terms of individual aspects of confidentiality, integrity, availability, and accountability (C-I-A-A).*
- *The C-I-A-A evaluation was used to drive an assessment of the specific threats and related vulnerabilities associated with these resources.*
- *The most likely and most severe risk exposures were identified, and these in turn were used to determine the overall risk exposure of a particular resource.*
- *The risk exposure ratings were used to determine recommended safeguards, which ultimately led to formation of the risk mitigation strategy.*

Hopefully, using these two very different approaches to describe the assessment process as a starting point, you can develop your own format that will highlight the important aspects of your assessment style and priorities. Remember also that this is meant to be one section of an *executive summary*, not a doctoral thesis, so try to keep it brief and to the point.

Findings Summary

The final section of the *executive summary* will be the *findings summary*. The *executive summary* needs to be brief and concise and the *findings summary* should be the major portion of it. This is your chance to highlight any systemic issues, themes that were seen across the organization, controls that would address multiple risks, or critical exposure points.

There are two common ways to organize this section of the executive summary. The first is by going through the risk areas one by one in order of criticality or possibly in the order in which they were discovered. A simple example of this style would be as follows:

There were 14 High and 2 Moderate level risk exposures identified that need to be addressed. Of those 14 High risk items, there are only a couple of issues that need to be addressed immediately. These are ...

The second approach is to organize the risks by threat source or threat activity. If you organize the findings summary by threat vector, you would, for example, group all the risks associated with weak authentication together rather than listing the risks for remote access separately and then describe the risks for internal servers. This technique can help you to identify a significant gap in control maturity for the organization, which may not be as clear if the authentication risks are spread out across various assets.

The following excerpt from an assessment report for XYZ Government Agency illustrates the threat focused format:

Information Disclosure by Weak Authentication:
A risk assessment of the external and internal security posture of XYZ Government Agency found that the present authentication system used by the company's employees to connect to the agency network remotely and to highly sensitive internal systems is vulnerable to compromise. Testers were able to successfully intercept and steal authentication credentials for several executives while connected to the company wireless network from the parking lot of the building and to subsequently use these stolen credentials to authenticate to the company's remote webmail service. Testers were also able to intercept and make use of authentication credentials to impersonate system administrators in order to gain full access to the HR database while plugged into an uncontrolled network connection in a conference room. Due to the high likelihood that these credentials can be stolen and used to compromise sensitive systems without detection, this is considered the biggest risk faced by the company.

When organizing an *executive summary*, it is crucial that you understand your audience. The reality is that executives aren't going to read pages of analysis, but

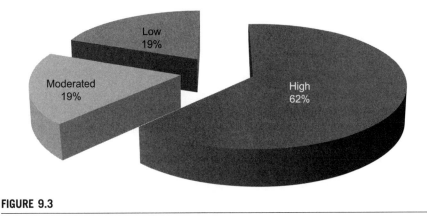

FIGURE 9.3

Sample risk pie chart.

you can catch their attention with meaningful (and colorful) graphs and charts that illustrate a severe control gap or area of great exposure.

One approach would be to use something like a pie chart to illustrate the overall percentage of high- versus low-exposure risks in the environment. Imagine that the high risks in the pie chart, in Figure 9.3, are bright red, whereas the medium and low risks are colored in blue and green, respectively. A lot of red in a report always captures an executive's attention and can help you get your point across quickly and meaningfully.

Figure 9.4 illustrates the risk exposures levels of each resource relative to the others. This particular graph would likely prompt a lot of good discussion when the report is reviewed about why such a critical resources as the *production servers* and *remote access* devices have such high-risk exposure. You might expect to find a lot of vulnerabilities in a desktop environment, but in this example, the servers have almost the same level of exposure. Aggregating all the findings per asset class like this can help for comparison sake, but be careful that this doesn't misrepresent what might be several lower risk findings adding up to surpass a single critical finding.

You might also try the report card or score card style shown in Table 9.2, almost as if you were back in elementary school again. Give each assessment area a grade from A to F and briefly highlight the justification for that grade. Again, no executive can miss a bunch of Ds and Fs in the report.

Ultimately, you will need to use all the tools at your disposal to summarize the most critical exposures and to help the organization to understand their weaknesses without casting blame or coming across as judgmental. The worst thing you can do is embarrass the IT or security team in a meeting with senior management. Always make sure that you review your findings and recommendations with them first and allow them to prepare for any presentation to senior management.

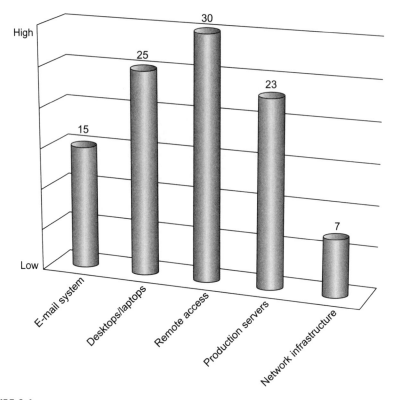

FIGURE 9.4

Sample risk graph.

Table 9.2 An Example of a Risk Score Card		
Topic	**Grade**	**Comments**
Physical	B	Physical security controls, resiliency considerations, and disaster recovery plans are well implemented; however, employees need an awareness training refresher. Testers were able to navigate unescorted into sensitive areas of the building without being challenged.
Internal	C	Several very old vulnerabilities were identified on internal systems, which indicate that the current patch management process is failing.
Remote access	D	Authentication system used to control remote access to the environment has multiple serious vulnerabilities that could lead to unauthorized access by external parties.
Overall Grade	**C**	

Body of the Report

It is common in the body of the report for the focus to be on the results of each individual vulnerability assessment activity, but this way of organizing the information misses the point of a risk assessment. Rather than going through each test and listing the findings, it is better to highlight the risks and include the assessment test findings that pertain to that risk exposure as a way to qualify the risks you are highlighting.

Appendices

The appendices are optional sections that can be used to capture changes in risk during a follow-up assessment, provide links to tools used and advisories referenced, and other resources to supply further context for the findings. It is good practice to include references to any vendor vulnerabilities that you cite in the body of the report. That way, the customer's technical team can do their own research and improve their knowledge of the weakness. Customers are paying for your knowledge and experience, so there is no need to try to keep your methods or tools a secret. Consider the report as another opportunity to spread awareness and provide education about good security hygiene.

You may also want to list some recommended control technologies in an appendix rather than in the body of the report, in order to keep it more objective and vendor neutral. Especially, if you are a consultant who also sells or implements security technologies, it is important to keep your recommendations neutral. Provide the client with several options and talk to them about the pros and cons of each.

Finally, an appendix with all the raw assessment results may be provided on separate media for the technical teams to review and recreate any findings.

Report Language and Style

Be careful about the choice of words and tone in the entire report. If you are performing a true audit, you would include words like "must," but if you are just providing an assessment, you would want to use "should" instead. It's important to set the right tone and give clients the opportunity to find their own solutions to the risks being identified. Even when you are formulating the mitigation strategy or action items, be conscious that these are recommendations and not mandates. Using terms like "recommends" will be received more easily than "will," "must," or even "should."

Executive Communication

Whenever you are analyzing a risk, whether it be as a third-party assessor or an internal employee, it is critical to be laser-focused on the business objectives and model of the organization.

For example, look at this company's business description:

AcmeHealth is a medium sized healthcare benefits software provider in the U.S. AcmeHealth's technology solutions reduce costs, provide market advantage, ensure compliance and improve consumer satisfaction. AcmeHealth's products and services help employers and employees manage complex decisions in an ever-changing healthcare benefits environment. AcmeHealth's Application Service Provider (ASP) solution provides integrated employee health and welfare benefits administration services for active, former and retired employees. Services include annual health plan enrollment, ongoing employee enrollment, benefits continuation, eligibility services, and flexible spending accounts.

Our fully integrated consumer-driven platform allows individuals to take control of their healthcare options through informative decision-making tools. AcmeHealth's applications automate business processes, reduce operating costs and provide access to accurate health information. AcmeHealth is proud of its ability to operate efficiently while responding quickly to the needs of its growing base of customers located in all 50 states and 16 countries. Headquartered in Boston, MA, AcmeHealth is proud to be the fastest growing technology company in the healthcare industry.

The business is an ASP model that deals with health benefits information for the employees of their clients. The flexible spending accounts likely will contain financial account information as well. This should bring to mind several regulations and laws that may be at play. If you were scoping an assessment project for this company, or preparing to present the results of an assessment to their executive team, you would want to focus on the sensitivity of someone's benefit information. In particular, you would want to note whether any of that data requires protection by law or even by contract with their clients. If you go into a meeting with executives focusing on technology deficiencies or even generally spouting industry best practices, you are going to lose the audience quickly. Nothing is worse than seeing the attention of your audience members drop off one by one to their BlackBerries as you try to describe the latest advancements in DLP (Data Leakage Prevention) technologies.

Try to put yourself in the shoes of the business team; is it likely that their clients would switch to another provider after a data breach of the benefits data? Even if it was publicized that internal company data unrelated to their clients were disclosed, how might this affect customer confidence in the organization?

You will always need to tailor your highlighted points to each organization's industry and business model. For example, if this organization provided a software product instead of a hosted service, the focus would be more on the security of their development and testing lifecycle and less on concerns about data disclosure (unless you are worried about the code being leaked). There is no single checklist for what to focus on or what to include in an executive briefing; just be sure to keep your choice of risk findings laser-focused on the mission of the organization. You never want to waste their time talking about risks with insignificant impact potential or negligible probability of occurrence. Save those items for the detailed report or offline discussions with the technical managers.

WRITING AUDIT RESPONSES

As anyone who works with auditors or regulators will tell you, dealing with an audit is a very different process from an internal risk review or engaging an outside consultant to perform an assessment. Auditors will base their review on some defined standard or checklist of controls that are expected to be in place. If you are lucky and get a security-savvy auditor, they may use a risk-based approach to drive which areas of the organization are targeted and which control categories should be highlighted. In general, however, this will be a very structured process involving sampling and validation that the prescribed controls are in place and operating as expected. In particular, this can be a great complement to an existing security baseline review process, which generally doesn't include validation through active testing.

Risk managers need to be closely involved in any active audits in your organization to ensure that existing controls and practices are being represented accurately by the SME to the auditors and that the auditors are aware of any risks that have already been assessed internally. For example, an auditor will want to know that a policy exception has already been granted for a particular area and you can't always rely on the technical SMEs to relay this information.

The typical flow for an audit is as follows:

1. Scope of audit and start date are established.
2. Auditors provide a list of preliminary evidence requests to the organization.
3. Audit begins with meetings and requests for evidence of controls.
4. Auditors review samples of the evidence and ask qualifying questions or request further evidence.
5. Draft report of findings is presented by auditors.
6. A discussion of the findings takes place between auditors and organization (sometimes multiple meetings with management and/or technical representatives).
7. Any revisions or clarifications are made and an audit report is published.
8. Organization writes their response (within 2 weeks or so).
9. Management response is included in the final report.

Any decent auditor is going to come up with some findings because, let's face it, no organization is perfect. The audit finding review and management-response stage is a critical time for risk managers to get involved with the audit process. The ability to effectively translate information between your technical SMEs, the organization's management, and the auditors in terms of risk management principles is both essential as well as rare. When presented with audit findings and recommendations from the auditors, you will need to consider several things, including the following:

- Whether or not you agree with the recommendation.
- How you plan to address it.
- Any compensating controls that you think already meet the intention or lessen the risk.

- Any technical or budget constraints on addressing it.
- Assigning responsibility for addressing the finding.
- Reasonable timeline within which to have it resolved.

Try to arrange with your auditors to review a draft version of the report with them before it is finalized so that you have an opportunity to tweak any language that might be too prescriptive or might not be completely accurate. It is better to correct these errors early on and not be forced to backtrack in your formal management response.

Once the findings are finalized, you will need to work with your management to write the management response. The first question you should ask yourself is whether or not you agree with the finding and/or recommendation. As mentioned earlier, it is better to address these concerns during a review of the draft report, but that isn't always possible. You might start your management response with one of the following:

- Management agrees/concurs …
- Based on our business model, management does not agree with the proposed solution …
- Management believes that the following factors were not accounted for during the assessment …

Next, you will need to lay out how you plan to address the finding. Hopefully, the auditor has left you some flexibility in deciding how to address each finding, but this will depend on the nature of the audit and the style of the auditor. Your management response might continue as follows:

- A high-level design for the solution will be drafted and circulated for internal review by [date] …
- An action plan for remediation will be developed and approved by [date] …
- Development has already begun to address the vulnerability and a fix will be included in the next software release in [date] …
- A review of the current issues and potential solutions will be conducted by [date] …
- A requirements document and project plan for remediation will be completed by [date] …
- We will work with the service provider to document a mutually agreed upon set of enhancements and publish a project plan for implementation by [date] …
- The affected policies and procedure documents will be updated to reflect the recommendations by [date] …
- A new pair of redundant routers has been purchased and will be implemented by [date] …
- Subsequent to the completion of the audit, the vulnerable services were reviewed and removed from the server …

A powerful tool in any audit is the ability to fix a critical issue between when it was identified and when the report is finalized. Especially, if this is a particularly embarrassing issue, or just really easy to fix, consider trying to address it quickly so you can note in your response that the finding has already been closed. When senior management is reading an audit report, this can really help your cause. Depending on the time lag between the audit and report being published, you might include these statements in your management response:

- A formal review process has been established and user awareness training is being rolled out in Q2 of 2012 ...
- IT and Security have researched the feasibility of implementing the recommended controls and determined that ...

Another situation that you might encounter is when you believe that there are already sufficient controls in place to mitigate a risk, but the controls may not match the standard being used by the auditors. Again, these discussions are best to have during the course of the audit or when reviewing the draft report, but sometimes that is not possible. If you think that you have a strong argument for the organization's existing compensating controls, then you might address the management response this way:

- Management believes that the identified risk is otherwise mitigated by the oversight role the *security* group performs by spot checking the assignment of access rights; therefore, the recommended control is not necessary ...
- The recommendation to implement token-based authentication is not necessary because the use of digital certificates is providing a data integrity and authentication check already ...

Even if you agree with the audit finding, it may not be practical for your organization to address the risk in the timeframe recommended by the auditors or in the manner specified. There might be resource, budget, technical, or even business constraints that would prevent you from addressing the risk as recommended. Some typical constraints include the following:

- Assets or environments outside your control
- Contracts or agreements with third party
- Budget/Financial
- Time
- Resources
- Environment
- International Laws

It is always better to be clear about these constraints in your management response and offer an alternative approach than to feel forced into a mitigation plan that has no chance of being successful.

All management responses that include a mitigation plan of any kind need to clearly list the responsible party. There will often be a risk (or finding) owner and also a primary contact for the mitigation actions. The responsible party could be cross-functional, is usually a group or role, and could be any combination of the following typical roles:

- IT group
- Security group
- Executive management
- Vendor management

There could be multiple parties involved in a mitigation plan, and the owner of the risk doesn't have to be in the same functional group as the contact person for the action items. Often, a business unit will own responsibility for a risk, while another group, such as the IT team, will be in charge of the mitigation action.

Another essential element of your management response is a specific timeframe for any mitigation actions. Depending on the format and preference of the auditor, this might be a specific calendar date or a target fiscal year and quarter (such as Q3 2012). One approach is to set a target such as "by the end of Q2" or "in the second half of 2011," but the auditors will generally ask for a more specific target date. At a minimum, any deliverables or commitments in your management response need to have a date and a responsible party clearly listed.

A general guideline for writing management responses is not to be more specific about a solution than you have to be. For example, it would be better to commit to "implementing two-factor authentication for remote access," instead of committing to "using RSA SecurID tokens for all employees to access the network remotely." In case something changes and you find a more appropriate or cost-effective solution, you don't want to be locked into something too prescriptive.

You can also often use generalities to your advantage. For example, you might specify the scope of a remediation action as applying to all "critical resources" versus all "production systems." This gives you the flexibility to use your risk model to determine which resources should be prioritized rather than referring solely to a one-dimensional distinction like which environment they are in; production devices might include a lot of systems of lower sensitivity that don't pose as much risk to the organization.

In responding to audit findings, people often make the mistake of committing to implementing a solution before any analysis has been done about the feasibility or effectiveness of that solution. An SSL VPN might seem like a good solution to your remote access problems during the audit, but you may discover that it doesn't meet all your requirements during the evaluation. If you have already agreed to this solution in your management response, this puts you in a tough position. Better to commit first to evaluating a solution, performing an analysis, or selecting a solution in your management response. This gives you some flexibility to take the time to find the solution that will be the right fit for your organization.

Another important strategy is to first commit to developing a plan or performing an analysis if you have no idea what it will take to resource a mitigation action. Some findings may require significant projects to remediate and it isn't always possible to plan for every step of that mitigation plan when writing your management response. Better to allow the proper time to really plan out the mitigation approach by first committing to developing the plan or strategy by a certain deadline instead of committing to a project completion date that may just be a shot in the dark. This type of management response might state the following:

- A plan will be developed to address ...
- The Security Group is reviewing the weaknesses in this ...
- Remediation of these weaknesses will be prioritized for Q? of this year ...
- IT is in the process of establishing a formal process for addressing ...
- An assessment that included recommendations for improvement and remediation plans will be completed by ...

With these guidelines in mind, hopefully you can show your value to the organization by minimizing the impact that poorly written and scoped management-response commitments can have on the organization. Ultimately, it should be your goal to stay ahead of the auditors in terms of identifying significant risks.

SUMMARY

During an assessment you may be tempted to do only the minimal amount of documentation to justify the risk analysis, but you also need to document any risk decisions that are made. You should have at least a few standard worksheets or forms that are used throughout the assessment process to capture basic analysis details that would help remind you later how you came to a particular conclusion. Generally, you won't be writing formal risk assessment reports for your own internal risk assessments; however, risk managers should be familiar with the basic rules about how to present the results effectively to senior management. Even as a risk manager, you will often have to manage consultants who are performing assessments for you, so it is important to set expectations for how those engagements should be run. As a consultant, the risk assessment report is your last chance to leave a positive lasting impression that will hopefully get you the next gig. You want to use a standard report format that highlights themes and systemic issues, and customize each report to ensure that the content doesn't come across as a boilerplate template. There were many recommendations for working with auditors in this chapter that you may want to share with other groups in your organization who are required to interact regularly with auditors. It can be very dangerous to rush the management-response process. Make sure that committed actions are reasonable and that you use flexible language that won't paint you into a corner.

Action Plan

After reading this chapter, you should consider taking the following actions in your own organization:

- Establish templates or implement existing worksheets to capture the justification for risk ratings and decisions throughout the assessment. Never rely on remembering the details to back up a decision.
- If you are a consultant offering risk assessment services, compare your assessment approach to the structured process in this chapter and fill any gaps.
- Any consultants, or risk managers who write risk reports, should go back through their last two executive summaries with a critical eye, looking for areas where it could be better organized or streamlined further.
- As a consultant, add a step to your project plan to read your client's mission statement before putting together the risk presentation for the senior managers and make sure your highlighted risks are obviously aligned with the client's objectives.
- At a minimum, require that a representative for your team is involved in the prep meetings and management responses for every audit.

References

[1] R.A. Caralli, J.F. Stevens, L.R. Young, W.R. Wilson, Introducing OCTAVE Allegro: Improving the Information Security Risk Assessment Process, Software Engineering Institute, 2007. www.sei.cmu.edu/reports/07tr012.pdf (accessed 01.02.10).
[2] Open Source Security Testing Methodology Manual. www.isecom.org/osstmm (accessed 01.28.11).

Risk Assessment Techniques

10

INFORMATION IN THIS CHAPTER

- Operational Assessments
- Project-Based Assessments
- Third-Party Assessments

INTRODUCTION

Once you have a risk model and a few assessments under your belt, you will want to start thinking strategically about how to manage the regular operational, project, and third-party assessments that will occupy most of your time as a risk manager or analyst. This can quickly become an overwhelming task if not approached strategically, making the best use of the tools and resources that are available. You will want to have a single risk model for the organization, but the actual assessment techniques and methods will need to vary based on the scope of the assessment. An assessment of risk during an incident investigation, for example, must be more streamlined than an architectural risk assessment of a new software application in development.

OPERATIONAL ASSESSMENTS

Do you think that you would use the exact same techniques to perform a risk assessment on a new application or system in development as you would use to assess an entire company during an acquisition? The answer is that you wouldn't. So far, we have established risk models and frameworks, which will be the foundation for any assessment, but how you go about performing that assessment will vary based on the size and nature of the target. It can be helpful to start thinking about categories of assessments, beginning with the distinction between operational assessments, meaning those ongoing day-to-day assessments that are occurring all year long, and project-based assessments which have a finite duration. The operational assessments will encompass regular assessments of emerging threats, newly announced vulnerabilities, and discovered standard violations, just to name a few. Operational assessments should not be confused with assessments of risks in the operations domain. In this context, operational describes the format of the assessment, indicating that these are ongoing and revolving assessments with no clear endpoint, as opposed to assessments of projects that have set completion dates. In contrast, an assessment of the operations domain would define the scope of the assessment, which would focus on threats to operations continuity. We are focusing on the former for the purposes of this discussion.

Some examples of operational risk assessment tasks in the information security space include the following:

- Threat analysis
- Vulnerability scanning
- Patch remediation
- Penetration Testing
- Incident prioritization
- Exception processing
- Compliance to standards reviews
- Certification and accreditation (C&A)
- Auditing (internal or external)
- Responses to client due diligence evaluations
- Vendor on-site reviews
- Regulatory gap analysis

As you can see, this list is rather diverse, and even so, it doesn't even begin to cover all the various tasks for which a security risk management team might be responsible. It just wouldn't be practical to use the exact same approach and techniques for each of these tasks, but fortunately, the fundamentals stay the same. It is really just the tools and format of the assessment that change with the type of task. For example, a vulnerability scan of your Internet presence is going to require a technical tool or service to perform security scanning of vulnerabilities, but an on-site review of a service provider's physical security controls is going to require a body with a clipboard and a list of required controls. Likewise, you aren't going to require an on-site physical assessment of Dell's facility just because they provide your server hardware, but you would want to perform that on-site assessment of an offshore development center that provides 80% of the code for your products. When you are establishing your risk management program, start by thinking about the different levels of resources that you will be assessing and map out which methodology will be most efficient for each.

Operational Techniques

For all those potential operational assessments, your options really come down to just a few assessment formats:

- Questionnaire
- Interview
- Passive testing

- Active testing
- Review of third-party assessment
- Acceptance of a certification

When it comes to internal or third-party assessments, you should consider mapping the depth and intrusiveness of the assessment technique to the risk sensitivity of the service being provided. For example, a review of an independent assessment report or a passive test, such as conducting a Google search for information about your organization, will usually be nonintrusive, requiring mostly only your own team's resources. For those resources that have lower risk sensitivities or have already been reviewed in the past without any significant findings, you may want to consider these approaches to minimize your impact on staff from other business units.

Questionnaires and Interviews

The first two techniques are questionnaires and interviews, and we will address them together since, ultimately, a questionnaire is just a passive version of an interview. Choosing which is appropriate can often be difficult and it may come down to trial and error to determine which one your organization responds to better, but hopefully, these guidelines will give you a good place to start. First, the benefit of an interview style assessment versus a questionnaire is that a skilled assessor can use the responses to a static question to guide their follow-up questions and direct which additional questions they ask. For instance, if you are assessing the IT environment and you have a series of questions about password controls (length, complexity, change history, expiration, initial distribution, reset procedures, and so on), but the system in question uses digital certificates or cryptographic keys instead, you can skip all the remaining password questions and drill into the key management questions on the fly. To do this with a questionnaire, you either need to program some logic into an online questionnaire or you will be doing a lot of back and forth follow-up questions about why they selected "N/A" for all your password questions.

Especially, if you are doing an internal assessment, you would be surprised how many additional risks you can uncover just by getting several people in a room at once and listening to them disagree about how something actually works. The manager will give you one answer, the engineer will correct him, and the junior engineer who recently joined the team will say "nobody told me that was the procedure." Of course, the above scenario assumes that some level of trust has already been established, that the culture supports healthy disagreement in public, and that your assessor understands the power of just listening. A side benefit of the interview technique can often be increased awareness among the team being assessed about what is expected from a security perspective and, as a result, bad practices can often be corrected right then. In contrast to that situation is the defensive interviewee or the subject who is actively offended that anyone would dare question their practices. If you suspect that might be the case, then a questionnaire might be the more effective way to go.

No matter how long you spend crafting the "perfect" questionnaire, you will always have questions that are misunderstood. If the question isn't clear, you will probably experience one of the following responses from the person answering the questionnaire (in order of likelihood, from most to least likely):

1. Skip the question altogether
2. Select "N/A" if it is an option
3. Give up on the questionnaire entirely and not finish it
4. Answer the question with a "No" just to be safe
5. Ask for clarification

You may wish that response 5 was more common, but with so many pulls on resources' time, you are probably going to have to hunt down the responder to find out that there was a question they didn't understand. You can minimize this situation by trying to provide organization-specific examples along with each question. A targeted example can go a long way toward clarifying the intent of the question. Of course, when conducting an interview, you can address any confusion immediately, which minimizes the time lost and the frustration experienced by both sides.

As a general rule, using an interview style is going to give you the richest and most accurate information in the shortest amount of time, assuming you can get the right people in a room all at once. It may seem onerous to schedule all these interviews and coordinate resources, but it gets you exposure to many critical functions in the organization and will be your quickest option. The challenge is that interviews don't scale well for large organizations, so you will need to prioritize where you use a questionnaire versus an interview. One approach is to use an interview for the first assessment and a questionnaire for each subsequent assessment for that same resource. That way, you get a detailed risk assessment and understanding of the resource up front, but can scale back the resource effort over time. Another approach is to send out a questionnaire and schedule an in person meeting with everyone involved to review the answers and discuss any follow-up questions. With this approach, you leverage the benefits of both assessment formats.

Active and Passive Testing

Questionnaires and interviews might work well for identifying policy violations or process weaknesses, but to really evaluate the technical vulnerabilities in your environment, you will need to perform some sort of security testing. Although passive testing sounds harmless, beware that the definition of passive is not always consistent across the field. There are definitely gray areas to be aware of; any testing should require appropriate senior management approval. Most security scanners or vulnerability scanners are tools with large databases of known attacks and weaknesses and will scan the environment for signs of vulnerabilities or compromises. These tools will also typically have the ability to identify missing patches, configuration mistakes, or denial-of-service weaknesses.

Security scanning tools are very common. Many will focus on general operating system and commercial application vulnerabilities, but others specialize in mapping environments or testing Web applications for weaknesses. Most will only look for signs of a weakness, while others also include the option to validate a vulnerability by actually exploiting it. Any tool that will actually verify a weakness by executing the exploit would be considered a penetration testing tool, not just a scanner. There are many open source and commercial scanners available. A few of the most common ones are as follows:

- Nessus (free and commercial versions available)
- NMap (free)
- ISS
- Retina
- Nexpose
- Foundscan
- Qualys
- Core Impact
- AppScan
- WebInspect

This list doesn't even come close to being inclusive, especially as you start to look at specialized scanners for targets like wireless networks and Web applications. A great list of the top 100 network security tools is available on Gordon Lyon's SecTools site [1], and many of these tools are security scanners of some kind. Gordon is the author of the NMap scanner, so he knows a little something about the topic.

The scope of an active or passive test can range greatly depending on your organization's particular concerns. For example, the following are all typical types of assessments:

- Enterprise vulnerability assessment (active)
- Penetration testing analysis (active)
- Wireless security assessment (active)
- Blackbox application testing (active)
- Malicious threat assessment (passive)
- Internet reconnaissance (passive)
- Application code security review (passive)

Most of these should have an obvious scope; however, *malicious threat assessment* and *Internet reconnaissance* both likely need some further explanation. Typically, a *malicious threat assessment* would involve putting a passive security device at key network aggregation points to review traffic for potential malicious activity or policy violations. This is sometimes accomplished by temporarily putting a specialized Network Intrusion Detection System (NIDS) device, or an anomalous network activity monitoring device like the Riverbed Cascade (formerly known as Mazu) analyzer, on the network, and reviewing the alarms that are triggered. This is a passive test because at no point is there any chance that the normal operations of the network can be impacted. Signatures and anomaly detection techniques aren't perfect, so it may be useful to conduct one of these tests every so often, even if you already have intrusion detection systems (IDS) deployed in your environment. Just having an analyst look at your network traffic for a week without the prejudices of what is expected or suspicious can often uncover unknown issues.

WARNING

No matter what kind of testing is proposed and how much the tester assures you that there will be zero impact to your environment, be very cautious. Even the deployment of a passive monitoring device on your network could impact operations if, for example, the device is accidently assigned an IP address that is already being used by another critical server. This may sound implausible, but be assured—it really happens! Better to be cautious and run installs of even passive monitoring devices through proper change management processes.

An *Internet reconnaissance* test should be focused on assessing the organization's profile based on what information is publicly available on the Internet. Domain registries, the organization's financial statements, career postings, and vendor case studies are all sources of information about an organization that could be used by an attacker. Google has actually become a primary tool for would-be attackers to profile an organization looking for weaknesses that can be exploited by technical means or through social engineering. Any organization needs to have some level of public presence, a point that is emphasized by the introduction of the White House as an active participant on Facebook during the Obama administration. The point of this type of testing is to have someone with the knowledge of typical data mining techniques look at the organization's profile from an Internet perspective and identify unnecessary information risks. Like other passive testing methods, this assessment presents no risk of an operational disruption to the organization.

Most active testing will involve either a tool or a person performing functions against a resource to look for known responses, which indicate that a vulnerability is present. For example, an active scan of your environment would look for known vulnerabilities and improper configurations that could allow an attacker unauthorized access to a resource. It is always recommended that you scan your environment both internally and externally so that you get an idea of what would be visible to any outside attackers as well as potentially malicious insiders. It is a good idea to publish a formal schedule for scanning and to communicate this to resource owners and administrators. You may need to do your scanning during off-hours or maintenance windows to avoid affecting a production service. After all, no matter how much time you put into tuning your scanner, you can't guarantee zero impact to the environment being scanned, and resource administrators need to be prepared to respond if needed to a disruption.

One focus of security testing needs to be to validate that current controls are behaving as expected. It isn't enough to just implement a set of controls; you need to evaluate those controls to ensure they are really reducing your risk exposure to the level you expect. Controls also require constant tuning and adjustment, especially with the growing sophistication and persistence of attackers, and you will need to be constantly monitoring each layer of controls to see which attacks are getting through. If you think that your firewall is locked down, run a port scan to verify. If you are relying on your anti-virus software to catch the latest threats, introduce a few sample pieces of malware into an isolated and controlled environment to see the detection rate (virtualization with no network connectivity can be a great test bed). If you think that peer review of application code is catching the violations of coding standards, have a security architect review a random sampling of code to validate. As they say, trust but verify.

In addition to regular scanning and other internal assessments, it is crucial to have outside experts come in periodically to assess different parts of the security program by performing penetration testing on the network or Web application, or by trying to bypass physical controls like gaining access to a secured area without a badge. This will help you to identify weak areas that need more attention and can also help you validate the threat vectors that you have assessed as most likely.

Third-Party Reviews and Certifications
When working with vendors and service providers, you are going to need to rely on other means of assessing the security posture of the third party. Most service providers aren't going to let you show up at their offices with a security scanner and just let you go nuts on their environment (at least we hope they won't!). Thus begins the negotiation of best evidence. You might think of this as a similar dilemma to what you would see in court. Direct evidence may not always be available, so you may need to rely on alternatives like maybe an expert witness. The same is often true when assessing a third-party provider—you may not be allowed to walk through their Security Operations Center (SOC) or run your own penetration test against their Internet-facing systems, but they should provide you some indication that they have had an independent third-party assessor perform these tests and that any high-risk findings are being addressed appropriately. The debate about the appropriate level of detail to require will be discussed in depth later in this chapter, but suffice to say for now that you likely shouldn't expect a copy of a penetration report, but it might be reasonable to request an executive summary. After all, the provider also has to manage the risks inherent in distributing active exploit details.

If report summaries from independent assessors are not available, the next best thing would be a certification that demonstrates a certain level of security posture and program maturity. For example, you might recognize an ISO 27001 or SAS70 Type II certification as being sufficient proof of robust security controls for the organization. Eventually, the industry will need to develop a certification that covers all the areas of review in the 800 to 3,000 question evaluations that some customers are requiring their providers to complete, but as a field, we aren't there yet. The SAS70 certification, for example, can be a fantastic evaluation of security controls, but the scope will vary between organizations depending on what they chose to include in the review and the level of detail in the report. This makes the certification hard for risk managers to use as a consistent indicator of excellence.

Baseline Reviews

In terms of operational risk assessments, another important focus is Certification and Accreditation (C&A). For many business professionals, these terms may not be meaningful, but don't worry: like with the term *information assurance*, you will most often see these terms in the context of the US federal government. Although the terminology isn't popular in private industry yet, the function actually is already in use. On the most basic level, C&A tasks require establishing a security baseline for each system in your environment, ensuring any new deployments are compliant with the baseline, monitoring the configuration of the system over time to be sure it doesn't deviate from the baseline, and documenting any areas where the system can't comply with the baseline. In essence, a C&A process is meant to formalize the standards for configuring a system securely and force an explicit review of those controls and authorization decision to allow it to operate in an environment.

Certification and accreditation are really both subsets of an overall *information security risk management* program. Risk management is the overall program for identifying weaknesses, threats to those weaknesses, and assessing the impact to the organization that might result from an exploitation of those weaknesses. Certification is the process of evaluating whether the system/application meets the minimum standards that have been established, and *accreditation* is the management decision process to determine if any deviations from standards are acceptable. When you think about this in basic terms, it essentially equates to a risk assessment followed by a risk decision. In the US federal government, there are very explicit job roles and positions involved in this process; however, most corporations use a combination of the resource owner or operator and a representative from the security team to negotiate these details.

There are two contexts in which the term "baseline" is used for Information Security. The first is referring to a point in time snapshot of the current state of the environment as a comparison point. The second is the minimum set of required configuration settings or controls to meet a desired level of security. In this chapter, we are using the latter definition—just think of it as a secure configuration template.

There are many activities required to make a C&A process run smoothly, and many of these tasks will be performed by the resource administrators or operations teams, with oversight from the Information Security team. As part of the change management process, the postimplementation steps of updating documentation such as network diagrams, server build documents, software hash libraries, standard build images, and so on should be performed. A good practice is to create a hash library of known good software in your environment; that way, when there is an investigation of a system compromise, you can easily identify software and configuration files that have not been tampered with because they match the unique hash you created in advance.

Many organizations also run regular (as often as nightly) scans of server configuration files to ensure they still meet the baseline, and if any deviations are found, they get escalated to management and the security team to investigate the cause. When a deviation from the baseline is required due to technical constraints or for specific business purpose, the justification, risk evaluation, and approval needs to be documented and processed like any other risk acceptance. This assessment needs to happen before the system/application "goes live" or is released and regularly until it is decommissioned. It is important to ensure that this requirement is communicated to all project managers and stakeholders so that they can account for this time upfront when they create a project schedule. You will also need to establish who has the authority to keep the system/application from going live or being released if there is a serious security issue. You may hear this authority referred to as the "red lever." This is the person who the organization has established as having the authority to stop a system from going into production or to shut down an existing system if the exposure warrants it. Accreditation is not a permanent state; the security of any system/application needs to be re-evaluated periodically, usually on a set schedule, the frequency of which should depend on the sensitivity of the resource. The NIST Special Publication 800-37 Revision 1 [2] is a great reference for anyone who is involved in C&A work. It has evolved in this revision from a rather static and inflexible process into a risk-focused lifecycle methodology.

Assessment Approaches for Different Sized Scopes

When you are faced with assessing a very large environment, "random sampling" should be the first words that come to mind. It may be feasible to perform full port and vulnerability scans on 20 systems in a reasonable amount of time without putting a dangerous load on the systems or the network, but think about the logistics if you needed to assess 2,000 systems. At that point, is there really any value in documenting the same weaknesses across all 2,000 systems? You don't need a sample size that big to establish a pattern. Especially if you are in a consultant role, you will want to very carefully consider what scope of assessment would be a productive use of time and resources. Remember that whatever you test, you will need to document and report on. Because of these considerations, and just like auditors have been doing forever, random sampling is the best approach.

Similarly, there are often debates about whether automated penetration testing is sufficient for a thorough assessment, as opposed to having a highly skilled ethical tester hacking away at the application or system manually. Clearly, the latter option is preferred, but it is also typically not possible as the only method of testing on large-scale assessments. If you are looking to assess a specific function in an application that uses a proprietary protocol, then maybe a purely manual penetration test is the right solution, but for large-scale assessments, any tester is going to use a hybrid of some level of automation along with manual testing.

PROJECT-BASED ASSESSMENTS

Chapters 11 and 12 will cover daily risk assessment activities that continue on a constant cycle, but for now, let's first look at how best to approach an assessment with a defined endpoint based on a single project. The three most common projects that will require a risk assessment are as follows. Each requires a slightly different approach and has its own challenges.

- Software development
- Software/technology acquisition
- Selection of third-party service provider

The scope of an assessment can vary greatly, from a new product enhancement to the acquisition of another company. However, the process and deliverables are going to be the same, even if the subject matter varies. The important distinction here is that this is a point-in-time assessment and not an on-going process like operational assessment activities, which we have previously discussed. Because of this, it is necessary to have a set project timeline and clear deliverables to guide the assessment.

Risk Assessments in the Project Lifecycle

Generally, the motivation for this type of risk assessment will be to demonstrate due diligence and assess the level of risk being undertaken by the project. These assessments need to be performed as early in the project's lifecycle as possible so that it can be properly influenced by the results of the assessments from the beginning. Otherwise, time and effort may be lost if the team is allowed to go too far down a flawed path. A security risk assessment can be performed by just about anyone involved in the project team if given the proper guidelines, and occasionally, the project may require an outside party to guide the assessment. Your organization's culture will strongly influence who should lead each assessment, but generally the responsibility will fall on the Information Security team.

The output of this assessment will include the identification of risks, threats, and general concerns from the team and, ultimately, recommendations for controls to mitigate those threats. The analysis and recommendations would then generally be presented to senior management or other project stakeholders to make the final decisions. You should notice that this is no different than any other assessment methodology that has been introduced so far, so what really distinguishes the project-based assessment is that it is time-boxed and is designed to be a point-in-time evaluation.

The FRAAP Approach

If you are interested in a structured approach to an accelerated assessment, Thomas Peltier has coined the term Facilitated Risk Analysis and Assessment Process (FRAAP) [3] to describe his approach to managing a risk assessment of a project in a short timeframe. Using this streamlined approach, you can cut down the time it takes to gather risk data and produce recommendations, while still getting the appropriate Subject Matter Experts (SMEs) involved. The goal is to conduct the assessment in a matter of 4 to 8 hours and then produce the recommendations within a few days of the assessment session. This can really help to keep projects on track and minimize the time requirements on the SMEs. Within this model, it is especially important to define a structured agenda and strict roles for each participant. In doing so, you can avoid risk discussions that can drag on and drift far from the focus area. The role of the Information Security representative is to facilitate the discussions rather than dictate the direction they take. Depending on the topic, there might be several business units or departments represented in the session. Some of them are listed here as follows:

- Functional owner
- Business analyst
- System engineer
- Database administrator
- Network administrator
- System programmer
- Application programmer
- Functional manager
- Information security
- Legal
- Human resources

If you are serving as the facilitator for the meeting, then it is best to have someone else on your team attend to represent Information Security. This way you can focus on the facilitator's responsibilities and not be perceived as pushing your own agenda. The idea behind the FRAAP format is to run a session that encourages the participants to raise issues and identify risks, without spiraling out of control with side discussions and tangents. Once the risks have been identified, the team analyzes the impacts and agrees on the likely consequences of those risks. Then, each risk is rated in terms of the priority to the organization.

For the most part, this analysis relies on the expertise and knowledge of the people in the room, including representatives from the security team, but it can also be influenced by other data about the resources or observed trends in the industry that were gathered prior to the assessment session. Activities like brainstorming serve an important role in Peltier's FRAAP approach, but there is also enough structure to the assessment format that it should be able to keep the session productive.

Prep Work

Before you lock everyone in a room for 8 hours talking about risks, you will need to do some preparation work. Set up a 1-hour pre-session meeting with the primary stakeholder, project lead, and session facilitator to discuss the goals, agenda, and format for the session. Keep this meeting short and focused. Peltier recommends five deliverables for this meeting:

- Draft a scope statement for the initiative and the assessment.
- Obtain visual diagrams of any resource components, inter-dependencies, or information flows.
- Select the team members for the actual assessment session.
- Decide on meeting logistics, such as location, timing, supplies, food, and so on.
- Agree on definitions of any controversial terms such as the following:
  - Confidentiality, integrity, availability, accountability
  - Risk
  - Threat
  - Vulnerability
  - Impact
  - Control

Having this defined up front and published to the assessment team will avoid wasting time at the beginning of the session trying to get everyone on the same page.

The assessment session itself should last between 4 and 8 hours, depending on the size of the project and shouldn't include more than 15 participants. If you can get everyone into a room off-site or at least away and disconnected from everyday distractions, then the sessions will be far more efficient. The last thing you want to see is everyone sitting around the table answering e-mails on their laptops or BlackBerries. Expectations need to be set early that this time will be dedicated to the project and the assessment activity.

The facilitator will want to come to the assessment session prepared with materials, such as flipcharts and markers, printed copies of the terminology definitions, a clear scope statement, and any visual diagrams that might be appropriate. It is recommended to distribute the materials from the pre-session meeting in advance. This gives the participants the opportunity to review them in advance, gather any information that they might need for the meeting, and also identify if they are not the right resource to be involved in the assessment. You should, however, also assume that the majority of people will not review the materials in advance, so plan to spend a few minutes summarizing the scope at the beginning of the meeting.

Running the Session

The assessment session itself should only last between 4 and 8 hours. You will have to consider your audience, scope of the assessment, and the culture of your organization when choosing the length of the session. Some assessments may be hard to complete thoroughly in just 4 hours, but you also have to account for people's attention span and other draws on their time. Scheduling any large group can be difficult, so the shorter the session, the better chance you have of getting everyone together. The session itself should have three deliverable goals. There is no one single way to capture this information, so experiment with a few approaches and choose the format that works best for you.

1. Identify the risks
2. Prioritize the risks
3. Identify controls to mitigate the top priority risks

One way to start off the session is to go around the room and ask each participant to identify any risks associated with confidentiality. Set a maximum time for this exercise (say 3 minutes per person) and capture all the ideas, then go around the room again and spend the same amount of time listing all the integrity risks. Repeat this process again for availability and accountability to create a comprehensive list of risks. Alternatively, you could begin by going around the room and asking each participant to list one issue or concern that they have with the project. When you're facilitating a session, keep in the mind the usual brainstorming tips, such as the following:

- Remain neutral at all times
- Don't judge or dismiss any ideas
- Ensure that all ideas are captured
- Solicit input from everyone
- Only let one person speak at a time
- Don't let any one person dominate the conversation

To keep the session moving forward, the facilitator needs to be very strict about following these general brainstorming guidelines. Especially for security professionals, it can be hard to stay in character as the facilitator and not comment on the issues or ideas being raised as you would when wearing your security hat, but this separation of roles is important to the success of the session. It can be difficult to find the balance between allowing participants to be creative and not letting any one personality dominate the discussion. A good way to avoid this is by cutting people off after 3 minutes or so. Otherwise, you may find the session spending too much time on a single issue and missing others. Be sure to have someone tasked with recording all the ideas and issues being raised, and defer those that are out of scope for this project. Finally, be sure to manage the group so that you only have one conversation going at a time; if the debate gets heated, you may need to mediate to keep the conversation productive and above the line.

Next, look at each identified risk and analyze the severity of each. Then, take each of those risks and rate it based on the likelihood of occurrence. Following this, you will want to prioritize the risks based on their risk rating and focus the rest of the session on the higher exposure items. The assessment and analysis will be captured in worksheets, similar to the worksheets provided as a part of OCTAVE Allegro, which we will explore in Chapter 11.

Sample Worksheets

Having a structured assessment approach is essential to the viability of the FRAAP approach; so, this section provides several worksheets that can be used to capture the artifacts of each step of the FRAAP session. Keep in mind that each worksheet has been slightly adapted from the typical FRAAP worksheet to meet the risk model used in this book, but the general concepts remain the same.

The first step in the session is to start identifying concerns or risks, assign them a risk type (C-I-A-A), and identify the resource affected by the risk. You can see an example of this in Figure 10.1.

Once you have completed the brainstorming, review the list of risks identified and eliminate any duplicates. You should now have a list of categorized risks with the associated resources identified. Next, on the *resource sensitivity profile* worksheet (Figure 10.2), you will start out by listing each resource from the first worksheet.

Once you have listed all of the resources, include a very short description of that asset's sensitivity or importance to the organization. Use this description to guide your rating of the resource's *confidentiality*, *integrity*, *availability*, and *accountability* sensitivities using the same Low-Moderate-High scale from our

		Risk description list	
#	Risk type	Risk description (vulnerability and consequences)	Resource
0	Confidentiality	Sensitive account information is discarded in the regular trash, which could lead to disclosure of customer financial accounts to unauthorized internal or external parties. Disclosure of this data violates several state privacy laws.	Paper statements
1	————	———— ————	————

FIGURE 10.1

Risk description list worksheet.

		Resource sensitivity profile					
#	Resource impacted	Sensitivity description	Confid	Integ	Avail	Acct	Overall
0	Paper copies of client account statements	Client account statements include the client's name, financial account number, address, and current balance. This information is protected by several regulations and privacy laws. Disclosure could lead to financial fraud and liability for the organization, or legal penalties.	High	Low	Low	Moderate	High
1	————	———— ————	——	——	——	——	——

FIGURE 10.2

Resource sensitivity profile worksheet.

#	Brief vuln desc.	Threat category	Threat activity	Risk exposure rating			
				Like	Sev	Sens	Exposure
0	Account information in trash	External targeted attack	A criminal could pull a few client's sensitive financial account information out of the dumpster behind the office and use it for fraudulent purposes.	High	Moderate	High	High
1	Account information in trash	Internal abuse	An employee could pull sensitive financial account information for all clients out of the trash cans in the office and use it for fraudulent purposes.	Moderate	High	High	High
2	_____	_____	_____ _____	___	___	___	___

FIGURE 10.3

Risk exposure rating worksheet.

earlier *security risk profile*. Finally, determine the overall sensitivity for the resource based on highest of the individual C-I-A-A values.

At this point, you have identified the risks and their associated resources and rated the sensitivity to risk for each resource. Next, you will need to break each risk into its threat and vulnerability components, as shown in Figure 10.3.

Notice in the example in Figure 10.3 that one initial risk has been separated into two different combinations of threat/vulnerability pairs with slightly different risk ratings. This illustrates how the combinations of threats and vulnerabilities can result in different risk exposures depending on the threat category. The threat categories being used are as follows:

- Natural disaster
- Infrastructure failures
- Internal abuse
- Accidents
- External targeted attacks
- External mass attacks

In this worksheet, the likelihood and severity of the threat/vulnerability pair is combined with the sensitivity of the resource from the previous worksheet to derive the final exposure rating.

You can use the qualitative mapping table from Chapter 6 to derive the exposure value from the likelihood, severity, and sensitivity ratings.

Once the risks have been captured and rated, you will need to identify the controls that will mitigate them. You can start with a list from one of the numerous industry resources available (for example, ISO, NIST, NSA) or you can build your own custom list. Often, organizations will publish a list of approved or existing controls and technologies. This can help to reduce the complexity of the environment and increase the reusability of previous investments.

A good place to start is with the *20 Critical Security Controls for Effective Cyber Defense* [4]. These Top 20 Controls were agreed upon by a consortium US government representatives, which included the National Security Agency (NSA), US Computer Emergency Readiness Team (US CERT), the Department of Defense Joint Task Force-Global Network Operations (DoD JTF-GNO), the Department of Energy Nuclear Laboratories, the Department of State, and the Department of Defense Cyber Crime Center, plus the top commercial forensics experts and penetration testers that serve the banking and critical infrastructure communities.

Use the *mitigating controls list* worksheet shown in Figure 10.4 to capture the mitigating controls that could be implemented to address the risks identified above, including the control type of *preventative*, *detective*, or *responsive*. You will use this worksheet to map each risk to the control that will adequately mitigate it. When choosing controls, follow these guidelines:

- Identify controls that address multiple risks
- Focus on cost-effective solutions
- The total cost of the control should be proportional to the value of the asset

In many cases, multiple controls will be needed to properly mitigate a single risk. Likewise, a single control may mitigate several risks. In the original FRAAP worksheets, there are a few interim worksheets to help illustrate the effects of mapping the controls to the risks and the risks to the controls. This can help you see the controls that will give you the most bang for your buck. For the sake of simplicity, those worksheets have been eliminated here and have been replaced with the single *action plan* worksheet in Figure 10.5. The last worksheet (Figure 10.4) was a simple list of each risk and the controls that could be used to mitigate it in the order the risks were identified. The *action plan* worksheet should summarize all the information that you have gathered so far for each of the priority items. These should be listed in order of importance.

You want to start by focusing on the risks with the highest ratings because they require the most immediate attention. The moderate risks will need attention soon and the low risks can be dealt with when time and resources are available. You may also focus on prioritizing the controls that mitigate the most risks. When you are recommending actions, remember to think about the time and resources

Mitigating controls list			
#	Brief risk desc	Control type	Control description
X	Insider stealing paper statements	Preventative	Paper cross-cut shredder in all the mail rooms
Y	Insider stealing paper statements	Preventative	Data classification and handling policy, requiring the use of a shredder for all sensitive documents
1	————————	————	————————————————————————————

FIGURE 10.4

Mitigating controls list worksheet.

				Action plan				
#	Brief risk desc	Risk type	Rating	Control	Priority	Owner action	By whom	When
1	Insider stealing paper statements	CONF, ACCT	High	X, Y	6	Buy a shredder and install in convenient location, and publish a handling policy	Administrative staff	4/30/07
2								

FIGURE 10.5

Action plan worksheet.

that will be required to execute on the plan. There is no value in listing action items that aren't practical.

Be sure to identify who is responsible for each item and include a deadline. As you are considering mitigating controls, always keep in mind that accepting a risk as-is may be an option as well.

Reporting

After the completion of the assessment session, your goal should be to have the report ready within 4 to 6 days. Because a template is being used to gather the information, it will be easier to compile into an assessment and recommendations report. The report is generally written by the session facilitator. Finally, a postsession meeting or meetings should be held with the stakeholders to present the report. This may be done in two or more meetings: one for an executive level overview and one to dive into more detail about each issue.

The FRAAP approach is just one technique for adding structure to your project-based risk assessments. Its value is in the defined agenda, roles, and worksheets for capturing, rating, and mitigating risks. As was illustrated here, the model is flexible enough to allow you to expand on the worksheets and risk scales themselves over time to incorporate them into a different risk model. If you expect to perform any project-based assessments, it is highly recommended that you read Peltier's book *Information Security Risk Analysis*.

THIRD-PARTY ASSESSMENTS

Earlier in this chapter, we started to lay out the challenges that quickly present themselves when dealing with third-party assessments. Almost every organization these days is experiencing this struggle from both sides of the relationship, as the client performing a due diligence evaluation and as the provider answering client or partner queries. This process can quickly become a huge drain on your resources if not managed properly. Let's pull back the curtain and look at the inner workings of this process from behind the scenes.

As noted earlier, the first issues you will encounter are the lack of an industry standard format for vendor risk assessment questionnaires and the lack of a universally accepted certification as an alternative to individual evaluations from clients. What makes it even worse is that even among clients who are looking for the same general information, each questionnaire will word the questions just differently enough that you can't even reuse your answers. So, you will need to have staff who are capable of crafting appropriate answers to these questions based on their knowledge of your security controls without giving away too much information, all the while responding in as positive a manner as possible so as to discourage follow-up questions. People with this skill are not easy to come by. To make matters even worse, you may get multiple questionnaires from different parts of the same company, and you can't even count on the questionnaires staying the same from year to year from a single client. As their programs grow and mature, they change the focus of their questions so that you basically end up having to start from scratch each year.

Industry Standard Assessments

Hopefully, you didn't just read that long list of issues and give up because solutions to these problems are available. Now that we have adequately framed out the context for the challenges, let's talk about these solutions. In the short-term, the solution that can have the largest positive impact would be creating a standardized set of vendor due diligence questions in a common format to eliminate the need for so many customized responses. This will greatly speed up the request turnaround time and allow service providers the ability to provide the most accurate answers possible. With so many ad hoc requests coming in, it can be challenging to always find the right SME to provide a definitive response and you can be sure that some clients ask some very obscure questions.

The good news is that there is a standard questionnaire emerging out of the financial services industry that could meet this need if adoption of it continues to expand quickly outside of this industry. Out of the BITS Financial Services Roundtable, there emerged a Standardized Information Gathering (SIG) questionnaire [5], which is aligned with the Federal Financial Institutions Examination Council (FFIEC) guidelines, and the Agreed Upon Procedures (AUP) report, which can be provided as a substitute for individual client tests of stated security procedures. The value of these tools has been proven by several large and small organizations; however, its usefulness all hinges on universal adoption of this format between businesses and their providers, and between businesses and their clients/partners. Version 6 of the SIG was released in 2010, but you will likely see organizations using a variety of versions from 3 to 5 as they transition to the newer version, which promises to have streamlined the number of questions down from several thousand to a more manageable number. The breadth of topics covered include the typical security operations and policy questions that you might expect, as well as sections ranging from physical security and business continuity to privacy. As a standard, the SIG is far from universal, but adoption is growing at a fast pace, to the point where some of the leading GRC tools have integrated it into their software offerings.

Levels of Assessment

This section certainly isn't meant to be an advertisement for the SIG, but there are several features of the implementation that make it worth highlighting. The first is (as of version 5) the flexibility to roll out three levels of detail, a level 1, a level 2, and a detailed version. Version 5's level 1 contains around 100 questions, which lends itself really well to a client due diligence request during the early stages of a vendor review when a Non-Disclosure Agreement (NDA) may not have been established yet and sales needs a really quick turnaround. Using the level 1 questionnaire, you can quickly identify if there are any red flags or show-stoppers that would cause you to reject the vendor as a candidate, without the vendor having to give away too much about their controls. The *version 5, level 2* questionnaire is more detailed, with closer to 400 questions, so this might be more appropriate for later in the contract negotiations, either after the contract has been signed or at least when an NDA is in place.

Another way to make use of the levels in the SIG is when you are performing due diligence reviews of your own vendors and service providers. It allows you to base the level of SIG required on the sensitivity level of the service being provided. One possible schedule for assessments is shown in Table 10.1.

This particular schedule might assume that there was no high-exposure risk found during the review in the first year. You could set a threshold for the number or level of the findings to determine the frequency and depth of the assessments performed. Another consideration to keep in mind is that vendors in your category of low sensitivity might not require a full formal review at all. Vendors who, for example, just provide you desktop and laptop hardware probably don't need to answer 20 questions about privacy controls; so, you might implement a modified version of the schedule, as shown in Table 10.2.

In this scenario, the SIG level 1 would be used only for the moderate-sensitivity vendors, and the low-sensitivity vendors would undergo any formal SIG assessment beyond the basic security questions that would be asked during

Table 10.1 SIG-Based Vendor Schedule—Example 1

Service Sensitivity	First Year	Second Year	Third Year	Fourth Year
High	SIG detailed	SIG level 2	SIG detailed	SIG level 2
Moderate	SIG level 2	N/A	SIG level 1	N/A
Low	SIG level 1	N/A	N/A	SIG level 1

Table 10.2 SIG-Based Vendor Schedule—Example 2

Service Sensitivity	First Year	Second Year	Third Year	Fourth Year
High	SIG detailed	SIG level 2	SIG detailed	SIG level 2
Moderate	SIG level 1	N/A	SIG level 1	N/A
Low	N/A	N/A	N/A	N/A

the vendor selection process specific to the service. However you slice it, the point is that use of a measure like the SIG allows you a lot of flexibility.

Now, imagine a world where you have three versions of the SIG prepared and ready to distribute to your clients and partners immediately upon request. This will never completely replace requests for individual assessments of some services or requirements up front to perform architectural reviews, and so on, but it can reduce the load on your teams significantly. Version 6 of the SIG was released in 2010, and at the time this book was published, it was still unclear how the improvements will affect the adoption rate in the industry. Of course, some clients still may not accept a standardized response like the SIG, no matter how detailed it is, or even a third-party certification; so, you will need to leverage internal risk assessment activities as sources of information when responding to these client queries.

Basing Assessments on Sensitivity

In Chapter 4, risk profiling and risk sensitivity were discussed in detail. This discussion touched on vendor profiling, but didn't get into specific questions that should be included in a third-party profile versus a security risk profile for an internal resource. Concerns around third-party providers are going to focus on a few areas, such as the following:

- Will the vendor store or process sensitive data at their site?
- Will the vendor have access to regulated information?
- Will the vendor's systems directly connect to your organization?
- Will the vendor's service or product be integrated into your offerings?
- Will the vendor's staff need access to your facilities?

These types of questions would be included in a vendor risk profile and then used to determine the sensitivity of the service being provided. You could even include more specific questions about the types of data involved in the service, such as the following:

- Will the vendor store or process sensitive employee data at the vendor location?
- Will the vendor store or process sensitive customer data at the vendor location?

With the introduction of the SIG, version 6, in 2010, there were several improvements made that eliminated one level of assessment detail and, at the same time, made it easier to structure the assessment detail level around the answers to your profiling questions. Version 6 of the SIG includes a SIG-Lite, which is similar to the previous SIG level 1, but no longer includes a SIG level 2 questionnaire for those moderate-sensitivity vendors. Instead, you can use the SIG-Lite as the base for all the assessments and then add individual topic-based questionnaires as needed. For example, you may structure your assessments as follows:

- If the vendor's risk sensitivity rating is High, then the following questionnaires need to be completed:
  - SIG-Lite
  - SIG-F. Physical and Environmental Security
    - required if the vendor will process or store any employee privacy data or client confidential data
  - SIG-G. Communications and Operations Management
    - required if the vendor's system or network will be directly integrated with your environment
  - SIG-I. Information Systems Acquisition Development and Maintenance
    - required if the vendor will have direct or indirect access to your production systems
  - SIG-J. Incident Event and Communications Management
    - required if the vendor will process or store any sensitive data
  - SIG-K. Business Continuity and Disaster Recovery
    - required if the vendor's service will be integrated into your offerings to customers or supports a critical service
  - SIG-L. Compliance
    - required if the vendor will process or store any regulated data at their site
  - SIG-P. Privacy
    - required if the vendor will process or store privacy data for your employees or your clients at their site
- If the vendor's risk sensitivity rating is Moderate, then the SIG-Lite questionnaire needs to be completed.
- If the vendor's risk sensitivity rating is Low, then no further assessment is required beyond the questions in the *vendor security risk profile*.

If you design your security risk profile for each vendor to capture this information from the business owner of the relationship, then you can easily determine the proper level of due diligence required. Of course, you could also create your own questions, but then you are contributing to the problem for service providers who have to respond to so many customized questionnaires. It is better to start with a standard question set and pick and choose which items to include in your subset.

Improving the Process

Having a single vendor assessment format is certainly not the silver bullet; there are several other efficiency improvements that you can make rather easily. The first is to develop a public-facing document that summarizes your security program at a high level, almost like a marketing brochure. This can be a very helpful tool for your sales team to able to provide to new prospective clients/partners before they get into the detailed analysis stage. Include brief summaries of aspects of your program like the general philosophy, alignment with any industry standards, and your high-level privacy policy. Again, this will not replace a detailed analysis later, but it may help to satisfy any concerns that the client's security team will have and help to build confidence that your organization takes security seriously.

Regardless of whether you choose to implement a standardized questionnaire like the SIG or not, you will need some repository for past client questionnaires and answers. If your organization is most often the vendor being reviewed, then you need a way to quickly search old questionnaires for already approved answers or, in the case of repeat client questionnaires, to reuse and refresh the answers from last time. Be cautious about reusing any answers without first viewing them because things change quickly in everyone's environment, and those answers could easily be out of date. Some sort of searchable database of past answers would be a useful investment so that your staff isn't forced to spend a lot of time writing new responses to the same questions. If a database is used as the client response repository, then it needs to be searchable by at least client name, date, and question keywords.

Another option is to align your internal risk assessment processes, such as a Certification and Accreditation review or internal audit function, to the standard assessment questionnaire to ensure that the information is being captured and kept fresh all year round. Otherwise, the task of refreshing it yearly can be significant when you have to break it up into pieces and get each operational team to review and approve their answers. Whenever you can combine assessments, or at least streamline them, you will earn appreciation from the business. If you find yourself in the situation where clients are commonly asking you questions that you have never asked internally, then you will probably want to update your own internal risk assessment process to incorporate these areas of concern. A good indicator of how the threat landscape is shifting is the trends in changing client due diligence focus areas. One year it might be high availability, and the next year, end-point data leakage protection controls. Being aware of these changes in focus can be invaluable when planning and prioritizing your own assessment focus areas.

One final piece of the overall process optimization is feeding any data gathered back into the policy and standard governance process. If your policies or standards seem to be out of line with what clients or partners are expecting, then you should flag these areas and entertain adjusting the internal policy to match.

Similarly, if all your providers are coming up short in your assessments in a certain area, then you might consider adjusting the expectations in your internal policy to allow for some kind of compensating control that provides equivalent protection.

SUMMARY

Whether to use a questionnaire or interview style of assessment can be an important decision that will affect how quickly you get answers back from the other business units and how detailed the responses are. Interviews will provide you the richest information, but the questionnaire is more scalable and less intrusive. Similarly, you should carefully consider at the beginning of every assessment whether you want to use an active testing technique that will produce the most reliable results, or use a less-intrusive passive testing method. When faced with a one-time assessment of a new project, strongly consider Peltier's FRAAP methodology for streamlining the process. Assessments of your program from clients and assessments of your own service providers can be a large resource drain if you don't implement a standardized approach. Try to maximize your resources by producing customer-facing documentation about your security program to minimize ad hoc requests.

Action Plan

After reading this chapter, you should consider taking the following actions in your own organization:

- Pick a few of your most sensitive business areas and schedule an in-person interview with the SMEs to perform the risk assessment, instead of sending them a questionnaire.
- Perform a targeted Google search for any information about your organization that is publically available.
- If you have any active monitoring devices in your environment, including intrusion detection systems or even logs from a firewall, pick a random sampling of data for, say, 30 minutes and review it for any anomalies.
- If you find that you are spending a lot of time assessing and remediating risks associated with the nonsecure configuration systems or software, initiate a project to establish security baselines that meet your standards and focus on automating compliance checks.
- For the next project-based assessment, try the FRAAP approach and worksheets.
- Download the BITS SIG and consider standardizing on it for assessments of your third-party providers and/or make a version available to your clients as a substitute for ad hoc reviews.
- Review your schedule for third-party assessments and ensure that the assessment frequency is directly tied to the sensitivity of the vendor service.

References

[1] Top 100 Network Security Tools. SecTools.Org. http://sectools.org (accessed 20.01.11).

[2] NIST 800-37, Guide for Applying the Risk Management Framework to Federal Information Systems. http://csrc.nist.gov/publications/nistpubs/800-37-rev1/sp800-37-rev1-final.pdf (accessed 29.12.09).

[3] T.R. Peltier, Information Security Risk Analysis, second ed., Auerbach Publications, Boca Raton, FL, 2005.

[4] SANS Institute, 20 Critical Security Controls for Effective Cyber Defense. www.sans .org/critical-security-controls (accessed 19.05.10).

[5] BITS Standardized Information Gathering (SIG) questionnaire. www.sharedassessments.org (accessed 02.02.11).

Building and Running a Risk Management Program

III

Threat and Vulnerability Management

## 11

INFORMATION IN THIS CHAPTER

- Building Blocks
- Threat Identification
- Advisories and Testing
- An Efficient Workflow
- The FAIR Approach

INTRODUCTION

If you are looking for an opportunity to apply the risk principles and techniques that we have introduced thus far into daily security activities, then the Threat and Vulnerability Management program is a great place to start. This is a basic function that every organization needs to have, so it makes a good candidate for a forum in which to roll out your revised risk model. Even a task as common as patch management can greatly benefit from a good dose of risk management.

BUILDING BLOCKS

If you think about the typical tasks for which an Information Security team is responsible, many of the operational activities will include processing of new vulnerability notifications, keeping up to date on the news and reports of the latest emerging threats, scanning the environment for vulnerabilities and unauthorized services, reviewing the results of penetration tests, and working with the operational teams to ensure that security patches are being rolled out. All of these activities can be grouped under the umbrella of a Threat and Vulnerability Management (TVM) program. This program is also often referred to as Threat and Vulnerability Assessment (TVA), but TVM is more accurate because the process needs to include more than just identifying and ranking the risk exposures. It also needs to include tracking findings through to remediation, prompting appropriate risk acceptance processes, and adjusting to shifts in threats over time. The idea is to tie together the various sources of intelligence about new threats and vulnerabilities being exploited and to correlate this with the discovered vulnerabilities in your own environment.

Discovery techniques take many forms, such as using a software inventory to validate the applicability of a new vendor vulnerability that was just announced or using a vulnerability scanner to look for instances of a vulnerable service. If done correctly, this information can be mapped to provide a true sense of the risks that are most applicable to your environment and are most imminent from a threat perspective. Consider the following scenario where

1. a vendor announces a new critical vulnerability in their Web application server software affecting a particular service;
2. you then read on the SANS Internet Storm Center diary [1] that there have been several confirmed exploits of that vulnerability in the wild;
3. you look through your software inventory and see that you run the affected version on all your Web servers;
4. you consult the most recent scan of your Internet presence and find that the particular vulnerable service is indeed running on your Web servers;
5. you confirm several failed attempts to exploit this service by consulting the Web server logs from your central log management system;
6. and, finally, you coordinate with your server management team to roll out the vendor patch that evening during a maintenance window.

This series of events could describe a typical day for the TVM program when a vendor announces new vulnerabilities. Of course, there could be a hundred variations to this scenario, but the point is that it is necessary to have all this information available so that you can immediately qualify a threat and vulnerability when needed. To make all of this possible, there are many pieces that need to be aligned and in place; otherwise, all you end up with is volumes of data with nothing actionable to show for it.

Program Essentials

The volume of TVM data to be assessed at any given time is always going to be a challenge. Even the most diligent security professionals can be tempted to take on too big of a scope too early. For example, many new security managers will try to assess the risk of a vulnerability individually for every asset in their environment right out of the gate, but this can quickly get complicated. As with much of what we are faced with in risk management, it is better to take a strategic approach by starting small. Establish a program to cover a very small scope (for example, start with a handful of Internet-facing servers or even just one workstation) and iron out any hiccups in the process before you expand the program to tackle the entire organization. You don't have to have the perfect solution to cover every possibility from the beginning. Most risk models will grow and can be revised over time. Especially if you are implementing a Threat and Vulnerability Management program from scratch in your organization, you don't want to tackle the whole environment from the start. Take the time to prioritize the target environment and flesh out the details of your intake and qualification processes to ensure a smooth experience for resource administrators.

Start with the following TVM development steps:

1. Establish an asset inventory
2. Profile your environments (sensitivity)
3. Define your risk scales
4. Define a workflow for assessing vulnerabilities

Try to establish an accurate asset inventory, and assign business owners and custodians if responsibilities are not already clear. You can't begin to assess the risk of new vulnerability notifications if you don't know what you have and don't have in your environment.

Before any risk analysis can be performed, a risk sensitivity score for each resource/environment needs to be assigned (profiling). This is another way to use the sensitivity concepts and Security Risk Profile from Chapter 4. The idea is for the business owner to rate the resource's importance to the organization from an information security perspective and relative to the enterprise environment. You might start by working with the business continuity or operations teams to leverage their assessments of which resources are critical to the functioning of the business. Resources that have been identified as important to the organization from a disaster recovery or continuity perspective will likely also end up at the top of your risk sensitivity list. In the context of a TVM program, you may want to break from the strategy of looking at your most sensitive resources and instead focus on either your most prevalent asset type (for example, a Windows desktop) or the asset type that is most exposed to threats (for example, laptops and other mobile devices). When an activity is so operational and vulnerability focused, the magnitude of the applicability will often out-weigh the importance of any one asset. Meaning that the percentage of the systems that are vulnerable can sometimes increase the likelihood so much that it makes the sensitivity of the asset irrelevant.

Next, you will need to define the qualitative risk scales for assessing the severity and likelihood of a given threat/vulnerability pair. These scales will vary based on your organization and the maturity of your program. Chapter 6 covered a qualitative risk model that will be expanded on in this chapter and applied to TVM activities specifically.

Finally, you need to define the workflow for processing any newly identified risks. How you implement this workflow is probably the single biggest factor for the success of your program. If you overwhelm the Subject Matter Experts (SMEs) or don't provide them with actionable data, then the TVM program will fall flat on its face.

WARNING

A high percentage of false positives can kill your credibility with system administrators. This outcome is completely avoidable! You should run numerous tests of any scanning or alerting device before anything is escalated to the system administrators to remediate. Take a small random sampling, or even just use your own system, and validate the findings first with these data. Tweak the tools as necessary to minimize false positives. It is easy to lose the confidence of the resource administrators, and often it's very hard to get it back.

Asset and Data Inventory

Having an asset and data inventory is a basic part of any security program, but in many cases, it looks easier than it is. Assets usually are tracked at some level by other functions, but often, these inventories don't include the information that you will need. At a minimum, you will want to capture this basic data in your inventory:

- System Type and Version
- Software (including Version)
- Physical and Logical Location
- Logical Network Addressing
- Owner
- Resource Administrator
- Data Sensitivity

For added efficiency, combining your inventory data with your Security Risk Profile can provide the TVM program with a single source for much of the data needed to verify applicability.

Let's imagine that a vulnerability notification for Apache Web server, version 2.0, is released. The first question you would need to ask is, "Does this apply in my environment?" If the answer is, "No," then you have nothing else to do; it isn't productive to spend a lot of your own and the administrator's time trying to track down and qualify vulnerabilities that turn out not to be applicable in your environment. If, on the other hand, the answer is, "I don't know," then you can't qualify the risk. For example, you may not run Apache directly on any of your Web servers, but a vendor product in your environment may use an Apache server as part of their application without you realizing it. So you can't rely solely on asset inventories that are based on records of what has been purchased, you also need to compare this to active discovery and scanning results.

There are many ways to start gathering inventory information if you don't already have a central database of assets:

- Vulnerability scanning data will tell you a lot about your environment, but not necessarily about the business context for applications.
- Infrastructure devices, such as DHCP, DNS, and NAC servers, can also be a good source of information.
- Many organizations have a naming convention for systems that can be helpful.
- Software licensing and maintenance contracts may also be helpful.
- Records of technology purchases from the acquisitions or finance department are always helpful.

Methods for putting together a data inventory are similar: you can do scans of your environment, passively monitor communications, interview business owners, and so on.

Resource Profiling

Before any risk assessment can be performed, you must first assign sensitivity ratings for the resources in question. An e-commerce organization, for example, is going to value the systems associated with their Web presence most highly, whereas a brick and mortar retail chain might prioritize the point-of-sale systems in each store. In general, try to think about the resources on which the organization is dependent in order to function, the resources with the most sensitive data, or even those that are the most visible to the public. Whatever your criteria are, the idea is to formalize them into levels of importance to your organization and use this information to prioritize any subsequent analysis work.

From a TVM perspective, the resource often will be an application or system, but it may be easier to start by assigning sensitivity values to environments, such as the database tier or an Internet DMZ network, instead. If you want to look at the class or type of asset instead, you might assign the printers a low sensitivity, the user PCs a moderate sensitivity, and the servers a high sensitivity. This sensitivity rating should take into account the potential impact of a compromise to the organization for that class of resource.

To do this, you may want to gather the following information about each asset or asset class:

- General Description
- Function and Features
- Information Classification
- Criticality to Organization
- Applicable Regulations
- User Community

All of these attributes will help you to differentiate the importance of each asset to the organization (risk sensitivity). Remember, the risk sensitivity is really a measurement of the resource's tolerance for risk or acceptable range of risk exposure. As before, start with a basic Low-Moderate-High scale, and don't be afraid to make broad assignments in this first pass. If this isn't granular enough for your organization, you can always expand the scale. One possible approach to assigning the sensitivity is to categorize your resources by servers, desktop/laptop, printers, and infrastructure devices as shown in Table 11.1.

There are two common ways to approach sensitivity ratings for a TVM program: the first is to look at each category of asset (for example, printer, PC, server, network device, and so on) and assign each an overall sensitivity value, and the second is to assign sensitivity ratings environment by environment. Assignments of sensitivity by environment (for example, research lab, Web server farm, sales laptops/mobile devices, backup servers/network) were demonstrated in

Table 11.1 Asset Class by Sensitivity

Asset Class	Sensitivity
Production servers	High
Desktop/Laptop	Moderate
Printers	Low
Infrastructure	High

Chapter 4 (see Figure 4.3) as part of the general risk profiling discussion. Either of the approaches is valid.

Keep in mind that for a qualitative risk model to be effective, you will need a clear definition of the rating scale. When you start assessing your assets, try the simple Low-Moderate-High scale we used in Chapter 4. Be careful not to over-rate your assets. Remember, the tendency is to always rate the importance of all your assets as high, which is why it is best to assess resources relative to the most important asset in your environment. If, for instance, the mainframe holds all your sensitive data and runs all your critical applications and if this resource has, therefore, been rated as highly sensitive, then you certainly couldn't justify rating your desktops and laptops as highly sensitive as well. To keep things in perspective, remind yourself that if a hacker compromised your central network switch or router that would be much worse for the organization than a compromise of any one desktop or laptop. As you rate the assets in your organization, it can be helpful to keep reminding yourself that you aren't evaluating their risk exposure, but just their sensitivity to risk.

Once you feel comfortable that your process is running smoothly, you can break free from these high-level categories of assets and start assigning more specific sensitivity scores at a system or application level. Start broad and set reasonable goals or you will quickly get overwhelmed.

THREAT IDENTIFICATION

In general, a threat describes the source of an exploit. Essentially, a threat has the potential to harm the resource. Another way to define a threat source is anything capable of acting against an asset in a manner that can result in harm. As described in Chapter 5, a threat source can take many forms, from a targeted attack to an infrastructure failure. Many organizations deal with mass attacks more often than the more highly publicized targeted attacks. There are many ways to evaluate threat exposure. You might focus on the aspects of threat that would affect the likelihood of an exposure, such as the sophistication of the attacker or size of the threat universe, or you might be more interested in the aspects of threat that affect the severity of a vulnerability, such as whether a threat is external or internal. Chapter 6 detailed the use of qualitative scales for both likelihood and severity to rate risk exposure, but even these scales leave room for error and interpretation. This can be dangerous, especially, if you have your more junior analysts doing the bulk of the TVM assessments, so it is important to develop clearer guidance for the analysts.

One alternative approach includes looking at threat intelligence reports that can help you to profile the vectors, motivations, and common frequencies for reported or observed threat activity. This might provide you with valuable data about where to focus your further assessment and mitigation efforts.

Another effective strategy is to use the data most pertinent to your organization by gathering statistics about the security incidents that have been observed within your own environment. Keeping detailed records of incidents with key identifier fields can allow you to profile the likely threats and paths based on your own historical data.

There is a ton of hype in the media and within the security industry about the latest threats to emerge in the field. Some are clearly trends that will come and go, but others are emerging as areas of concern. In Chapter 5, we discussed information warfare, cyber terrorism, organized crime, and the growing sophistication of insider attacks. These are all threats to keep in mind when thinking about threat evaluation as a part of your TVM program. As you go through your own threat modeling exercises, keep the categories of threat and also these emerging trends in mind. Try to think about the vulnerabilities in your environment that may be targets of these threats, as well as resources that could be used against another organization, and take this information into account as you develop your recommendations for management.

Threat Data Sources

There are many good sources of threat information these days; in fact, it sometimes seems like there are almost too many. The following are just a few periodic reports that can provide a broad perspective on trends:

- Verizon Business Data Breach Investigations Report
- CSI Computer Crime and Security Survey
- Symantec Internet Security Threat Report
- Sophos Security Threat Report
- Trend Micro Future Threat Report

The anti-malware vendors are a good source for information because they monitor many threats on the Internet; however, you should also look at companies that provide managed security monitoring and response services. These service providers will have great cross-client aggregated data regarding events and incidents that have been investigated. You might also use resources like the CERT Coordination Center and the Internet Storm Center to provide more real-time updates on threat sources and the latest vectors. In reality, all these resources only scratch the surface of what is available currently. You will want to do your own research to find the data sources that are most pertinent to your organization. For example, if you work for a state government in the United States, you would want to consider joining the Multi-State Information Sharing and Analysis Center (MS-ISAC) [2] for regular intelligence that is specifically targeted at your industry.

Whichever resources you decide to use, when you review these periodic reports or advisories, look for both trends that support your own suspicions and initiatives, as well as data that don't support your assumptions about the most likely threats. It is important to understand the questions being asked, the criteria for the analysis, and the source of the data. For example, in some cases, human error may have been a leading cause of small data breach, but these data may not have been included in the sample; potentially only large reported disclosures were included. Knowing this will help you to better assess the applicability of these findings to your own environment.

ADVISORIES AND TESTING

As previously discussed, sources of vulnerability data range from security intelligence services to vendor announcements and from data published by security researchers to testing of your own environment. Most commonly, you will be processing vulnerability announcements from vendors or sifting through the volumes of data created by a vulnerability scan. In either case, you need to have a comprehensive risk model and solid criteria in place for each risk qualification level.

Rating Vulnerabilities

What makes one vulnerability different from another? If you are going to adjust the industry rating of a vulnerability to your own environment, you need to know how to analyze a vulnerability report for details that affect both the likelihood and the severity of the potential exposure. Consider some of the following questions:

- Is the vulnerability applicable in our environment?
- Is there a virus or IDS signature for it?
- Does it require tricking a user to be effective?
- Is authentication required prior to exploit?
- Does it affect servers, as well as desktops?
- How widely deployed is the vulnerable software or system?
- Does it allow a limited scope of control or arbitrary code execution?

These particular questions are mentioned again here because they apply directly to a TVM program; refer back to Chapter 6 for a more comprehensive list of likelihood and severity-qualifying questions.

Most vulnerability notification services and scanners provide some kind of default rating for the findings, and the more sophisticated ones even include a confidence rating, but it is crucial that you rate these vulnerabilities for your own environment. The most efficient approach is to use the default or vendor-supplied ratings as a way to narrow down your focus from hundreds or even thousands to a more manageable number. Then, you can analyze the risks of each exposure to your organization and adjust the rating accordingly. Taking several passes to qualify the vulnerabilities may seem like more work, but the idea is to perform a more detailed level of analysis with each pass.

This section began with some sample questions to ask when analyzing each advisory. These are just some of the factors that need to be considered and accounted for in your risk model. Armed with this knowledge, you can better focus your administrators' efforts on those risks that are most likely to be exploited and those likely to do the most damage.

The simple severity and likelihood scales that were introduced in Chapter 6 are a good place to start, but your risk analysts are going to need a lot more guidance than that when they are sorting through large volumes of vulnerability data. To address this need, the following severity and likelihood scales have been developed and tested over the course of several years. Each level of the scale is the same as before, but additional guidance has been added to help analysts choose the most appropriate severity and likelihood ratings for each vulnerability or combination of vulnerabilities.

Table 11.2 shows the severity criteria on a 4-level low-critical scale (based on Table 6.11):

Additional guidelines could be provided to analysts about how to handle the combination and aggregation of multiple vulnerabilities. Similarly to the expanded

---

Table 11.2 Qualitative Vulnerability Severity Scale, 4-Level

Level
Low – May be a deviation from recommended practice or an emerging standard. May lack a security governance process or activity, but have no direct exposure.
• Deviation from a recommended practice or emerging standard. • May be the lack of a security process or procedure to govern or manage security-related activities. • No direct exposure.
Moderate – May indirectly contribute to unauthorized activity or just have no known attack vector. May result in a degradation of service and/or a noticeable decrease in service performance.

Continued...

Table 11.2 Qualitative Vulnerability Severity Scale, 4-Level (*Continued*)

Level

- Weaknesses that can be combined with other vulnerabilities to have a higher impact.
- Disclosure of information that could aid an attacker.
- Any vulnerability that could hinder the detection or investigation of higher impact exploit.

High – May allow limited access to or control of the application, system, or communication, including only certain data and functionality. May result in a short disruption of service and/or denial of service for part of the user community.

- The attacker can access the sensitive data or functionality of a user, either limited to specific data and/or a specific user.
- An outside attacker can execute arbitrary code at the level of the user.
- Allows a user to access unauthorized functionality.
- Allows limited modification or destruction of critical/sensitive data, either limited to specific data and/or a specific user.
- Severe degradation of services.
- Exposure of sensitive system or application information that provides implementation details that may be used to craft an exploit.

Critical – May allow full access to or control of the application, system, or communication, including all data and functionality. May result in a prolonged outage affecting all users of the service.

- The attacker is not limited in access after execution; they may be able to escalate privileges.
- Disclosure of all sensitive or confidential information is likely.
- Allows modification or destruction of all critical/sensitive data.
- May result in a total shutdown of services.

severity scale, the Negligible-Very High likelihood scale from Chapter 6 (see Table 6.9) has been enriched with additional guidance specific to vulnerability analysis in Table 11.3.

Notably, the criteria for these likelihood levels are intended to provide guidance for several types of information security scenarios, from software vulnerabilities to flaws in procedures, so not every item in the level will necessarily apply to each threat or vulnerability.

Remember, whenever there is a documented occurrence of a vulnerability having been exploited in the past within the organization, the likelihood level should automatically be increased from the initial assessment rating, unless further mitigations have been put in place since the incident. Similarly, if an instance has been documented in the organization's industry, the likelihood level should be set to at least Moderate.

Table 11.3 Qualitative Vulnerability Likelihood Scale, 5-Level

Level

Negligible – The threat source is part of a small and trusted group, or controls prevent exploitation without physical access to the target, significant inside knowledge is necessary, or purely theoretical

- Small and trusted population has access to the vulnerability.
- Vulnerability can be exploited with local physical access only and resources have strong physical access controls.
- A series of strong authentications or multifactor authentication are required for exploit.
- Possible only with a significant amount of likely detectable guesswork or tightly controlled internal information.
- Attack is theoretical in nature, and no known exploit or potential of exploit is currently proven or expected.

Low – The threat source lacks motivation or capability, or controls are in place to prevent, or at least significantly impede, the vulnerability from being exercised

- General corporate population could exploit the vulnerability.
- Vulnerability can be exploited through the internal company network only.
- Single strong authentication is required for exploit.
- Possible only with a significant amount of guesswork or internal information.
- Vulnerability can be exploited with local physical access only, and resources have physical access controls, but are still accessible to a large number of people.

Moderate – The threat source is motivated and capable, but controls are in place that may impede successful exercise of the vulnerability

- Vulnerability can be exploited by limited and known population.
- Vulnerability can be exploited through the internal company network or client connection only.
- Simple authentication is required for exploit.
- Vulnerability requires a user to be "tricked" into taking some action (for example, a targeted phishing message or a request to go to a Web site and download a file).
- Possible only with detailed internal information or reasonable guessing.
- Expert technical knowledge is needed, such as knowledge of available attack tools.

High – The threat source is highly motivated and sufficiently capable, and controls to prevent the vulnerability from being exercised are ineffective

- Vulnerability can be exploited by extended corporate population.
- Vulnerability can be exploited by anyone who can reach the network, where no authentication is required.
- Vulnerability can only be exploited from related networks to which the organization does not control access.
- Simple (easily guessable) authentication may be required for exploit.
- Possible with limited knowledge of target configuration.
- Basic attack skills are needed, such as an automated attack.

Continued...

Table 11.3 Qualitative Vulnerability Likelihood Scale, 5-Level (*Continued*)

Level
Very high – Exposure is apparent through casual use or with publicly available information, and the weakness is accessible publicly on the Internet
• Can be exploited by large anonymous population (any Internet host).   • Vulnerability can be exploited from the general Internet.   • Possible with only publicly available information.   • No specific attack skills are required, such as general user knowledge.

TIPS & TRICKS

Always account for the threat vector when considering the likelihood of a risk. The activity that would cause the vulnerability to be exploited may not be an activity that is normal for the system or environment. For instance, downloading a file from a certain Web site or reading a malicious attachment are examples of activities that would be far less likely to affect production servers than desktop systems.

It is important to note that the criteria for each level of the qualitative scales are not like policies or standards, which stay relatively static. The scales should be dynamic documents such that members of your team can add or adjust criteria as needed over time. You will want to be careful not to change the number of levels too frequently because that can wreak havoc on previously assessed risks, but you should feel free to update the criteria as you deem appropriate.

Even though the severity and likelihood scales have been expanded to include more specific criteria, the risk matrix from Chapter 6 (see Figure 6.2) can still be used to determine the final risk rating for each threat/vulnerability combination. These same risk scales can be used to assess vulnerability advisories, scanning findings, penetration testing results, or even vulnerabilities that are discovered as part of an incident investigation.

ANALYZING A VULNERABILITY NOTIFICATION

One of the most fundamental functions in Information Security is performing risk analysis on new vulnerability advisories, and this is also a major focus of a TVM program. Time and resources are always going to be limited, so you need to prioritize which vulnerabilities you spend time trying to patch or otherwise mitigate. The key to this decision is risk analysis. For this, you need clear and repeatable criteria for both severity and likelihood, as presented in Tables 11.2 and 11.3. The trick is to use a common set of guidelines to help analysts consistently rate the risk of new vulnerabilities to your particular environment. Management needs to be comfortable that the vulnerabilities are being rated consistently regardless of the experience level or background of the particular analyst.

Read through this actual vulnerability notification regarding an Adobe product and try to rate this vulnerability based on your gut feeling:

Adobe Acrobat and Reader Multiple Remote Code Execution Vulnerabilities
Initial Risk Rating: High
Multiple vulnerabilities in Adobe Reader 9 and Acrobat 9 could allow remote attackers to *crash the application* or potentially *control affected systems*. According to the vendor, one of these issues (JBIG2 input validation) is *currently being exploited* and could potentially lead to remote code execution.
Adobe recommends its users to update to Adobe Reader/Acrobat 9.1.
UPDATE 4/6/2009: (CVE-2009-0927) Symantec has detected *active exploitation attempts of this issue in the wild*. Administrators are advised to apply the appropriate updates as soon as possible.
UPDATE 4/14/2009: Sun has acknowledged these vulnerabilities in Solaris 10 (SPARC platform). A final resolution is pending completion. A workaround and an interim fix are currently available.
CVE Details: Heap-based buffer overflow in Adobe Acrobat Reader 9 before 9.1, 8 before 8.1.4, and 7 before 7.1.1 allows *remote attackers to execute arbitrary code* via a PDF file with a malformed JBIG2 symbol dictionary segment.
http://cve.mitre.org/cgi-bin/cvename.cgi?name=CVE-2009-0193

Assuming a 4-level (Low-Moderate-High-Critical) scale for risk exposure, how would you rate this vulnerability in your environment? Some key aspects of the advisory have already been highlighted to help you get started. Does your gut assessment compare with the default rating of high from the notification service? Try to use the severity and likelihood scales from this chapter (see Tables 11.2 and 11.3) to evaluate the vulnerability again and note any differences between your ratings and the default rating.

There are many factors to consider about your own environment when evaluating the risk exposure for this scenario. For example, if your Active Directory Domain Controller happens to have a vulnerable version running on it, a scanner might flag this as a high risk, but most of these exploits require opening a specially crafted PDF file on the server to be successful. What are the chances that an administrator is going to download or get e-mailed a malicious PDF and decide to open it on your Domain Controller? Probably not high. Looking at your desktops and laptops, however, the likelihood of exposure is high, so that's where you should focus your efforts.

Consider how your evaluation would change if you could verify that your anti-virus controls would detect these specially crafted PDF files. Would that change your rating? If there were malware scanning at your e-mail gateway and active scanning on your desktops, then having a signature for this attack would greatly decrease the likelihood as well. You might also look at the effectiveness of internal awareness training as a compensating control. To be able to consider this scenario fully, you would need to have collected metric data about past Phishing and SPAM attacks, and about how often your user community was a victim of these attacks.

For this Adobe vulnerability, it is actually easier to assess the severity than the likelihood, which is exactly why the risk model distinguishes between sensitivity, severity, and likelihood. The sensitivity is going to differ based on the resource in question (for example, servers have high sensitivity, whereas desktops have moderate sensitivity). Likewise, the likelihood will depend on the details of your environment (for example, strong malware detection and proven user awareness could make the likelihood Low, but the lack of these controls could make it Moderate). For the purposes of the Adobe example, suppose you are assessing the risk exposure as it pertains to your desktop environment and that you have no specific compensating controls to prevent this exploit. Using the qualitative scales, you would get the following results:

- Risk Sensitivity = Moderate
- Likelihood = Moderate (exploit requires tricking the user, see Table 11.3)
- Severity = High (crash the application, allows arbitrary code execution and could allow full control, see Table 11.2)
- Risk Exposure = High (see risk matrix in Figure 6.3)

Note that if the vulnerability advisory had stated more clearly that an attacker exploiting this vulnerability could gain full control of a system, which would have pushed the severity rating of this exploit up to the Critical level, then the resulting risk exposure would stay the same.

Now, assume instead that you are assessing this vulnerability for your Windows Domain Controller server:

- Risk Sensitivity = High
- Likelihood = Low (the usage model of PDFs on these servers might lower this level from that in the previous example)
- Severity = High (this doesn't change)
- Risk Exposure = Moderate (see risk matrix in Figure 6.3)

There are a couple of interesting comparisons to note here. First, notice that the overall exposure is reduced from high to moderate in this example, even though the server has a higher sensitivity. This is because the vulnerability is far less likely to be exploited on the server because of current administrator practices. Administrators most likely don't download PDF files or open e-mail attachments on the servers. Also, notice that the severity rating didn't change from one example to the next, even though the compensating controls and resource sensitivity are different. Finally, notice that the default industry risk rating doesn't hold up when applied to this organization's servers, but that the severity rating for each example remained consistent.

There are two traps to avoid when analyzing vulnerabilities. It is easy to under-estimate the current level of compensating controls and spend time remediating issues that aren't very important. It is just as easy to overestimate the effectiveness of your controls and get bitten by a vulnerability that you knew about but had decided to deprioritize. You can try to avoid both of these scenarios by carefully documenting your compensating controls, with particular note of the ways in which they affect severity or likelihood ratings, and testing and/or tracking their effectiveness.

AN EFFICIENT WORKFLOW

Now that you have a feeling for how to rate vulnerabilities as they come in from advisories, it is worth briefly discussing what else is needed to make a Threat and Vulnerability Management program successful. There are three basic activities in which every TVM program should be engaging, which are as follows:

1. Monitoring advisories from a trusted service.
2. Performing regular security scanning of your environment, both internally and externally.

3. Using the advisories and scanning to ensure that regular patching of critical systems is being performed according to the risk of each threat/vulnerability pair.

There are many additional activities that may be within the purview of the TVM program, such as enterprise penetration testing and Internet reconnaissance, but these three duties are essential. Of course, just scanning an environment or monitoring an advisory service isn't enough, you also need to act on these information sources.

There are several commercial and free sources available for security alerts, including the following:

- US CERT: www.us-cert.gov/cas/techalerts/index.html
- Microsoft: www.microsoft.com/technet/security/advisory/default.mspx
- Secunia: http://secunia.com/
- iDefense: http://labs.idefense.com/intelligence/
- SANS: http://isc.sans.edu/xml.html

TIPS & TRICKS

When you are presenting the results of your TVM program to management, keep the metrics very simple. Include a listing of the top 10 most prevalent vulnerabilities, as well as the metric showing how the operational groups are doing with patching systems according to the Service Level Agreement (SLA) you have established internally. You want management to see that systems are getting patched in a timely manner, and then expand your metrics to cover other areas once the organization is comfortable with these initial metrics.

Defining a Workflow

Once you have defined your scales and formulas for calculating the real risk exposures of vulnerabilities, you need to define a workflow for handling them (see Figure 11.1). Assuming a four-tier risk model, a good place to start is by looking at just the Critical- and High-level risks, setting aside the Moderate and Low findings for now. Hopefully, you will have very few risks in the Critical category, but it is likely you will have a good number of High risks.

Next, you will need to qualify each vulnerability for applicability to your environment. This will usually require some research on the part of your technical staff if you don't have a good asset inventory that includes software and operating system versions. If you do have a comprehensive asset inventory, your job will be a lot easier and the filtering can potentially even be automated.

Once you have a list of vulnerabilities that are rated either Critical or High and you have determined that they are applicable to your environment, you will need to re-rate them. This is where a formal risk model is crucial. You will need to determine in advance how many risk levels you will have, what variables your risk formula will include, and which criteria you will use to categorize vulnerabilities at each level.

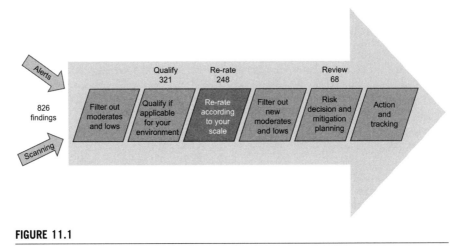

FIGURE 11.1

Vulnerability qualification workflow.

For example, when one organization used this methodology, they started with 826 findings, narrowed those down to 321 that needed to be qualified, eliminated 73 as false positives, and after qualification and re-rating, they were left with 68 findings to address. Imagine if they had started out by trying to rate and analyze all 826 findings!

Exceptions

There are always going to be vulnerabilities that either don't have a fix (patch or workaround), or for which the fix will require a long-term plan to address and test the solution. So how do you handle and track these so that they don't get lost? To deal with these scenarios, you can implement the existing Security Policy Exception/Risk Acceptance Process we reviewed in Chapter 8. This will help you to fully assess the risk of operating in the current state, consider any mitigating controls that may reduce your risk and get senior management to sign-off on it. Further, this process should also include a tracking mechanism so that you can set an expiration date for the acceptance and make sure that the solution is being worked on. Most findings from the TVM program will likely have a clear remediation action, such as a configuration change or patch, but you need to be prepared for the ones that can't be fixed, either because a solution hasn't been released by the vendor or because the nonsecure configuration is required for some business purpose.

THE FAIR APPROACH

Factor Analysis of Information Risk (FAIR) is an interesting model of risk assessment because it does a great job of breaking risk down into its various components (referred to as "risk factoring"), but keeps the analysis steps simple enough that they can still be practical for typical assessment work. In his publication *Introduction to the FAIR Framework*, the author, Jack Jones, uses the fantastic metaphor of a bald tire that can be viewed as a weakness in the context of a car, but as irrelevant when the tire is being used as a swing. The attention to the nuances of risk language and perspectives in the FAIR model has made it a frequently cited reference for many in the Information Security field. In fact, you may remember that the definition of risk exposure, which has been used throughout this book, is based on the definition of risk from FAIR. However, the FAIR framework goes far beyond a glossary of terms; its significance is in its approach to measuring risk.

The FAIR framework can be applied to both qualitative and quantitative analysis models, but its real value is in providing an approachable structure for quantitative analysis, which few other models have been able to achieve. FAIR begins with two basic factors to measure risk:

1. Loss Event Frequency (LEF)
2. Probable Loss Magnitude (PLM)

These terms may sound very similar to many of the concepts covered thus far in this book, as well as the simple ALE formula mentioned in Chapter 6, but there are some important distinctions. Throughout the qualitative model discussion, frequency and probability have been lumped together into likelihood. As you will see, the focus on LEF increases the complexity of the analysis, but it also increases the precision. Earlier in this chapter, a series of questions and criteria were used to qualify the appropriate level of likelihood for each threat/vulnerability pair. LEF adds structure to this analysis by breaking down the equivalent of our likelihood rating into four fundamental factors:

> **The frequency with which threat agents come into contact with the assets (Contact)** – this speaks to the threat surface for the asset in question.
> **The probability that threat agents will act against the assets (Action)** – this addresses the motivation factor that is seen in other risk frameworks.
> **The probable nature (type and severity) of impact to the assets (Threat Capability)** – this accounts for the specific type of threat and how severe it will be (that is, the capability of the threat agent).
> **The probability of threat agent actions being successful in overcoming protective controls (Control Strength)** – this takes into account any compensating controls that may reduce the likelihood of exploit.

Similarly, the PLM factor includes a very detailed and structured approach to measuring the equivalent of the risk sensitivity score used throughout this book. When it comes down to it, each approach accounts for the same considerations but organizes it differently.

Measuring Risks

Back in Chapter 6, we tried to apply the Annualized Loss Expectancy (ALE) formula to assess several risks, but that was where quantitative analysis broke down. There wasn't enough information available to properly calculate the rate of occurrence. Looking at the vulnerability advisory example from this chapter, let's see if FAIR can help us where ALE came up short.

FAIR provides a very comprehensive framework for analyzing information risks, including a step-by-step process for qualifying risks with several reference tables to get you started. The very basic reference tables will be briefly explained in this chapter to illustrate the depth of the FAIR analysis model even in its simplest form. To calculate the Threat Event Frequency (TEF), you could use the simple progression of quantitative frequency ranges from FAIR shown in Table 11.4. Like the qualitative likelihood scale used earlier in this chapter, the TEF scale uses five levels.

The next two variables are aspects of the vulnerability that will affect the Loss Event Frequency: Threat Capability (Tcap) and Control Strength (CS), shown in Tables 11.5 and 11.6, respectively. You may notice that both of these variables were considered components of the likelihood rating in the earlier qualitative model.

In order to calculate the Vulnerability variable, which together with the Threat Event Frequency will determine the Loss Event Frequency, you will need to compare the capability of the threat source with the strength of the existing controls to prevent the exploitation. This is mapped in a table similar to the risk matrices used earlier for the qualitative models, except in this case a rating of Very Low for

Table 11.4 FAIR Threat Event Frequency Table

Level	Description
Very low	<.1 times per year (less than once every 10 years)
Low	Between .1 and 1 times per year
Moderate	Between 1 and 10 times per year
High	Between 10 and 100 times per year
Very high	>100 times per year

Table 11.5 FAIR Threat Capability Table

Level	Description
Very low	Bottom 2% when compared against the overall threat population
Low	Bottom 16% when compared against the overall threat population
Moderate	Average skill and resources (between bottom 16% and top 16%)
High	Top 16% when compared against the overall threat population
Very high	Top 2% when compared against the overall threat population

Table 11.6 FAIR Control Strength Table

Level	Description
Very low	Only protects against bottom 2% of an average threat population
Low	Only protects against bottom 16% of an average threat population
Moderate	Protects against the average threat agent
High	Protects against all but the top 16% of an average threat population
Very high	Protects against all but the top 2% of an average threat population

Table 11.7 FAIR Vulnerability Table

		Control Strength				
		Very Low	**Low**	**Moderate**	**High**	**Very High**
Threat capability	Very low	Moderate	Low	Very low	Very low	Very low
	Low	High	Moderate	Low	Very low	Very low
	Moderate	Very high	High	Moderate	Low	Very low
	High	Very high	Very high	High	Moderate	Low
	Very high	Very high	Very high	Very high	High	Moderate

control strength is bad and a rating of Very High for threat capability is bad, as shown in Table 11.7. The best case is that the threat capability is rated Very Low and the control strength is rated Very High. The final Loss Event Frequency rating is determined using a second mapping table, shown in Table 11.8, comparing the Vulnerability and Threat Event Frequency values.

The last factor for measuring the risk is the Probable Loss Magnitude (PLM) rating. Here too, FAIR takes a practical approach to estimating loss by providing ranges rather than trying to identify a precise value. The table in Table 11.9 shows one possible implementation of this factor. The appropriate ranges will be different depending on the organization, so this table may need to be tweaked for your organization.

Once the PLM and LEF are calculated, the final step is to determine the risk exposure using one last mapping table, shown in Table 11.10. Again, this matrix doesn't differ much from the risk matrix used in Chapter 6 (Figure 6.2), except that FAIR uses several more levels of PLM than is used for Severity or Sensitivity in the qualitative model. When you think about the fundamental differences in the approaches, this makes a lot of sense, as a quantitative model lends itself better to more precise evaluations of these variables than a qualitative model does. In the qualitative model, it is important to make it abundantly clear which level is

Table 11.8 FAIR Loss Event Frequency Table

		Vulnerability				
		Very Low	**Low**	**Moderate**	**High**	**Very High**
Threat event frequency	Very low	Very low	Very low	Very low	Very low	Very low
	Low	Very low	Very low	Low	Low	Low
	Moderate	Very low	Low	Moderate	Moderate	Moderate
	High	Low	Moderate	High	High	High
	Very high	Moderate	High	Very high	Very high	Very high

Table 11.9 FAIR Probable Loss Magnitude (PLM) Table

Magnitude	Range Low End	Range High End
Very low	$0	$999
Low	$1,000	$9,999
Moderate	$10,000	$99,999
Significant	$100,000	$999,999
High	$1,000,000	$9,999,999
Severe	$10,000,000	—

Table 11.10 FAIR Risk Exposure Table

		Loss Event Frequency				
		Very Low	**Low**	**Moderate**	**High**	**Very High**
Probable loss magnitude	Very low	Low	Low	Moderate	Moderate	Moderate
	Low	Low	Low	Moderate	Moderate	Moderate
	Moderate	Low	Moderate	Moderate	High	High
	Significant	Moderate	Moderate	High	High	Critical
	High	Moderate	High	High	Critical	Critical
	Very high	High	High	Critical	Critical	Critical

appropriate, but when you are using hard numbers, it becomes more obvious where a risk falls on the scale.

What FAIR considers the PLM value is equivalent to the risk sensitivity rating and components of the severity rating used throughout this book. So where Sensitivity, Likelihood, and Severity variables were used in our qualitative model to rate the risk exposure, FAIR is using a similar approach with Probable Loss Magnitude, Threat Event Frequency, and Vulnerability, respectively. They are different ways of approaching the problem, but in the end, they account for the same factors. You can find detailed guidance for each of the 10 steps of the basic FAIR workflow on the author's, Jack Jones, Web site [3].

Using the FAIR methodology can help you properly qualify many factors that affect the probability and severity of a given risk. You certainly wouldn't want to go to this level of granularity for every vulnerability that is announced; after all, you could have 10 advisories in one day! But this model provides a great way to approach an in-depth analysis of the vulnerabilities that are most highly rated using the quicker qualitative model.

In a way, the value of FAIR is in its granularity; it addresses each factor of risk individually. But, this is also what makes FAIR difficult to implement on a wide scale. It provides too many options for a quick assessment, such as what is needed in a TVM program.

ANALYZING A VULNERABILITY NOTIFICATION USING FAIR

First, let's review a quick summary of the vulnerability advisory that was used earlier in this chapter to demonstrate rating a risk with the qualitative model introduced in the second part of this book. The highlights are as follows:

- Affects Adobe Acrobat and Reader
- Initial Risk Rating was High
- Allow remote attackers to
  - Execute arbitrary code
  - Crash the application
  - Potentially control the system
- Currently being exploited in the wild
- Uses a heap-based buffer overflow attack

Using the qualitative scales, this risk was rated as a High for desktop systems and Moderate for servers. Now, let's try using the FAIR approach and compare the results. Luckily, both models use the same final four-level scale for risk—Low-Critical—so it should be easy to compare the two.

To begin, we need to determine the Threat Event Frequency (TEF) using the scale in Table 11.4. Based on the information in the advisory (you may want to look back at the full description earlier in this chapter), it would seem that this vulnerability is currently being exploited in the wild; so at a minimum, you can expect a breach to occur at least once in the next year. According to the FAIR model, this puts you in the Moderate TEF rating level (between 1 and 10 times). At this point, in the model, you aren't yet considering other controls (for example, user awareness) that might be in place to prevent this breach from occurring.

Next, the Threat Capability (Tcap) needs to be determined. Crafting a PDF document to abuse the buffer overflow in Acrobat is not the kind of skill possessed by just anyone off the street. Some advisories will indicate whether the exploit code is readily available on the Internet, whether someone has published instructions, or if an attack kit or script is being circulated. If that were the case, you would be looking at the lower end of the Tcap scale. Given the information provided in this case, we must assume that none of those resources are yet available to potential attackers. So, for this attack, you are probably looking at advanced, but not elite, hackers and programmers, who would put you in the High Tcap level.

Now, we need to account for the strength of existing controls. A signature to detect and block these malicious PDF files would certainly put the Control Strength rating in at least the High level. But there is no indication about whether that signature exists in this scenario, so our existing controls currently involve relying solely on the awareness of the user community not to open suspicious PDF files. The effectiveness of awareness programs is improving over time as we develop better methods of educating the general user community, but there is still a very high rate of users getting tricked. To be generous to our users, let's rate the control strength as Moderate.

According to our matrices, a TEF rating of Moderate, a Tcap rating of High, and a CS rating of Moderate yields a Vulnerability rating of High and Loss Event Frequency rating of Moderate.

Then, at this point, only one more variable remains, and that is the Probable Loss Magnitude (PLM). FAIR provides a very detailed methodology for looking at various aspects of loss, including productivity, replacement cost, fines, damage to reputation, and so on. This list should sound familiar to you from our discussions of risk sensitivity. We already estimated that, in the worst case scenario, this breach might happen 10 times in one year, which means possibly 10 desktops or servers becoming infected, and with servers likely having a lower probability of being exploited. Assume that the most likely case is that a system is crashed or even damaged such that it needs to be rebuilt, and that this will mostly impact productivity for the desktops. If an employee making $80,000 per year loses one day of work, you might estimate that this comes to around $300–$400 per day of lost productivity. If the breach occurs the maximum expected 10 times during the year, that puts the PLM in the $1,000 through $9,999 range. On the other hand, execution of arbitrary code can have many implications depending on the motivation of the attacker. They could use it to infect other systems on the same network, steal the user's authentication credentials, or even steal sensitive data from the system. You can see where this analysis could start getting even more complicated once you begin to take all of these possibilities into account. For the sake of simplicity, let's say that you determine the worst case scenario PLM is in the Significant range; in this case, your final risk score will be High.

To summarize, for the desktops, this vulnerability likely presents a Moderate risk, and in the worst case, a High-risk exposure. This puts the worst case FAIR analysis in line with our earlier qualitative results, but the more likely case according to the FAIR analysis actually comes out at a lower risk rating. You can try this exercise yourself and see what you come up with for the Domain Controller server. Compare that to the earlier result if you want to further examine the relationship between the two models.

SUMMARY

The primary focus of a TVM program should be on monitoring threat intelligence for its applicability to your organization and constantly assessing the vulnerabilities that might be exploited. While other areas of the risk management program will focus on more long-term or project-based assessments, on-going short operational assessments, including security scanning, patch management, and monitoring of security detection controls, are more characteristic of a TVM program. Without a strategy for quickly filtering out the lower risk items and the items that just don't apply to your environment, you will almost immediately drown in information. Of all the risk management activities, TVM has the most potential to leverage the automation of data correlation and feeds from systems, such as asset management systems or security scanners. Although quantitative analysis may be difficult for process and practice-focused risks, the FAIR framework provides a practical approach to assess vulnerabilities with greater precision than traditional qualitative models.

Action Plan

After reading this chapter, you should consider taking the following actions in your own organization:

- Choose one security advisory service, as specific to your industry as possible, and monitor that for new threats and vulnerabilities.
- Provide the qualitative scales to your analysts to use for every vulnerability assessment.
- If you aren't evaluating advisories or scanning reports now, implement this addition on a very small scale and run that for 6 months before expanding the scope.
- Immediately implement the qualification workflow to filter out the lower risk items.
- For your highest-rated risks (that is, Critical level exposures), which should also be your smallest category of risks, implement the more precise FAIR model to assess just those risks in greater detail.

References

[1] SANS Internet Storm Center, Handler's Diary. http://isc.sans.edu/diary.html (accessed 30.01.11).
[2] Multi-State Information Sharing and Analysis Center (MS-ISAC). www.msisac.org (accessed 20.01.11).
[3] Risk Management Insight Web site http://riskmanagementinsight.com (accessed 06.03.10).

Security Risk Reviews

## 12

INFORMATION IN THIS CHAPTER

- Assessing the State of Compliance
- Implementing a Process
- Process Optimization: A Review of Key Points
- The NIST Approach

INTRODUCTION

Unfortunately, it isn't enough for security teams to publish a volume of policies and standards and then expect compliance. With any policy or standard that is established, you should expect some level of noncompliance that needs to be evaluated and addressed. Different organizations may refer to the ongoing gap analysis process by different names, but a simple term is a Security Risk Review (SRR). You may hear this process referred to as a Compliance to Standards review, which although accurate sends the wrong message about its intent. The goal is never 100% compliance with every aspect of every security standard. The point of an SRR process is to identify the areas where there is a gap and determine if it is acceptable for the organization. This is not an audit with a new name, but it is an internal activity that needs to be performed to ensure there is proactive monitoring of security risks in the areas that have already been deemed critical enough to establish a security policy covering it. If the TVM program is focused on looking for the signs of issues and analyzing emerging threats, then the SRR is a complementary risk activity whose purpose is to identify and address more strategic issues and systemic root causes.

ASSESSING THE STATE OF COMPLIANCE

Any organization will have a long list of policies and standards on paper, and these should all accurately represent the desired state of the organization, but, honestly, some policies have more impact on the security posture of the organization than other policies. A Security Risk Review is, in essence, just a gap analysis. Think of it like a piece of paper with two columns: you would list the active standards on first column and the current practices in the second column, and then highlight any discrepancies. This is different than an audit in several ways, the first being that it is meant to be a collaborative process between the security team and the business to identify where enforcement of a standard is and isn't appropriate. It isn't a performance evaluation in any way. Think of it as an audit without judgments. This review should be marketed within the organization as a tool to increase the understanding of security expectations and prioritize the areas of greatest exposure. All standards are not the same, and when it really comes down to it, the risk manager or analyst needs to help the business figure out which requirements are must-haves and which are nice-to-haves, given the current environment and with the understanding that this focus may change over time.

Balancing Security and Risk

At this point, you may be wondering how this is different from how you run your Information Security program today; the distinction is actually in the approach. For the sake of simplicity and consistency, the security field has evolved toward using a cookbook-type approach. Everyone gets the same recipe and is expected to execute on it in the same way, but we don't live in a one-size-fits-all world. Instead of blindly applying so-called "best practices" across the board, use some risk analysis techniques to determine the most appropriate controls. A preventative control may be the "best" option that is specified in a standard, but by keeping an open mind and through analysis of the actual presenting risk, you may determine that a detective control reduces the exposure to an acceptable level. These are the types of discussions and debates that a Security Risk Review process should foster. The desired end state isn't necessarily always going to be "compliance"; success needs to be determined by the objectives of the business.

As a risk manager or analyst, there are many factors to consider when evaluating any deviation from an established standard. Let's review some of these factors as follows:

- Do you understand the technical and process related vulnerabilities and threats?
- Is a proposed change better or worse than the current state?
- Does it meet the intent of the standard?
- Could additional controls mitigate any risks?

If you do not have a technical background, make sure that you either fill your staff with some analysts with that skill-set or build strong relationships with some technical staff in other functions who can help you. It is guaranteed that you will be presented with many risk scenarios that will require at least a basic technical background that will lead you to ask the right questions and properly evaluate the options. After all, engineers are notorious for telling management that something is impossible if they don't think that you have the background to call their bluff.

When presented with a request to make a change to an environment that would cause a system to come out of compliance with established standards, an often overlooked part of the analysis process is to consider that the current state, though compliant, may have its own problems. Standards are written for the general case with the best intentions, but they can't possibly account for every scenario, and there is a tendency to implement compliant configurations without considering their applicability or appropriateness. You will particularly encounter this if you inherit a security program that had formerly been run by a security novice.

Another approach is to look back at the standard in the context of the policy and try to determine if the proposed changes meet the intent of the standard. Many times, a single statement from a standard may be taken out of context, leading you to enforce a level of control that was never intended. If the altered controls provide the same level of protection, but in a different way, then this may be a good candidate for an exception stating those compensating controls. Occasionally, the standard itself may be too prescriptive and will require a slight modification.

Finally, you will always want to be thinking about creative solutions to meet the protection requirements without having to say "no" to the business. An answer of "yes" with additional requirements will always be better received than a flat "no." Try to think of an alternative preventative control, or else a supplementary detective or responsive control, to lower the risk to an acceptable level and not slow down the business unnecessarily.

Recall the discussion of the password lockout scenario from the sidebar in Chapter 2. This example is a good illustration of the mindset of identifying the real weaknesses and devising creative solutions to meet the business' needs, but it doesn't help you to articulate the risks associated with accepting the control change proposal or how additional controls could lessen any additional risk of deviating from the current standard. For that, a structured methodology is needed to apply the general risk lifecycle workflow steps to an on-going gap analysis exercise.

Qualifying the Risk

With the general guidelines established about how to keep a balance when analyzing a deviation from standards, the focus now needs to shift to a comprehensive methodology for qualifying that risk. As a quick refresher about how we qualify risks, the same three variables apply to a Security Risk Review as to any other risk analysis:

- Assess the sensitivity of the asset
- Assess the likelihood of the exploit
- Assess the severity of the vulnerability

Just like the TVM approach, we need to rate the risk in terms of the value of the resource, the likelihood of the exploit, and the severity of the vulnerability. The lower risk items need to be set aside so that the proper focus can be devoted to the higher risk exposures. Also like TVM, the complexity and volume of data makes the process impossible unless you first implement a workflow that can use levels of assessment depth to filter out those lower risk items. You wouldn't perform a full FAIR assessment on every vulnerability you discover in a security scan, nor would you go into that depth for a Security Risk Review.

IMPLEMENTING A PROCESS

The purpose of the Security Risk Review (SRR) process is to identify areas where your security standards are not being met. The focus initially should be on applications and supporting infrastructure that are most critical to the organization. This risk analysis process will follow five high-level steps:

- Assess Resources (Profiling)
- Generate Findings
- Analyze Risk
- Risk Decision
- Risk Exceptions

Think of this process like an organization-wide gap analysis exercise. The intent is not to make judgments about the compliance of any one group or to suddenly bring the entire enterprise into compliance with every single security standard, but rather to get a general picture of the compliance state of the organization and start to identify areas of focus.

All too often, we follow a checklist of security controls or program components without taking the time to determine the areas of highest risk to our organizations. The goal with the SRR is to prioritize not only the resources being evaluated but also the importance of the standards themselves. The standard requiring a log of all guest accesses to the data center may be rightly deemed less critical than the requirement to have swipe card access to the data center. Reviews should be performed periodically or whenever new policies/standards are adopted by the organization. Similar to the application security assessments, a schedule should be established for security reviews based on the risk profile of the resource. One provision in an organization's Information Security Policy may be that all high-sensitivity resources must be assessed annually, all moderate-sensitivity resources every 2 years, and all low-sensitivity resources every 5 years, but be sure to leave yourself the flexibility to decide how that review should be executed.

Workflow Steps

The workflow introduced here for Security Risk Reviews is derived from the general risk management lifecycle in Chapter 3, with each step expanded to address the activities of an SRR review lifecycle specifically:

1. At the beginning of the year, the business owner for each resource must establish with the security team a schedule to assess their assets.

2. The security team generates a questionnaire for the particular resource and notifies the primary contact. The primary contact has 2 weeks to complete the questionnaire and submit it. The primary contact may be the business owner or may be another more technical resource.

3. The security team reviews the questionnaire for completeness and finalizes it. At this time, they generate the findings (out-of-compliance items), which the security team has 2 weeks to review any additional information provided and prequalify each finding. The prequalification includes an initial risk rating based on the provided information and establishing any follow-up questions.

4. The security team documents every follow-up action or question and assigns it to a primary contact. The security team sends a list of these tasks to each primary contact and the business owner, giving them 2 weeks to provide the additional information needed to qualify the risk. As an alternative, the primary contact may organize a meeting with the security team to qualify the findings.

5. On the basis of this information, the security team establishes the final risk ratings for each finding and filters out the lower risk items.

6. The security team meets with each primary contact and business owner to discuss the remaining risks and to decide how to address them.

7. The primary contact and business owner then have 1 week to establish an action plan or request a policy exception.

8. A risk is considered "addressed" when any of the following criteria are met:
   a. Approval of a Risk Exception Request (Exception)
   b. Approval of a Plan for Mitigating Controls (Mitigation)
   c. Implementation of a Vulnerability Fix (Remediation)

The workflow diagram in Figure 12.1 lists each step, a short description, and also includes the roles responsible for carrying out that step.

In the workflow figure, possible turnaround times have been suggested (in weeks) to help illustrate that these activities need to have set deadlines to avoid the pitfalls of the never-ending assessment. However, these timeframes can be adjusted based on the needs of your organization. They are just meant as guidelines to ensure expectations are set in advance for a reasonable turnaround time.

Establish Schedule

Setting the schedule strategically can mean the difference between a productive year and a year of struggle and conflict. It is important to work with the resource owners and administrators to establish a schedule for when each resource will be reviewed. Try to give the business units some autonomy to choose their own timing for the reviews, as long as this will leave enough time to complete the analysis by the end of the year. For example, if you are assessing some internally built applications, they may want to work the review around their development schedule, avoiding the months with big releases. Have some flexibility when establishing the schedule, but then monitor it closely throughout the year to keep each review from

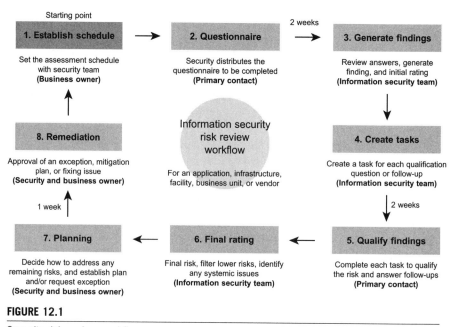

FIGURE 12.1

Security risk review workflow.

slipping to the end. You will also have to manage your own resources, so you'll have to influence the business' desired schedule with what you can support. Having all the reviews scheduled in November clearly won't work!

Similar to the TVM process, you will want to prioritize the most critical resources to be reviewed. Once you are comfortable that those risks are well defined, then start adding some of the less sensitive resources to the scope. You will find that you will have the best success if this review isn't seen as just a security initiative. Try to get senior management to show their support by establishing a company-wide objective to perform the review and address the findings annually.

TIPS & TRICKS

When you are scheduling the Security Risk Reviews with each business owner, don't allow any to be scheduled past the third quarter of the year. This way you allow yourself both time to review and address all the findings by the end of the year, and you also allow a buffer for those review dates, which will inevitably slip due to some resource conflict or other priority.

Distribute a Questionnaire

The easiest place to start is by distributing a questionnaire to each of the resource owners or custodians. This questionnaire should cover your policy/standard set, but be careful not to make it too long or you will overwhelm the business. Each question should have a simple Yes/No format so that you don't have to spend a lot of time interpreting the answers. It is also recommended to include an "N/A" option for questions that may not apply and leave a field for comments. There are many ways to organize these reviews from a questionnaire perspective, for example, nesting questions, so that areas that don't apply can easily be skipped and making sure that the questions are logically grouped. You also want to design different questionnaires for each of the resource types. For example, a review of a business unit will generally focus on process and procedural controls, whereas a review of an environment may focus on network device configuration and backup methods.

There are tools to help you deliver the questionnaires, but a simple Excel document can work just fine. Refer to Chapter 10 for more information about designing a questionnaire to get the best results. It is good practice to require the creation of SRR questions with any new security policy or standard that the organization adopts. Whoever proposes the new policy/standard should also be responsible for identifying the related questions that are most important to include in future reviews.

Generate Findings

On the basis of any noncompliant responses to the questions, a finding should be generated. This finding will become the record for documenting the risk of noncompliance. Among the information that should be tracked for each finding are as follows:

- Finding Identifier (Some unique number to reference the finding, such as CTS0001)
- Target Resource (application, infrastructure component, process, environment, facility, and so on)
- Status of the Finding (open, researching, owner analysis complete, closed with exception, closed false positive, closed by mitigation, and so on)
- Category (access control, change management, physical security, business continuity, secure development, and so on)
- Control Standard (Reference the actual Policy/Standard being violated)
- Question Identifier (Some unique number to reference the question such as SRR0501)
- Question Content ("Do all data centers implement nonwater-based fire suppression systems?")
- Question Response ("No")
- Question Comments ("Water sprinklers are implemented in data center ABC …")

The more information you can gather in the comments section up front, the more time you will save qualifying the risks later. You will likely want to spot check the answers to ensure that none have been skipped and that there are no anomalies. For example, if the resource owner has marked "N/A" for several modem questions, and then answered others, you might go back to them to clarify.

Once the questions have all been answered and the findings identified, you will need to perform the initial rating process. For each finding, the risk exposure needs to be assessed and qualified. On the basis of the information provided in the questionnaire and your knowledge of the environment, you should assign each finding an initial rating. Remember that this rating will be based on predetermined scales of likelihood and severity initially. The sensitivity of the resource will come later.

You may not have enough information to make an educated assessment of the risk for every finding at this time, but that's expected. Assign values based on a general case or your best judgment of the situation. Try to err on the high side of the risk because you can always lower it later during the qualification process. Be sure to document your reasoning for each risk rating. It is guaranteed that six (or even three) months down the road, you won't remember why you rated the finding as a Moderate in this case, and documentation will also help to justify your assessments with auditors.

Once you have given each finding an initial risk exposure rating, you will want to filter out the lower risk findings to start with, just like during the TVM process. This will help your team and the organization to focus on high-priority issues and not get distracted by less critical areas. The first time through the process, you should filter out any Moderate- or Low-risk findings and focus your efforts on the High- and Critical-risk exposures. Chances are that there will be enough of these to keep you very busy. This is not meant to imply that the lower risk items will be ignored or that there is an explicit permission to resource owners to be out of compliance, but you need to start somewhere. When you have a handle on the higher risk items, you can go back and start addressing the Moderate-risk items.

Once you have filtered out the findings based on an initial or default rating, you will need to start the process of describing and evaluating the risk of each finding. You may discover answers that are contradictory or that you know to be wrong, so you may close some findings out right away as false positives. When you are rating each finding, be sure to account for any existing controls that would limit or lessen the risk in some way. Also, be aware of any themes that emerge within one review or across the environment.

Create Tasks

Next, the security team must work with the resource owners to understand the risk to the organization for each remaining finding and identify any existing mitigating or compensating controls that may affect the assessment of risk. Generally, you will not have enough information just from the questionnaire to properly rate the finding, so this is your chance to gather additional information and ask follow-up questions.

On the basis of this additional information, you should be able to rate the risk exposure; however, these responses may also prompt additional follow-up questions. For this reason, holding a meeting or conference call for the qualification process is recommended. Send the questions to the resource owners in advance, but meet to discuss their responses. This way you can raise any additional concerns right in the meeting and save time going back and forth.

You will also likely come across several false positives during the qualification process. This typically happens when the original question was misunderstood or the person answering it didn't know the answer so they just responded "No" to be safe. If you can confirm this with the resource owners and SMEs, then you can just close out that finding and document it as a false positive. This may also be an indication that the original question needs to be revised.

In some cases, a risk finding may be seen across several applications or represent a systemic problem; in this case, a thematic risk will be created to track the individual risk findings. This thematic risk may also be used to escalate critical risks to senior management. Generally, it would be too overwhelming for senior management if you were to list every individual finding in the executive summary, so you will instead want to group them by theme to show management the trends and help call out standard areas that aren't being met across several parts of the organization.

RISK DEEP DIVE

Creating Tasks

Imagine that you have distributed an SRR questionnaire to the server administration team in your organization, and they answered "No" to the following question:

Do all system-to-system (or service) account passwords expire automatically at least annually?

You will need to ask several follow-up questions to better understand the scope and impact of this standard violation. These might include the following:

- Do the passwords ever expire?
- Is there a schedule established to change the passwords manually?
- Are they initially set randomly and with complexity?
- Where are the passwords stored?
- What are these accounts used for?
- How are the passwords transmitted?
- Please list the accounts that don't comply

All these questions cover some aspect of related controls that may increase the chance of a password misuse or disclosure. Think about how answers to these questions will affect your assessment of severity and/or likelihood. If these passwords have full administrator access to your database server, then the severity is going to be much higher than an account that is used to automate the transfer of a log files to an archive server.

Many of the other questions will affect the evaluation of the likelihood that not changing a password at least annually will put it at risk. However, maybe the expiration and change isn't automated, it is done manually on a set schedule; if this is the case, this could be a good candidate for an exception. This is just one example of the follow-up questions you might ask to further qualify a risk before giving it a final rating.

Qualify Findings

Sometimes the hardest step in the entire Security Risk Review workflow will be following up on all the tasks that you have assigned to various groups within the organization. Especially, if you aren't careful to make your follow-up questions crystal clear, you may have a lot of back and forth asking the business owners and resource administrators for more information.

When you created each task, you should have had a good idea what information was missing to allow you to assess the risk properly. Maybe your finding was that backup tapes are not encrypted when taken offsite, but you don't know if the sensitive data are encrypted in the database before it is backed up. Now, you need to review the additional information that was provided and determine if you have enough to properly qualify the finding. In particular, you will be looking for compensating controls and contributing factors that might decrease or increase the likelihood of occurrence, or contain or expand the scope of the exposure.

Final Rating

By the time you get to this step, you should have the proper context to understand the full extent of the exposures and any constraints that have prevented compliance thus far. Consider the compensating controls for this possible SRR finding:

Resource administrators don't verify the integrity of the information resource patches through such means as comparisons of cryptographic hashes to ensure the patch obtained is the correct, unaltered patch.

Let's assume that you have talked to the resource administrator for the server, and they tell you that the server runs the IBM AIX operating system. How might this affect your assessment of the risk? Let's also assume that all patches and updates are first applied to a development and then QA environment before being implemented in production. How would that change your assessment?

You might describe the compensating controls as follows:

"Although the operating system updates are not checked for integrity using cryptographic hashes, all updates are obtained directly from the vendor's site (IBM in this case for the AIX servers) and all patches are thoroughly tested in DEV, and QA environments before being installed in Production. This limits the likelihood of a transmission corruption causing damage to critical systems. By using only IBM's website to obtain software updates (as opposed to forums and other third-party sites), the chance of obtaining maliciously altered code is reduced but not eliminated."

When accounting for compensating or mitigating controls, there are a few ways that a risk exposure level can be reduced:

Lower the severity of the vulnerability
- Limit or contain the effects of the vulnerability
- May include isolation of the vulnerable component

- May include logging or monitoring
- May include incident response or disaster recovery plans
- May include increasing the redundancy or removing a dependency

Decrease the likelihood of exploitation

- Increase the difficulty of exploiting the weakness
- Decrease the threat surface
- Decrease the attractiveness of the target

Notice that there are many ways to reduce either the severity or the likelihood of the risk. Many controls will actually lower both the severity and likelihood. For example, a database monitoring tool might be able to detect and alert security staff immediately about an abuse by an administrator. This would reduce the severity because the security staff can respond immediately to contain the incident before too much damage is done. It may also lower the likelihood because administrators will know about this monitoring and be discouraged from insider attacks.

As previously noted, there is also the option of lowering the risk sensitivity of the resource, but this is very rarely possible. This would require a significant change to the application, such as removing sensitive data or the elimination of an applicable regulation. We see this most often in the PCI world, where retail companies will segment their systems that are in scope for PCI compliance from the rest of the network using a firewall. That immediately changes the sensitivity of the non-PCI systems because those penalties no longer apply.

Planning

Together with the resource owner, and maybe even members of senior management, the security team now needs to negotiate a plan to reduce the risk or accept it. This can often be the longest step in the process because budgets may already be set for the year and resources allocated, and other risks may also require work. All this has to be balanced and informed decisions need to be made. For each finding, a risk decision needs to be made regarding how to address each risk. Remember, there are three choices, which are as follows:

Accept the Risk – This requires submitting a formal request through the risk exception process (exceptions are temporary).
Remediate the Risk – This requires coming into compliance with the standard (short-term fix).
Mitigate the Risk – This requires implementing controls to lessen the severity or likelihood of the risk (long-term strategy).

The artifacts of this step of the process will include either a documented mitigation plan or a policy exception, or more than likely, both. The exception process has been covered in detail in Chapter 8, but essentially, you need to at least document the following information during this step:

- Action (accept, remediate, mitigate)
- Mitigation/Remediation Plan (with dates and owners)

- Status (not started, in progress, under review, pending exception, complete, and so on)
- Risk Exception (for further details, see Chapter 8)

Again, this can be tracked in spreadsheets, MS Word documents, SharePoint, databases, or GRC applications; it really doesn't matter as long as it is capturing the right information and can be made available to the people who are on the hook to fix the risks. Being able to provide some kind of risk dashboard is key. An SME will want to see all the actions for which they are responsible regardless of whether it came from a Security Risk Review or a TVM finding. Business owners will want to see the current security posture of all the resources for which they are responsible.

The security team will meet with each resource owner or SME to discuss the remaining risks and decide how to address them. A risk is considered "addressed" when any of the following criteria are met:

- Approval of a Risk Exception Request (exception)
- Approval of a Plan for Mitigating Controls (mitigation)
- Implementation of a Vulnerability Fix (remediation)

If we go back to our example of the administrators not verifying the hash of the software updates after downloading them, then we can think about our options to address this risk in terms of three main choices, as follows:

- Consider the current compensating controls as sufficient, meaning that they may not meet the letter of the standard, but they provide equivalent protection in line with the intent of the standard.
- Accept the risk as is, which will require a formal policy exception.
- Develop an action plan to address the risks with additional mitigating controls, a transference of risk or plan to avoid the risk entirely.

For our example, you might consider implementing a procedure to scan the system for vulnerabilities and configuration changes after implementing any new updates. In this way, you would hopefully catch any malicious backdoors that are being implemented on the system. This solution would be considered a mitigating control. You might also want to implement a procedure to back up the system prior to installing updates in order to lessen the impact of a corrupt software update causing data loss or extended outages. This solution would also be considered a mitigating control.

If the existing compensating controls are deemed sufficient, then the next step is to document the compensating controls and how they meet the intent of the protection requirement. This should probably include filing an exception to document the acceptance of those controls or suggesting that the policy/standard be adjusted to allow for these equivalent controls. However, if the risk is deemed as acceptable to the organization without further mitigation, then an exception definitely needs to be filed. You should have established in advance the workflow for approval of exceptions (see Chapter 8), and it is recommended that the approval workflow accounts for the different risk exposure levels. Remember that exceptions must always be temporary and should never be approved without an expiration date set. When an exception expires, it needs to be reviewed and a decision made about whether it is still needed, should be extended, or should be modified in some way.

Most often, there will be some mitigation plan or action plan established to address the risks. If you think about the effects that mitigating controls can have on risks, they have the potential to lower the magnitude of any one or all of the variables used to calculate risk exposure. A preventative control may change the likelihood of a vulnerability being exploited, but do nothing to change the severity of a successful exploit, whereas a reactive control may not lessen the likelihood at all, but it could limit the severity by constraining the scope of the exploit once it is detected. Detective controls can sometimes have the effect of a deterrent that lowers likelihood, but generally, they will limit the impact of the exploit by allowing the organization to quickly respond to the attack. Recall that residual risk is the remaining risk exposure level after implementing the recommended controls. Each mitigation plan should indicate the expected risk reduction so that management can decide whether the action is sufficient and whether it is worth the effort.

Remediation

This final step of the workflow involves tracking of the mitigation action items by the security team and execution on the mitigation plan by the business owner or SME. These actions can take many forms depending on the plan. It is best to establish distinct milestones for any long-term projects, to provide a mechanism to identify actions that are in jeopardy of not meeting their commitment date.

PROCESS OPTIMIZATION: A REVIEW OF KEY POINTS

There are many ways to approach each aspect of a Security Risk Review, from roll-out to exception handling. The following are just a few areas where you can benefit from the experience of several other failed attempts:

- Prioritize findings and assets
- Assign the questions a default risk rating
- Tailor the questionnaires to the assets
- Use resources strategically

First, you will want to start by establishing a threshold to filter out the lower risk findings. As you reduce the number of critical and high risks, you can start focusing on the moderate risks, and so on. Similarly, prioritize which assets you include in the review initially. You should have an intuitive feeling for which of your resources are critical to the organization, so start by assessing them. Don't take on too much the first time through. Keep the scope small until you feel comfortable that the process is working smoothly. If this is your first year performing these reviews, start with at most three resources to assess. This will allow you to focus on improving the process instead of rushing through the assessments to meet some aggressive goal.

Once you decide which resources to prioritize, there are many practical ways to make this process more efficient. The first is to assign each of your review questions a default likelihood and severity. This way, when you create your initial findings, you have a risk rating to start with. You can use this default rating to filter out the lower risk items and focus your attention on the high-exposure findings. Just remember that you will want to err on the high side, when assigning the default ratings. Assume, maybe not the worst case possible, but the worst case that is likely for non-compliance with each question, and then rate the risk based on this generic scenario. Then, when you are assessing the actual finding, you can adjust your rating. Chances are that you will have more findings that go down in their final rating than go up.

You may not want to reassess lower sensitivity assets each year; maybe put them on a 3- or 5-year cycle. Similarly, you may not want to re-ask the entire question set every year. You could, for example, use the full set the first year, and then only ask the higher risk questions the next year. Especially, if you are only going to focus on the higher risk findings, why ask the lower risk questions each year and ignore the findings?

You could even nest the questions to save time. For example, ask a high-level question that is very basic and if that is answered negatively, then trigger more in-depth questions. For example, if a vendor answers "No" to: "Do all external connections pass through a stateful firewall," then you might have some concerns and ask several in-depth questions. You have likely seen questionnaires with 20 questions related to modems, but if you don't use modems, it can get tedious to read them all and mark "N/A" for each.

Another trick is to tailor your questionnaires to different resources. For example, a different set of questions may apply at an application, infrastructure, facility, or even vendor level. So you may want to create a few questionnaires for each resource type. That way you don't waste people's time selecting "N/A" for a bunch of questions. Keep the question set as tight and small as possible if you want to minimize resistance from the organization.

TIPS & TRICKS

Each year, solicit feedback from your primary contacts in the organization about how the questionnaires, and the process in general, can be improved. There are always opportunities to clarify questions, better organize the sections, or approach the process differently.

Finally, try to use your resources as strategically as possible. You may have one or two people in the organization with a general knowledge of several different resources. They may not be able to answer every question, but maybe they can give you 80% of the answers without having to bother several individual SMEs. You might guess that the enterprise architects and even members of the security team may have a lot of the answers already. If you can use them first, you can minimize the strain on the SMEs who are usually highly constrained resources. You could even look at past audit reports, security scans, or client questionnaires to find answers to questions. The business will appreciate it if you can narrow down the questions in advance or just ask them to verify the answers you have given.

Prioritization always needs to be a critical focus. There are a couple of indicators that a risk should go to the top of your list besides the obvious rating of a Critical-risk exposure:

- Same issue seen across multiple environments or systems
- An easy, low-cost mitigating control is available
- A single mitigating control will address multiple risks
- An issue continually presents on customer due diligence evaluations
- Risk is directly linked to an annual objective for the organization

Use these high-level guidelines to help filter which risks you escalate to the attention of senior management and push the business to mitigate, and you should see success in your program.

THE NIST APPROACH

Back in Chapter 10, Certification and Accreditation (C&A) was introduced in the context of an operational assessment of security baselines. If this sounded familiar, it is because this is basically what a Security Risk Review is focused on; only a C&A has a much narrower mission. This may seem like a strange time to re-review the baselines discussion, but in the context of assessing your organization's compliance with its own policies and standards, the security baseline can be a great tool to streamline the review process. The formal process of C&A is most often implemented in the US federal government, and the leading standards for this practice are published by the National Institute of Standards and Technology (NIST). NIST is a standards organization that is sponsored by the US federal government. It regularly publishes many guidelines and standards related to all kinds of Information Security topics from cryptography to incident response processes. If you are not familiar with the resources available for NIST, you should look through the wealth of free resources on their Web site [1]. You will find that many government standards in the United States are based on the guidelines developed by NIST.

The NIST Evolution

The original NIST guidelines for risk management (SP800-30—*Risk Management Guide for Information Technology Systems*) were based on an eight-step lifecycle, which is very similar to the lifecycle approach that was introduced in Chapter 3. This is one of the first frameworks that focused specifically on risk management in an Information Security context. Back in 2002, when it was published, risk management wasn't the buzzword that it is now. Approaches were still very perimeter focused and security controls frameworks were very prescriptive. Even when a related specification for Certification & Accreditation (NIST SP800-37 revision 0) came out in 2004, it had clearly not embraced a risk-based approach yet. However, NIST has recently released a new revision of their Certification and Accreditation (C&A) guidance (NIST SP800-37 revision 1—*Guide for Applying the Risk Management Framework to Federal Information Systems, A Security Life Cycle Approach*) that now focuses on a risk management approach with a more comprehensive lifecycle (now six steps) for C&A. This updated approach (based on the process first described in NIST SP800-39—*Managing Risk from Information Systems, An Organizational Perspective*) is summarized as follows:

1. Categorize System
2. Select Controls
3. Implement Controls
4. Assess Controls
5. Authorize System
6. Monitor Controls

As written in this revision of SP800-37, "The risk management process described in this publication changes the traditional focus from the stovepipe, organization-centric, static-based approaches to C&A and provides the capability to more effectively manage information system-related security risks in highly dynamic environments of complex and sophisticated cyber threats, ever increasing system vulnerabilities, and rapidly changing missions" [2]. Clearly, there is recognition that previous approaches were not flexible enough to accommodate the quickly changing environments of today.

The evolution of the NIST approach to C&A represents a very significant shift in approaches to operational security practices from one of the institutions that has the most influence over global information security standards. It is only a matter of time, then, before the risk-based approach begins to influence other organizations' standards and processes as well.

The goal of NIST's revised Risk Management Framework is to transform the traditional Certification and Accreditation (C&A) process into a six-step process that emphasizes building security controls into information systems, maintaining awareness through monitoring, and providing intelligent data to leaders to better make informed decisions about risk. Like other risk management approaches, NIST has explicitly called out the information system owner and security control providers to take responsibility for driving and supporting the risk management process; it is not left only to the security function to be accountable for assessing protection needs on an on-going basis.

Focus of the NIST Process

Generally, when you think about a C&A process, baselines and configuration guidelines come to mind. Most often, this work is associated with hardening systems and verifying that the configuration meets established standards, but this is really just a specific implementation of a more general risk management activity.

The NIST framework is focused on the following objectives:

- Real-time risk management and continuous monitoring
- Automated tools to inform decisions
- Integration with enterprise architecture and Software Development Lifecycle (SDLC)
- Equal emphasis on all stages of the lifecycle
- Normalizing information risks with other enterprise risks
- Clearly establishing accountability for controls

Like many corporations, the federal government has recognized that Information Security risk initiatives need to be in alignment with the goals of the organization as a whole and not operate in a vacuum. Using a common risk management framework across the entire organization and with specific models for different functions, the organization can achieve a more cohesive and consistent level of protection that addresses the real risk exposures for that organization at that time. It is vitally important to get senior leaders deeply involved in risk decisions, but in order for that to happen, security professionals need to provide actionable data to management so that they can weigh the trade-offs appropriately. NIST seems to be taking a big step in that direction with this revised risk framework.

Figure 12.2 illustrates the lifecycle that SP800-37 recommends. Notice that this process follows the same flow as the lifecycle we discussed in Chapter 3 (shown

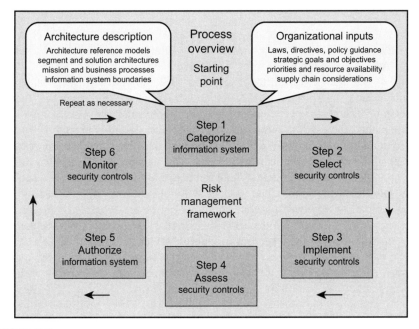

FIGURE 12.2

NIST C&A process overview.

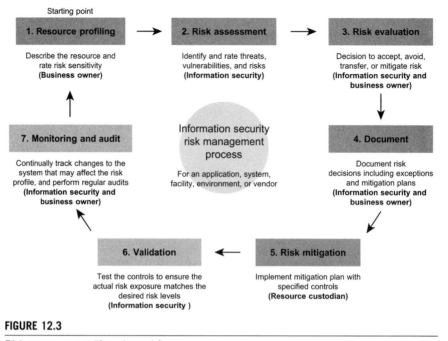

Starting point

1. Resource profiling

Describe the resource and
rate risk sensitivity
(Business owner)

2. Risk assessment

Identify and rate threats,
vulnerabilities, and risks
(Information security)

3. Risk evaluation

Decision to accept, avoid,
transfer, or mitigate risk
**(Information security and
business owner)**

7. Monitoring and audit

Continually track changes to the
system that may affect the risk
profile, and perform regular audits
**(Information security and
business owner)**

Information security
risk management
process

For an application, system,
facility, environment, or vendor

4. Document

Document risk
decisions including exceptions
and mitigation plans
**(Information security and
business owner)**

6. Validation

Test the controls to ensure the
actual risk exposure matches the
desired risk levels
(Information security)

5. Risk mitigation

Implement mitigation plan with
specified controls
(Resource custodian)

FIGURE 12.3

Risk management lifecycle workflow.

again in Figure 12.3), but in some cases, it may organize the individual activities
differently or use different names for the steps of the process. For example, steps 4
and 5 (Assess and Authorize) from NIST have been combined into step 6 (Validation) of our model. In addition, our model calls out a specific step (step 4) to
document the risk exposure information and decisions while recognizing that, in
reality, this documentation is compiled as each step is completed.

Ultimately, the C&A process should be the mechanism for preventing vulnerable systems from going live in your environment and for continually monitoring
their compliance with established baselines. This can be accomplished either by
various tools or manually, using change management systems or even security
event monitoring systems. The idea is to identify when a configuration has
deviated from the approved baseline so that it can be reviewed and remediated if
necessary. Unlike an audit, a Security Risk Review usually does not include any
hands-on validation of the responses to the assessment questionnaires, so you will
need to find other creative ways to verify that the answers you are receiving are
accurate. By reviewing the baselines used for C&A instead of reviewing each and
every system or application in your environment during a Security Risk Review,
you can streamline the process and eliminate a lot of topics from your questionnaires that have already been addressed in the baselines. At this point, all you will
need to ask is whether the target resource has implemented the baseline. There is
much more to the NIST 800-37 risk framework than we have the space to cover

here, so it is recommended that you read that publication in its entirety and think about how you might implement a similar process for your organization.

SUMMARY

Writing and distributing security policies and standards are just the beginning. You also need to evaluate the organization's compliance to those standards. Unlike an audit, this is meant to be an internal assessment of where the gaps are and which ones present a large enough risk to require some sort of mitigation. This is an on-going process that will start with a small focus, but it needs to continue to regularly assess new standards as they are published and account for any changes in the risk landscape. If you focus on the highest risk areas and structure your questionnaires as clearly as possible, you will encounter less resistance from the business. Ultimately, this process should be seen as a proactive exercise to stay ahead of emerging threats and potential incidents, and of course, the auditors. To do this, you will want to promote a culture of self-identification and self-discovery of risks. Along with the Security Risk Review process comes the latest evolution of the NIST C&A guidance, which can provide tools, such as security baselines, to further optimize your gap analysis activities.

Action Plan

After reading this chapter, you should consider taking the following actions in your own organization:

- Establish a Security Risk Review program and workflow, based on your existing Information Security policy and standard set.
- Choose three of your most critical resources and schedule them for a Security Risk Review within 1 year.
- Develop an assessment questionnaire based on the standards that have the most potential for exposure or the areas where you know the organization is weakest; keep the questionnaire to no more than 50 questions to start.
- If you don't have the equivalent of a C&A program in your function, review the NIST documentation and use it to assess which components your organization is currently missing, and then establish a phased plan to implement security baselines and the associated validation checks for critical applications and systems.

References

[1] NIST. http://csrc.nist.gov (accessed 20.01.11).
[2] NIST 800-37, Guide for Applying the Risk Management Framework to Federal Information Systems. http://csrc.nist.gov/publications/nistpubs/800-37-rev1/sp800-37-rev1-final .pdf (accessed 29.12.09).

A Blueprint for Security

13

INFORMATION IN THIS CHAPTER

- Risk in the Development Lifecycle
- Security Architecture
- Patterns and Baselines
- Architectural Risk Analysis

INTRODUCTION

How do you validate the design of new applications before coding even begins? Do you have a formal methodology to assess the fundamental design of third-party applications or services? The key to these issues is defining an enterprise-wide approach to security architectural risk analysis. *Information security architecture* is not a new concept, but it is still a relatively immature discipline with few effective models available. This chapter introduces a new model that can help organizations to tackle this kind of analysis without having to employ a team of security architects.

RISK IN THE DEVELOPMENT LIFECYCLE

Security architectural risk analysis is a very specific skill set that isn't found widely within security groups except in the largest and most mature organizations. In this chapter, we will get down to the nuts and bolts level of conducting an architectural risk assessment, so if you don't come from a technical background, just do your best to glean the major points and the process-level concepts. Also keep in mind, however, that this activity is recognized as one of the three fundamental control activities in a secure development lifecycle, so it is important that you begin to think about these processes.

Ultimately, the goal of this chapter is to provide a new model as a reference to architects who are tasked with performing risk assessments of software, systems, and networks. Specifically, the hope is that by the end of this chapter, even the nontechnical audience will be able to do the following:

- Understand how architectural risk analysis fits into the three basic security functions every mature organization needs to ensure a secure environment.

- Through real-world examples and experiences, learn how security architectural risk analysis should be integrated into an existing Software Development Lifecycle (SDLC) and other design processes.
- Understand core security architecture concepts and goals.
- Develop an understanding of how risk analysis can be used practically to assess the fundamental design choices made by third-party solutions.
- Understand how this approach can help to prioritize projects and help organizations to focus on the most critical risk exposures.
- Learn some techniques to consistently determine security control requirements and the acceptable placement of components based on risk levels and predefined baselines.
- Apply these practical techniques in their own organizations to improve the lifecycle of any technology project.
- Be empowered, regardless of the size of their organization, to improve efficiency and reduce costs.

Architectural risk analysis is an often neglected discipline across the industry today and typically has only been adopted in the most mature organizations, such as the financial services and defense industries. However, because of the inclusion of this analysis in their security programs, these organizations have enjoyed increased efficiency of the development process, found fewer weaknesses during quality testing and postdeployment testing, and have developed a common language for risk that can be communicated to executives. This chapter will describe how a well-focused and flexible security architecture program can result in measurable gains for the organization by introducing an innovative approach to developing and assessing security architectures, building reusable patterns, and consistently making risk decisions about exposures. The first steps toward success are to clearly define what the program will include, how it will be integrated into existing processes, and how it can benefit the business' objectives.

It is typical for security professionals to skip right to technologies to solve any issue that arises, resulting in inconsistent risk decisions, a myriad of technologies that can't be managed effectively, and, ultimately, an audit nightmare. A security architecture should describe the vision for how security can support the business mission and provide a reusable template for designers and business stakeholders. And, as noted earlier, architectural risk analysis is one of the three essential components of any secure application development program:

1. Architectural risk analysis
2. Code review
3. Penetration testing

Fundamentally, architectural risk analysis follows the same general stages as risk management (that is, resource profiling, qualifying exposures, and validating controls); however, applying these stages to an architectural risk analysis can seem like a daunting task for any organization. Luckily, this chapter includes a methodology that has been developed over many years and across several organizations and industries. The approach provides structured guidance for making this analysis streamlined and consistent. Essentially, this chapter aims to provide a starting point for implementing this process in your own organization and to give you a roadmap for how to evolve that practice over time as the risk management program matures.

Analysis Workflow

The process for defining security requirements should begin with a *security risk profile* of the proposed application/system. This exercise will help identify any sensitive information being processed or stored by the target system as well as any other assurance needs. Following the completion of the profiling process, the *security architecture risk analysis process* should be initiated as part of the application design process. Figure 13.1 describes the steps included in the architecture workflow.

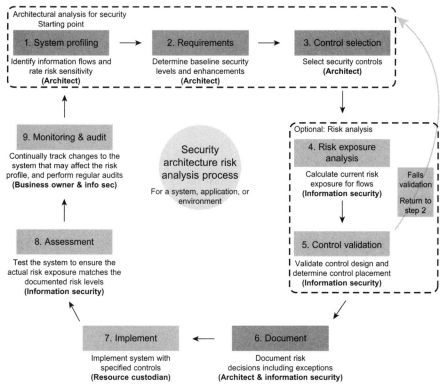

FIGURE 13.1

Security architecture risk analysis workflow.

This is a cyclical workflow that guides the business owner or designer through all the steps of

- determining the individual security needs of each system component
- calculating risk exposures and matching them to the appropriate level of security controls
- choosing solutions that meet the security functional requirements
- documenting any exceptions to the process
- assessing the posture of the implemented solution
- monitoring them on an ongoing basis to trigger re-evaluation if any aspect of the risk profile changes

For most projects, steps 2, 3, 4, and 5 of the workflow (shown in Figure 13.1) can be bypassed if established architectural or design patterns are used. However, wherever projects deviate from an established pattern, a formal architectural analysis must be performed. Similarly, a formal risk analysis (steps 4 and 5) may not be necessary for every project. The architect and members of the security team will work together to determine which projects warrant a formal risk assessment.

Steps 1 to 8 of this workflow should be directly integrated into the application/system design process or SDLC. As functional and nonfunctional requirements for the project are defined, the risk implications should also be considered and the appropriate controls chosen early in the lifecycle to reduce the time spent redesigning a system right before implementation, or worse yet, having to change the system after deployment because of an unmitigated vulnerability.

During an application/system's lifetime, the risk profile may change due to many factors such as changes to its functionality, new regulations, or newly discovered vulnerabilities. All changes should be reviewed to determine how they affect the risk decisions made during the system's initial design, and any significant changes should prompt a re-evaluation of this process to ensure the existing security controls still meet the assurance requirements.

In general, the security architecture should frame a common concept and measurement of risk exposure, which will guide risk decisions across the organization. Several points in a system's lifecycle will require guidance from the enterprise information security architecture (EISA), including the following:

- Design stage – after a new system is proposed
- Evaluation stage – after a system is implemented, but before it goes "live"
- Re-evaluation stage – anytime a significant change is made to the system's risk profile, or on a regularly scheduled basis
- Audit stage – whenever an audit is performed on a system

Upon adoption of the architecture, legacy systems will be brought into compliance over time based on their priority to the organization.

SECURITY ARCHITECTURE

Traditional information security practices have always been primarily concerned with perimeter control. The assumption was that the outside world was un-trusted and the inside was trusted. As environments have grown more complex, however, it has become necessary to separate different portions of the internal environment based on sensitivity to the risk that is imposed by or upon other parts of the environment. The increasing recognition of the number of security breaches initiated by malicious insiders and the rising transitive risk imposed by one line of business on another through differing security decisions have forced organizations to define a defense in depth strategy that can help to mitigate those risks. Early attempts of many organizations to address these issues without a common security framework have lead to the implementation of point solutions and ad hoc implementations that have not been consistent across the enterprise and, in some cases, have not been the best solution to meet the organization's business goals.

Goal of Security Architecture

Although many good risk decisions may have been made, and in many cases best of breed controls have been put in place to protect the organization and its clients, without a common framework to measure the effectiveness of these controls or ensure consistency of implementation, there is no assurance that the real risks are being addressed. Without a common vision and standard methodology for integrating security into the business environment, disparate implementations and inconsistencies can present undue risk to the business.

The need for a unifying security vision and consistent methods to mitigate what is a complex set of risks has led to recognition of a need for the development of an EISA. To realize a unified vision of information security across the entire business that can grow and scale over time, several design priorities must be established. At a high level, the EISA must

- provide guidance for tactical security projects
- facilitate the security policy and process initiatives
- lead the standardization of risk decisions and technology across the organization
- better establish security standards for the design of new systems, environments, and services
- establish basic security principles that limit access by default and diversify protection techniques
- improve the security of the organization

These priorities should guide every step of both the architecture development and its application over time.

Security architecture can be a catalyst for increasing the level of risk consciousness in the organization. It can also provide every business owner or system designer with the tools for determining the necessary security controls based on business objectives rather than just industry trends. The result is a cohesive environment with practical security standards and reusable design patterns that can accelerate the development process and simplify the audit process.

The purpose of the EISA is to inform the enterprise of the strategy for how and when to protect sensitive data and critical resources. The key characteristics of the security architecture framework are that it

- provides the strategic roadmap and long-term view for security across the organization
- translates business objectives and processes into security context
- informs the organization of recommended practices and conventions, some of which may already be in use and can subsequently be
  - more uniformly and efficiently applied
  - more effectively communicated to key stakeholders
  - more clearly defined and tracked for auditing purposes
  - used to improve the security posture of the entire environment
- provides the methods, mechanisms, and tools to assist auditors and business owners to ensure the proper use of controls for specific resources based on standardized risk decisions
- provides the business owner and security service provider a more comprehensive awareness of information security needs and the types of functions that may be used to provide adequate control
- provides a standard design reference and list of recommended technologies for the entire enterprise
- enables the organization to audit compliance to designated security baselines and standards enterprise-wide
- expands on industry standard and proven best practices from inside the organization as well as other organizations such as NIST, IETF, ISO, CERT, SANS, SABSA, ISC^2, and others
- translates security stipulations from all contracts, local laws, industry regulations, and national or international laws into security requirements for protecting client, company, and employee information
- is organized in a modular manner that allows for maximum reusability between implementations and maximum lifetime for each architecture component

Developing an Architecture

Like other areas of risk management, the architecture development and implementation review processes need to be driven by particular business requirements for assuring various levels of *confidentiality*, *integrity*, *availability*, and *accountability* based on the risk to a particular resource.

There are many ways to organize and represent a security architecture. The following lays out a very formal approach; however, this level of detail is not essential for a program to be successful. The formality and structure of your architecture are going to depend a lot on your business needs. The organization's Information Security Policy is the highest level articulation of the business goals and the ways in which security can help facilitate those goals. All levels of the EISA should be in line with this organizational direction and should provide a path to accomplish the goals of the policy. Similarly, the security policy mandates that all business owners and system designers make use of the security architecture and meet its standards. The EISA facilitates the organization's ability to satisfy the following requirements that were set forth in the Information Security Policy:

- Security architecture shall enable the organization and its business units to perform business processes electronically and deliver secure services to their customers.
- Business requirements and security policies, not the technology itself, should drive the choice of security controls.
- Security levels applied to data and resources shall, at a minimum, be commensurate with their business value and sufficient to contain risk to an acceptable level.
- Security architecture shall be based on industry-wide, open standards, where possible, and accommodate needs for varying levels of security.
- Security is a critical component of individual business unit and organization systems interoperability.
- Information systems security will be built into systems from their inception rather than "bolted on" after system implementation.
- To achieve the benefits of an enterprise-standards-based architecture, all information technology investments shall conform to the established EISA that is designed to ensure the protection and interoperability of information technologies across the organization.

As seen in Figure 13.2, the highest level is always going to be driven by the organization's guiding policies.

The *target architecture* is the first step or highest level artifact in the overall EISA. The *target architecture* provides the foundational concepts, principles, and models similar to the topics covered at the beginning of Chapter 7. This is meant to guide further development of more specific architectural patterns and design documents. The next level is the *reference architecture*, which addresses the same concepts as the target but at a logical level. The reference level document should reflect and represent all of the major security strategies from the target level, including in which security zone to place resources, choosing an appropriate access control model, and the functional requirements for the associated security controls. This will then be applied to specific environments and scenarios in individual *architectural pattern* documents. Each *architectural pattern* should translate the *reference architecture* into technology level specifications for a particular part of the environment and address any specific considerations that differentiate the data and resource risks in this environment

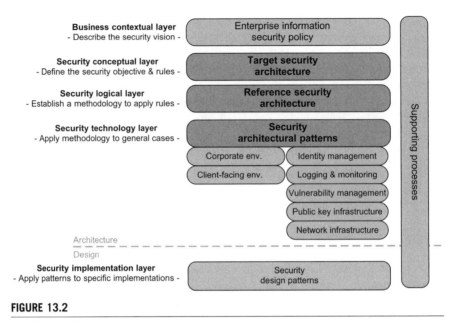

Business contextual layer
- Describe the security vision -

Security conceptual layer
- Define the security objective & rules -

Security logical layer
- Establish a methodology to apply rules -

Security technology layer
- Apply methodology to general cases -

Architecture

Design

Security implementation layer
- Apply patterns to specific implementations -

Enterprise information security policy

Target security architecture

Reference security architecture

Security architectural patterns

Corporate env. | Identity management
Client-facing env. | Logging & monitoring
Vulnerability management
Public key infrastructure
Network infrastructure

Supporting processes

Security design patterns

FIGURE 13.2

Architecture hierachy.

from the rest of the enterprise. From these architectural documents, *design patterns* will be created for specific implementations. A *design pattern* should translate the technology specifications from the *architectural patterns* into detailed designs. These designs will specify the desired products that meet the higher level architectural goals and should be reusable across many implementation projects. *Design patterns* are not considered part of the suite of architecture documents because of their level of specificity.

Notice in this model that security supporting processes are addressed at every layer of the architecture as needed. Along with the specific documents associated with each layer of the architecture in the Figure 13.2, the EISA framework also includes artifacts such as worksheets, templates, and tools to support the implementation of the architectural standards.

When establishing such an architecture, you will also need to develop a migration strategy and perform an assessment of current state in order to guide adoption of the architecture. This migration strategy should provide high-level objectives for dealing with legacy systems that do not currently match the architecture and also define steps for integrating a standardized security architecture review process into new system development and acquisition. This is not a process that will be completed overnight, but rather is a lengthy initiative with milestones defined along the way. For example, many organizations have found the architecture to be a good reference when performing risk analysis of existing systems, whereas others have chosen to apply it only to new development.

Security Architecture Principles

The following are foundational security principles that should influence the development of the architecture and patterns, as well as their implementations:

- Should be in alignment with security policies
- Security policies should drive the selection and implementation of security controls (process or technical)
- Should be risk-based

Information systems (including software, computing platforms, systems, data, and networks) should maintain a level of security that is commensurate with the risk and magnitude of the harm that could result from the inaccessibility, loss, misuse, disclosure, or modification of information. The selection of controls should also be based on a business risk analysis and risk management decision. Security without adequate business or risk justification should be avoided.

Operational Considerations

Technical security controls should not be recommended without the implementation of associated management and operational controls. This may include support and maintenance functions, or response and audit processes. A technical security control should only be considered viable if the associated management and operational processes are also deemed practical for the organization.

Measurement

All security requirements that define how a system or product should function must also provide criteria to measure how well it performs the given security function. In the past, target metrics were usually only identified for performance needs, making it difficult to measure the efficiency and effectiveness of a security control or process in reducing risk.

Modularity

Components of the architecture itself should be re-usable between particular implementation projects and should be modular to prevent advances in technology from requiring updates to the entire architecture. The lower layers of the architecture should specify controls in more detail and will therefore be more susceptible to technology changes. Without substantial changes in business need or risk, it is anticipated that the security services will not fundamentally change.

Separation by Risk Profile

A security zone is a physical or logical grouping of resources, which share the same risk profile and business function. The boundaries between zones are implemented using security controls, which are meant to filter inbound or outbound communications and mediate access to sensitive resources. These boundaries may exist within a larger application/system or be network level controls between different resources.

Virtual controls can be used to create security zones that are able to share some physical infrastructure and location. The boundary of the security zone is defined by the controls, the strength of enforcement, and the traffic they allow or prevent.

The EISA should provide guidance and tools for determining the proper placement of security zone boundaries and determining the criteria for controls at those boundaries and within the perimeter (such as application controls within a system or communications between systems in the same zone).

The decision to place a resource, component, application, or service into a particular zone is determined by any or all of the following factors:

- The need to avoid exposure to risk
- The need to avoid imposing risk on other resources, components, applications, or services
- The need to meet business requirements that can only be satisfied by a dedicated environment

Examples of zone boundary implementations include networks separated by network layer controls, virtual machines separated by virtual machine controls, or processes separated by process controls. In each case, the risk is isolated from other applications and data of disparate risk.

The abstract notion of a security zone is useful in that it can be used to communicate business level risks and controls as well as technical level risks and controls. Additionally, it allows for the risks and controls to be documented in a consistent and comprehensive manner. Another strength of this definition of a security zone is that it can also be used at many levels of granularity. Security zones can be applied to groups of resources or to distinct subcomponents or individual devices in a system.

Other business factors also can drive separation into security zones. While some business factors are not risk motivated, they can and often do affect the risk environment in which a resource exists. These can include cost factors or specialized performance requirements. The degree of separation also depends on performance and high-availability requirements for systems and networks, the need to protect systems with weak self-defenses, and the level of required C-I-A-A assurance.

Rules of Data Movement

The motion of data between zones with different risk profiles (often inter-security zone) is subject to the rules of data motion in the architecture, namely:

1. Data may only pass between resources or components via a security control or service, even if they remain within the same security zone.
2. If a security zone boundary is traversed, security controls must be used to ensure the data's C-I-A-A needs are preserved at the strictest level defined by the source zone's risk profile.
3. Both the initiator of a communication and the recipient may impose security constraints on the other party, depending on the differences in risk profile between the two entities.

The criteria for applying these rules should rely on the recognition that the data will traverse a path or system with a different risk profile or function, or travel outside the direct control of its owner. These are very high-level rules for information exchange that can help to protect data throughout an entire lifecycle, regardless of the path they take or systems they traverse.

Information Flow Control Model

Access control models look at security from the perspective of users and objects and their associated attributes pertaining to the authorization to access certain resources. The *information flow control* model looks at the same environment from the perspective of what information is authorized to be transferred between entities. The rules of data movement form the basis for defining security requirements in the *information flow control* model. In this model, security controls help to ensure that information transfers involving an information system are not made from a higher security level object to an object of a lower security level without proper mitigation of the inherent risks. In this model, the risks associated with interactions between users and resources are analyzed from a data communications perspective. Every information flow has an initiator, a target, and a path. This may be across a network or just within the memory space of a single system; either way the same concepts apply.

Nontraversable Boundaries

The majority of security designs and considerations focus on defining the necessary controls to ensure that an essential communication is protected and limited to the expected participants and activities. In many cases, there are resources with no business need to communicate. In these cases, the infrastructure must in some way prevent a communications path from being available to those entities in order to limit transitive risk and adhere to the principle of least privilege. Like network flow controls that filter and restrict permitted traffic, there are different levels of strength within the space of controls to enforce nontraversable boundaries. For example, virtual segmentation controls can be overcome or bypassed given very specific conditions; however, proper configuration and design precautions should minimize these risks. The risk sensitivity of the resources in question should dictate the strength of nontraversable boundary controls needed to separate them.

Trust Relationships

The following three aspects influence the threat that an information flow presents to a resource:

1. Type of flow initiator – human user versus automated
2. Endpoint/medium – interval versus external, and inter-zone versus intra-zone
3. Privilege level – basic, privileged, or management

FIGURE 13.3

Degrees of trust.

The ways in which these attributes can affect risk decisions for a business owner are described in more detail below.

Type of Flow Initiator

The flow initiator (or principal) encompasses both human users and automated processes. An automated process is viewed as somewhat less threatening, in that it is more likely to originate from an established endpoint to make a routine type of request, and therefore is less prone to human error in keystrokes. As with a device (endpoint), the more information that can be established about the initiator (through the use of controls, including the necessary authentication strength), the more trust that can be leant to the communication. Figure 13.3 illustrates the trust level spectrum for these characteristics.

It is also typically easier to define what is expected activity or traffic when dealing with an automated process than when dealing with a human. Thresholds and limits can be set more specifically with an automated process because interactions are programmatic (which is not to say that an automated process can't perform an unexpected action, of course). In contrast, human interactions can be harder to predict and sometimes require a larger range of acceptable activity. However, predictability can have its security drawbacks as well. For instance, an automated and scheduled process may be easier to intercept or impersonate once the malicious attacker has determined the pattern of occurrence when compared with user interactions, which tend to be more sporadic.

Endpoint/Medium

Along with the flow initiator, there is also the device (endpoint), from which the flow initiates, and network (transport medium), which the flow traverses, to consider. Generally speaking, a device maps to some level of compliance with organizational policies for approved configurations, installed protections, and so on. The risk profile of the transport medium will vary based on the organization's level of knowledge about or control over that path.

For this second aspect of trust, the possible categories vary between "Internal" and "External" parties and between "Inter-Zone" and "Intra-Zone."

Internal/External

Considerations about whether the access device is owned and maintained by the organization ("Internal") are a particularly important aspect in determining the risk it imposes on a resource. A device not actually controlled by the organization can

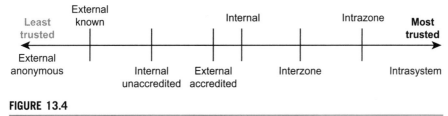

FIGURE 13.4

Degrees of endpoint trust.

still be checked for its adherence to policy. Compliance would indicate that similar risk protection decisions have been made, in which case they may be treated as "Internal" access devices. The same is true for a network outside the organization's control, although in these cases, documentation, accreditations, and regular audits are used more often than active checks on each connection. In general, flows traversing nonmanaged networks ("External") will require a higher level of controls. In reality, there is no longer a clear distinction between internal and external, but rather a continuum of trust based on the mentioned considerations.

Intra/Inter
The distinction between intra- and inter-zone is similar to the distinction between internal and external, except that all traffic occurs within an environment controlled by the organization. However, the important considerations are the same. The risk profiles of systems sharing the same zone are more likely to be more similar than those in separate zones, and therefore the risk decisions are more likely to have been similar and sufficient for each; so, an intra-zone data flow requires fewer mitigating controls. Figure 13.4 illustrates the trust level spectrum for these characteristics.

In general, the closer the endpoint and medium come to meeting the risk profile and assurance requirements of the target resource, the less stringent the required controls over the ensuing communications.

Privilege Level: The Initiator's Assigned Rights
Special and higher authorizations allow the flow initiator greater levels of control either over a business application or the configuration of the resource itself. The basic user will have the most typical assurance needs to protect their interactions with the resource that will often match the risk sensitivity rating of the overall target resource. Since they comprise the broadest category, basic users will also necessitate higher levels of controls to limit activity than a more tightly controlled and trusted group such as management users. Privileged or management users, indicating administrative access levels (not executive management), have a much greater level of control over the applications and resources with which they interact. Because of this, initial access is granted to a limited group, and the particular risk sensitivities of these flows will require certain controls to adequately protect

them. A privileged user may have more access to an application (for example, application administrator or role administrator) than a basic user, but they would not have full administrative privileges to the underlying system like a management user would.

At a minimum, basic user controls focus on limiting the scope of access to only authorized activity, and management controls emphasize the strength of authentication, confidentiality of information retrieved, integrity of any configuration changes, and accountability of all activities. The management baseline is more clearly defined because it is a more specific case, whereas a basic user's C-I-A-A requirements will vary more greatly between resources.

These three primary characteristics—type of flow initiator, endpoint/medium, and privilege level, together—comprise the basic combinations that define the possible trust levels for a data flow.

Security Zones

Segregation of resources into security zones (also called enclaves or domains) should be the default, not the exception. Users should remain in their own zone, separate from any services that are offered. Every application should be in a zone dedicated to providing services, separated from the user machines, and isolated by risk sensitivity and exposure levels. Co-location of applications that can share risk will serve as both an economic advantage and a means of simplifying management of application environments. In the desktop environment, the same rules of least privilege should apply, meaning that any communications path between users or access devices should be denied unless there is a specific business need for that service to exist. In most environments, it is rare that a direct peer-to-peer service is needed; so, preventing it can also help to eliminate many threat vectors such as internal abuse of privileges, inadvertent sharing of sensitive data, or the spread of malware.

The concept of segregation by zones can also be extended into the user space. These zones can divide user groups by risk and requirements as determined for applications. Some of the user associated groupings may include the following:

- Users on public networks
- Customers and partners on private networks
- Guests (nonemployee) on internal networks
- Limited access staff (including "nonstandard" internal users) on internal networks
- General access staff on standard platforms
- Privileged access staff on internal networks
- Infrastructure management staff on internal networks

Each of these may have specific security controls and would require explicit controls for any communications directly between users. The separation of application tiers and zones also requires that users, both internal and external, be separated from the service environments. Users should not be commingled with servers, just as servers of differing risk should not share the same unrestricted resources. In all cases, a boundary requiring authentication and authorization will exist between users and services. In addition, access to an internal user network should be limited to authorized users and machines and should limit the access of unknown and unauthorized machines that may be used to gain access (either directly or indirectly) to authorized resources.

PATTERNS AND BASELINES

The following terms and concepts are provided to help guide architectural decisions regarding risk in any environment.

Services (Payload) Traffic

Services traffic is business data and communications exchanged between a service and its intended business clients, directly related to fulfilling the business purpose for which the service was created. This traffic includes the delivery of services to end users, the communications necessary to deliver the business service to the end users, or data exchanged between the component entities that deliver the business service.

A service is generally the final target of a traffic (flow) request or may itself be an automated initiator of a flow to another service resource. Automated flows from one service system make business requests for data or services from another resource, such as an Application server requesting services from a Database, Messaging, or Web Service within the same or across another service zone. Service resources that host business-mission applications usually have three functional tiers: data storage, business logic processing, and user interface functionality.

Examples of this traffic include the following:

- Communications (traffic) to and from a corporate application
- Authentication and directory services (this category of traffic also includes a special subset called Infrastructure Common Services)
- Application database replication (within this category of traffic, management-resource databases are a special subset); on-demand or scheduled replication of data

Management traffic and *infrastructure common services* are both considered to be specialized subsets of service traffic that are treated separately because of their unique attributes and security requirements.

Management Traffic

Management traffic is any service that makes direct contact to another asset (which becomes the "managed resource"), either to retrieve or interface with the configuration and status of hardware components, the core operating system, features of user interfaces to the OS, or the business application, sometimes taking subsequent action to maintain or change configurations. All actions ultimately provide underlying support to the service being delivered by the managed resource to its users. This highly privileged access will usually allow either modification and/or viewing of sensitive system configurations. Management traffic includes three categories: management, monitoring, and data backups and restores.

Infrastructure Common Services

Common services are services used by multiple applications, data flows, zones, and tiers. They are focused on application use (as opposed to management use). Examples may be date/time synchronization, authentication and directory services, network address assignment, and network name resolution.

External versus Internal Traffic

In today's networked world, the distinction between "external" and "internal" users, networks, and services has become blurred. Government agencies apply the term "external" to any network or system that lies outside of what is known as the accreditation boundary—outside of the area in which the agency or company can monitor, test, review, and maintain visibility and control over security posture. In the context of this architecture, "external" will no longer refer to the physical location, but rather the level of control over the security posture of the endpoint device or user.

This is a conceptual perspective on security segregation by general risk profile and function. Boundaries should exist between these zones in order to delineate a high-level view of security control placement and separation by risk profile.

Transitive Risk Considerations

As portions of infrastructure are designed, built, or redesigned, the risk imposed by neighboring resources and communicating resources needs to be considered. In particular, as controls and zones are shared between resources to save money and reduce complexity, the varying assurance requirements of the data need to be accounted for. Resources should be separated if their defined security requirements are distinct from those of their neighbors. Three primary reasons to separate resources using security zones are as follows:

1. Outside risk (cannot accept risk) – the content of the zone is subject to external risk and must be protected.
2. Inside risk (generates risk to others) – the content of the zone poses additional risk to the environment and therefore requires separation.
3. Nonsecurity related – business requirements dictate isolation of the environment (for availability, throughput, and so on).

Risk to a particular asset, system, application, or set of data needs to be assumed by the business owner, but if that risk cannot be contained within the boundary of that entity, the risk will also have to be considered by any affected business owners. In terms of a general case, a few key instances of this relationship are worth considering.

Shared Zones

An important transitive risk exposure scenario would involve resources that share a common zone. In this case, the principle of least privilege recommends that there should be no traversable data paths between the resources if there is no need for them to communicate directly. If there is a need for interaction, the paths between them should be tightly restricted only to those flows that are necessary. This prevents a situation where users of one resource have a free reign to navigate to all the systems in a particular zone. If business owners decide that their systems should reside together for economic or operational benefits, then the threat universe and vulnerabilities of those neighboring systems must be taken into account when calculating the risk exposure for each resource in the group.

Risk to Other Interfaces

Similar to the transitive risk threat between resources in a shared zone, the risk that a flow may impose on other network flows on that system must also be considered. Accepting risk on a particular service interface may have implications for other services related to that asset. If a user interface is exposed to a risk that is exploited, this could leave other flows such as a back-end connection to another server or a management server vulnerable as well. The value of defense-in-depth measures is to minimize the impact of a compromise to a given service, and network controls alone may not be sufficient to fully mitigate the risk. For this reason, whenever a risk decision is made regarding the protection of a single data flow, the implications on the asset overall and any related resources must also be considered to contain the risk exposure.

Traversing Risk Sensitivity Boundaries

In an enterprise environment, it will often be necessary for systems of differing risk sensitivity levels to communicate with each other. In these cases, the proper controls should be put in place based on the determination of the specific information flow's sensitivity to risk. Since this determination relies not only on the impact of the data itself but also on the level of control over the system that is exposed on the flow, the flow controls must be appropriate to protect both parties involved.

Combining Security Controls

Often, it will be beneficial to share or combine security controls for multiple resources, either to reduce operational complexity or for economic reasons. In fact, effective design and planning of zones should identify the logical boundaries that resources can share when they require the same level of protection. When considering the benefits of shared or combined controls, it is important to also account for the availability requirements of that interaction—the potential impact for each resource of relying on a single path through a set of controls if those controls suffer a failure or denial-of-service attack, for example.

Aggregate and Partial Data

Assessing the risk sensitivity of a data flow requires focusing well beyond the risk sensitivity of the asset as a whole and beyond even that of any one application or function of that resource. The specific characteristics of the individual flow need to be considered. There are two primary aspects of a flow to consider: the sensitivity of the data in that flow or directly accessible by that flow and the privilege to the asset or application that the flow allows. These two factors will help guide risk assessment decisions made regarding the application of security controls.

In fact, a particular flow may have access only to a very specific interface on an application, one for instance that displays a small subset of data from a system, which is determined to be less risk sensitive than the larger collection of data. A certain system may gather data from many resources of varying risk sensitivity and the compiling system should assume the risk sensitivity of the most sensitive source with which it communicates. The particular data that are gathered and compiled must be reviewed to determine the risk sensitivity of the compiled set. For example, a billing system may gather data from highly risk-sensitive resources, but the actual cost-center and usage statistics information may be deemed to be low risk because only partial data have been gathered. A similar example would be a performance monitoring system that tracks the uptime of a resource. This performance data may be classified as low sensitivity even though the systems it monitors are determined to be highly risk sensitive.

Similarly, the risk sensitivity of the aggregated data should be considered based on the combined value of individual information. Often, seemingly nonsensitive data can be combined into more meaningful groupings that may have higher risk sensitivity in their aggregated form and therefore require stronger protections. All these behaviors should be considered when resources of varying risk sensitivity need to communicate and share data.

Multidevice Systems

When a system is distributed across several physical assets for functional or availability purposes, communication across the network presents an additional opportunity for risk; it exposes the data flows to observation, tampering, blocking, and misdirection. In particular, clustered and highly available systems may include several physical assets that are connected over the network for synchronization and health-check functionality. If these components communicate over a shared network space, they may be exposed to the risks listed above and you may therefore need to account for these issues when making risk management decisions. It is recommended that appropriate information flow controls be applied to any flows on shared networks or within systems, but if operational or business reasons preclude these measures, then the business owners need to be aware of the risks and make decisions accordingly. This intra-system but inter-asset communication could be secured by segmenting the traffic either physically or logically to limit the participation to only the authorized system components.

Front-End versus Back-End Application Tiers

Based on software development best practices and to achieve improved functionality and flexibility, a three-tier application approach also increases the ability to protect various components of the system from each other using information flow controls between them. In some cases, the business owners may determine that the components can reside in the same zone based on their risk profile and functional needs to communicate; however, other instances may require the different parts of the application to be separated by zone boundaries due to differing risk postures such as an exposure to external entry that is deemed too risky for the back-end components directly.

Public-Facing Resources

Services available to external entities can be generally categorized into two groups: those that are made available to the public in an anonymous fashion and those that are only accessible by a predetermined and restricted user community. The risk profiles of these two sets of services differ greatly due to the difference in threat universe, data sensitivity, and assurance needs. Security controls around public access services should be mostly focused on protecting the availability of the data and the integrity of the asset itself from compromise rather than on the other assurance needs of the public data. In general, risk sensitivity ratings are mostly based on the degree of impact if the data were disclosed to unauthorized parties; however, there is no unauthorized audience for public resources. Given that these public-facing resources have such a different risk profile, and therefore their owners have had to make very different risk decisions than for externally facing systems with restricted user populations, it is necessary to separate public/anonymous resources from nonpublicly accessible resources with security controls. Commonly, this segmentation is referred to as a DMZ. Whenever other internal resources need to communicate with externally accessible assets, their threat universe and risk exposure should be accounted for when determining the necessary security controls on that communication.

Internal Nonstandard Clients

When considering the risk exposures from clients accessing a particular service, it should be noted that not all internal systems adhere to the same standard client profile and standards. In any organization, there are usually nonstandard client systems in the environment that deviate from the normal client system build and typical usage profile in order to support specific business purposes. Any service owner should determine the appropriate security requirements for users of their resource, and any flow to a client that does not meet those requirements may require additional network flow controls to mitigate the exposure. Examples of nonstandard clients might be users running a different operating system or users who have connections to outside resources that are more risk prone than the typical user.

ARCHITECTURAL RISK ANALYSIS

To fully realize its potential, the EISA needs to be fully integrated into each process for application development, system design, technology solution implementation, and related business processes. Starting at the initiation of a new project, information assurance needs must be considered along with any other nonfunctional requirements. In fact, the security needs of an application, system, or environment should directly support a particular business requirement, such as a need to protect customer account numbers from unauthorized access during transactions. In this way, superfluous constraints, or security for security's sake paradigms, can be avoided.

Detailed Risk Analysis Workflow

The workflow diagram (Figure 13.5) mentioned earlier in this chapter is included again as a reference when reviewing the process steps in more detail. The risk analysis process is intended to present a sensible progression for determining security needs, choosing controls, and validating the protection decisions. The process can help to identify gaps in controls, map out various scenarios for securing access to a resource, weigh the results of each, and make informed decisions accordingly. The workflow lays out the approach to applying the security architecture to a system or environment's lifecycle and the progression of the workflow (see Figure 13.5).

This workflow represents the confluence of tools and techniques within a security architecture with existing operational evaluation and planning activities, including portions of other risk assessment processes and development systems such as a typical Information Security Risk Management Program and SDLC. An overall profile of the resource in question should be completed before beginning this process. The output from the architecture risk analysis process can then be leveraged to further document risk management decisions in the later steps of an overall asset risk assessment process or to support decisions during an audit scenario.

The following section contains brief descriptions of each activity shown in the workflow diagram. Reference tables have been provided in *Appendix C—Architectural*

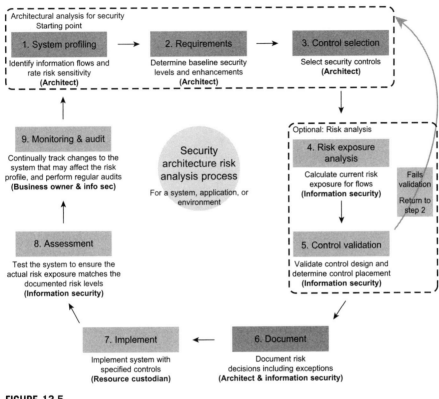

FIGURE 13.5

Security architecture risk analysis workflow.

Risk Analysis Reference Tables, which you may want to refer as you review the risk analysis workflow.

Primary Workflow

The following workflow describes the steps that will be taken for new resources and throughout those same resources' entire lifecycle from inception to retirement.

1. System Profiling
   In this stage, the information flows are identified and risk sensitivity for each one is rated. It is important to characterize the target resource and identify any functionality, data classifications, and system/user interactions. This general information will be important when making risk decisions and control determinations throughout the process.
   1.1 Each applicable type of information flow is identified and categorized.
   1.2 Assign four individual C-I-A-A risk sensitivity ratings for each flow of the resource. Also, determine the overall risk sensitivity rating for each flow based on the C-I-A-A ratings.

2. Requirements

   In this stage, the *baseline security levels* and *enhancements* are determined.

   2.1 Use the matrix in *Appendix C* to determine the *baseline security level* for each flow based on the overall risk exposure rating. Fill in the corresponding functional assurance requirements for each flow.

   2.2 Use the matrix in *Appendix C* to determine the *enhancements* to the *baseline security levels* for each flow based on the C-I-A-A risk sensitivity ratings.

3. Control Selection

   In this stage, the appropriate controls are selected according to the functional requirements identified in the last step.

   3.1 Combine any *enhancement* requirements with the *baseline security level* specifications to form the complete control selection criteria. Select controls that satisfy these functional requirements (baseline and enhancements) and document how each requirement has been met. Any exceptions should be noted, and the compensating controls or risk acceptance approval should also be noted.

4. Risk Exposure Analysis

   In this stage, the current level of risk exposure is calculated for each flow

   4.1 Determine the *threat universe* (TU) rating for each flow.

   4.2 Assign a *vulnerability* (VU) rating for each flow, with known weaknesses noted.

   4.3 Populate the overall *risk sensitivity* (RS) rating for each flow.

   4.4 Calculate the current *risk exposure* rating, which is the product of the *threat universe* rating, *vulnerability* rating, and *risk sensitivity* rating.

5. Control Validation and Placement

   In this stage, the control design will be validated and the security value measured.

   5.1 Recalculate the risk exposure rating, accounting for the security controls selection criteria identified by the *baseline security level* and *enhancements*.

   5.2 Measure the security benefit (that is, reduction in risk) by comparing the risk exposure rating before and after the application of security controls.

   5.3 Determine the appropriate placement of the resource, given its risk profile and function.

6. Document Risk Decisions

   Use the resulting risk data and functional requirements from the *risk analysis process* to support the risk management decisions in the general approved risk management process.

7. Implement

   Implement the resource according to the appropriate development lifecycle, such as an SDLC, and include the designated security controls as part of the rollout.

8. Assessment

Once a control or set of controls are rolled out, but before going "live," an assessment needs to be performed to validate that risk exposure has been reduced to the expected level. The assessment process involves the following:

- Compiling evidence that the controls are implemented correctly and operating as intended.
- Validating that the controls are producing the desired outcome with respect to meeting the security requirements of the system.
- Presenting this evidence in a manner that decision makers are able to use effectively in making credible, risk-based decisions about the operation or use of the system.

An assessment procedure consists of a set of assessment objectives, each with an associated set of assessment methods and assessment objects. An assessment objective includes a set of determination statements related to the particular security control under assessment. The determination statements are closely linked to the content of the security control (that is, the security control functionality) and the assurance requirements, which were identified in earlier steps, to ensure traceability of assessment results back to the fundamental control requirements. The application of an assessment procedure to a security control produces assessment findings. These assessment findings are subsequently used in helping to determine the overall effectiveness of the security control.

The assessment should begin with a review of the risk assessment documentation from the system's development and should verify that not only have the specified controls been implemented but also the controls are configured and behaving as expected. Assessment activities usually include examinations, interviews, and hands-on testing. This will often take the form of vulnerability or penetration testing to validate technical controls. Paper exercises or dry runs can also be effective for policy and process controls.

9. Monitoring and Auditing

It is necessary to perform ongoing monitoring of the controls to ensure they are still providing the expected level or assurance and to regularly audit the controls to ensure they are complete and still appropriate for the risk profile of the resource being protected. As aspects of the resource change and grow through natural evolution and additional development, this may cause the risk profile of the resource to change. In addition, new threats and vulnerabilities emerge constantly, also necessitating a re-evaluation of the protections that have been put in place. All security controls should have a clearly defined set of criteria against which to measure their performance. Monitoring and reporting should be in place to validate that the control is meeting the expectations laid out in these criteria.

As you might imagine, step 9 is not the "last" step in this process; rather, the process should be ongoing, constantly monitoring performance and reassessing the resource's needs both over time and when major modifications to its profile occur. With this workflow, every business owner has the opportunity to explore the ways the owned resource is accessible as well as how it affects the other systems.

The *baseline security level* and *enhancement* tables (provided in *Appendix C*) have been derived from the NIST 800-53 document [1].

Risk Exposure Analysis

One aspect of this approach to architectural risk analysis will certainly require a little more explanation and that is step 4—*risk exposure analysis*. This is represented as an optional step in the workflow because steps 4 and 5 can be bypassed if established architectural or design patterns are used. However, wherever projects deviate from an established pattern, a formal architectural analysis must be performed. Similarly, a formal risk analysis (steps 4 and 5) may not be necessary for every project. The architect and members of security team will work together to determine which projects warrant a formal risk assessment.

The risk exposure is calculated for each information flow using the values in Figure 13.6. This is done first without considering any compensating controls and then again in step 5 with the compensating controls included. The comparison of the risk exposure values from steps 4 and 5 demonstrate the value of those controls by calculating the reduction in risk exposure and the residual risk level can be compared to the asset's risk tolerance range for further validation.

An example of how this flow analysis might look on a worksheet is shown in Figure 13.7. In this example, the *cross site scripting* vulnerability is outside of the recommended risk exposure range, but the *internal IP address leak* is within the acceptable range. Then, by applying the controls that would be selected in step 3, this raw risk exposure should be reduced to an acceptable level.

This same risk analysis methodology can also be used to determine when one resource in a particular environment might be introducing too much transitive risk

Risk exposure (based on the CVSS scoring scale)		
Threat universe × Vulnerability risk × Risk sensitivity = Risk exposure		
Threat universe scale: 1 = 1–50 potential users 2 = 51–500 3 = 501–2000 4 = 2001–32000 5 = 32001 or more potential users	**Vulnerability scale:** 1 = negligible vulnerability/controls implemented 2 = low-risk vulnerability 3 = moderate-risk vulnerability 4 = high-risk vulnerability	**Risk sensitivity scale:** 2 = a low sensitivity to risk 3 = moderate sensitivity to risk 4 = a high sensitivity to risk
Risk exposure scale: Low = 1–8 Moderate = 9–25 High = 26–39 Extreme = 40+	**Recommended risk exposure levels:** Risk sensitivity Recommended exposure range Low Low–high = 1–39 Moderate Low–moderate = 1–25 High Low = 1–8	

FIGURE 13.6

Risk exposure reference for information flows.

ID	Threat universe	Vulnerability risk	Risk sensitivity	Risk exposure
1	22,000 users 4	Cross site scripting 4	Moderate 3	**Extreme** 48
1	22,000 users 4	Leaks internal IP address 2	Moderate 3	**Moderate** 24
____	____ users ____	____ ____	____	____

FIGURE 13.7

Risk analysis worksheet example.

to another resource. For example, if the resource in Figure 13.7 had these same vulnerabilities that were not addressed, think how that would affect another resource on the same network segment that had a high-risk sensitivity.

Legacy Migration Workflow

The same *security architecture risk analysis* workflow described above applies to the general process for bringing legacy resources into compliance with the security architectural standards. The primary difference here is that, for existing systems, applications, or environments, active vulnerability assessments can be performed to educate the risk exposure calculations. Once the necessary controls have been identified in step 3, a gap analysis should be included to determine whether current controls in place meet the same standard and intent, or whether additional controls are needed. The resulting documentation step would then include a plan for applying controls based on priority or risk and the effort involved, and this plan would then be carried out in the implementation step.

To really make this process effective, supplementary documentation will need to be provided, including workflows and worksheets to aid business owners with the task of determining a system's risk profile and evaluating its risk exposure. Many of the quantifications resulting from the risk analysis tools and techniques may be useful to the business owner outside of this process as well.

SUMMARY

Architectural risk analysis isn't just an activity that your architects need to worry about, this should be a core aspect of your risk management program whenever there are systems and applications being developed or acquired. Some level of vulnerabilities are going to exist and by looking at them from the perspective of the associate information flows, you can better assess the necessary controls to protect them and the appropriate placement for them in your environment. Using the analysis workflow in this chapter, you can efficiently leverage existing patterns to shorten the analysis cycle and help the architects and designers by defining high-level control requirements based on the risk exposure level of the flow.

Action Plan

After reading this chapter, you should consider taking the following actions in your own organization:

- Document reusable patterns for any common architectures or designs, such as a central authentication or Web-based application model, which meet your organization's security goals.
- Use the principles in this chapter to define a high-level target architecture document that can be used as a reference for new system/application design.
- Formally integrate an architectural risk analysis into the very early stages of your development lifecycle.
- Identify existing gaps by performing an architectural risk assessment of your most critical or exposed information flows.

Reference

[1] NIST 800-53, Revision 3. Recommended Security Controls for Federal Information Systems and Organizations. http://csrc.nist.gov/publications/nistpubs/800-53-Rev3/sp800-53-rev3-final_updated-errata_05-01-2010.pdf (accessed 21.11.10).

Building a Program from Scratch

14

INFORMATION IN THIS CHAPTER

- Designing a Risk Program
- Prerequisites for a Risk Management Program
- Risk at the Enterprise Level
- Linking the Program Components
- Program Roadmap

INTRODUCTION

Knowing how to assess a risk is clearly an essential skill for risk managers and analysts, but this knowledge in no way guarantees that you will be successful at building a security program around risk activities. Traditionally, guidelines for security leaders have focused on such aspects of a security program as awareness or budgeting, but how can any of this be properly prioritized without first establishing a basic risk profile for your organization? Sure, you can publish some basic security policies, roll out introductory awareness training, and start to budget for additional resources and technologies, but in the end, you still need some fundamental risk assessments to ensure that these initiatives are focused on the most critical weaknesses of your organization.

DESIGNING A RISK PROGRAM

Consider the organizations that have been involved in the major data breaches receiving media attention over the last few years (we won't name them here because, really, they have suffered enough), and you will discover that it wasn't that these organizations weren't spending enough money on security, they just weren't focusing their resources in the right areas. In fact, the US economic crisis that began in 2008 has caused many to challenge the viability of risk management principles in general. Many have claimed that the risk management principles that failed the financial community shouldn't be trusted to help the *information security* industry. The problem with that argument is that the success or failure of any risk model is really a matter of implementation. Even the most brilliant and perfect theory, principle, model, or technology can be misused in practice or, in many cases, ignored. The good news is that there are many very capable professionals diligently working on developing new models and frameworks for assessing and evaluating *information security* risks. The gap that still exists, and that this book has been specifically written to address, is how to take these developments and put them into practice across a diverse industry. The approach taken in this book has been to provide guidance for managers and analysts about how to build and operate a risk-based security program that is agnostic of the particular risk model or techniques. It doesn't matter if you come from a qualitative background, prefer a quantitative approach, or use a hybrid of the two; this book provides a high-level methodology and program-level view of risk management, and the analysis techniques are meant to be interchangeable. If you don't like the qualitative mapping tables in previous chapters, substitute a table from OCTAVE Allegro or even use a formula from FAIR. The basic principles and structure of the program will work regardless of your preference.

With all of that said, the structure of and the activities in the program become an important focus for anyone who is responsible for running an *information security* program. As you might expect, a good risk management program can't stand on its own without a good basic foundational infrastructure. Throughout this chapter, we will focus on several basic building blocks for any good *information security risk management program*, including the prerequisites for starting one. Since formal security risk management programs are still not very common, we will also look at approaches to building a program from scratch and where to focus resources initially. Whether you are building out an entire security program from the ground up, or just trying to mature an existing program to follow a risk model, this will give you the step-by-step implementation plan. At this point, you should already be comfortable with the techniques involved in performing risk assessments, but now we need to add approaches for measuring the value of security and qualifying the current risk level for presentation to executive level management. As each risk program component is introduced in this chapter, be thinking about whether your own organization does or doesn't already incorporate the activity, and if not, how they could be integrated into your current program. By the end of this chapter, you should have a solid understanding of how security risk assessment fundamentals and tools can be implemented holistically to properly manage the *information security* risks that exist in your own organization. Basically, you should be able to articulate how you will focus your efforts so that your resources will be directed in the right places and used most efficiently.

Risk Is the Core

It is essential for any security professional to understand how a risk model can become the center of a mature *information security* program. The evolution of the threat landscape and security field into a more mature discipline requires that a risk-based focus be pervasive throughout your information security program.

There are many components of a typical security program, including event monitoring, penetration testing, code reviews, awareness and training, metric reporting, policies and standards, and security architecture, and all of these map nicely to different aspects of risk management. Most of your days as a security professional are spent trying to prevent vulnerabilities from being exploited and identifying new ones or, on bad days, catching vulnerabilities being exploited. Risk management should be the umbrella for all these activities, but it should be more closely focused on making risk decisions based on what is an acceptable level of risk for the organization and what the priorities of the business are.

If policies are a foundational component of any mature security program, then risk management is the core. Policies lay out the security expectations for the organization and these policy statements should inform the focus of risk management activities. For example, you might have a policy about the proper protections for sensitive data that your organization processes and a standard detailing how it should be handled securely. Risk activities would then be implemented to identify and rate the sensitivity of various data types and assess any gaps in handling practices, after which mitigation plans would be implemented to address the most critical exposures. Although it used to be common for security managers to force controls and restrictions on their organizations based on so-called "best practices," without truly researching and understanding the real risks to that organization's mission, you should now be promoting a risk mindset throughout the organization. You will know that this paradigm shift from best practices to a risk-based program has been successful when you start to encounter challenges from the business that are more than the typical resistance to encountering security constraints and are, instead, well-thought-out risk arguments. When business units start using your own risk tools against you to rationalize not implementing a security control, take a step back and realize that you have finally penetrated the business culture of the organization. This is the level of discussion and debate that should be encouraged.

Program Goals

All too often, *information security* is forced on an organization, and this approach creates resistance, leading to limited success in actually improving security posture. By shifting the focus away from blindly applying industry standards across the board and enforcing minimal compliance with regulations, the *information security* function can help to identify and address the risk exposures that are most likely to impact the organization. Think about the fundamental goals of an *information security risk management program*:

- Improve the security posture of the organization
- Empower business units to identify and remediate risks
- Help prioritize remediation tasks
- Educate the organization regarding real threats and weaknesses
- Increase visibility and capability to track risks

- Improve the consistency of risk assessment approaches
- Establish a common formula for risk evaluations
- Meet audit, regulatory, and customer expectations

Notice that the word "control" isn't used once in this list of goals. Although security controls are an important tool in risk management, controls are never a goal, but rather a means to an end. This is important to keep in mind because, as an industry, we are constantly losing focus on our most basic responsibilities to our organizations. It is too easy to get caught up in thinking only about what controls we have in place and which ones are missing, rather than focusing on enabling the business objectives of the organization. We need to avoid what is sometimes called the "big hammer" approach to security, when best practices are forced down the business' throat. Security should be framed in terms the business understands and honestly weighed against other goals for the organization. If our expectations are nothing short of an *information security* utopia, then we are going to fail. Well-thought-out and properly implemented risk management methodologies will finally help us to break free from the best practices mentality because what is considered best for the industry may not even be applicable to your organization.

Risk management is a lifecycle approach, meaning that the process of evaluating, remediating, and assessing exposures never ends. It is all about knowing how, when, and where to apply security measures. Once you realize that there is no such thing as totally "secure" (because you can never eliminate all risks) and that the responsibility for decisions about how to protect data ultimately falls on the data owner (you are just the data custodian), then you can start to put things into perspective and not take management decisions too personally.

Most security teams will participate in some form of annual planning meeting. This is a great opportunity to read through that list of program goals again and reset your focus. It can be all too easy to get caught up in your daily activities and not lift your head up to assess whether you are still being effective. For example, if you are running a *threat and vulnerability management* program, are you taking the time to look for trends and alignment with business objectives? More than likely, if you aren't careful, you are charging forward at 110% to accomplish the goals that you set out at the beginning of the year. Unfortunately, looking at your alignment and focus annually just isn't enough. This examination really should be more of a quarterly review activity. Get your team together every quarter and review a common set of metrics that will identify themes or systemic issues that need focus. This is also a good opportunity to adjust for any changes in the organization's initiatives. Remember, close alignment with the business strategy is the key to a successful program.

Starting from Scratch

Even with the right attitude, just having the right components is not enough to build a successful program; you will also need to know how to make the most of the limited time and resources that you have to work with. You can save yourself a lot of pain and effort by following these simple rules:

1. Don't run a security scan of the entire environment and throw the resulting 200 page report down on the CIO's desk expecting it to all get fixed – you just made an enemy for life.
2. Don't try to identify and profile every system and data type all at once – comprehensive inventories aren't built overnight.
3. Don't try to build a comprehensive risk model that will account for every possible scenario and special case imaginable before you start looking for critical risks – that feared security breach may happen before your perfect model is complete.
4. Don't take on large-scale assessments until you have proven your methodology is effective and repeatable on a small scale; otherwise, you will continually be wasting resources struggling with fundamental process issues.

You can sum up all this advice in one statement: you only get one opportunity to make a first impression on the organization—so don't waste it by taking on too much. For example, when faced with building a program from the ground up, many people will try to assess the sensitivity of every asset in the organization right out of the gate. As you can imagine, this process gets complicated quite quickly. Start small, establish some successes, and then expand. The first solution doesn't have to be the perfect solution to cover every possibility right from the beginning. You should expect your risk model to grow and be revised over time.

The following are the essential steps for a young security risk management program:

1. Establish an asset inventory
2. Define your risk scales
3. Profile your environments (sensitivity)
4. Define a workflow for assessing vulnerabilities

Keep in mind that these four steps are just the bare minimum to get started, but it can be a challenge to stay focused on establishing these foundational components without getting distracted. You will need to have the discipline to suppress the tendency to just start fixing the obvious stuff before you have these basics in place.

A good example of this dependency, on the four steps, is that before any risk evaluation can be performed, a *security risk profile* must first be created for the resource/environment in question. As discussed in earlier chapters, the security risk profile gathers information about the resource to help rate its sensitivity to security risks. The profile relies heavily on having an accurate inventory of systems, applications, or data in your environment. Ideally, the resource owner would provide basic information about the asset, such as a description of its purpose, applicable environments, user community, applicable regulations, and so on, and would rate the resource's importance to the organization from an *information security* perspective.

It might already be apparent to you why defining the risk scales is the next essential step. There really is no basis for resource owners to evaluate the importance of any asset if you haven't defined the risk level scales yet; with no scales, a rating of High versus Low is meaningless. Remember that our guidance is to start small, so rather than starting the risk profiling process at a server or application level, begin by profiling the environments as a whole. You need to start prioritizing and filtering somewhere, so pick a level and begin there.

Now you might think that you are ready to press the **Start** button on that Nessus scan of your network, but all that data are no good to you without a workflow to process it. You need to have a solid procedure in place to leverage your risk scales, to perform initial assessments of the vulnerabilities, and to allow you to focus on the ones with the greatest risk. You never want to be the one trying to force the desktop support team to patch every single vulnerability, from high to low, all at once. Worse yet, you don't want to give the desktop support team a list of vulnerabilities to fix, only to find out that they are all false positives that could have easily been identified if you had an accurate asset inventory. Remember, you only have one chance for that first impression, and trust is much easier to lose than to earn. It is all about picking your battles and justifying the risk.

Comparing the Models

So far in this book, four industry frameworks have been discussed: OCTAVE Allegro, FAIR, FRAAP, and NIST. Each risk framework has its benefits and drawbacks, so the most common solution is to take the best of each and leave the rest behind. The NIST lifecycle of stages fits most security programs the best when you are trying to implement a comprehensive risk management program. If you are just performing a single assessment of an environment or project, then the steps of the OCTAVE methodology may be a better fit. Especially for third-party assessors and consultants, the diligence of OCTAVE shows real value to clients, but it can also be overkill for smaller projects so you will likely want to combine several of the activities and worksheets.

One approach is to take the profiling activities and several of the worksheets from the OCTAVE Allegro framework. The level of detail in the worksheets can be excessive for some assessments, so simplifying the threat modeling by using the high-level categories will help. The NIST framework best defines postmitigation steps, and FAIR has the best scoring methodology.

Risk management is complex topic including many activities that touch on all aspects of any business, so you will likely find that each of the popular industry frameworks is better suited for particular situations. The key differentiators are

- NIST
  - High-level approach evolved into C&A solution
  - Comprehensive lifecycle
  - Automated implementations are successful
- OCTAVE Allegro
  - Detailed worksheets and questionnaires
  - Best suited for projects and one-time assessments

- FAIR
  - Detailed quantitative and probabilistic method
  - May be overwhelming for novices without integration into a tool
- FRAAP
  - Focused on project scale assessments
  - Style and structure are easily adaptable to other analysis methods
  - Format encourages collaborative brainstorming of risks in a structured setting

NIST 800-30 provides a very high-level and flexible workflow for risk management complete with some detailed process tasks and responsibilities defined; however, OCTAVE Allegro goes one step further by providing detailed artifacts such as risk worksheets to get you started. Of course, the strength of the OCTAVE Allegro method is also its weakness: although it provides good structure, it can also overwhelm risk novices with its many activities and worksheets. FAIR is one of the most comprehensive and intuitive models available; however, it can also be resource intensive when you are trying to assess a large number of risks very quickly. If we start to see the FAIR methodology integrated into security tools, its rate of adoption will likely increase quickly.

If you want to implement a program of *information security* risk management, you would likely start with the NIST 800-30 approach to qualify the bulk of your risks quickly, and then use the FAIR approach to really dig deeper into the critical or systemic risks to validate the initial assessment. However, if you are assessing a single critical application/system deployment, you should probably draw on the OCTAVE Allegro framework instead because it integrates very well into an existing software/system development process.

The newer NIST 800-37 approach to C&A seems to lend itself best to for any operational risk activities like analyzing vulnerability notifications from vendors or assessing systems for compliance to a baseline. The risk scoring based on essential controls is a good way to track the vulnerability level of your organization, but it has limitations. Lastly, for a more general IT-based approach, there is also a new emerging governance model from ISACA called RiskIT [1].

There are entire books and courses dedicated to teaching each of these models, but hopefully this overview gives you a good place to start and will help you to understand the major strengths and weaknesses of each approach.

PREREQUISITES FOR A RISK MANAGEMENT PROGRAM

Before you can even start talking seriously about a putting together a risk management program, you will need to have these following components in place:

- Security policies and standards
- Information resources inventory
- Security liaisons

- Common risk formula
- Enterprise risk committee
- Mapping of risk domains to business objectives
- Other security processes tied to risk
- Risk and exception tracking system

These have been listed in a rough successive order, but there really isn't any dependence between them. It is recommended that you start with a basic policy and standard set because this will set the tone for your security program. After that, the order isn't so important.

Security Policies and Standards

Very basically, you need to set out the expectations before you can assess your organization's compliance. If you are building a program from scratch, you shouldn't even bother with any other aspects of risk management until the most basic policies around Acceptable Use and Data Classification are established.

In the federal government, they have very clear guidelines for classifying information into different levels of sensitivity. Along with each classification level, there are specific protection and handling requirements. Nonfederal organizations usually adopt a three- or four-level system with Public-Internal-Confidential and sometimes Restricted categories. The right mix depends on the business model of your organization. Regardless of how many levels you employ or what you call them, the key is to define the levels based on differences in handling practices. There is no advantage to classifying two data types at different levels if the handling requirements are exactly the same. Simplicity is the key when developing your model. Remember, the classification system needs to be accessible to your average employee to make daily decisions about the sensitivity of the data they are handling. Just keep it simple because ultimately it will fail if users can't easily classify data on a daily basis. The levels should be logical and meaningful to your average employee.

Information Resources Inventory

Having an asset and data inventory is a basic part of any security program, but in many cases, it looks easier than it is. Assets usually are tracked at some level by other functions, but this often doesn't include the information that you will need. For example, your organization may have an inventory that is maintained by an operational or finance team, but does it include these details?

- Systems
- Software
- Versions
- Location
- Addressing

- Owner
- Regulated data

As a risk manager, inventories become critical for many reasons. We already discussed the need for an accurate system inventory when establishing a TVM program or implementing security risk profiles, but they can also be critical for several other tasks like answering client due diligence questions or assessing the priority of a real-time security alert.

Imagine that you receive an alert indicating multiple failed logins to the root account on server srvnyc001. If you don't know what environment that system is in, what services it provides, or what data are stored on it, then how can you possibly decide the criticality of responding to the alert? Even worse, imagine that you don't even get a server name, you just have an IP address, but that network range doesn't show up on any of your network diagrams, and you don't know who the system owner or administrator is…. This is unfortunately an all too common scenario, and as you can imagine, it really slows down any subsequent risk qualification process.

You may not appreciate how important an accurate inventory can be until you start considering tying together different risk assessments tasks. For example, you may identify an SSL cipher weakness on a particular Web server when running a security scan through your TVM program, identify the lack of compliance with cryptographic standards during a *security risk review* for a particular Web application, and get written up during an internal audit for allowing SSLv2 in a different Web application, only to find out that both applications run on the same Web server and that, therefore, these are really three findings from different sources all related to the same risk. Being able to tie these findings together through a common inventory that includes all the details mentioned above will be essential as your program expands and matures.

Likely, your team will not own the asset inventory for your organization, but you will want to work with the team that maintains it to add some additional information that will be useful in a risk management program and find a way to link this inventory to your profiling process. For example, you may want to enrich a standard inventory with another field indicating which applications a particular server supports. Or you may want to track the highest classification of data that is processed or stored by that resource. Inventories can also be used to populate other security tools like vulnerability scanners or log management systems. The value of a comprehensive inventory shouldn't be underestimated, but beware that stale data can often be more deadly than no data at all. Lastly, when you are assessing your own inventory, keep in mind that this should cover information resources as well as physical assets like hardware and software. After all, what we are protecting is really the data, not the physical containers.

Security Liaisons

Hopefully, a theme that you have seen woven throughout this book is the focus on doing more with less. Security leaders should be careful not to be seen as trying to build their own empire of security staff. When the size of the security team starts to dwarf some equally critical functions, you are just putting your team at risk for an undesirable level of scrutiny. With that said, the demands on the security function certainly aren't going to be decreasing any time soon, and it can be challenging to reconcile these two facts. One tactic is to establish a role of a *security liaison* (also called a *security maven* or *information security lead*) within other business units. This role is responsible for ensuring some aspects of executing security risk management activities and aspects of the *information security* program in general, within their own business unit. The scope of responsibilities will vary between organizations, but typically the role is responsible for and accountable for the oversight of security administration activities within their assigned functional areas, including some responsibility, along with the resource owners, for security risk profiling of the information resources. A *train the trainer approach* has become a common term in businesses who are looking for ways to save on the cost of education and training for their employees, and this role follows the same concept. The security team is responsible for training the liaisons and keeping them up to date with the latest developments and trends, and they can then rely on the liaisons to carry these messages to their own groups and translate them into terms that will be more meaningful to their teams.

Some possible responsibilities for this role might include the following:

* Oversee risk assessments in their function
* Review and approve policy exceptions
* Ensure audit issues are resolved
* Delegate security tasks within their function
* Maintain inventory of information resources
* Represent function to security committees and review boards
* Principle contacts for security issues
* Educate function on security policies and initiatives

Essentially, the idea is that since the security team can't be in every meeting or be involved in every decision, we need to enable liaisons from the various business units or functions to represent security interests on a daily basis. Liaisons are the key to execute a risk management program with limited staff.

Of course, you can't expect this role to be successful without up front and ongoing training and education. This includes not only the knowledge, skills, time, tools, and contacts needed to fulfill their role but also the clear authority and support from the executive level so that this doesn't become a meaningless title. Liaisons can be a great way to expand the reach of the security function without additional headcount, so you should be able to free up some budget to ensure they have a steady stream of targeted training to keep them current. Also, you will want to keep a focus on keeping them informed about incidents, trends, changes in standards, and any new regulatory or legal requirements. Plan regular meetings and training sessions with them, and integrate them into your risk activities as much as possible. Of course, these responsibilities must also be formalized as part of their personal performance objectives if you really want to see engagement.

Keep in mind that as security liaison positions are volunteer roles, they will need to get support from their own management to take on these responsibilities in addition to their current job function, so try to choose them carefully. You can often minimize the additional burden on these individuals by nominating those who already have close ties and complementary job roles to *information security*. For example, someone from the legal staff may already be responsible for negotiating the security clauses in contracts and ensuring they are sufficient; so, that individual might be a logical choice for a liaison. Similarly, someone in a business continuity or access provisioning role who works closely with the security team already would make an excellent security liaison for their function.

RISK AT THE ENTERPRISE LEVEL

Before you can even hope to tackle risk management at an enterprise level or integrate your security risk management program into an enterprise level view, you need to convince the organization of the value of a common risk formula.

Common Risk Formula

Whether you are a financial analyst looking at credit risk or a member of the human resources team analyzing the high percentage of critical processes being supported by contractors, you ultimately need to have a common formula or method for calculating risk. Even though the details of the model vary between these functions and you can't expect the financial analyst and the human resources staff to have the exact same criteria for a high-severity risk, at the enterprise level there has to be some way to compare them. In fact, the *information security* risk models that have been used throughout this book would never be directly applicable to other risk domains such as operations or finance, but the framework for the levels and exposure mapping methodology is reusable. All of the evaluation steps are somewhat modular, in that you could substitute in your own risk calculations into the lifecycle workflow.

It is very important to establish a common language for risk across the organization. You may have different descriptions of a high severity between the domains, but terms like severity, threat, likelihood, exposure, and vulnerability need to be consistent or you will never be able to have productive discussions about priorities across business units.

With a single format for tracking risks and a single calculation method, you can derive a means of normalizing risks identified by different functions at an enterprise level to get a true picture of the organization's posture. A critical risk for the financial liquidity of assets from the accounting team needs to be equivalent to a critical exposure on a Web service from the *information security* team. Before you bother implementing any actual risk activities or assessments, start by surveying the different risk models already in use within your organization and align them to a common formula and definition for risk terminology.

Enterprise Risk Committee

In most organizations, the Enterprise Risk Committee is made up of senior management or their representatives. All the different functions should be represented, including *information security*, *legal*, *compliance*, *HR*, *operations*, *finance*, and *vendor management*. Typical characteristics for an enterprise risk committee include the following:

*   Looks at risks across the entire organization
*   Most senior management levels
*   *Information security* is just one member
*   Only the highest level risks are reported
*   Often systemic or thematic risks are highlighted
*   Usually reports risks to the *board of directors*

Often, at this level, risks will be broken up by *risk domain* (such as *brand/reputation* or *legal/regulatory*) and then maybe more specific subcategories or *risk areas*.

The topic of enterprise risk management is beyond the scope of this book, so we will focus on the role of *information security* in this program. Most importantly, there need to be clear criteria defined for how and when significant risks will be escalated to this group. You will want to start out by only escalating the most serious risks to this level (those rated as critical risk exposure, for example) because you will want to make sure that you direct attention and focus to those issues. If you present too many risks, they will just get lost and the committee will lose focus. As your program matures and you eliminate critical risks, you may start presenting some key lower level risks, but be careful not to appear to be dominating the risk committee. There are risks from many domains that executives need to understand and balance against any security exposures.

It is a good idea to keep the risk committee current with the security posture of the organization. One approach to this is to present a "state of the company" type of report to the risk committee, in which you look at the risk posture and exposure level across the organization. It is essential to realize that *information security* issues are just one source of risks that need to get prioritized and weighed against other business risks.

Mapping Risk Domains to Business Objectives

A risk domain is a high-level grouping of risk areas that is generally tied to an overall business goal for the organization. For example, a business goal might be to increase the efficiency of service/product delivery to customers. So, an appropriate risk domain might be titled *product delivery* and would include all aspects of product development, project management, and product rollout, including some security components. In this case, a security risk to product delivery might be that there is no security testing performed until the product is ready for go-live, at which point a penetration test is performed, leaving no time to fix any issues that are discovered.

Some possible business objectives that you might use to define your risk domains are as follows:

- Make money (maintain a profit margin)
- Don't break any laws/regulations (keep regulators happy)
- Stay ahead of our competition
- Grow into new markets/diversify your revenue
- Increase/protect the brand value
- Deliver your products and services as expected
- Maintain operational excellence

Notice that we don't categorize *information security* as its own domain, but rather as a source of risk in many domains. If risk domains are mapped to business goals, then security doesn't make the list. Being secure intentionally isn't listed as a risk domain for the organization because security is generally a component that will contribute to other risk areas like reputation or financial loss. But there are certainly security components within many other business goals, especially in the legal and regulatory functions. Think about the impact to the organization of a security breach from the risk profiling exercises. It all comes down to financial loss, damage to reputation, legal penalties, and so on. Once you realize that the risks identified through your *information security risk management* program really impact domains not owned by the security team, this will allow you to better align your initiatives and concerns with the priorities of the business.

Operational risk is a typical risk domain for most organizations. This domain might include business continuity concerns such as disasters, service outages, supply chain failures, third-party dependencies, single points of failure, degradation of service, and so on. Typically, the operational domain is concerned with availability, but there are also other *information security* risks that will present within this domain.

Damage to *brand/reputation* is often a concern whenever a security risk is identified. The impact to the organization can be difficult to predict in all cases, but it is important to track this as a domain if appropriate. Of course, there are some organizations that are more insulated against reputational impact because customers might not have an alternative. These are all factors to account for in your risk model.

Some potential categories of security risk within each domain are as follows:

- Potential for exposure of sensitive information
- Potential for failure of a legal/regulatory obligation
- Potential for failure of a key process

It is critical to define the organization's business objectives, define the related domains of risk, and tie your security initiatives directly to them. This will make it clear to the business leaders exactly how your efforts are supporting the goals of the organization. Anything that doesn't map to these objectives should be discarded.

Examples of Risk Areas

Within the scope of technology, there are several key *risk areas* (some examples are listed) that can be used to categorize similar risk types. These groupings of risks help us to identify similar risks in our modeling exercises and for reporting purposes.

* Asset management
* Business continuity
* Change management
* Vendors and outsourcing
* Privacy and data protection
* Physical and environmental

For example, a security risk in the *change management* area may include unauthorized changes to an environment or it may involve ignoring a designated maintenance window. *Information security* risks will typically show up in many domains and various risk areas under those domains, so it is important to add risk areas as appropriate for your organization.

Operational, compliance, and legal concerns are usually at the top of the list for security professionals, but we must also consider other factors, like physical threats to outsourced functions or inability to recover data during a disaster situation. These all may fall under the umbrella of *information security* to identify and oversee, but the accountability lies with other risk domain owners to facilitate the qualification of the risks and oversee the progress of the mitigation plans to address them at the enterprise level.

LINKING THE PROGRAM COMPONENTS

So far, we have discussed several prerequisites for an *information security risk management* program; the last two can be grouped together under the category of linking what would otherwise be individual security activities and implementing a system to track them.

Tying Other Security Processes to Risk

Alignment amongst all the various *information security* activities and functions should have obvious value, but the best way to link these individual activities together isn't always as clear. These are just some of the activities that should feed information into the risk management program by identifying potential risk exposures:

* Vulnerability scanning
* Incident notification and response
* Application code reviews

- Architectural and design reviews
- Compliance to standards review
- Security event monitoring
- Internal audit reviews

In addition, the execution of each activity should be guided and shaped by the framework set out by the risk management program. For example, your *threat and vulnerability management* program should use the same scale and formula for rating risks as your *security risk review* or *architectural review* processes. The criteria and guidance for each level of the scale may vary between activities, but they should still use a common calculation of risk.

You really don't need to have an incredibly sophisticated solution in all of these areas to start seeing value. Just keep in mind that each activity needs to feed identified risks into the overall risk management program in order to truly get an accurate view of the organization's security posture at any given time. For example, if you are continually finding weak passwords on one production server through regular password cracking tests, then those data need to get fed into the *security risk review* process to create a new finding to investigate whether the server is out of compliance with the password complexity standards. More mature programs will automate these feeds through an oversight and tracking system.

Risk and Exception Tracking System

You will need to establish a system for tracking the state of risks in your environment. This doesn't have to be anything particularly complicated to start, but it does need to capture basic analysis information and mitigation plans. There are several commercial products in the Governance, Compliance, and Risk (GRC) space to fit this need, but use of these products is not necessary for success. At a minimum, you need a system that will allow you to

- document risk decisions
- capture reasons for risk rating
- document compensating controls
- provide tracking of mitigation plans

At a basic level, you will want to track risks associated with different resources and document all the details of the analysis. You will especially want to capture the reasoning for rating a risk at a certain level, any compensating controls, and details of the mitigation plan. This documentation could be as simple as a spreadsheet or SharePoint site or as complex as a commercial GRC system like Archer or Agliance. The power of a commercial GRC solution is the ability to directly link your risk assessments and exceptions to your incident or vulnerability tracking systems. In an ideal world, you would also have the capability to link your risk assessments to resource inventories, security risk profiles, and even SEIM systems.

If you spend your time developing or implementing any component of a GRC solution, you should consider starting with an exception workflow tool. In any healthy risk management program, there are always going to be exceptions. One way to improve the efficiency and ensure the appropriate visibility for exception requests is to base the level of approval on the level of risk exposure. If it is a high exposure, then that might require multiple signatures from executive management, but a lower exposure risk may just require a manager from the security team to sign off on it. This is another great opportunity to get *security liaisons* involved in the risk management process, by including them in the review workflow. You can also map the acceptability or need for mitigating controls to the risk level. For example, if you use a four-level risk scale, the lowest level may require no mitigating controls, the next might be acceptable with controls, the next level up may be executive management judgment and require remediation within a short timeframe, and the top level may be unacceptable to the organization without the highest level of approval, and even so, only temporarily.

Policy exceptions and risk acceptance criteria have been covered in detail earlier in this book, but the following are recommendations about some minimal fields to include in a tracking system:

- Standard form describing the risk details, including the risk rating
- Identify the owner of the risk and/or mitigation plan
- Description of the mitigation plan, including milestone dates
- Approval signatures
- Expiration date for the exception

The more complex you get with the logic of the approval workflow, to be determined by aspects of the exception such as the risk rating, the more you will want to somehow automate the exception process for simplicity and auditability.

PROGRAM ROADMAP

There have been a lot of concepts, suggestions, and approaches introduced throughout this book, and the many options available may make you wonder where to go after you implement the basic prerequisite program components. In an effort to give you the benefit of a several year view of a program's development, the following timeline is proposed as one path you might take your program, as shown in Table 14.1.

By the end of the third year, you should have a fairly mature risk program that is running smoothly with visible metrics. At this point, it is a good time to reevaluate the program and give it a facelift. Spend the time working with your own team and your contacts in other business units to assess what is working well and what needs improvement. For example, if you look at the last year of audit findings and all the same items were not caught by your internal risk assessments, you need to address why this is failing. Also, you might notice a trend in the due diligence questions that you are getting from your customers and decide to shift

Table 14.1 Security Risk Program 3-Year Roadmap

Date		Actions
Year 1	1st half	1. Develop a plan to address any missing prerequisite items (inventory, policies, and so on)
		2. Implement a very basic *threat and vulnerability management* (TVM) program
	2nd half	3. Expand your TVM program to highest sensitivity environments and establish measurable metrics
		4. Complete *security risk profiles* for your most critical resources
		5. Distribute a security risk review (SRR) questionnaire for just those most critical resources and focus on qualifying highest risk findings
Year 2	1st half	6. Refine TVM process and set metrics for all environments
		7. Expand the SRR process to include other high-sensitivity resources
		8. Implement a third-party SRR process with a more targeted list of questions (different from internal questionnaire) and target most critical vendors
	2nd half	9. Focus on identifying systemic and risk themes from TVM and SRR and escalate these to senior management
Year 3	1st half	10. Sponsor an initiative to develop security baselines for critical systems/applications and use these to streamline SRR internally
		11. Focus on ways to validate the SRR findings, such as reviewing event logs or scanning results
	2nd half	12. Document an Enterprise Security Architecture, or at least patterns for well-established implementations
		13. Identify strong risk indicators, and start tracking them
		14. Gather feedback internally about ways to improve the program

some assessment focus into those areas. You will find the most value when you can pull all of your risk information from all the various sources into one dashboard of risk. If you haven't gotten to this point after 3 years of operating the program, then this needs to be a priority.

Lessons from the Trenches

Very simply, risk management is a complex topic and there are a lot of areas that could easily trip you up as you begin to roll out your own program. This book is intended to provide a detailed roadmap for developing your own implementation, but in case you get seduced by the many distractions and misconceptions being propagated in the industry, try to keep these simple guidelines in mind:

- Start small
- Start with industry scales and ratings before developing your own

- Focus on oversight, security can't fix everything
- Tie security initiatives to business objectives

You have to keep focused on a small scope of assessments to start. A good place to start is by looking at just the highest level risks, setting aside the "Moderate" and "Low" findings at first. Similarly, don't try to assess risks for your entire organization right out of the gate. Many people make the mistake of trying to take on too much too quickly, and they fail. It is better to keep your scope small to start and then expand once you have a proven and stable process.

We have discussed at length how to develop your own risk models and scales, but it can be helpful to use an established framework to start. Once you get going, you can focus on customizing it over time as you identify areas where the framework doesn't meet your needs.

As the field is maturing, we are finding that the *information security* function is evolving into more of an oversight role and the operational duties are becoming more decentralized. The sooner you accept that you won't be able to fix every risk—and that the security team shouldn't always be responsible for remediation—the better.

Finally, you can't truly be successful unless you map your security initiatives directly to the business objectives of the organization. Showing this alignment will naturally encourage executive management support and provide the best chance for funding. Armed with these basic guidelines, you can now go out and improve the security posture of your organization, one risk at a time.

SUMMARY

Hopefully, now that you have reached the end of this book, you will agree that building a program around risk, and not just discussing risk analysis models, has value for any organization. You should be able to use this chapter to pull together the various risk models, assessment techniques, activities, and processes from the entire book and develop your own strategy for turning these into an actual program. As hard as it might be to assess some risks, you will find that the real challenge is integrating all of these components into your existing security program and showing real value to the rest of the business. This chapter presents several of the prerequisites for a risk management program and also offers one possible roadmap for implementing a program that will result in as little resistance as possible from the business.

Reference

[1] ISACA. The Risk IT Framework Excerpt. www.isaca.org/Knowledge-Center/Research/Documents/RiskIT-FW-Excerpt-8Jan09.pdf (accessed 20.01.11).

Appendix A: Sample Security Risk Profile

Resource Name: _____

Business Owner: _____

Information Security Team Contact: _____

A. GENERAL INFORMATION

1. Please select which groups of individuals have access to your information resource:
   - ☐ Employees
   - ☐ External Clients
   - ☐ Partners
   - ☐ Outsourcers
   - ☐ Regulators
   - ☐ Government Agencies
   - ☐ Vendors
   - ☐ Other
2. Has a penetration test been performed on the application?
   - ☐ Yes
   - ☐ No
   - **2.1** Please enter the date of the most recent penetration test: _____
   - **2.2** Who performed the most recent penetration test? _____
   - **2.3** Please briefly describe any outstanding security issues: _____
   - _____
   - _____

B. INFORMATION SENSITIVITY

3. Please specify the client data used or collected (select all that apply):

Client Data	Contains Data Value (YES/NO)
Financial institution account information	
Credit card information	

Continued...

(Continued)

Client Data	Contains Data Value (YES/NO)
International identifying number (for example, Social Security)	
Home address	
Home or cell phone	
Medical information	
Birth date	
Personal private information (for example, mother's first/middle/maiden name, city of birth, first school, and so on)	
Cultural information (racial or ethnic origin, political opinion, religion, trade union membership, sexual preference, criminal record)	

4. Please specify the employee data used or collected: (select all that apply)

Employee Data	Contains Data Value (YES/NO)
Birth date	
Credit card information	
Cultural information (racial or ethnic origin, political opinion, religion, trade union membership, sexual preference, criminal record)	
Dependents or beneficiaries	
Financial institution deposit information	
Hire date	
Home address	
Home or cell phone	
International identifying number (for example, Social Security)	
Marital status	
Medical information	
Performance reviews/evaluations	
Personal private information (for example, mother's first/middle/maiden name, city of birth, first school, and so on)	
Salary/compensation information	

5. Please specify the type of corporate (internal business information) data used or collected (select all that apply):

Corporate Data	Contains Data Value (YES/NO)
Client lists	
Financial forecasts	
Legal documents/contracts	
Merger or acquisition plans	
Strategic plans	

6. Please specify the type of third-party data used or collected (select all that apply):

Third-Party Data	Contains Data Value (YES/NO)
Intellectual property	
Licensed software in internally developed applications	
Subject to Non-Disclosure Agreement (NDA)	

7. Does the information resource use or process any other confidential or restricted data?

☐ Yes, please specify: _____

☐ No

8. Does the information resource administer use or grant access to sensitive data (or privileges) on other systems?

☐ Yes

☐ No

8.1 Please describe how this application administers access to sensitive data on other systems or grants access to sensitive data:

_____

_____

9. Does the information resource process any financial transactions?

☐ Yes

☐ No

9.1 If information resource initiates or accepts financial transaction (noncustomer transactions – internal to the organization only), please specify approximately how much money is processed:

☐ < $10,000

☐ $10,000 to $49,999

☐ $50,000 to $499,999

☐ $500,000 to $1,000,000

☐ > $1,000,000

10. Could mishandled information damage the organization by resulting in faulty business transactions, loss of money, or jail time?
- ☐ Yes
- ☐ No

    10.1 If information was compromised by an unauthorized outside party, select the resulting level of potential damage:
- ☐ Criminal Prosecution
- ☐ < $500,000
- ☐ $500,000 to $999,999
- ☐ $1,000,000 to $4,999,999
- ☐ $5,000,000 to $9,999,999
- ☐ > $10,000,000

C REGULATORY REQUIREMENTS

11. Is the information resource subject to any regulatory requirements?
- ☐ Yes
- ☐ No

    11.1 Please select the *regulatory requirements* that are applicable (select all that apply):
- ☐ Federal Financial Institutions Examination Council (FFIEC)
- ☐ Gramm-Leach-Bliley Act (GLBA)
- ☐ Health Insurance Portability and Accountability Act (HIPAA)
- ☐ Office of Foreign Asset Control (OFAC)
- ☐ Subject to regulation in multiple jurisdictions (that is, European Union, BAFIN, Asia Pacific)
- ☐ Other, please specify: _____

    11.2 Please briefly describe which aspects of the regulation apply to the information resource:

_____

_____

12. Are there any other *requirements* (for example, contractual) that mandate information security controls for confidentiality, integrity, availability, or accountability?
- ☐ Yes
- ☐ No

    12.1 Please provide any detail on other requirements that may be applicable for the information resource:

_____

_____

D. BUSINESS REQUIREMENTS

13. Please rate the overall <u>confidentiality</u> needs (the consequence of unauthorized disclosure or compromise of data stored, processed, or transmitted by the resource) of the information resource:
- ☐ High
- ☐ Moderate
- ☐ Low

14. Please rate the overall <u>integrity</u> needs (basically the consequences of corruption or unauthorized modification/destruction of data stored, processed, or transmitted by the resource) of the information resource:
- ☐ High
- ☐ Moderate
- ☐ Low

15. Please rate the overall <u>availability</u> needs (basically the consequences of loss or disruption of access to data the resource stores, processes, or transmits) of the information resource to <u>non-Company</u> users:
- ☐ High
- ☐ Moderate
- ☐ Low
- ☐ N/A

16. Please rate the overall <u>availability</u> needs (basically the consequences of loss or disruption of access to data the resource stores, processes, or transmits) of the information resource to <u>Company</u> users (excluding access to support the application or system itself):
- ☐ High
- ☐ Moderate
- ☐ Low
- ☐ N/A

17. Please rate the overall <u>accountability</u> needs (basically the consequences of the inability or compromised ability to hold users accountable for their actions in the resource) of the information resource to its <u>general users</u>:
- ☐ High
- ☐ Moderate
- ☐ Low

18. Please rate the overall <u>accountability</u> needs (basically the consequences of the inability or compromised ability to hold users accountable for their actions in the resource) of the information resource to its <u>support or administrative users</u>:
- ☐ High
- ☐ Moderate
- ☐ Low

19. Please rate the overall reputational damage to the organization if it was known to the user community or industry that the information resource has been breached or defaced in some manner:
- ☐ High
- ☐ Moderate
- ☐ Low

E. DEFINITIONS

Use the following definitions for Low, Moderate, and High ratings in this questionnaire:

Rating	Definition
Low	A compromise would be limited and generally acceptable for the organization, resulting in minimal monetary, productivity, or reputational losses There would be only minimal impact on normal operations and/or business activity
Moderate	A compromise would be marginally acceptable for the organization, resulting in certain monetary, productivity, or reputational losses Normal operations and/or business activity would be noticeably impaired, including the potential for breaches of contractual obligations
High	A compromise would be unacceptable for the organization, resulting in significant monetary, productivity, or reputational losses The ability to continue normal operations and/or business activity would be greatly impaired, potentially resulting in noncompliance with legal or regulatory requirements and/or loss of public confidence in the organization

Appendix B: Qualitative Risk Scale Reference Tables

Aspects of the qualitative risk scales are spread throughout several chapters in this book. The following is a consolidated reference for these scales, which can be used in your own assessments:

Table 4.2 Qualitative Risk Sensitivity Scale

Level	Criteria
High	A compromise would be unacceptable for the organization, resulting in significant monetary, productivity, or reputational losses
	The ability to continue normal operations and/or business activity would be greatly impaired, potentially resulting in noncompliance with legal or regulatory requirements and/or loss of public confidence in the organization
Moderate	A compromise would be marginally acceptable for the organization, resulting in certain monetary, productivity, or reputational losses
	Normal operations and/or business activity would be noticeably impaired, including the potential for breaches of contractual obligations
Low	A compromise would be limited and generally acceptable for the organization, resulting in minimal monetary, productivity, or reputational losses
	There would be only minimal impact on normal operations and/or business activity

Table 4.4 Risk Tolerance Levels

Risk Sensitivity	Risk Tolerance (Risk Exposure Range)	Risk Threshold (Risk Exposure Upper Bound)
Low	Negligible–High	High
Moderate	Negligible–Moderate	Moderate
High	Negligible–Low	Low

Table 6.11 Qualitative Severity Scale, 4-Level

Level	Description
Low	May be a deviation from recommended practice or an emerging standard. May lack a security governance process or activity but have no direct exposure.
Moderate	May indirectly contribute to unauthorized activity or just have no known attack vector. May result in a degradation of service and/or a noticeable decrease in service performance.

Continued...

Table 6.11 Qualitative Severity Scale, 4-Level (*Continued*)

Level	Description
High	May allow limited access to or control of the application, system, or communication, including only certain data and functionality. May result in a short disruption of service and/or denial of service for part of the user community.
Critical	May allow full access to or control of the application, system, or communication, including all data and functionality. May result in a prolonged outage affecting all users of the service.

Table 6.12 Qualitative Likelihood Scale, 5-Level

Level	Description
Negligible	The threat source is part of a small and trusted group; controls prevent exploitation without physical access to the target; significant inside knowledge is necessary, or purely theoretical
Low	The threat source lacks motivation or capability, or controls are in place to prevent, or at least significantly impede, the vulnerability from being exercised
Moderate	The threat source is motivated and capable, but controls are in place that may impede successful exercise of the vulnerability
High	The threat source is highly motivated and sufficiently capable, and controls prevent the vulnerability from being exercised are ineffective
Very High	Exposure is apparent through casual use or with publicly available information, and the weakness is accessible publicly on the Internet

		Severity			
		Critical	**High**	**Moderate**	**Low**
Likelihood	**Very high**	Critical	Critical	High	Moderate
	High	Critical	Critical	High	Low
	Moderate	High	High	Moderate	Low
	Low	Moderate	Moderate	Low	Low
	Negligible	Low	Low	Low	Low

FIGURE 6.2

Qualitative mapping table, 4/5-level, no sensitivity.

Likelihood	Severity	Risk sensitivity		
		Low	Moderate	High
Negligible	Low	Low	Low	Low
Negligible	Moderate	Low	Low	Low
Low	Low	Low	Low	Low
Negligible	High	Low	Moderate	Moderate
Low	Moderate	Low	Moderate	Moderate
Moderate	Low	Low	Moderate	Moderate
Negligible	Critical	Low	Moderate	Moderate
High	Low	Low	Moderate	Moderate
Very high	Low	Low	Moderate	Moderate
Moderate	Moderate	Moderate	Moderate	Moderate
Low	High	Moderate	Moderate	Moderate
High	Moderate	Moderate	Moderate	High
Low	Critical	Moderate	Moderate	High
Moderate	High	Moderate	High	High
Very high	Moderate	Moderate	High	Critical
High	High	Moderate	High	Critical
Moderate	Critical	Moderate	High	Critical
Very high	High	High	Critical	Critical
High	Critical	High	Critical	Critical
Very high	Critical	Critical	Critical	Critical

FIGURE 6.3

Qualitative mapping table, 4/5-level.

Appendix C: Architectural Risk Analysis Reference Tables

Chapter 13 outlined the workflow of security architectural risk analysis and referenced several reference tables for baseline security requirements and mappings to risk sensitivity. These tables have been consolidated in this appendix for ease of reference.

BASELINE SECURITY LEVELS AND SAMPLE CONTROLS

Table C.1 lists the Baseline Security Level requirements (from S5 to S1), along with some sample controls that might meet those requirements.

Table C.1 Security Baseline Levels	
Functional Requirements	**Security Technology Controls**
S5: Application Protocol and Session Filtering, Inspection, and Validation	
S5.1. Traffic should be terminated, inspected, and reinitiated at the application level (OSI Layers 6 and 7).	**Application Proxy:** breaks the application session and reinitiates it to the target system. It also verifies that it is the expected type of traffic at the application layer and below.
S5.2. Application level protocol decoding and policy enforcement.	**Application Proxy:** uses session identifiers to track the state of communications and only allows certain requests to pass. Any encrypted communications should be decrypted by the proxy and re-encrypted if needed to the target.
S5.3. Enforce authorization policies based upon user identity, endpoint security state, and/or network information.	**Application Proxy:** uses a combination of user/device authentication and current endpoint state checks to filter access to protected resources. The proxy may use a combination of network address, ports, and protocols to filter access to protected resources.
S5.4. Validation of proper application behavior.	**Application Proxy:** uses an application-aware logic to verify that application requests and calls are valid and authorized.

Continued...

Table C.1 Security Baseline Levels (*Continued*)

Functional Requirements	Security Technology Controls
S5.5. Protect against and eradicate malicious code transmission, and automatically updates protection.	**Application Proxy with Anti-malware:** uses either a built-in or third-party scanning mechanism to inspect all authorized traffic for malware including viruses, worms, trojans, and spyware.
S5.6. Detect application layer attacks using signature-based, anomaly-based, or behavior-based methods.	**Application Proxy with IDS:** uses intrusion detection features to detect common network exploits.
S5.7. Include mechanisms (should be automated) to isolate and eliminate application attacks and exploits.	**Application Proxy with IPS:** uses intrusion prevention features to automatically block common network exploits.
S5.8. Audit activity based upon user identity, endpoint security state, and/or network information.	**Application Proxy:** uses system logs to track activities based on the account login of the user or source network/device. Also uses system logs to track the accepted and blocked traffic flows based on the identity of the user and the application calls and data transmitted.
S5.9. Prevent the unauthorized release of information or any unauthorized communication when there is an operational failure of the control mechanism.	**Control:** fails closed when there is an operational failure to prevent unauthorized users from accessing protected resources.

S4: Network Protocol and Session Filtering, Inspection, and Validation

Functional Requirements	Security Technology Controls
S4.1. Traffic should be terminated, inspected, and reinitiated at the network session level (OSI Layers 2 to 5).	**SSL VPN Gateway:** breaks the network session and reinitiates it to the target system. It also verifies that it is the expected type of traffic at the network session layer and below. **TCP Proxy:** breaks the network session and reinitiates it to the target system. It also verifies that it is the expected type of traffic at the network session layer and below. **Web Proxy:** breaks the network session and reinitiates it to the target system. It also verifies that it is the expected type of traffic at the network session layer and below.
S4.2. Participate in and track communications state, and filter accordingly.	**SSL VPN Gateway:** uses session identifiers to track the state of communications and only allows certain protocols to pass. **Stateful Firewall:** uses TCP session or UDP sudo-session tables to track the state of communications and only allows known connections to pass.

Table C.1 Security Baseline Levels (*Continued*)

Functional Requirements	Security Technology Controls
	TCP Proxy: uses session identifiers to track the state of communications and only allows certain protocols to pass. **Web Proxy:** uses session identifiers to track the state of communications and only allows certain protocols to pass.
S4.3. Enforce authorization policies based upon user identity, endpoint security state, and/or network information.	**SSL VPN Gateway:** uses a combination of user/device authentication and current endpoint state checks to filter access to protected resources. **Stateful Firewall:** uses a combination of network address, ports, and protocols to filter access to protected resources. **TCP Proxy:** uses a combination of user/device authentication and current endpoint state checks to filter access to protected resources. **Web Proxy:** uses a combination of user/device authentication and current endpoint state checks to filter access to protected resources.
S4.4. Protect the authenticity of communications sessions; this includes the endpoints and the communication between.	**Firewall with IPSec VPN:** uses encryption, digital signing of data transmissions, and digital certificate verification for source device and control. **SSL/HTTPS:** uses encryption, digital signing of data transmissions, and digital certificate verification for source device and control. **SSL VPN Gateway:** uses SSL encryption, digital signing of data transmissions, and digital certificate verification for source device and control.
S4.5. Ensure a trusted communications path.	**SSL/HTTPS:** uses encrypted tunnel to encapsulate traffic. Firewall with IPSec VPN: uses encrypted tunnel to encapsulate traffic. **SSL VPN Gateway:** uses SSL VPN tunnel to encapsulate traffic.
S4.6. Detect network layer attacks using signature-based, anomaly-based, or behavior-based methods.	**Stateful Firewall with IDS:** uses intrusion detection features to detect common network exploits.
S4.7. Include mechanisms (should be automated) to isolate and eliminate network attacks and exploits.	**Stateful Firewall with IPS:** uses intrusion prevention features to automatically block common network exploits.

Continued...

Table C.1 Security Baseline Levels (*Continued*)

Functional Requirements	Security Technology Controls
S4.8. Audit activity based upon user identity, endpoint security state, and/or network information.	**SSL VPN Gateway:** uses system logs to track activities based on the account login of the user or source network/device. **Stateful Firewall:** uses system logs to track the accepted and blocked traffic flows based on the network address, ports, and protocols of the source and destination network/device. **TCP Proxy:** uses system logs to track activities based on the account login of the user or source network/device. **Web Proxy:** uses system logs to track activities based on the account login of the user or source network/device.
S4.9. Prevent the unauthorized release of information or any unauthorized communication when there is an operational failure of the control mechanism.	**Control:** fails closed when there is an operational failure to prevent unauthorized users from accessing protected resources.
S3: Network Protocol Filtering, Inspection, and Validation	
S3.1. Identify and authorize a source (device, network, or location) based on a network (OSI Layers 2 to 4) attribute, such as a Media Access Control (MAC) address, physical switch port, IP address, port, protocol, and so on.	**Stateful Firewall**: uses a combination of network address, ports, and protocols to filter access to protected resources.
S3.2. Observes and tracks communications state and filters accordingly.	**Stateful Firewall:** uses TCP session or UDP sudo-session tables to track the state of communications and only allows known connections to pass.
S3.3. Validation of adherence to network (OSI Layers 2 to 4) protocol standards.	**Stateful Firewall:** blocks or rejects packets that are incorrectly formed according to protocol standards.
S3.4. Limit access to specific network paths and protocols.	**Client-to-Client VPN:** uses VPN tunnel to encapsulate traffic. **Network Protocol:** uses VPN tunnel to encapsulate traffic. **Network Segmentation:** use physical or logical network segmentation to prevent user traffic from being accessible by other users. **Stateful Firewall:** restrict flows to expected network ports and protocols.

Table C.1 Security Baseline Levels (*Continued*)

Functional Requirements	Security Technology Controls
S3.5. Detect network layer attacks using signature-based, anomaly-based, or behavior-based methods.	**Stateful Firewall with IDS:** uses intrusion detection features to detect common network exploits.
S3.6. Include mechanisms (should be automated) to isolate and eliminate network attacks and exploits.	**Stateful Firewall with IPS:** uses intrusion prevention features to automatically block common network exploits.
S3.7. Audit activity based on a source network (OSI Layers 2 to 4) attribute, such as a Media Access Control (MAC) address, physical switch port, IP address, port, protocol, and so on.	**Stateful Firewall:** uses system logs to track the accepted and blocked traffic flows based on the network address, ports, and protocols of the source and destination network/device.
S3.8. Prevent the unauthorized release of information or any unauthorized communication when there is an operational failure of the control mechanism.	**Control:** fails closed when there is an operational failure to prevent unauthorized users from accessing protected resources.
S2: Network Protocol Filtering	
S2.1. Identify and authorize a source (device, network, or location) based on a network (OSI Layers 2 to 4) attribute, such as a Media Access Control (MAC) address, physical switch port, IP address, port, protocol, and so on.	**Access Point:** uses a combination of network address, ports, protocols, and wireless channels to filter access to protected resources. Both users and devices are authenticated. Virtual LAN (VLAN) segmentation is used to separate users while they are being processed. **NAC System:** uses both user and device authentication to validate source identity with back-end authentication system. **Switch/Router:** uses a combination of network address, ports, and protocols to filter access to protected resources. Virtual LAN (VLAN) segmentation is used to separate users while they are being processed.
S2.2. Infers communication state and filters accordingly.	**Access Point:** uses access control lists tied to specific ingress and egress interfaces/channels to make directional and filtering decisions. 802.1x is used to filter out any nonauthentication traffic at the data link layer when access sorting is being performed. **Switch/Router:** uses access control lists tied to specific ingress and egress interfaces to make directional and filtering decisions.

Continued...

Table C.1 Security Baseline Levels (*Continued*)

Functional Requirements	Security Technology Controls
S2.3. Limit access to specific network entry points and paths.	**Access Point:** restricts flows to expected network ports, protocols, wireless channels, and segments. Controls can be implemented on the access point itself or another policy enforcement point. **Network Protocol:** uses VPN tunnel to encapsulate traffic. **Switch/Router:** restricts flows to expected network ports, protocols, interfaces, and segments. Controls can be implemented on the physical port level if needed.
S2.4. Audit activity based on a network (OSI Layers 2 to 4) attribute, such as a Media Access Control (MAC) address, physical switch port, IP address, port, protocol, and so on.	**NAC System:** uses system logs to track the accepted and blocked access requests based on the network address, ports, and protocols of the source and destination network/device. **Switch/Router:** uses system logs to track the accepted and blocked traffic flows based on the network address, ports, and protocols of the source and destination network/device.
S2.5. Prevent the unauthorized release of information or any unauthorized communication when there is an operational failure of the control mechanism.	**Control:** fails closed when there is an operational failure to prevent unauthorized users from accessing protected resources.
S1: Open	
Security measure not specified/indicated (unrestricted and anonymous access).	N/A

Each sample information flow control in the right-hand column provides one example of a satisfactory control. In these examples, single control devices are used to meet the functional security requirements; however, this will not always be the case. The requirements could also be met either by combining functionality in a single device or by using multiple devices.

SECURITY ENHANCEMENT LEVELS AND SAMPLE CONTROLS

Table C.2 lists sample controls to meet the flow's Confidentiality, Integrity, Availability, and Accountability requirements beyond what the baselines provide.

Table C.2 Security Enhancement Levels

Functional Requirements	Security Technology Controls
C: Confidentiality	
C2.1. Employ medium strength cryptographic mechanisms to limit unauthorized disclosure of information.	**Client-to-Client VPN:** a client-based VPN tunnel can be used to encrypt data transmissions from end to end. **Firewall with IPSec VPN:** a client-based IPSec VPN tunnel can be used to encrypt data transmissions. **Management Protocol:** the specific management protocol implements encryption of data transmissions. **Network Protocol:** IPv6 implementations of IPSec tunneling can be used to encrypt data transmissions from end to end. **SSL:** use of SSL by the application implements tunneling, which is used to encrypt data transmissions from end to end. **SSL VPN Gateway:** uses SSL encryption of data transmissions.
C2.2. Establish a trusted communications path between communication endpoints.	**Firewall with IPSec VPN:** uses encrypted tunnel to encapsulate traffic. **Network Segmentation:** use physical or logical network segmentation to prevent payload traffic from traversing untrusted network paths. **SSL VPN Gateway:** uses SSL VPN tunnel to encapsulate traffic.
C2.3. Employ authentication mechanisms to limit unauthorized disclosure of information.	**Network Protocol:** uses device authentication such as digital certificates to verify the identity of both the source device and control itself. **SSL:** uses user or device authentication such as digital certificates to verify the identity of both the source and the control itself.

Continued...

Table C.2 Security Enhancement Levels (*Continued*)

Functional Requirements	Security Technology Controls
	SSL VPN Gateway: uses user authentication and a strong password policy to permit/deny access to protected assets, along with digital certificates to verify the identity of both the source device and control itself. **Stateful Firewall with Authentication:** uses device authentication such as digital certificates to verify the identity of both the source device and control itself. **Stateful Firewall:** uses device authentication such as digital certificates to verify the identity of both the source device and control itself.
C3.1. Employ high-strength cryptographic mechanisms to prevent unauthorized disclosure of information.	**Access Point:** uses an encryption protocol such as AES-CCMP (part of WPA2 or 802.11i)), which tunnels all transmissions to protect user communications in transit. AES-CCMP employs methods such as Counter Mode to avoid a typical weakness in wireless communications from repeating ciphertext. **IPSec VPN Concentrator:** a client-based IPSec VPN tunnel can be used to encrypt data transmissions. **SSL VPN Gateway:** uses SSL encryption of data transmissions.
C3.2. Establish a trusted communications path between communication endpoints.	**Access Point:** uses mutual authentication between wireless clients and access points. Mutual authentication prevents a wireless LAN client from joining a rogue WLAN. **IPSec VPN Concentrator:** uses encrypted VPN tunnel to encapsulate traffic. **SSL VPN Gateway:** uses SSL VPN tunnel to encapsulate traffic.
C3.3. Employ strong multifactor authentication mechanisms to limit unauthorized disclosure of information.	**Access Point:** uses 802.1x to authenticate the user, user's access device, and the wireless access point. User authentication is performed with a source external to the access point such as a Radius server. **IPSec VPN Concentrator:** uses device authentication such as digital certificates to verify the identity of both the source device and control itself. Users are authenticated by the VPN using a multifactor method.

Table C.2 Security Enhancement Levels (*Continued*)

Functional Requirements	Security Technology Controls
	SSL VPN Gateway: uses multifactor user authentication and a strong password policy to permit/deny access to protected assets, along with digital certificates to verify the identity of both the source device and control itself. **Wireless Policy System:** the NAC system and access point use an encrypted tunnel between them for all transmissions to protect user credentials in transit.
T: Integrity	
T2.1. Services resources are uniquely identified and authenticated by the client.	**IPSec VPN Concentrator:** uses a preshared key to identify the server as authentic during tunnel negotiations.
T2.2. Employ medium-strength cryptographic mechanisms to recognize changes to information during transmission.	**Client-to-Client VPN:** uses digital signing of data transmissions. **Firewall with IPSec VPN:** uses digital signing of data transmissions. **Management Protocol:** the specific management protocol implements digital signing of data transmissions. **Network Protocol:** IPv6 uses digital signing of data transmissions. **SSL:** uses digital signing of data transmissions. **SSL VPN Gateway:** uses digital signing of data transmissions.
T3.1. Service resources are uniquely identified and authenticated by the client using strong authentication methods.	**SSL VPN Gateway:** uses a server-side certificate to validate the service as authentic.
T3.2. Employ high-strength cryptographic mechanisms to recognize changes to information during transmission.	**Access Point:** use an encryption protocol such as CBC-MAC message integrity method to ensure communications have not been tampered with between the client and access point. **IPSec VPN Concentrator:** uses digital signing of data transmissions. **SSL VPN Gateway:** uses digital signing of data transmissions.
T3.3. Source endpoint health/policy verification and enforcement.	**IPSec VPN Concentrator:** uses remote evaluation or on-host agents to assess the health and compliance of the access device based on Omgeo policy. The results of these checks affect the subsequent authorization and enclaving decisions.

Continued...

Table C.2 Security Enhancement Levels (*Continued*)

Functional Requirements	Security Technology Controls
	SSL VPN Gateway: uses remote evaluation or on-host agents to assess the health and compliance of the access device based on Omgeo policy. The results of these checks affect the subsequent authorization and enclaving decisions.
	Wireless Policy System: uses remote evaluation or on-host agents to assess the health and compliance of the access device based on Omgeo policy. The results of these checks affect the subsequent authorization and enclaving decisions.
A: Availability	
A2.1. Limit the effects of typical denial-of-service attacks using software controls.	**Stateful Firewall with IPS:** uses intrusion prevention features to automatically block common network DOS exploits.
A2.2. Manage capacity, bandwidth, or other redundancy to limit the effects of information flooding types of denial-of-service attacks.	**Stateful Firewall:** uses bandwidth and session thresholds to limit the effects of a DOS attack. The firewall itself also implements controls in its software and hardware to protect itself from DOS attacks.
A2.3. Moderate level of redundancy in the control itself (such as dual-power supplies).	**Control:** contains dual-power supplies and spreads connections across multiple physical interface cards for redundancy.
A3.1. Comply with Omgeo standards for Distributed Computing High Availability.	**Various Controls:** it is out of the scope of this document to specify which control will meet the high-availability standards. Various controls such as firewalls, network segmentation, site redundancy, clustering, and load balancing can meet the typical availability requirements.
A3.2. Limit the effects of typical denial-of-service attacks using software controls, and path and hardware redundancy.	**Stateful Firewall:** uses bandwidth and session thresholds to limit the effects of a DOS attack. The firewall itself also implements controls in its software and hardware to protect itself from DOS attacks.
	Load Balancers: dynamically distribute traffic across several resources, network paths, or sites based on the current load levels.

Table C.2 Security Enhancement Levels (*Continued*)

Functional Requirements	Security Technology Controls
A3.3. Manage capacity, bandwidth, or other redundancy to limit the effects of information flooding types of denial-of-service attacks.	**Stateful Firewall:** uses bandwidth and session thresholds to limit the effects of a DOS attack. The firewall itself also implements controls in its software and hardware to protect itself from DOS attacks.
A3.4. High level of redundancy in the control itself (such as clustering).	**Control:** at least two devices are configured for high availability in a cluster. Each device contains dual-power supplies and spreads connections across multiple physical interface cards for redundancy.
A3.5. Limit the use of resources by service priority.	**Router/Switch:** uses Quality-of-Service controls to prioritize critical business traffic to have guaranteed bandwidth. **WAN Accelerator:** uses Quality-of-Service controls to prioritize critical business traffic to have guaranteed bandwidth.
A3.6. Stateful traffic failover capability on control device.	**Control:** any session-oriented traffic will failover statefully from one cluster member to another. Users will not have to reinitiate connections when one control device fails.
N: Accountability	
N2.1. Users or source systems are uniquely identified and authenticated.	**Application Proxy:** uses multifactor user authentication along with digital certificates to verify the identity of the source user and device, respectively. **SSL VPN Gateway:** uses multifactor user authentication along with digital certificates to verify the identity of the source user and device, respectively. **Stateful Firewall:** uses a combination of source network address, ports, and protocols for identification. **IPSec VPN Concentrator:** uses device authentication such as digital certificates to verify the identity of both the source device and control itself. Users are authenticated by the VPN using a multifactor method. **NAC System:** uses both user and device authentication to validate source identity with back-end authentication system protocols for identification.

Continued...

Table C.2 Security Enhancement Levels (*Continued*)

Functional Requirements	Security Technology Controls
	TCP Proxy: uses source authentication such as digital certificates or preshared keys to verify the identity of the source device. **Web Proxy:** uses user authentication along with digital certificates to verify the identity of the source user and device, respectively.
N2.2. Determine if information originated from an individual, or if an individual took specific actions or received specific information.	**IPSec VPN Concentrator:** uses user authentication to track access to protected assets and activities. **NAC System:** tracks assignment of network addresses, port connections, and authorizations for each user/ device. **SSL VPN Gateway:** uses user authentication to track access to protected assets and activities, along with digital certificates to verify the identity of the source device. **Stateful Firewall:** uses identified network attributes to track access to protected assets and activities. **TCP Proxy:** uses source authentication to track access to protected assets and activities and identify the source device. **Web Proxy:** uses user authentication to track access to protected assets and activities, along with digital certificates to verify the identity of the source device. **Application Proxy:** uses user authentication to track access to protected assets and activities, along with digital certificates to verify the identity of the source device.
N2.3. Produce audit records that contain sufficient information to establish what events occurred, the sources of the events, and the outcomes of the events.	**Firewall with IPSec VPN:** uses digital certificates to verify the identity of the source device. **NAC System:** uses audit records to show events by user and by resource, and also administrator activities. **SSL VPN Gateway:** uses audit records to show events by user and by resource, and also administrator activities.

Table C.2 Security Enhancement Levels (*Continued*)

Functional Requirements	Security Technology Controls
	Stateful Firewall: uses system logs to track the accepted and blocked traffic flows based on the network address, ports, and protocols of the source and destination network/device. **Stateful Firewall with Authentication:** uses user authentication to track access to protected assets and activities. **TCP Proxy:** uses audit records to show events by user and by resource, and also administrator activities. **Web Proxy:** uses audit records to show events by user and by resource, and also administrator activities.
N2.4. Ability to select the type of events to be audited.	**Control:** uses log entry categorization levels to set a baseline of events to capture, such as "critical" or "debug" levels.
N2.5. Log entries should be formatted to allow for the appropriate compiling of time-correlated audit trails.	**Control:** uses standard log formats and timestamping to allow for correlating of events by time.
N2.6. Ability to send audit records to a centrally managed system for retention and analysis.	**Control:** uses standard syslog service to send log entries to a central logging server.
N2.7. Timestamps (including date and time) of audit records are generated using internal system clocks.	**Control:** uses internal system clock to timestamp each log entry.
N2.8. System times should be synchronized regularly with a trusted source.	**Control:** uses Network Time Protocol (NTP) to synchronize the system clock.
N3.1. Users or source systems are uniquely identified and authenticated using strong multifactor authentication methods.	**Application Proxy:** uses multifactor user authentication along with digital certificates to verify the identity of the source user and device, respectively. **SSL VPN Gateway:** uses multifactor user authentication along with digital certificates to verify the identity of the source user and device, respectively. **Stateful Firewall:** uses a combination of source network address, ports, and protocols for identification. **IPSec VPN Concentrator:** uses device authentication such as digital certificates to verify the identity of both the source device and control itself. Users are authenticated by the VPN using a multifactor method.

Continued...

Table C.2 Security Enhancement Levels (*Continued*)

Functional Requirements	Security Technology Controls
	NAC System: uses both user and device authentication to validate source identity with back-end authentication system protocols for identification. **TCP Proxy:** uses source authentication such as digital certificates or preshared keys to verify the identity of the source device. **Web Proxy:** uses user authentication along with digital certificates to verify the identity of the source user and device, respectively.
N3.2. Determine if information originated from an individual, or if an individual took specific actions or received specific information.	**IPSec VPN Concentrator:** uses user authentication to track access to protected assets and activities. **NAC System:** tracks assignment of network addresses, port connections, and authorizations for each user/device. **SSL VPN Gateway:** uses user authentication to track access to protected assets and activities, along with digital certificates to verify the identity of the source device. **Stateful Firewall:** uses identified network attributes to track access to protected assets and activities.
	TCP Proxy: uses source authentication to track access to protected assets and activities and identify the source device. **Web Proxy:** uses user authentication to track access to protected assets and activities, along with digital certificates to verify the identity of the source device. **Application Proxy:** uses user authentication to track access to protected assets and activities, along with digital certificates to verify the identity of the source device.
N3.3. Produce audit records that contain sufficient information to establish what events occurred, the sources of the events, and the outcomes of the events.	**Firewall with IPSec VPN:** uses digital certificates to verify the identity of the source device. **NAC System:** uses audit records to show events by user and by resource, and also administrator activities. **SSL VPN Gateway:** uses audit records to show events by user and by resource, and also administrator activities.

Table C.2 Security Enhancement Levels (*Continued*)

Functional Requirements	Security Technology Controls
	Stateful Firewall: uses system logs to track the accepted and blocked traffic flows based on the network address, ports, and protocols of the source and destination network/device. **Stateful Firewall with Authentication:** uses user authentication to track access to protected assets and activities. **TCP Proxy:** uses audit records to show events by user and by resource, and also administrator activities. **Web Proxy:** uses audit records to show events by user and by resource, and also administrator activities.
N3.4. Ability to select the type of events to be audited.	**Control:** uses log entry categorization levels to set a baseline of events to capture, such as "critical" or "debug" levels.
N3.5. Log entries should be formatted to allow for the appropriate compiling of time-correlated audit trails.	**Control:** uses standard log formats and timestamping to allow for correlating of events by time.
N3.6. Ability to send audit records to a centrally managed system for retention and analysis.	**Control:** uses standard syslog service to send log entries to a central logging server.
N3.7. Timestamps (including date and time) of audit records are generated using internal system clocks.	**Control:** uses internal system clock to timestamp each log entry.
N3.8. System times should be synchronized regularly with a trusted and authenticated source.	**Control:** uses Network Time Protocol (NTP) to synchronize the system clock.

Note that several levels mention cryptographic strength, but do not define it further. This should be further specified by the organization's information security standards.

MAPPING SECURITY LEVELS

As it was explained in Chapter 13 the minimum level of security controls needed to protect the resource can be determined using the mapping process that uses the category of flow and Risk Sensitivity ratings of the resource to determine the necessary functional control requirements:

Table C.3 Baseline Security Level Mapping

	Privilege Level																	
	Basic						Privileged						Management					
	Human			Automated			Human			Automated			Human			Automated		
Endpoint/ Medium	L	M	H	L	M	H	L	M	H	L	M	H	L	M	H	L	M	H
External anonymous	S3	S5	S5															
External unaccredited	S3	S4	S5	S3	S4	S5	S4	S4	S5	S4	S4	S5	S4	S4	S5	S3	S4	S5
Internal unaccredited	S2	S4	S5				S3	S4	S5	S3	S3	S5	S3	S4	S5	S3	S4	S5
External accredited	S3	S4	S5	See Table C.4			S3	S3	S5	See Table C.4			S4	S4	S5	See Table C.4		
Internal	S2	S3	S5				S3	S3	S5	S3	S3	S5	S3	S4	S5	S3	S4	S5

Note that certain combinations in the Table C.3 are blocked out indicating that this scenario should never be permitted in the environment. Internal automated flows are represented in the following matrix:

Table C.4 Baseline Security Level Mapping, Internal Automated Flows

Endpoint/ Medium	Privilege Level								
	Basic			Privileged			Management		
	L	M	H	L	M	H	L	M	H
Inter-zone	S2	S3	S4	S2	S3	S4	S3	S3	S4
Intra-zone	S2	S2	S3	S2	S2	S3	S2	S2	S3
Intra-system	S2	S2	S2	S2	S2	S2	S2	S2	S2

Mapping for the Risk Sensitivity level to the Enhancements requirements for each C-I-A-A tenant (Table C.5) are listed as follows:

Table C.5 Enhancement Security Level Mapping

C-I-A-A	Security Level Enhancements	
	Risk Sensitivity— Moderate	Risk Sensitivity—High
Confidentiality	C2	C3
Integrity	T2	T3
Availability	A2	A3
Accountability	N2	N3

Note that a risk sensitivity level of Low is not listed in Table C.5 because there is no enhancement requirement for that sensitivity rating.

Risk exposure (based on the CVSS scoring scale)		
Threat universe × Vulnerability risk × Risk sensitivity = Risk exposure		
Threat universe scale: 1 = 1–50 potential users 2 = 51–500 3 = 501–2000 4 = 2001–32000 5 = 32001 or more potential users	**Vulnerability scale:** 1 = negligible vulnerability/controls implemented 2 = low-risk vulnerability 3 = moderate-risk vulnerability 4 = high-risk vulnerability	**Risk sensitivity scale:** 2 = a low sensitivity to risk 3 = moderate sensitivity to risk 4 = a high sensitivity to risk
Risk exposure scale: Low = 1–8 Moderate = 9–25 High = 26–39 Extreme = 40+	**Recommended risk exposure levels:** Risk sensitivity Recommended exposure range Low Low–high = 1–39 Moderate Low–moderate = 1–25 High Low = 1–8	

FIGURE C.6

Step 4 Calculate Risk Exposure Rating for Flows

Step 4 of the architectural risk analysis workflow involves calculating the current level of risk exposure given several variables. For each information flow of the resource, data for Threat Universe (TU), Vulnerability (VU), and Risk Sensitivity (RS) ratings (in the resource's current state) are evaluated and are used to derive a Risk Exposure rating. Values and ranges for this calculation are provided in Table/Figure C.6.

Index

A

Acceptance, 150
Access control, 130, 143, 269
   content-based access control, 131
   discretionary access control, 130
   RBAC, 130
   rule-based access control, 130–131
   security services, 132
   see also Assurance model; Security control
     principles; Security services
Access Control List (ACL), 95, 130
Access device control, 270–271
Accountability, 10
   qualitative severity scale, *110*
   severity, 110
   see also Integrity; Confidentiality; Availability
Accreditation, 196
ACL, *see* Access Control List (ACL)
Addressed risk, 250
Addressing the risk, 250
Agreed Upon Procedures (AUP), 206
ALE, *see* Annualized Loss Expectancy (ALE)
Annualized Loss Expectancy (ALE), 123, 231
Anti-malware vendors, 221
Appendices, 181
Application layer protocol information, 131
Application Service Provider (ASP), 182
Architectural pattern, 265
Architectural risk analysis, 313–330
Asset class, *220*
Asset-based threat profiles, 169
   areas of concern, 171, *171*
   business security requirements, 170, *170*
   making, 170, 171
   resources, 169
   risk pie chart, 179, *179*
   steps, 169
   see also Vulnerability identification
Assurance model, 129
   C-I-A-A model, 129
   Positive Security Model, 130
   see also Access control; Security control
     principles; Security services
Audit logs, 119
Audit responses, 183
   constraints, 185
   critical issue fixing, 184

   cross-functional role, 186
   flow for audit, 183
   plan development, 187
   risk manager's involvement, 183
   SSL VPN, 186
   timeframe for mitigation actions, 186
   writing management response, 184–185, 187
AUP, *see* Agreed Upon Procedures (AUP)
Authentication, 137
Authorization, 138
Automated process, 270
Availability, 10
   qualitative severity scale, *108*
   severity, 107–108
   see also Accountability; Confidentiality;
     Availability
Avoidance, 149

B

Baseline, 196–197
Best practices, 4–5, 22
BIA, *see* Business Impact Assessment (BIA)
Big hammer, 288
Biomedical research company, 80–81
BITS, 32
Blacklist security model, *see* Negative security model
Blueprint for Security, 259–284
Brand/reputation damage, 297
Business Impact Assessment (BIA), 43, 48–50
   resource profiling, 48–50
Business security requirements, 170, *170*
Business-driven security program, 28–34
   annual business objectives, 29
   decision making, 32–34
   employees background checks, 32
   guidelines, 31
   positioning information security, 30
   regulations and compliance pressures, 30
   risk-based approach, 29
   service provider hiring, 32
   smart work, 28–29
   vocabulary, 30
   WPA2 protection, 31

C

C&A, *see* Certification and Accreditation (C&A)
Center of Internet Security (CIS), 145
Certification, 196

Note: Page numbers in *italics* indicate figures and tables.

331